Fodor's 98

Paris

The complete guide, thoroughly up-to-date

Packed with details that will make your trip

The must-see sights, off and on the beaten path

What to see, what to skip

Vacation itineraries, walking tours, day trips

Smart lodging and dining options

Essential local do's and taboos

Transportation tips

Key contacts, savvy travel advice

When to go, what to pack

Clear, accurate, easy-to-use maps

Books to read, videos to watch, background essay

Fodor's Travel Publications, Inc.
New York • Toronto • London • Sydney • Auckland
www.fodors.com/

Fodor's Paris '98

EDITOR: Natasha Lesser

Editorial Contributors: Robert Andrews, Roberta Beardsley, Robert Blake, David Brown, K. Neil Cukier, Audra Epstein, Laura M. Kidder, Simon Hewitt, Suzanne Rowan Kelleher, Alexander Lobrano, Jennifer Paull, Heidi Sarna, Helayne Schiff, M. T. Schwartzman (Gold Guide editor), Dinah Spritzer

Editorial Production: Laura M. Kidder

Maps: David Lindroth, *cartographer;* Bob Blake, *map editor*

Design: Fabrizio La Rocca, *creative director;* Guido Caroti, *associate art director;* Jolie Novak, *photo editor*

Production/Manufacturing: Rebecca Zeiler

Cover Photograph: Philip Gould/Corbis

Text Design: Between the Covers

Copyright

Special Sales

CONTENTS

ON THE ROAD WITH FODOR'S

WE'RE ALWAYS THRILLED to get letters from readers, especially one like this:

It took us an hour to decide what book to buy and we now know we picked the best one. Your book was wonderful, easy to follow, very accurate, and good on pointing out eating places, informal as well as formal. When we saw other people using your book, we would look at each other and smile.

Our editors and writers are deeply committed to making every Fodor's guide "the best one"—not only accurate but always charming, brimming with sound recommendations and solid ideas, right on the mark in describing restaurants and hotels, and full of fascinating facts that make you view what you've traveled to see in a rich new light.

About Our Writers

Our success in achieving our goals—and in helping to make your trip the best of all possible vacations—is a credit to the hard work of our extraordinary writers and editors.

Simon Hewitt, who first wrote much of this book, headed to Paris straight from studying French and art history at Oxford. It was a return to base: His grandmother was French, as are his wife and daughter. He recently moved to Versailles to gain a different perspective on life in and around the French capital. When not contemplating the Sun King's bigger-than-life Baroque home, his thoughts often turn to cricket—he is captain of the French national team.

Roberta Beardsley has lived in Paris for 26 years, enough time to have had at least two lives and many more residences. Seven years near Les Halles has convinced her that where you live has a lot to do with how you spend your evenings. With a little help from her friends, she has scoped out all of *the* best places to see a play, hear some music, or have a drink.

K. Neil Cukier is a French-American, Paris-based journalist who has lived on both sides of the Atlantic. His previous professions have included deck hand on a private yacht on the Mediterranean, ski bum in the French alps, grape picker in the South of France, and philosophy student at La Sorbonne.

Suzanne Rowan Kelleher traded bagels for croissants four years ago when she moved from New York to Paris. A wayfarer by nature, Suzanne is a travel writer who contributes to *Esquire* and *Travel Holiday.* She has good news about shopping and lodging in Paris, reporting that France's recession has forced the city to become increasingly value-oriented.

Editor **Natasha Lesser** has lived, among other places, in Washington, DC, San Francisco, Iowa City, Nairobi, and Paris. After exploring every boulevard and back rue of this great capital, she has stayed long enough at her desk in New York to pass her knowledge on to you.

Alexander Lobrano has lived in Paris for 11 years, after eating his way through Boston, New York, and London. He writes a weekly dining column for *Paris Time Out* and has reported on French food and restaurants for many British and American publications, including *Departures, Bon Appetit,* and *Condé Naste Traveler.* His best meal in Paris? Last year at Philippe Detourbe.

New This Year

This year we've added terrific Great Itineraries that will lead you through the best of the city, taking into consideration how long you have to spend.

Simon Hewitt has also added new walking tours, covering more parts of Paris than ever before. In addition, a list of the best of Paris cafés has been added to Chapter 3 and a selection of fine art galleries has been added to Chapter 6. And, as always, Alexander Lobrano and Suzanne Rowan Kelleher have added exciting, new hotels and restaurants.

And this year, Fodor's joins Rand McNally, the world's largest commercial mapmaker, to bring you a detailed color map of Paris. Just detach it along the perforation, and drop it in your tote bag.

On the Web, check out Fodor's site (www.fodors.com/) for information on major destinations around the world and travel-savvy interactive features. The Web site also lists the 80-plus radio stations nationwide that carry the *Fodor's Travel Show,* a live call-in program that airs every weekend. Tune in to hear guests discuss their wonderful adventures, or call in for answers to your most pressing travel questions.

How to Use This Book

Organization

Up front is the **Gold Guide,** an easy-to-use section divided alphabetically by topic. Under each listing you'll find tips and information that will help you accomplish what you need to in Paris. You'll also find addresses and telephone numbers of organizations and companies that offer destination-related services and detailed information and publications.

The first chapter in the guide, Destination: Paris, helps get you in the mood for your trip. What's Where gets you oriented, New and Noteworthy cues you in on trends and happenings, Pleasures and Pastimes describes the activities and sights that really make Paris unique, Great Itineraries leads you through the best of the city, Fodor's Choice showcases our top picks, and Festivals and Seasonal Events alerts you to special events you'll want to seek out.

The Exploring chapter is subdivided by neighborhood; each subsection recommends a walking tour and lists neighborhood sights alphabetically, including sights that are off the beaten path and on the fringe of the city. The remaining chapters are arranged in alphabetical order by subject (dining, lodging, nightlife and the arts, shopping, and side trips).

At the end of the book you'll find a Portrait, a wonderful essay about Paris, followed by suggestions for any pretrip research you want to do, from recommended reading to movies on tape with Paris as a backdrop.

Icons and Symbols

★ Our special recommendations
✕ Restaurant
🏨 Lodging establishment
🐤 Good for kids (rubber duckie)
☞ Sends you to another section of the guide for more information
✉ Address
☎ Telephone number
FAX Fax number
☉ Opening and closing times
💰 Admission prices (those we give apply to adults; substantially reduced fees are almost always available for children, students, and senior citizens)

Numbers in white and black circles that appear on the maps, in the margins, and within the tours correspond to one another.

Credit Cards

The following abbreviations are used: **AE,** American Express; **DC,** Diners Club; **MC,** MasterCard; and **V,** Visa.

Please Write to Us

You can use this book in the confidence that all prices and opening times are based on information supplied to us at press time; Fodor's cannot accept responsibility for any errors. Time inevitably brings changes, so always confirm information when it matters—especially if you're making a detour to visit a specific place. In addition, when making reservations be sure to mention if you have a disability or are traveling with children, if you prefer a private bath or a certain type of bed, or if you have specific dietary needs or other concerns.

Were the restaurants we recommended as described? Did our hotel picks exceed your expectations? Did you find a museum we recommended a waste of time? If you have complaints, we'll look into them and revise our entries when the facts warrant it. If you've discovered a special place that we haven't included, we'll pass the information along to our correspondents and have them check it out. So send us your feedback, positive *and* negative: E-mail us at editors@fodors.com (specifying the name of the book on the subject line) or write the Paris editor at Fodor's, 201 East 50th Street, New York, New York 10022. Have a wonderful trip!

Karen Cure
Editorial Director

Paris with Arrondissements

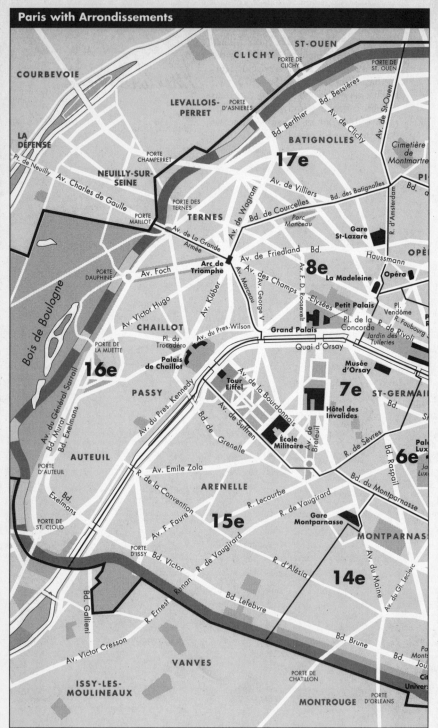

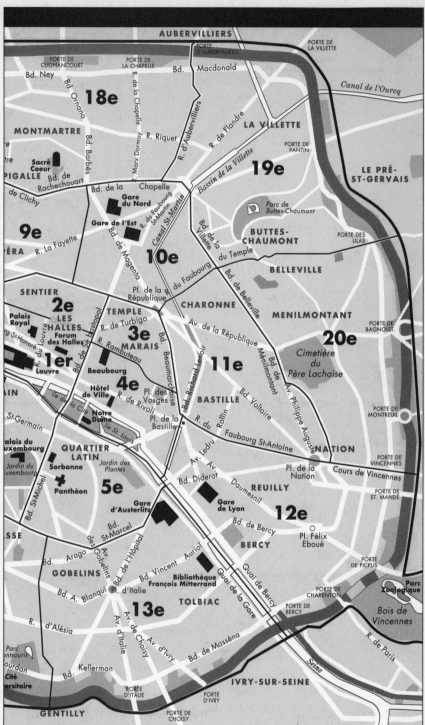

AUBERVILLIERS

PORTE DE
LA VILLETTE

PORTE
D'AUBERVILLIERS

Bd. Macdonald

Canal de l'Ourcq

PORTE DE
CLIGNANCOURT

PORTE DE
LA CHAPELLE

Bd.

Bd. Ney

R. de la Chapelle

R. d'Aubervilliers

R. de Flandre

LA VILLETTE

PORTE DE
PANTIN

18e

R. Riquet

R. Marx Dormoy

Bd. Ornano

Bd. Barbès

Bassin de la Villette

19e

LE PRÉ-
ST-GERVAIS

MONTMARTRE

Sacré
Cœur

Parc de
Buttes-Chaumont

PIGALLE

Bd. de
Rochechouart

Bd. de la   Chapelle

Gare
du Nord

R. du Faubourg
St-Martin

Canal St-Martin

PORTE DES
LILAS

de Clichy

BUTTES-
CHAUMONT

Bd. de la Villette

9e

Gare de l'Est

Bd. de Magenta

BELLEVILLE

R. La Fayette

10e

du Temple

Pèra

Pl. de la
République

R. du Faubourg

Bd. de Belleville

MENILMONTANT

SENTIER

CHARONNE

PORTE DE
BAGNOLET

2e

TEMPLE

20e

LES
HALLES

Bd. de Sébastopol

R. de Turbigo

Av. de la République

Palais
Royal

3e

Cimetière
du
Père Lachaise

Forum
des Halles

R. Rambuteau

MARAIS

Bd. de Ménilmontant

Av. Philippe Auguste

Bourg St-Honoré

1er

Beaubourg

Bd. Beaumarchais

11e

Bd. Voltaire

Louvre

4e

Pl. des
Vosges

R. Richard Lenoir

Hôtel
de Ville

R. de Rivoli

BASTILLE

Ile de la Cité

Notre
Dame

Pl. de la
Bastille

R. du   Rollin

NATION

AIN

Ile St-Louis

R. du Faubourg St-Antoine

PORTE DE
VINCENNES

Palais du
Luxembourg

QUARTIER
LATIN

Av. Ledru

Av.

PORTE DE
MONTREUIL

St-Germain

Sorbonne

Jardin des
Plantes

Bd. Diderot

Daumesnil

Pl. de la
Nation

Cours de Vincennes

Jardin du
Luxembourg

Panthéon

5e

REUILLY

PORTE DE
ST-MANDÉ

Bd. St-Michel

Gare
d'Austerlitz

Gare
de Lyon

12e

ISSE

Bd.
St-Marcel

Bd. de Bercy

Pl. Félix
Eboué

Bd.   Arago

Av. des Gobelins

Av. de l'Hôpital

BERCY

PORTE
DE PICPUS

Bd.

GOBELINS

Bd. Vincent   Auriol

Quai de la Gare

Quai de Bercy

Parc
Zoologique

Bd. A. Blanqui

Bibliothèque
François Mitterrand

PORTE DE
CHARENTON

Pl. d'Italie

R. d'Alésia

13e

TOLBIAC

Bois de
Vincennes

Av. de Choisy

Av. d'Italie

Bd. de Masséna

PORTE DE
BERCY

Seine

R. de Paris

Parc
ontsouris

ourdan

Bd. Kellerman

Cité
versitaire

PORTE
D'ITALIE

IVRY-SUR-SEINE

GENTILLY

PORTE DE
CHOISY

PORTE
D'IVRY

Paris Métro

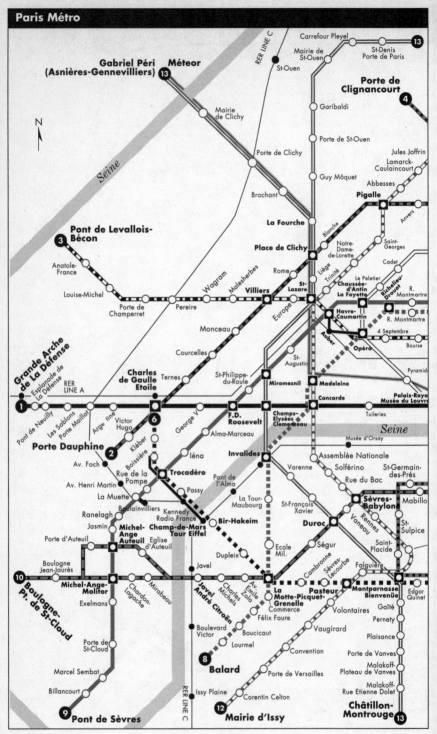

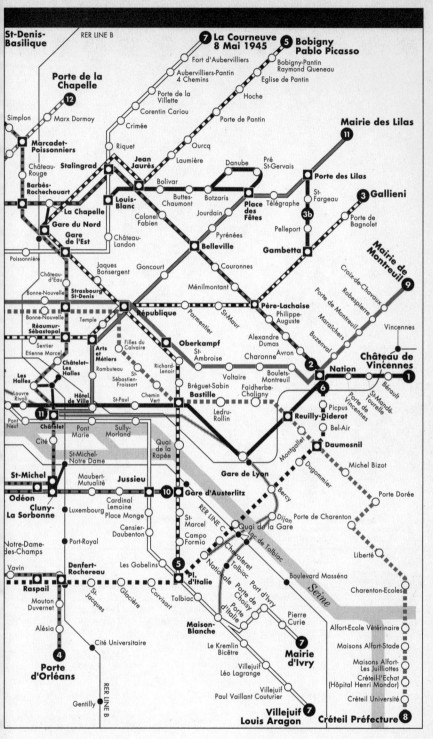

World Time Zones

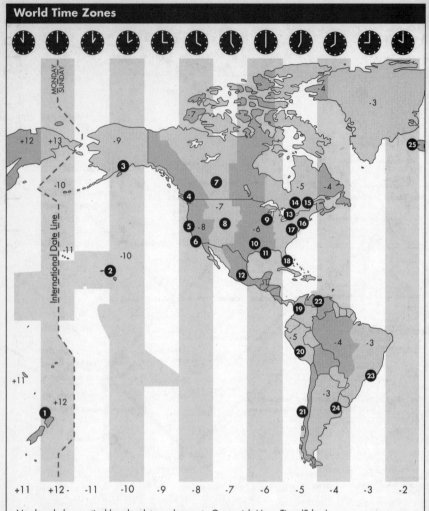

Numbers below vertical bands relate each zone to Greenwich Mean Time (0 hrs.).
Local times frequently differ from these general indications,
as indicated by light-face numbers on map.

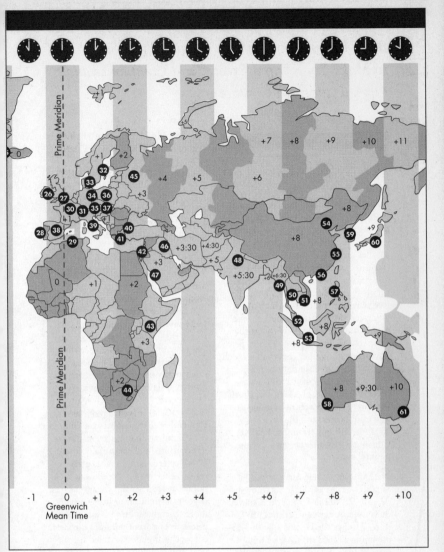

Mecca, **47**
Mexico City, **12**
Miami, **18**
Montréal, **15**
Moscow, **45**
Nairobi, **43**
New Orleans, **11**
New York City, **16**

Ottawa, **14**
Paris, **30**
Perth, **58**
Reykjavík, **25**
Rio de Janeiro, **23**
Rome, **39**
Saigon (Ho Chi Minh City), **51**

San Francisco, **5**
Santiago, **21**
Seoul, **59**
Shanghai, **55**
Singapore, **52**
Stockholm, **32**
Sydney, **61**
Tokyo, **60**

Toronto, **13**
Vancouver, **4**
Vienna, **35**
Warsaw, **36**
Washington, D.C., **17**
Yangon, **49**
Zürich, **31**

SMART TRAVEL TIPS A TO Z

Basic Information on Traveling in Paris, Savvy Tips to Make Your Trip a Breeze, and Companies and Organizations to Contact

A

AIR TRAVEL

MAJOR AIRLINE OR LOW-COST CARRIER?

Most people choose a flight based on price. Yet there are other issues to consider. Major airlines offer the greatest number of departures; smaller airlines—including regional, low-cost, and no-frill airlines—usually have a more limited number of flights daily. Major airlines have frequent-flyer partners, which allow you to credit mileage earned on one airline to your account with another. Low-cost airlines offer a definite price advantage and fewer restrictions, such as advance-purchase requirements. Safety-wise, low-cost carriers as a group have a good history, but **check the safety record before booking** any low-cost carrier; call the Federal Aviation Administration's (FAA's) Consumer Hotline (☞ Airline Complaints, *below*).

➤ MAJOR AIRLINES: **Air France** (☎ 800/237–2747 in the U.S., ☎ 08–02–80–28–02 in France) to Charles de Gaulle. **American Airlines** (☎ 800/433–7300 in the U.S, ☎ 08–00–23–00–35 in France) to Charles de Gaulle, Orly. **Continental** (☎ 800/231–0856 in the U.S., ☎ 01–42–99–09–09 in France) to Charles de Gaulle. **Delta** (☎ 800/241–4141 in the U.S., ☎ 01–47–68–92–92 in France) to Charles de Gaulle. **Northwest** (☎ 800/225–2525 in the U.S., ☎ 01–42–66–90–00 in France) to Charles de Gaulle. **TWA** (☎ 800/892–4141 in the U.S., ☎ 01–49–19–20–00 in France) to Charles de Gaulle. **United** (☎ 800/538–2929 in the U.S., ☎ 01–41–40–30–30 in France) to Charles de Gaulle. **USAirways** (☎ 800/428–4322 in the U.S., ☎ 01–49–10–29–00 in France) to Charles de Gaulle.

➤ FROM THE U.K.: **Air France** (☎ 0181/742–6600 in the U.K., ☎ 08–02–80–28–02 in France). **British Airways** (☎ 0345/222–111 in the U.K., ☎ 08–02–80–29–02 in France). **British Midland** (☎ 0181/754–7321 or 0345/554–554 in the U.K., ☎ 01–48–62–55–65 in France). **Air U.K.** (☎ 0345/666–777 in the U.K., ☎ 01–44–56–18–08 in France).

GET THE LOWEST FARE

The least-expensive airfares to Paris are priced for round-trip travel. Major airlines usually require that you **book far in advance and stay at least seven days** and no more than 30 to get the lowest fares. Ask about "ultrasaver" fares, which are the cheapest; they must be booked 90 days in advance and are nonrefundable. A little more expensive are "supersaver" fares, which require only a 30-day advance purchase. Remember that penalties for refunds or scheduling changes are stiffer for international tickets, usually about $150. International flights are also sensitive to the season: **plan to fly in the off season** for the cheapest fares. If your destination or home city has more than one gateway, **compare prices to and from different airports.** Also price flights scheduled for off-peak hours, which may be significantly less expensive.

To save money on flights from the United Kingdom and back, **look into an APEX or Super-PEX ticket.** Both sorts should be booked in advance and have certain restrictions, though they can sometimes be purchased right at the airport.

DON'T STOP UNLESS YOU MUST

When you book, **look for nonstop flights** and **remember that "direct" flights stop at least once.** International flights on a country's flag carrier are almost always nonstop; U.S. airlines often fly direct. Try to **avoid connecting flights,** which require a change of plane. Two airlines may jointly operate a connecting flight, so ask if your airline operates every segment—you may find that your preferred carrier flies you only part of the way.

USE AN AGENT

Travel agents, especially those who specialize in finding the lowest fares (☞ Discounts & Deals, *below*), can be especially helpful when booking a plane ticket. When you're quoted a price, **ask your agent if the price is likely to get any lower.** Good agents know the seasonal fluctuations of airfares and can usually anticipate a sale or fare war. However, waiting can be risky: The fare could go *up* as seats become scarce, and you may wait so long that your preferred flight sells out. A wait-and-see strategy works best if your plans are flexible, but if you must arrive and depart on certain dates, don't delay.

CHECK WITH CONSOLIDATORS

Consolidators buy tickets for scheduled flights at reduced rates from the airlines then sell them at prices that beat the best fare available directly from the airlines, usually without advance restrictions. Sometimes you can even get your money back if you need to return the ticket. Carefully read the fine print detailing penalties for changes and cancellations, and **confirm your consolidator reservation with the airline.**

➤ CONSOLIDATORS: **United States Air Consolidators Association** (✉ 925 L St., Suite 220, Sacramento, CA 95814, ☎ 916/441–4166, FAX 916/441–3520).

AVOID GETTING BUMPED

Airlines routinely overbook planes, knowing that not everyone with a ticket will show up, but sometimes everyone does. When that happens, airlines ask for volunteers to give up their seats. In return these volunteers usually get a certificate for a free flight and are rebooked on the next flight out. If there are not enough volunteers the airline must choose who will be denied boarding. The first to get bumped are passengers who checked in late and those flying on discounted tickets, so **get to the gate and check in as early as possible,** especially during peak periods.

Always **bring a photo ID to the airport.** You may be asked to show it before you are allowed to check in.

ENJOY THE FLIGHT

For more legroom, **request an emergency-aisle seat;** don't however, sit in the row in front of the emergency aisle or in front of a bulkhead, where seats may not recline.

If you don't like airline food, **ask for special meals when booking.** These can be vegetarian, low-cholesterol, or kosher, for example.

To avoid jet lag try to maintain a normal routine while traveling. At night **get some sleep.** By day **eat light meals, drink water (not alcohol), and move about the cabin** to stretch your legs.

Some carriers have prohibited smoking throughout their systems; others allow smoking only on certain routes or even certain departures from that route, so **contact your carrier regarding its smoking policy.**

COMPLAIN IF NECESSARY

If your baggage goes astray or your flight goes awry, complain right away. Most carriers require that you file a claim immediately.

➤ AIRLINE COMPLAINTS: U.S. Department of Transportation (DOT) **Aviation Consumer Protection Division** (✉ C-75, Washington, DC 20590, ☎ 202/366–2220). **FAA** Consumer Hotline (☎ 800/322–7873).

AIRPORTS & TRANSFERS

The major airports are **Orly** (☎ 011–33–1/4975–1515) and **Charles de Gaulle** (☎ 011–33–1/4862–1212).

Flying time is 7 hours from New York, 9½ hours from Chicago, and 11 hours from Los Angeles. Flying time from the United Kingdom is 1½ hours.

TRANSFERS

From the Charles de Gaulle airport, **the easiest way to get into Paris is on the RER-B line,** the suburban express train, which leaves from right beneath Terminal 2. Trains to central Paris (Les Halles, St-Michel, Luxembourg) depart every 15 minutes. The fare (including métro connection) is 45 francs, and journey time is about 35 minutes. Note that you have to carry your luggage down to the train track, and trains can be crowded if you arrive at rush hour.

A convenient and pleasant **bus service between Charles de Gaulle airport and the city is operated by Air France.** Buses run every 15 minutes between the airport and Montparnasse, as well as between the airport and the Arc de Triomphe, with a stop at the Air France air terminal at Porte Maillot. The fare is 55 francs, and journey time is about 40 minutes. The **Roissybus, operated by the Paris Transit Authority, runs between Charles de Gaulle and the Opéra** every 15 minutes; the cost is 40 francs. Rush-hour traffic can make traveling by bus slow and frustrating.

At the airport, **taxis are readily available.** Journey time is around 30 minutes, depending on the traffic, and the fare is between 150 and 200 francs. Ask what the fare will be before getting in the taxi. For the same price as a taxi for two or more people, **Paris Airports Service can meet you on arrival in a private car** and drive you to your destination.

By train, **the most economical way to get to Paris from Orly is to take the RER-C line;** take the free shuttle bus from the terminal to the train station. Trains to Paris leave every 15 minutes. The fare is 28 francs, and journey time is about 35 minutes.

Another option is to **take the new monorail service, Orlyval,** which runs between the Antony RER-B station and Orly airport every 7 minutes. The fare to downtown Paris is 54 francs.

From Orly airport, **Air France buses run every 12 minutes** to the Air France air terminal at Les Invalides on the Left Bank. The fare is 40 francs, and journey time is between 30 and 45 minutes, depending on traffic. The Paris Transit Authority's **Orlybus leaves every 15 minutes for the Denfert-Rochereau métro station;** cost is 30 francs.

In light traffic, **taxis take around 25 minutes;** the fare will be about 160 francs. Be sure to ask about the fare before getting in the taxi. With reservations, **Paris Airports Service can pick you up at Orly** and drive you directly to your destination.

➤ SHUTTLE SERVICE: **Paris Airports Service** (☎ 01–49–62–78–78); reservations must be made two to three days in advance, and Master-Card and Visa are accepted.

B

BICYCLING

Bicycles can be rented in the Bois de Boulogne (at the Jardin d'Acclimatation) and the Bois de Vincennes as well as from some RER stations, the Bateaux-Mouches embarkation point by place de l'Alma, and Paris-Vélo. Rental rates are 80 francs per day, 195 francs per weekend, and 420 francs per week. There is a 2,000-franc deposit for rental, which can be put on a credit card. Passports and national identity cards are also often accepted as alternative forms of deposit. *See* Chapter 1 for more information about bicycling in Paris.

➤ BICYCLE RENTAL: **Paris-Vélo** (✉ 2 rue du Fer à Moulin, 5ᵉ, ☎ 01–43–37–59–22).

BUS TRAVEL

IN PARIS

Although it's slower than the métro, **traveling by bus is a convenient, scenic way to get around the city.** Paris buses are green and white; route number and destination are marked in front and major stopping-places along the sides. Most routes operate from 7 AM to 8:30 PM; some continue to midnight. Ten Noctambus, or night buses, operate hourly (1:30–5:30 AM) between Châtelet and various nearby suburbs; they can be stopped by hailing them at any point on their route.

The brown bus shelters, topped by red and yellow circular signs, contain timetables and route maps. Paris-Visite/Formule 1 passes are valid, otherwise it costs 30 francs. Regular buses accept métro tickets, or you can buy a single ticket on board. If you have individual tickets, you should **be prepared to punch one or more tickets in the red and gray machines on board the bus.** You need to show (but not punch) weekly, monthly, and Paris-Visite/Formule 1 (☞ Métro, *below*) tickets to the driver as you get on.

Take the Montmartrobus for a tour of some of the most charming streets around the *butte*. The terminus is at the Pigalle métro station. The Balabus, a public bus that runs between May and September, gives an interesting tour around the major sights. Terminus: La Défense or Gare de Lyon.

FROM THE U.K.

It is possible to take a bus (via ferry) to Paris from the U.K. Eurolines operates a nightly service from London's Victoria Coach Station, via the Dover–Calais ferry, to Paris. Departures are at 9 AM, arriving at 6 PM; noon, arriving at 9 PM; and 10 PM, arriving at 7 AM. Fares are £60 round-trip (under-25 youth pass £56), £35 one-way. Hoverspeed offers up to four daily departures from Victoria Coach Station. Fares are £60 round-trip, £38 one-way. Reservations can be made in person at any National Express office or at the Coach Travel Centre.

➤ BUS COMPANIES: **Coach Travel Centre** (⊠ 13 Regent St., London SW1 4LR, ☎ 0171/824–8657 to make credit-card reservations). **Eurolines** (⊠ 52 Grosvenor Gardens, London SW1W 0AU, ☎ 0171/730–0202). **Hoverspeed** (⊠ International Hoverport, Marine Parade, Dover CT17 9TG, ☎ 01304/240241).

BUSINESS HOURS

During the **weekdays, banks are open,** but there's no strict pattern to their hours of business. Generally, they're open from 9:30 AM to 4:30 or 5 PM.

Most Paris **museums close one day a week**—usually either Monday or Tuesday—and on national holidays. Usually, they're open from 10 AM to 5 or 6 PM. A few museums close for lunch (noon–2) and are open Sunday only in the afternoon. Many of the large museums have one *nocturne* opening per week when they close at 9:30 or 10 PM.

Generally, **large shops are open from 9:30 or 10 AM to 6 or 7 PM** and don't close at lunchtime. Many of the large department stores stay open until 10 PM on Wednesday or Thursday. Smaller shops and many supermarkets often open earlier (8 AM) but

take a lengthy lunch break (1 PM–3 PM); small food shops are often open Sunday mornings, 9 AM–1 PM. Some corner grocery stores stay open until about 10 PM. Most shops close all day Sunday, except some around the Marais, the Bastille, the Latin Quarter, and the Ile de la Cité.

C

CAMERAS, CAMCORDERS, & COMPUTERS

Always **keep your film, tape, or computer disks out of the sun.** Carry an extra supply of batteries, and **be prepared to turn on your camera, camcorder, or laptop** to prove to security personnel that the device is real. Always **ask for hand inspection of film,** which becomes clouded after successive exposure to airport x-ray machines, and **keep videotapes and computer disks away from metal detectors.**

➤ PHOTO HELP: **Kodak Information Center** (☎ 800/242–2424). *Kodak Guide to Shooting Great Travel Pictures,* available in bookstores or from Fodor's Travel Publications (☎ 800/533–6478; $16.50 plus $4 shipping).

CUSTOMS

Before departing, **register your foreign-made camera or laptop with U.S. Customs** (☞ Customs & Duties, *below*). If your equipment is U.S.-made, call the consulate of the country you'll be visiting to find out whether the device should be registered with local customs upon arrival.

CAR RENTAL

Rates in Paris begin at $60 a day and $196 a week for an economy car with air-conditioning, manual transmission, and unlimited mileage. This does not include tax on car rentals, which is 20.6%. Your best bet is to **make reservations before you go;** you can generally get a much better deal.

➤ MAJOR AGENCIES: **Alamo** (☎ 800/522–9696, 0800/272–2000 in the U.K.). **Avis** (☎ 800/331–1084, 800/879–2847 in Canada). **Budget** (☎ 800/527–0700, 0800/181181 in the U.K.). **Dollar** (☎ 800/800–4000; 0990/565656 in the U.K., where it is known as Eurodollar). **Hertz** (☎ 800/654–3001, 800/263–0600 in

Canada, 0345/555888 in the U.K.).
National InterRent (☎ 800/227–3876; 0345/222525 in the U.K., where it is known as Europcar Inter-Rent).

CUT COSTS

To get the best deal, **book through a travel agent who is willing to shop around.**

Also **ask your travel agent about a company's customer-service record.** How has it responded to late plane arrivals and vehicle mishaps? Are there often lines at the rental counter, and, if you're traveling during a holiday period, does a confirmed reservation guarantee you a car?

Be sure to **look into wholesalers,** companies that do not own fleets but rent in bulk from those that do and often offer better rates than traditional car-rental operations. Prices are best during off-peak periods. Rentals booked through wholesalers must be paid for before you leave the United States.

➤ RENTAL WHOLESALERS: **Auto Europe** (☎ 207/842–2000 or 800/223–5555, FAX 800/235–6321). **Europe by Car** (☎ 212/581–3040 or 800/223–1516, FAX 212/246–1458). **DER Travel Services** (✉ 9501 W. Devon Ave., Rosemont, IL 60018, ☎ 800/782–2424, FAX 800/282–7474 for information or 800/860–9944 for brochures). The **Kemwel Group** (☎ 914/835–5555 or 800/678–0678, FAX 914/835–5126).

NEED INSURANCE?

When driving a rented car you are generally responsible for any damage to or loss of the vehicle. Before you rent, **see what coverage you already have** under the terms of your personal auto-insurance policy and credit cards.

Collision policies that car-rental companies sell for European rentals typically do not cover stolen vehicles. Before you buy additional coverage for theft, find out if your credit card or personal auto insurance will cover the loss.

BEWARE SURCHARGES

Before you pick up a car in one city and leave it in another, **ask about drop-off charges or one-way service fees,** which can be substantial. Note, too, that some rental agencies charge extra if you return the car before the time specified on your contract. To avoid a hefty refueling fee, **fill the tank just before you turn in the car,** but be aware that gas stations near the rental outlet may overcharge.

MEET THE REQUIREMENTS

In Paris **your own driver's license is acceptable.** An International Driver's Permit is a good idea; it's available from the American or Canadian automobile association, or, in the United Kingdom, from the Automobile Association or Royal Automobile Club.

THE CHANNEL TUNNEL

Short of flying, the "Chunnel" is the fastest way to cross the English Channel (La Manche, to the French): 35 minutes from Folkestone to Calais, 60 minutes from motorway to motorway, or 3 hours from London's Waterloo Station to Paris's Gare du Nord.

➤ CAR TRANSPORT: **Le Shuttle** (☎ 03–21–00–60–00, in France; 800/388–3876 in the U.S.; 0990/353535 in the U.K.).

➤ PASSENGER SERVICE: In France, **Eurostar** (☎ 01–42–81–43–27). In the U.K., **Eurostar** (☎ 0345/881881), **InterCity Europe** (✉ Victoria Station, London, ☎ 0171/834–2345, 0171/828–0892 for credit-card bookings). In the U.S., **BritRail Travel** (☎ 800/677–8585), **Rail Europe** (☎ 800/942–4866).

CHILDREN & TRAVEL

CHILDREN IN PARIS

Many restaurants serve children's portions and have high chairs, and larger hotels will provide cribs free to guests with young children. (This is often not the case in pensions and smaller hotels.) Paris has plenty of diversions for the young, and **almost all museums and movie theaters offer discounted rates** to children.

Getting around **Paris with a stroller can be a challenge.** Not all métro stations have escalators. Buses are a better bet in off-peak hours since they are often not as crowded as the métro and have adequate space for strollers and carriages. Many museums will require you to check strollers at the entrance. You won't have a problem finding items such as disposable diapers (*couches à jeter*) or baby food in Paris; supermarkets carry several major brands of each, and after-hours pharmacies provide the essentials.

Be sure to plan ahead and **involve your youngsters** as you outline your trip. When packing, include things to keep them busy en route. On sightseeing days try to schedule activities of special interest to your children. If you are renting a car don't forget to **arrange for a car seat** when you reserve.

➤ LOCAL INFORMATION: Contact the **CIDJ** (✉ Centre d'Information et de Documentation pour la Jeunesse, 101 quai Branly, 75015 Paris, ☎ 01–44–49–12–00) for information about activities and events for youngsters in Paris. *Le Pariscope* and *L'Officiel* are two weekly publications with English sections on entertainment for children.

➤ BABY-SITTING: **Ababa** (✉ 8 av. du Maine, 15ᵉ, ☎ 01–45–49–46–46). **Allo Maman Poule** (✉ 55 rue Emile Landrin, Boulogne, ☎ 01–46–04–13–13). **Baby Sitting Service** (✉ 18 rue Tronchet, 8ᵉ, ☎ 01–46–37–51–24). **Bebe Cool** (✉ 4 rue Faustin Halie, 16ᵉ, ☎ 01–45–04–27–14). All can provide English-speaking baby-sitters with just a few hours notice. The hourly rate is approximately $6 plus an agency fee of $10.

HOTELS

Most hotels in Paris allow children under a certain age to stay in their parents' room at no extra charge, but others charge them as extra adults; be sure to **ask about the cutoff age for children's discounts.**

The Novotel chain allows up to two children under 15 to stay free in their parents' room, and many properties have playgrounds. Sofitel hotels offer a free second room for children during July and August and over the Christmas period.

➤ BEST CHOICES: **Novotel** (☎ 800/221–4542 for international reservations). **Sofitel** (☎ 800/221–4542 for international reservations).

FLYING

As a general rule, infants under two not occupying a seat fly at greatly reduced fares and occasionally for free. If your children are two or older **ask about children's airfares.**

In general the adult baggage allowance applies to children paying half or more of the adult fare. When booking, **ask about carry-on allowances for those traveling with infants.** In general, for babies charged 10% of the adult fare you are allowed one carry-on bag and a collapsible stroller, which may have to be checked; you may be limited to less if the flight is full.

According to the FAA it's a good idea to use safety seats aloft for children weighing less than 40 pounds. Airlines, however, can set their own policies: U.S. carriers allow FAA-approved models but usually require that you buy a ticket, even if your child would otherwise ride free, since the seats must be strapped into regular seats. Airline rules vary regarding their use, so it's important to **check your airline's policy about using safety seats during takeoff and landing.** Safety seats cannot obstruct any of the other passengers in the row, so get an appropriate seat assignment as early as possible.

When making your reservation, **request children's meals or a free-standing bassinet** if you need them; the latter are available only to those seated at the bulkhead, where there's enough legroom. Remember, however, that bulkhead seats may not have their own overhead bins, and there's no storage space in front of you—a major inconvenience.

GROUP TRAVEL

If you're planning to take your kids on a tour, look for companies that specialize in family travel.

➤ FAMILY-FRIENDLY TOUR OPERATORS: **Grandtravel** (✉ 6900 Wisconsin Ave., Suite 706, Chevy Chase, MD 20815, ☎ 301/986–0790 or 800/247–7651) for people traveling with grandchildren ages 7–17. **Families Welcome!** (✉ 92 N. Main St., Ashland, OR 97520, ☎ 541/482–2442 or 800/326–0724, FAX 541/482–0660).

CONSUMER PROTECTION

Whenever possible, **pay with a major credit card** so you can cancel payment if there's a problem, provided that you can provide documentation. This is a good practice whether you're buying travel arrangements before your trip or shopping at your destination.

If you're doing business with a particular company for the first time, **contact your local Better Business Bureau and the attorney general's offices** in your state and the company's home state, as well. Have any complaints been filed?

Finally, if you're buying a package or tour, always **consider travel insurance** that includes default coverage (☞ Insurance, *below*).

➤ LOCAL BBBS: **Council of Better Business Bureaus** (✉ 4200 Wilson Blvd., Suite 800, Arlington, VA 22203, ☎ 703/276–0100, FAX 703/525–8277).

CUSTOMS & DUTIES

When shopping, **keep receipts** for all your purchases. Upon reentering the country, **be ready to show customs officials what you've bought.** If you feel a duty is incorrect, appeal the assessment. If you object to the way your clearance was handled, get the inspector's badge number. In either case, first ask to see a supervisor, then write to the port director at the address listed on your receipt. Send a copy of the receipt and other appropriate documentation. If you still don't get satisfaction you can take your case to customs headquarters in Washington.

ENTERING FRANCE

If you're coming from outside the European Union (EU), you may import duty free: (1) 200 cigarettes or 100 cigarillos or 50 cigars or 250 grams of tobacco (twice that if you live outside Europe); (2) 2 liters of wine and, in addition, (a) 1 liter of alcohol over 22% volume (most spirits) or (b) 2 liters of alcohol under 22% volume (fortified or sparkling wine) or (c) 2 more liters of table wine; (3) 50 milliliters of perfume and 250 milliliters of toilet water; (4) 200 grams of coffee, 100 grams of tea; and (5) other goods to the value of 300 francs (100 francs for those under 15).

If you're arriving from an EU country, you may be required to declare all goods and prove that anything over the standard limit is for personal consumption. Since January 1993, however, there is no longer any limit or customs tariff imposed on goods carried within the EU.

Any amount of French or foreign currency may be brought into France, but foreign currencies converted into francs may be reconverted into a foreign currency only up to the equivalent of 5,000 francs.

ENTERING THE U.S.

You may bring home $400 worth of foreign goods duty-free if you've been out of the country for at least 48 hours and haven't already used the $400 allowance or any part of it in the past 30 days.

Travelers 21 and older may bring back 1 liter of alcohol duty-free. In addition, regardless of your age, you are allowed 200 cigarettes and 100 non-Cuban cigars. (At press time, a federal rule restricting tobacco access to persons 18 years and older did not apply to importation.) Antiques, which the U.S. Customs Service defines as objects more than 100 years old, enter duty-free, as do original works of art done entirely by hand, including paintings, drawings, and sculptures.

You may also send packages home duty-free: up to $200 worth of goods for personal use, with a limit of one parcel per addressee per day (and no alcohol or tobacco products or perfume worth more than $5); label the package PERSONAL USE, and attach a list of its contents and their retail value. Do not label the package UNSOLICITED GIFT, or your duty-free exemption will drop to $100. Mailed items do not affect your duty-free allowance on your return.

➤ INFORMATION: **U.S. Customs Service** (Inquiries, ✉ Box 7407, Washington, DC 20044, ☎ 202/927–6724; complaints, ✉ Commissioner's Office, 1301 Constitution Ave. NW, Washington, DC 20229; registration of equipment, ✉ Resource Management, 1301 Constitution Ave. NW,

Washington DC, 20229, ☎ 202/927–0540).

ENTERING CANADA

If you've been out of Canada for at least 7 days you may bring in C$500 worth of goods duty-free. If you've been away for fewer than 7 days but more than 48 hours, the duty-free allowance drops to C$200; if your trip lasts 24–48 hours, the allowance is C$50. You may not pool allowances with family members. Goods claimed under the C$500 exemption may follow you by mail; those claimed under the lesser exemptions must accompany you.

Alcohol and tobacco products may be included in the seven-day and 48-hour exemptions but not in the 24-hour exemption. If you meet the age requirements of the province or territory through which you reenter Canada you may bring in, duty-free, 1.14 liters (40 imperial ounces) of wine or liquor *or* 24 12-ounce cans or bottles of beer or ale. If you are 16 or older you may bring in, duty-free, 200 cigarettes and 50 cigars; these items must accompany you.

You may send an unlimited number of gifts worth up to C$60 each duty-free to Canada. Label the package UNSOLICITED GIFT—VALUE UNDER $60. Alcohol and tobacco are excluded.

➤ INFORMATION: **Revenue Canada** (✉ 2265 St. Laurent Blvd. S, Ottawa, Ontario K1G 4K3, ☎ 613/993–0534, 800/461–9999 in Canada).

ENTERING THE U.K.

If your journey was wholly within EU countries you needn't pass through customs when you return to the United Kingdom. If you plan to bring back large quantities of alcohol or tobacco, check on EU limits beforehand.

➤ INFORMATION: **HM Customs and Excise** (✉ Dorset House, Stamford St., London SE1 9NG, ☎ 0171/202–4227).

D

DISABILITIES & ACCESSIBILITY

ACCESS IN PARIS

Though the city of Paris is doing much to ensure that public facilities accommodate people with mobility problems, it still has a long way to go. Some sidewalks now have low curbs, and many arrondissements have public rest rooms and telephone boxes that are wheelchair accessible. Some monuments, hotels, and museums, especially those constructed in the past decade, are equipped with ramps, elevators, and special toilet facilities. However, it is best to ask in advance about access, particularly about elevators, since many smaller, older hotels do not have them. Taxi drivers are required by law to assist travelers with disabilities in and out of their vehicles. Unfortunately, not all métro and RER stations are wheelchair accessible, nor many buses.

➤ LOCAL RESOURCES: An RER and métro access guide is available at most stations, as well as from the **Paris Transit Authority** (RATP) kiosk (✉ 53 bis quai des Grands Augustins, 6ᵉ or ✉ pl. de la Madeleine, 8ᵉ, ☎ 08–36–68–41–14).

TIPS & HINTS

When discussing accessibility with an operator or reservationist, **ask hard questions.** Are there any stairs, inside *or* out? Are there grab bars next to the toilet *and* in the shower/tub? How wide is the doorway to the room? To the bathroom? For the most extensive facilities meeting the latest legal specifications, **opt for newer accommodations,** which are more likely to have been designed with access in mind. Older buildings or ships may offer more limited facilities. Be sure to **discuss your needs before booking.**

➤ COMPLAINTS: **Disability Rights Section** (✉ U.S. Department of Justice, Box 66738, Washington, DC 20035–6738, ☎ 202/514–0301 or 800/514–0301, FAX 202/307–1198, TTY 202/514–0383 or 800/514–0383) for general complaints. **Aviation Consumer Protection Division** (☞ Air Travel, *above*) for airline-related problems. **Civil Rights Office** (✉ U.S. DOT, Departmental Office of Civil Rights, S-30, 400 7th St. SW, Room 10215, Washington, DC, 20590, ☎ 202/366–4648) for problems with surface transportation.

TRAVEL AGENCIES & TOUR OPERATORS

The Americans with Disabilities Act requires that travel firms serve the

THE GOLD GUIDE / SMART TRAVEL TIPS

needs of all travelers. That said, you should note that some agencies and operators specialize in making travel arrangements for individuals and groups with disabilities.

➤ TRAVELERS WITH MOBILITY PROBLEMS: **Access Adventures** (✉ 206 Chestnut Ridge Rd., Rochester, NY 14624, ☎ 716/889–9096), run by a former physical-rehabilitation counselor. **Accessible Journeys** (✉ 35 W. Sellers Ave., Ridley Park, PA 19078, ☎ 610/521–0339 or 800/846–4537, FAX 610/521–6959), for escorted tours exclusively for travelers with mobility impairments. **Hinsdale Travel Service** (✉ 201 E. Ogden Ave., Suite 100, Hinsdale, IL 60521, ☎ 630/325–1335), a travel agency that benefits from the advice of wheelchair traveler Janice Perkins. **Wheelchair Journeys** (✉ 16979 Redmond Way, Redmond, WA 98052, ☎ 206/885–2210 or 800/313–4751), for general travel arrangements.

DISCOUNTS & DEALS

Be a smart shopper and **compare all your options before making a choice.** A plane ticket bought with a promotional coupon may not be cheaper than the least expensive fare from a discount ticket agency. For high-price travel purchases, such as packages or tours, keep in mind that what you get is just as important as what you save. Just because something is cheap doesn't mean it's a bargain.

LOOK IN YOUR WALLET

When you use your credit card to make travel purchases you may get free travel-accident insurance, collision-damage insurance, and medical or legal assistance, depending on the card and the bank that issued it. American Express, MasterCard, and Visa provide one or more of these services, so **get a copy of your credit card's travel-benefits policy.** If you are a member of the American Automobile Association (AAA) or an oil-company-sponsored road-assistance plan, always **ask hotel or car-rental reservationists about auto-club discounts.** Some clubs offer additional discounts on tours, cruises, or admission to attractions. And don't forget that auto-club membership entitles you to free maps and trip-planning services.

DIAL FOR DOLLARS

To save money, **look into "1-800" discount reservations services,** which use their buying power to get a better price on hotels, airline tickets, even car rentals. When booking a room, always **call the hotel's local toll-free number** (if one is available) rather than the central reservations number—you'll often get a better price. Always ask about special packages or corporate rates.

When shopping for the best deal on hotels and car rentals **look for guaranteed exchange rates,** which protect you against a falling dollar. With your rate locked in you won't pay more even if the price goes up in the local currency.

➤ AIRLINE TICKETS: ☎ 800/FLY-4–LESS.

➤ HOTEL ROOMS: **Hotels Plus** (☎ 800/235–0909). **Hotel Reservations Network** (HRN; ☎ 800/964–6835). **International Marketing & Travel Concepts** (IMTC; ☎ 800/790–4682).

SAVE ON COMBOS

Packages and guided tours can both save you money, but don't confuse the two. When you buy a package your travel remains independent, just as though you had planned and booked the trip yourself. Fly-drive packages, which combine airfare and car rental, are often a good deal. In cities, ask the local visitors bureau about hotel packages. These often include tickets to major museum exhibits and other special events.

JOIN A CLUB?

Many companies sell discounts in the form of travel clubs and coupon books, but these cost money. You must use participating advertisers to get a deal, and only after you recoup the initial membership cost or book price do you begin to save. If you plan to use the club or coupons frequently you may save considerably. Before signing up, find out what discounts you get for free.

➤ DISCOUNT CLUBS: **Entertainment Travel Editions** (✉ Box 1068, Trumbull, CT 06611, ☎ 800/445–4137; $28–$53, depending on destination). **Great American Traveler** (✉ Box 27965, Salt Lake City, UT 84127, ☎ 800/548–2812; $49.95 per year).

Moment's Notice Discount Travel Club (✉ 7301 New Utrecht Ave., Brooklyn, NY 11204, ☎ 718/234–6295; $25 per year, single or family). **Privilege Card International** (✉ 201 E. Commerce St., Suite 198, Youngstown, OH 44503, ☎ 330/746–5211 or 800/236–9732; $74.95 per year). **Sears's Mature Outlook** (✉ Box 9390, Des Moines, IA 50306, ☎ 800/336–6330; $14.95 per year). **Travelers Advantage** (✉ CUC Travel Service, 3033 S. Parker Rd., Suite 1000, Aurora, CO 80014, ☎ 800/548–1116 or 800/648–4037; $49 per year, single or family). **Worldwide Discount Travel Club** (✉ 1674 Meridian Ave., Miami Beach, FL 33139, ☎ 305/534–2082; $50 per year family, $40 single).

PASSES

Paris Tourist Offices, railroad stations, major métro stations, and participating museums sell the **Carte Musées et Monuments,** which offers unlimited access to more than 60 museums and monuments in Paris over a one-, three-, or five-day period; the cost, respectively, is 70, 140, and 200 francs. Temporary exhibitions are not included in this pass. *See also* Métro *and* Train Travel, *below.*

DRIVING

FROM THE U.K.

There are a number of different driving routes to Paris. The Dover–Calais route includes the shortest Channel crossing; the Newhaven–Dieppe route requires a longer Channel crossing but a shorter drive through France.

Driving distances from the French ports to Paris are as follows: from Calais, 290 km (180 mi); from Boulogne, 243 km (151 mi); from Dieppe, 193 km (120 mi); from Dunkerque, 257 km (160 mi). The fastest routes to Paris from each port are via the N43, A26, and A1 from Calais; via the N1 from Boulogne; via the N15 from Le Havre; via the D915 and N1 from Dieppe; and via the A25 and A1 from Dunkerque.

E

ELECTRICITY

To use your U.S.-purchased electric-powered equipment, **bring a converter and adapter.** The electrical current in France is 220 volts, 50 cycles alternating current (AC); wall outlets take continental-type plugs, with two round prongs.

If your appliances are dual-voltage, you'll need only an adapter. Don't use 110-volt outlets, marked FOR SHAVERS ONLY, for high-wattage appliances such as blow-dryers. Most laptops operate equally well on 110 and 220 volts and so require only an adapter.

EMBASSIES & EMERGENCIES

➤ EMBASSIES: **U.S. Embassy** (✉ 2 av. Gabriel, 8ᵉ, ☎ 01–43–12–22–22). **Canadian Embassy** (✉ 35 av. Montaigne, 8ᵉ, ☎ 01–44–43–29–00). **British Embassy** (✉ 35 rue du Faubourg St-Honoré, 8ᵉ, ☎ 01–44–51–31–00).

➤ EMERGENCIES: **Fire** (☎ 18); locals tend to call the fire department for any type of emergency as it has fully trained medical teams and is very efficient. **Police** (☎ 17). **Ambulance** (☎ 15 or ☎ 01–45–67–50–50). **Doctor** (☎ 01–47–07–77–77). **Dentist** (☎ 01–43–37–51–00).

➤ HOSPITALS: **The American Hospital** (✉ 63 bd. Victor Hugo, Neuilly, ☎ 01–46–41–25–25) has a 24-hour emergency service. **The Hertford British Hospital** (✉ 3 rue Barbès, Levallois-Perret, ☎ 01–46–39–22–22) also offers a 24-hour service.

➤ PHARMACIES: **Dhéry** (✉ Galerie des Champs, 84 av. des Champs-Elysées, 8ᵉ, ☎ 01–45–62–02–41) is open 24 hours. **Pharmacie des Arts** (✉ 106 bd. Montparnasse, 14ᵉ) is open daily until midnight. **Pharmacie Matignon** (✉ rue Jean Mermoz, at the Rond-Point de Champs-Elysées, 8ᵉ) is open daily until 2 AM.

F

FERRY & HOVERCRAFT TRAVEL

There are a number of different ferry and hovercraft routes between the United Kingdom and France. Driving distances from the French ports to Paris are as follows: from Calais, 290 km (180 mi); from Boulogne, 243 km

THE GOLD GUIDE / SMART TRAVEL TIPS

(151 mi); from Dieppe, 193 km (120 mi); from Dunkerque, 257 km (160 mi). The fastest routes to Paris from each port are via N43, A26, and A1 from Calais and the Channel Tunnel; via N1 from Boulogne; via N15 from Le Havre; via D915 and N1 from Dieppe; and via A25 and A1 from Dunkerque.

➤ DOVER–CALAIS: **Hoverspeed** (✉ International Hoverport, Marine Parade, Dover CT17 9TG, ☎ 01304/240241) operates up to 15 crossings a day by Hovercraft and catamaran. The crossings take 35 minutes (Hovercraft) or 55 minutes (catamaran). **P&O European Ferries** (✉ Channel House, Channel View Rd., Dover, Kent CT17 9TJ, ☎ 0181/575–8555) has up to 25 sailings a day; the crossing takes about 75 minutes. **Sealink** (✉ Charter House, Park St., Ashford, Kent TN24 8EX, ☎ 01233/646801) operates up to 25 sailings a day; the crossing takes about 90 minutes.

➤ FOLKESTONE–BOULOGNE: **Hoverspeed** (☞ Dover–Calais, *above*) is the sole operator on this route, with 10 35-minute crossings a day.

➤ NEWHAVEN–DIEPPE: **Sealink** (☞ Dover–Calais, *above*) has as many as four sailings a day, and the crossing takes four hours.

➤ PORTSMOUTH–LE HAVRE: **P&O European Ferries** (☞ Dover–Calais, *above*) has up to three sailings a day, and the crossing takes 5½ hours by day, 7½ by night.

➤ RAMSGATE–DUNKERQUE: **Sally Line** (✉ Argyle Centre, York St., Ramsgate, Kent CT11 9DS, ☎ 01843/595522) has up to six 2½-hour crossings a day.

G

GAY & LESBIAN TRAVEL

In Paris, **several gay and lesbian organizations provide information** on events and medical care or counseling. A number of informative newspapers and magazines that cover the Parisian gay/lesbian scene are available at stores and kiosks in the city. *Paris Exit* is a well-rounded newspaper that discusses issues of interest; publishes an up-to-date calendar of events; regularly reviews new clubs, bars, restaurants, and cultural events

and lists services from travel agents to saunas. The *Gai Guide* lists gay bars, parties, and other events. The popular *Gai Pied Hebdo,* a weekly magazine, produces a summer guidebook (about 50 francs). *Lesbia,* a monthly magazine, has a wide range of listings, reviews, and contacts.

➤ GAY & LESBIAN ORGANIZATIONS: **Agora** (✉ 33 bd. Picpus, 12ᵉ, ☎ 01–43–42–19–02) provides information on events, meetings, and rallies. **Association des Médecins Gais** (☎ 01–48–05–81–71) and **Ecoute Gaie** (☎ 01–44–93–01–02 after 6 PM) offer advice and information over the phone. **Centre du Christ Libérateur** (✉ 5 rue Crussol, 11ᵉ, ☎ 01–48–05–24–48) provides medical care and counseling. **Centre Gai et Lesbien** (✉ 3 rue Keller, 11ᵉ, ☎ 01–43–57–21–47) offers a wide range of information on events. **FAACTS** (Free Anglo-American Counseling Treatment Support) at the American Church (✉ quai d'Orsay, 7ᵉ) has weekly meetings for people infected or affected by HIV.

➤ TOUR OPERATORS: **Gays Randonneurs & Voyageurs** (✉ BP 68 75462, Paris Cedex 10) and **Rando's** (✉ BP 419 75870, Paris Cedex 18, ☎ 01–42–26–08–04) plan weekend hikes and trips from Paris. **R.S.V.P. Travel Productions** (✉ 2800 University Ave. SE, Minneapolis, MN 55414, ☎ 612/379–4697 or 800/328–7787), for cruises and resort vacations for gays.

➤ TRAVEL AGENCIES: **Advance Damron** (✉ 1 Greenway Plaza, Suite 800, Houston, TX 77046, ☎ 713/682–2002 or 800/695–0880, ℻ 713/888–1010). **Club Travel** (✉ 8739 Santa Monica Blvd., West Hollywood, CA 90069, ☎ 310/358–2200 or 800/429–8747, ℻ 310/358–2222). **Islanders/Kennedy Travel** (✉ 183 W. 10th St., New York, NY 10014, ☎ 212/242–3222 or 800/988–1181, ℻ 212/929–8530). **Now Voyager** (✉ 4406 18th St., San Francisco, CA 94114, ☎ 415/626–1169 or 800/255–6951, ℻ 415/626–8626). **Yellowbrick Road** (✉ 1500 W. Balmoral Ave., Chicago, IL 60640, ☎ 773/561–1800 or 800/642–2488, ℻ 773/561–4497). **Skylink Women's Travel** (✉ 3577 Moorland Ave., Santa Rosa, CA 95407, ☎ 707/585–

8355 or 800/225–5759, FAX 707/
584–5637), serving lesbian travelers.

H
HEALTH

MEDICAL PLANS

No one plans to get sick while traveling, but it happens, so **consider signing up with a medical-assistance
company.** Members get doctor referrals, emergency evacuation or repatri-
ation, 24-hour telephone hot lines for
medical consultation, cash for emergencies, and other personal and legal
assistance. Coverage varies by plan,
so **review the benefits carefully.** *See*
also Embassies and Emergencies,
above.

➤ MEDICAL-ASSISTANCE COMPANIES:
International SOS Assistance (✉ Box
11568, Philadelphia, PA 19116, ☎
215/244–1500 or 800/523–8930; ✉
Box 466, pl. Bonaventure, Montréal,
Québec H5A 1C1, ☎ 514/874–7674
or 800/363–0263; ✉ 7 Old Lodge
Pl., St. Margarets, Twickenham TW1
1RQ, England, ☎ 0181/744–0033).
MEDEX Assistance Corporation (✉
Box 5375, Timonium, MD 21094, ☎
410/453–6300 or 800/537–2029).
Traveler's Emergency Network (✉
3100 Tower Blvd., Suite 1000B,
Durham, NC 27707, ☎ 919/490–
6055 or 800/275–4836, FAX 919/
493–8262). **TravMed** (✉ Box 5375,
Timonium, MD 21094, ☎ 410/453–
6380 or 800/732–5309). **Worldwide
Assistance Services** (✉ 1133 15th St.
NW, Suite 400, Washington, DC
20005, ☎ 202/331–1609 or 800/
821–2828, FAX 202/828–5896).

HOLIDAYS

With 11 national holidays (*jours
feriés*) and 5 weeks of paid vacation,
the French have their share of repose.
In May, there is a holiday nearly
every week, so be prepared for stores,
banks, and museums to shut their
doors for days at a time. Bastille Day
(July 14) is observed in true French
form. Celebrations begin on the
evening of the 13th and finish the
next day with an annual military
parade down the Champs-Elysées and
a fireworks display, usually at Trocadéro.

January 1 (New Year's Day); April 13
(Easter Monday); May 1 (Labor
Day); May 8 (VE Day); May 21

(Ascension); June 1 (Pentecost Monday); July 14 (Bastille Day); August
15 (Assumption); November 1 (All
Saints); November 11 (Armistice);
December 25 (Christmas).

I
INSURANCE

Travel insurance is the best way to
protect yourself against financial loss.
The most useful policies are trip-
cancellation-and-interruption, default,
medical, and comprehensive insurance.

Without insurance you will lose all or
most of your money if you cancel
your trip, regardless of the reason. It's
essential that you **buy trip-cancella-
tion-and-interruption insurance,**
particularly if your airline ticket,
cruise, or package tour is nonrefundable and cannot be changed. When
considering how much coverage you
need, look for a policy that will cover
the cost of your trip plus the nondis-
counted price of a one-way airline
ticket, should you need to return
home early. Also **consider default or
bankruptcy insurance,** which protects
you against a supplier's failure to
deliver.

Medicare generally does not cover
health-care costs outside the United
States, nor do many privately issued
policies. If your own policy does not
cover you outside the United States,
**consider buying supplemental medical
coverage.** Remember that travel
health insurance is different from a
medical-assistance plan (☞ Health,
above).

Citizens of the United Kingdom can
buy an annual travel-insurance policy
valid for most vacations during the
year in which it's purchased. If you
are pregnant or have a preexisting
medical condition, make sure you're
covered.

If you have purchased an expensive
vacation, particularly one that involves travel abroad, comprehensive
insurance is a must. **Look for comprehensive policies that include trip-delay
insurance,** which will protect you in
the event that weather problems cause
you to miss your flight, tour, or
cruise. A few insurers sell waivers for
preexisting medical conditions. Companies that offer both features include

Access America, Carefree Travel, Travel Insured International, and Travel Guard (☞ *below*).

Always **buy travel insurance directly from the insurance company;** if you buy it from a travel agency or tour operator that goes out of business you probably will not be covered for the agency or operator's default, a major risk. Before you make any purchase, **review your existing health and home-owner's policies** to find out whether they cover expenses incurred while traveling.

➤ TRAVEL INSURERS: In the U.S., **Access America** (☒ 6600 W. Broad St., Richmond, VA 23230, ☎ 804/285–3300 or 800/284–8300), **Carefree Travel Insurance** (☒ Box 9366, 100 Garden City Plaza, Garden City, NY 11530, ☎ 516/294–0220 or 800/323–3149), **Near Travel Services** (☒ Box 1339, Calumet City, IL 60409, ☎ 708/868–6700 or 800/654–6700), **Travel Guard International** (☒ 1145 Clark St., Stevens Point, WI 54481, ☎ 715/345–0505 or 800/826–1300), **Travel Insured International** (☒ Box 280568, East Hartford, CT 06128–0568, ☎ 860/528–7663 or 800/243–3174), **Travelex Insurance Services** (☒ 11717 Burt St., Suite 202, Omaha, NE 68154-1500, ☎ 402/445–8637 or 800/228–9792, FAX 800/867–9531), **Wallach & Company** (☒ 107 W. Federal St., Box 480, Middleburg, VA 20118, ☎ 540/687–3166 or 800/237–6615). In Canada, **Mutual of Omaha** (☒ Travel Division, 500 University Ave., Toronto, Ontario M5G 1V8, ☎ 416/598–4083, 800/268–8825 in Canada). In the U.K., **Association of British Insurers** (☒ 51 Gresham St., London EC2V 7HQ, ☎ 0171/600–3333).

L

LANGUAGE

The French study English at school for a minimum of four years (often longer) but to little general effect. However, **English is widely understood in major tourist areas,** and at least one person in most hotels can explain things to you. Young people usually speak more English than their parents' generation. Be patient, and speak slowly.

The French may appear prickly at first to English-speaking visitors, but they usually will try to help out, especially when you **at least make an effort to speak a little French.** So even if your own French is terrible, try to master a few words. *See* the French Vocabulary and Menu Guide at the back of the book.

LODGING

APARTMENT & HOUSE RENTALS

If you want a home base that's roomy enough for a family and comes with cooking facilities, **consider a furnished rental.** These can save you money, however some rentals are luxury properties, economical only when your party is large. Home-exchange directories list rentals (often second homes owned by prospective house swappers), and some services search for a house or apartment for you (even a castle if that's your fancy) and handle the paperwork. Some send an illustrated catalog; others send photographs only of specific properties, sometimes at a charge. Up-front registration fees may apply.

➤ RENTAL AGENTS: **Europa-Let/Tropical Inn-Let** (☒ 92 N. Main St., Ashland, OR 97520, ☎ 541/482–5806 or 800/462–4486, FAX 541/482–0660). **Hometours International** (☒ Box 11503, Knoxville, TN 37939, ☎ 423/690–8484 or 800/367–4668). **Interhome** (☒ 124 Little Falls Rd., Fairfield, NJ 07004, ☎ 201/882–6864, FAX 201/808–1742). **Property Rentals International** (☒ 1008 Mansfield Crossing Rd., Richmond, VA 23236, ☎ 804/378–6054 or 800/220–3332, FAX 804/379–2073). **Rental Directories International** (☒ 2044 Rittenhouse Sq., Philadelphia, PA 19103, ☎ 215/985–4001, FAX 215/985–0323). **Vacation Home Rentals Worldwide** (☒ 235 Kensington Ave., Norwood, NJ 07648, ☎ 201/767–9393 or 800/633–3284, FAX 201/767–5510). **Villas and Apartments Abroad** (☒ 420 Madison Ave., Suite 1003, New York, NY 10017, ☎ 212/759–1025 or 800/433–3020, FAX 212/755–8316). **Villas International** (☒ 605 Market St., Suite 510, San Francisco, CA 94105, ☎ 415/281–0910 or 800/221–2260, FAX 415/281–0919). **Hideaways International** (☒ 767 Islington St.,

Portsmouth, NH 03801, ☏ 603/430–4433 or 800/843–4433, FAX 603/430–4444) is a travel club whose members arrange rentals among themselves; yearly membership is $99.

HOME EXCHANGES

If you would like to exchange your home for someone else's, **join a home-exchange organization,** which will send you its updated listings of available exchanges for a year and will include your own listing in at least one of them. Making the arrangements is up to you.

➤ EXCHANGE CLUBS: **HomeLink International** (✉ Box 650, Key West, FL 33041, ☏ 305/294–7766 or 800/638–3841, FAX 305/294–1148) charges $83 per year.

M

MAIL

Post offices, or PTT, are scattered throughout every arrondissement and are recognizable by a yellow sign that says La Poste. They are usually open weekdays 8 AM–7 PM, Saturday 8 AM–noon.

➤ POST OFFICES: **Main office** (✉ 52 rue du Louvre, 1ᵉʳ), open 24 hours. **Champs-Elysées post office** (✉ 71 av. des Champs-Elysées, 8ᵉ), open until 11 PM.

RATES

Airmail letters to the United States and Canada cost 4.40 francs for 20 grams, 8.20 francs for 40 grams, and 13 francs for 60 grams. Letters to the United Kingdom cost 3 francs for up to 20 grams, as they do within France. Postcards cost 3 francs within France and EU countries, and 4.40 francs to the United States and Canada. Stamps can be bought in post offices and cafés sporting a red TABAC sign.

RECEIVING MAIL

If you're uncertain where you'll be staying, have mail sent to American Express (if you're a card member) or to Poste Restante at any post office.

MÉTRO

Métro stations are recognizable either by a large yellow *M* within a circle or by the distinctive curly green Art Nouveau railings and archway bear-ing the full title (Métropolitain). Taking **the métro is the most efficient way to get around Paris.**

There are 13 métro lines crisscrossing Paris and the suburbs (and a 14th in the works), and you are seldom more than 500 yards from the nearest station. It is essential to **know the name of the last station on the line you take, as this name appears on all signs.** A connection (you can make as many as you like on one ticket) is called a *correspondance.* At junction stations, illuminated orange signs bearing the name of the line terminus appear over the correct corridors for each correspondance. Illuminated blue signs marked *sortie* indicate the station exit. Be sure not to pass through any of the gates or *limites,* as your tickets are only valid inside these.

Métro service starts at 5:30 AM and continues until 1:00 AM, when the last train on each line reaches its terminus. Some lines and stations in the less salubrious parts of Paris are a bit risky at night, in particular Lines 2 and 13. But in general, the métro is relatively safe throughout, providing you **don't walk around with your wallet hanging out of your back pocket or (especially women) travel alone late at night.** The biggest nuisances you're likely to come across will be the wine-swigging *clochards* (homeless) blurting out drunken songs as they bed down on platform benches.

The métro network connects at several points in Paris with the RER (Réseau Express Régional, or the Regional Express Network). RER trains, which race across Paris from suburb to suburb, are a sort of supersonic métro and can be great timesavers.

All **métro tickets and passes are valid for RER and bus travel within Paris.** Métro tickets cost 8 francs each; a *carnet* (10 tickets for 46 francs) is a better value. If you're staying for a week or more and plan to use the métro frequently, the best deal is the weekly (*coupon jaune*) or monthly (*carte orange*) ticket, sold according to zone. Zones 1 and 2 cover the entire métro network; tickets cost 72 francs a week or 243 francs a month. If you plan to take suburban trains to visit places in the Ile-de-France, consider a four-zone (Versailles, St-Germain-en-Laye; 126 francs a week) or six-zone (Rambouillet, Fontainebleau; 170 francs a week) ticket. For these weekly/monthly tickets, you will need a pass (available from rail and major métro stations) and a passport-size photograph.

Alternatively, there are one-day (Formule 1) and three- and five-day (Paris Visite) unlimited travel tickets for the métro, bus, and RER. Their advantage is that, unlike the coupon jaune, which is good from Monday morning to Sunday evening, Formule 1 and Paris Visite passes are valid starting any day of the week and also give you discounts on a limited number of museums and tourist attractions. The price is 40 (one-day), 70 (two-day), 105 (three-day), and 165 (five-day) francs for Paris only; 170, 230, and 315 francs, respectively, for suburbs including Versailles, St-Germain-en-Laye, and Disneyland Paris.

Access to métro and RER platforms is through an automatic ticket barrier. Slide your ticket in and pick it up as it pops out. Be certain to **keep your ticket during your journey**; you'll need it to leave the RER system and in case you run into any green-clad ticket inspectors who can not only be very nasty if you don't have a ticket or a photo with your pass, but they can also impose a big fine on the spot.

MONEY

The units of currency in France are the franc (fr) and the centime. Bills are in denominations of 500, 200, 100, 50, and 20 francs. Coins are 20, 10, 5, 2, and 1 francs and 50, 20, 10, and 5 centimes. Note that the old 10-franc coin has been changed and replaced by a smaller, two-tone version. At press time (1997), the exchange rate was about 5 francs to the U.S. dollar, 3.75 to the Canadian dollar, and 7.75 to the pound sterling.

ATMS

ATMs are fairly common in Paris and are among the easiest ways to get francs. You may, however, have to look around for Cirrus and Plus locations. Try to get a list of locations from your bank before you go. Also before leaving home, **make sure that your credit cards and ATM cards have been programmed for ATM use in Paris.** Note that Discover is generally not accepted in France. Local bank cards often do not work overseas or may access only your checking account; **ask your bank about a Master-Card/Cirrus or Visa debit card,** which works like a bank card but can be used at any ATM displaying a Master-Card/Cirrus or Visa logo. These cards, too, may tap only your checking account; check with your bank about their policy.

➤ ATM LOCATIONS: **Cirrus** (☎ 800/424–7787). A list of Plus locations is available at your local bank.

COSTS

As in most capital cities, **life in Paris is more expensive than anywhere else in the country** (except the Riviera). Yet, unlike central London, for instance, Paris is a place where people live as well as work; Parisians, who shop and lunch locally, are not prepared to pay extravagant rates, and if you avoid the obvious tourist traps you will not have to pay those rates, either.

Prices tend to reflect the standing of an area in the eyes of Parisians; much sought-after residential arrondissements such as the 7ᵉ, 16ᵉ, and 17ᵉ—of limited tourist interest—are far more expensive than the student-oriented, much-visited Latin Quarter. The tourist area where value for money is most difficult to find is the 8ᵉ arrondissement, on and around the Champs-Elysées. Places where you can be virtually certain to shop, eat, and stay without overpaying include the streets surrounding Montmartre (not the Butte, or hilltop, itself); the St-Michel/Sorbonne area on the Left Bank; the mazelike streets around Les Halles and the Marais in central Paris; and the Bastille area and eastern Paris.

Note that in cafés, bars, and some restaurants, it is less expensive to eat or drink standing at the counter than it is to sit at a table. Two prices are listed, *au comptoir* (at the counter) and *à salle* (at a table). A cup of coffee, standing at a bar, costs from 6 francs; if you sit, it will cost from 10 francs. A glass of beer costs from 10 francs standing and from 15 francs sitting; a soft drink costs between 10

francs and 20 francs. A ham sandwich will cost between 17 francs and
30 francs. Expect to pay 35–40
francs for a short taxi ride.

CURRENCY EXCHANGE

For the most favorable rates, **change
money at banks or get money from
ATMs.** Although fees charged for
ATM transactions may be higher
abroad than at home, Cirrus and Plus
exchange rates are excellent, because
they are based on wholesale rates
offered only by major banks. You
won't do as well at exchange booths
in airports or rail and bus stations, in
hotels, in restaurants, or in stores,
although you may find their hours
more convenient. To avoid lines at
airport exchange booths, **get a small
amount of local currency before you
leave home.**

➤ EXCHANGE SERVICES: **International
Currency Express** (☎ 888/842–0880
on the east coast or 888/278–6628
on the west coast for telephone orders). **Thomas Cook Currency Services** (☎ 800/287–7362 for
telephone orders and retail locations).

TRAVELER'S CHECKS

Whether or not to buy traveler's
checks depends on where you are
headed. **Take cash if your trip includes
rural areas** and small towns, traveler's checks to cities. If your checks
are lost or stolen, they can usually be
replaced within 24 hours. To ensure a
speedy refund, buy your checks
yourself (don't ask someone else to
make the purchase). When making a
claim for stolen or lost checks, the
person who bought the checks should
make the call.

P

PACKING FOR PARIS

Although you'll usually have no
trouble finding a baggage cart at the
airport, luggage restrictions on international flights are tight, and baggage
carts at railroad stations are not
always available. So **pack light.**

Over the years, **casual dress has
become more acceptable,** although
Paris is still the world's fashion capital and people dress accordingly.
There is no need to wear a tie and
jacket at most restaurants (unless
specified), even fancy ones, and jeans

are de rigueur at the new Bastille
Opéra (a jeans-and-sneakers outfit,
however, may raise eyebrows). Shorts
are seldom worn in Paris—**if you are
wearing shorts, you may be denied
admission to churches and cathedrals.**
More and more people are wearing
sneakers, though you will still stand
out as a tourist if you have them on.
Otherwise, pack as you would for a
major American city.

It can be hot in Paris in summer and
cold in winter. Since it rains all year
round, **bring a raincoat and umbrella.**

Wear sturdy walking shoes for sightseeing: Paris is full of cobblestone
streets, and many historic buildings
are surrounded by gravel paths. Keep
in mind that you may be running in
and out of warm, crowded métros. To
protect yourself against purse snatch-
ers and pickpockets, take a handbag
with long straps that you can sling
across your body, bandolier-style,
with a zippered compartment for
your money and passport—French
law requires that you carry identification at all times.

Bring an extra pair of eyeglasses or
contact lenses in your carry-on luggage, and if you have a health problem, **pack enough medication** to last
the entire trip or have your doctor
write you a prescription using the
drug's generic name, because brand
names vary from country to country.
It's important that you **don't put
prescription drugs or valuables in
luggage to be checked**: it might go
astray. To avoid problems with customs officials, carry medications in
the original packaging. Also, don't
forget the addresses of offices that
handle refunds of lost traveler's
checks.

LUGGAGE

In general, **you are entitled to check
two bags on flights within the United
States and on international flights
leaving the United States.** A third
piece may be brought on board, but it
must fit easily under the seat in front
of you or in the overhead compartment.

If you are flying between two foreign
destinations, note that baggage allowances may be determined not by
piece but by weight—generally 88
pounds (40 kilograms) in first class,

66 pounds (30 kilograms) in business class, and 44 pounds (20 kilograms) in economy. If your flight between two cities abroad *connects* with your transatlantic or transpacific flight, the piece method still applies.

Airline liability for baggage is limited to $1,250 per person on flights within the United States. On international flights it amounts to $9.07 per pound or $20 per kilogram for checked baggage (roughly $640 per 70-pound bag) and $400 per passenger for unchecked baggage. Insurance for losses exceeding these amounts can be bought from the airline at check-in for about $10 per $1,000 of coverage; note that this coverage excludes a rather extensive list of items, which is shown on your airline ticket.

Before departure, **itemize your bags' contents** and their worth, and label the bags with your name, address, and phone number. (If you use your home address, cover it so that potential thieves can't see it readily.) Inside each bag, **pack a copy of your itinerary.** At check-in, **make sure that each bag is correctly tagged** with the destination airport's three-letter code. If your bags arrive damaged or fail to arrive at all, file a written report with the airline before leaving the airport.

PASSPORTS & VISAS

Once your travel plans are confirmed, **check the expiration date of your passport.** It's also a good idea to **make photocopies of the data page;** leave one copy with someone at home and keep another with you, separated from your passport. If you lose your passport, promptly call the nearest embassy or consulate and the local police; having a copy of the data page can speed replacement. Remember that **in France, you are required by law to carry identification at all times.**

U.S. CITIZENS

All U.S. citizens, even infants, need only a valid passport to enter France for stays of up to 90 days.

➤ INFORMATION: **Office of Passport Services** (☎ 202/647–0518).

CANADIANS

You need only a valid passport to enter France for stays of up to 90 days.

➤ INFORMATION: **Passport Office** (☎ 819/994–3500 or 800/567–6868).

U.K. CITIZENS

Citizens of the United Kingdom need only a valid passport to enter France for stays of up to 90 days.

➤ INFORMATION: **London Passport Office** (☎ 0990/21010) for fees and documentation requirements and to request an emergency passport.

PUBLIC TRANSPORTATION

Paris is relatively small as capital cities go, and most of its **monuments and museums are within easy walking distance of one another.** Walking is also a wonderful way of discovering the many pedestrian streets, beautiful courtyards, and other hidden pleasures off the beaten path. However, **the most convenient form of public transportation is the métro,** with stops every few hundred yards. Buses are a slower but more pleasant alternative, as you see more of the city. Taxis are relatively inexpensive and convenient, but not always easy to hail, particularly on Saturday nights after the last métro. Private car travel within Paris is best avoided; parking is extremely difficult.

Maps of the métro/RER network are available free from any métro station and in many hotels. They are also posted on every platform, as are maps of the bus network. Bus routes are also marked at bus stops and on buses. For more information, *see* Bus Travel *and* Métro, *above.*

To help you find your way around Paris, we suggest you **buy a *Plan de Paris par Arrondissement*** (about 40 francs), a city guide with separate maps of each district, including the whereabouts of métro stations and an index of street names. They're on sale in newsstands, bookstores, stationers, and drugstores.

If you're trying to determine the arrondissement of an address, here's a **hint: The last two digits of Paris zip codes are the number of the arrondissement;** for example, the zip code 75005 indicates an address in the 5^e arrondissement, 75011 is in the 11^e arrondissement, and so forth. In addresses in this guide, arrondissements are noted as follows: "1er" indicates the first arrondissement;

"2ᵉ," the second; "3ᵉ," the third; and so on.

S

SENIOR-CITIZEN TRAVEL

To qualify for age-related discounts, **mention your senior-citizen status up front** when booking hotel reservations (not when checking out) and before you're seated in restaurants (not when paying the bill). Note that discounts may be limited to certain menus, days, or hours. When renting a car, **ask about promotional car-rental discounts,** which can be cheaper than senior-citizen rates.

Older travelers to Paris can take advantage of many discounts, such as reduced admissions of 20%–50% to museums and movie theaters. For rail travel outside of Paris, the Carte Vermeil entitles travelers 60 years or older to discounts (☞ Train Travel, *below*).

➤ EDUCATIONAL TRAVEL PROGRAMS: **Elderhostel** (✉ 75 Federal St., 3rd Floor, Boston, MA 02110, ☎ 617/426–7788). **Interhostel** (✉ University of New Hampshire, 6 Garrison Ave., Durham, NH 03824, ☎ 603/862–1147 or 800/733–9753, FAX 603/862–1113). **Overseas Adventure Travel** (✉ Grand Circle Corporation, 625 Mt. Auburn St., Cambridge, MA 02138, ☎ 617/876–0533 or 800/221–0814, FAX 617/876–0455).

SIGHTSEEING

There are many ways to see Paris on a guided tour: by bike, by boat, by bus, by private minivan, and on foot.

Boat trips along the Seine run throughout the day and evening, and many include lunch or dinner for an average cost of 300 francs–600 francs. Wine and service are often factored into the lunch and dinner prices.

For a two-hour orientation tour by bus, the standard price is about 150 francs. The two largest bus tour operators are Cityrama and Paris Vision; for a more intimate-albeit-expensive-tour of the city, Cityrama also runs several minibus excursions per day. Paris Bus gives tours in a London-style double-decker bus. You can catch the bus at any of nine pickup points; tickets cost 125 francs

and allow you unlimited use for two days. A copy of the timetable is available from the main Paris Tourist Office (☞ Visitor Information, *below*). RATP (Paris Transit Authority) also gives guide-accompanied excursions in and around Paris.

Luxury minibuses (for 4 to 15 passengers) that will take you around Paris and its environs for a minimum of four hours can be arranged through Paris Bus and Paris Major Limousine.

A list of walking tours is available from the the Caisse Nationale des Monuments Historiques, or check the weekly magazines *Pariscope* and *L'Officiel des Spectacles* list walking tours under the heading "conférences;" most are in French, unless otherwise noted, and cost between 40 and 60 francs.

➤ BIKE TOURS: **Paris A Vélo, C'est Sympa** (✉ 41 bd. Henri IV, 4ᵉ, ☎ 01–48–87–60–01) runs a three-hour bike tour for 150 francs. **Paris Bike** (✉ 83 rue Daguerre, 14ᵉ, ☎ 01–45–38–58–58) organizes daily bike tours around Paris and its environs (Versailles, Chantilly, and Fontainebleau) for about 195 francs per person.

➤ BOAT TOURS: **Bateaux-Mouches** (✉ Pont de l'Alma, 8ᵉ, ☎ 01–42–25–96–10) boats depart from the Pont de l'Alma (Right Bank) 10–noon, 2–7, and 8:30–10:30. The price is 40 francs. Lunch is served on the 1 PM boat and costs 300 francs (150 francs children under 12). Dinner on the 8:30 service costs 500 francs (reservations essential).

Bateaux Parisiens-Tour Eiffel (✉ Pont d'Iéna, 7ᵉ, ☎ 01–44–11–33–44) boats depart from the Pont d'Iéna (Left Bank) every half hour in summer and every hour in winter, starting at 10 AM. The last boat leaves at 9 PM (11 PM in summer). The price is 45 francs during the day. Lunch service costs 300 francs. Dinner cruises on the 8 PM service cost 560 francs.

Bat-O-Bus (☎ 01–44–11–33–44), a trip along the Seine without commentary, has the advantage of allowing you to get on and off at any one of five stops along the river, including Trocédero, Musée d'Orsay, the Louvre, Notre-Dame, and Hôtel de Ville. Take it one stop for 12 francs, or pay 65 francs for a full-day ticket (25 francs for children under 12). Operating from April to September only, the Bat-O-Bus departs every half hour between 10 and 6.

Canauxrama (✉ 5 bis quai de la Loire, 19ᵉ; ✉ Bassin de l'Arsenal, 12ᵉ; ☎ 01–42–39–15–00) organizes leisurely canal tours in flat-bottom barges along the picturesque St-Martin and Ourcq canals in East Paris. Departures from the quai de la Loire are at 9:15 and 2:45, and departures from the Bassin de l'Arsenal (opposite 50 boulevard de la Bastille) are at 9:30 and 2:30. The trip lasts about 2½ hours. The price is 75 francs (60 francs on weekend afternoons). Reservations should be made in advance.

Paris Canal (✉ 19 quai de la Loire, 19ᵉ, ☎ 01–42–40–96–97) runs three-hour trips with bilingual commentary between the Musée d'Orsay and the Parc de La Villette, between April and mid-November only. The price is 95 francs. Reservations are essential.

Vedettes du Pont Neuf (✉ Ile de la Cité, 1ᵉʳ, ☎ 01–46–33–98–38) boats depart every half hour from the Square du Vert Galant 10–noon, 1:30–6:30, and 9–10:30 from March to October. The price is 45 francs during the day.

Yachts de Paris (✉ Port de Javel, ☎ 01–44–37–10–20) organizes two-hour "gourmet cruises." There is a fixed menu at 790 francs (wine included). Reservations must be made in advance.

➤ BUS TOURS: **Air France** (✉ 119 av. des Champs-Elysées, 8ᵉ, ☎ 01–44–08–22–22). **American Express** (✉ 11 rue Scribe, 9ᵉ, ☎ 01–47–77–77-07). **Cityrama** (✉ 4 pl. des Pyramides, 1ᵉʳ, ☎ 01–44–55–61–00). **Paris Bus** (☎ 01–42–30–55–50). **Paris Vision** (✉ 214 rue de Rivoli, 1ᵉʳ, ☎ 01–42–60–31–25). **RATP** (✉ pl. de la Madeleine, 8ᵉ; ✉ 53 bis quai des Grands-Augustins, 6ᵉ, ☎ 08–36–68–41–14; both offices are open daily 9–5). **Wagons-Lits** (✉ 31 rue Colonel Pierre Avia 15ᵉ, ☎ 01–41–33–68–00).

➤ PERSONAL GUIDES: **Paris Bus** (✉ 22 rue de la Prevoyance, Vincennes, ☎ 01–43–65–55–55). **Paris Major Limousine** (✉ 6 pl. de la Madeleine,

8ᵉ, ☎ 01–42–45–34–14), the price varies by time and number of passengers. Reservations are essential. The price varies from 1,300 to 2,200 francs.

➤ SPECIAL-INTEREST TOURS: **Cityrama** and **Paris Vision** (☞ Bus Tours, *above*) offer a variety of thematic tours ("Historic Paris," "Modern Paris," "Paris-by-Night") lasting from 2½ hours to all day and costing between 150 and 300 francs (more if admission to a cabaret show is included).

➤ WALKING TOURS: **Caisse Nationale des Monuments Historiques** (✉ Bureau des Visites/Conférences, Hôtel de Sully, 62 rue St-Antoine, 4ᵉ, ☎ 44–61–20–00).

SPORTS

The Paris Tourist Office (☞ Visitor Information, *below*) publishes a useful booklet, *Guide du Sport à Paris,* that lists sports facilities in the city. *See* also Chapter 1 for more information on Sports and Outdoor Activities in Paris.

The World Cup in soccer, to be held in June and July at the Parc des Princes and the Stade de France in St-Denis (☞ Spectator Sports, *below*), is the biggest event of 1998. Contact the French Government Tourist Office (☞ Visitor Information, *below*) for information about tickets and matches.

➤ BICYCLING: ☞ Bicycling, *above.*

➤ HEALTH CLUBS: **Aquaboulevard** (✉ 4 rue Louis-Armand, 15ᵉ, ☎ 01–40–60–10–00; 🎟 70 frs; ⊙ Daily 9 AM–11 PM) is a giant multisports complex with swimming pool, Jacuzzi, squash courts, and bowling alley, as well as a gym.

Club Jean de Beauvais (✉ 5 rue Jean-de-Beauvais, 5ᵉ, ☎ 01–46–33–16–80; ⊙ Weekdays 7 AM–10:30 PM, Sat. 8:30–7, Sun. 9:30–5), one of the oldest health clubs in Paris, is also one of the best. An entire floor is devoted to cardiovascular and strength-training equipment, and the range of programs includes low-impact aerobics and special back-care classes. The cost is 200 francs for a one-day pass; 600 francs per week.

Club Quartier Latin (⊠ 19 rue de Pontoise, 5ᵉ, ☎ 01–43–54–82–45; ⏱ Mon.-Thurs. 10 AM–midnight, Fri. 10–10, weekends 9:30–7:30) has a 33-meter skylighted pool, a climbing wall, squash courts, and exercise equipment. Seventy francs per day entitles you to use of the gym and pool; add another 75 francs per hour for squash (15-franc racquet rental). The pool only is 23 francs.

Espace Vit'Halles (⊠ pl. Beaubourg, 48 rue Rambuteau, 1ᵉʳ, ☎ 01–42–77–21–71; ⏱ Weekdays 8 AM–10 PM, Sat. 10–7, Sun. 11–4) in the 1ᵉʳ arrondissement offers a broad range of aerobics classes (100 francs per class, 800 francs for 10), exercise machines, sauna, and steam room (100 francs a day, 10-franc towel rental).

➤ HOTEL FITNESS CENTERS: The best fitness facilities are in the newer hotels on the edges of the city center. **Hôtel Nikko** (⊠ 61 quai de Grenelle, 15ᵉ, ☎ 01–45–75–25–45) has a 17-meter pool, health club, and weight room. The facilities are open to the public for 100 francs (50 francs for pool only). **Sofitel Paris** (⊠ 8 rue Louis-Armand, 15ᵉ, ☎ 01–45–54–79–00) has a 15-meter pool, a sauna, a steam room, and a Jacuzzi, plus a stunning view of the Paris skyline, (180 francs per day, the club is free to hotel guests) in its Vitatop Club.

➤ POOLS: **Aquaboulevard** (☞ Health Clubs, *above*). **Piscine des Halles** (⊠ pl. de la Rotonde, Forum des Halles, 1ᵉʳ, ☎ 01–42–36–98–44; ⏱ Mon. and Wed. 11:30–8; Tues, Thurs., Fri. 11:30–10; weekends 9–5) is a beautiful 50-m pool inside one of the largest shopping centers in the city. Admission is 24 francs and you can stay as long as you like; it can, however, get crowded. Every arrondissement also has its own pool; ask for the Paris Tourist Office's *Guide du Sport à Paris* for a list of pools near you.

➤ SPECTATOR SPORTS: **Palais Omnisports de Paris-Bercy** (⊠ 8 bd. de Bercy, 12ᵉ, ☎ 01–44–68–44–68, métro Bercy) hosts a wide range of sporting events; look for listings in the weekly ***Pariscope.*** **Roland-Garros** (⊠ 2 av. Gordon Bennett, 16ᵉ, ☎ 01–47–43–48–00). **Parc des Princes** (⊠ 24 rue du Cdt. Guilbaud, 16ᵉ, ☎ 01–42–02–76). **Stade de France** (⊠

Contact the St-Denis Tourist Office, 1 rue de la République, St-Denis, ☎ 01–42–43–33–55).

Students are a noticeable presence in the capital, where intellectuals are the French equivalent of American movie stars. The area surrounding the Sorbonne in the bohemian Latin Quarter is filled with students discoursing in smoke-filled cafés or browsing in crowded bookshops. Visiting students should have no trouble meeting their Parisian counterparts.

To save money, **look into deals available through student-oriented travel agencies.** To qualify you'll need a bona fide student ID card. Members of international student groups are also eligible. For a detailed listing of deals for students in Paris, ask for the brochure ***"Jeunes à Paris"*** from the main tourist office (☞ Visitor Information, *below*). **France-USA Contacts** (FUSAC) is a twice-monthly publication, available free in restaurants and in most American and British bookstores, with useful information for visiting students.

➤ HOSTELING: **Hostelling International–American Youth Hostels** (⊠ 733 15th St. NW, Suite 840, Washington, DC 20005, ☎ 202/783–6161, FAX 202/783–6171). **Hostelling International–Canada** (⊠ 400-205 Catherine St., Ottawa, Ontario K2P 1C3, ☎ 613/237–7884, FAX 613/237–7868). **Youth Hostel Association of England and Wales** (⊠ Trevelyan House, 8 St. Stephen's Hill, St. Albans, Hertfordshire AL1 2DY, ☎ 01727/855215 or 01727/845047, FAX 0171–844126). Membership in the U.S., $25; in Canada, C$26.75; in the U.K., £9.30).

➤ STUDENT IDs AND SERVICES: **Council on International Educational Exchange** (⊠ CIEE, 205 E. 42nd St., 14th floor, New York, NY 10017, ☎ 212/822–2600 or 888/268–6245, FAX 212/822–2699), for mail orders only, in the United States. **Travel Cuts** (⊠ 187 College St., Toronto, Ontario M5T 1P7, ☎ 416/979–2406 or 800/667–2887) in Canada.

➤ STUDENT TOURS: **Contiki Holidays** (⊠ 300 Plaza Alicante, Suite 900, Garden Grove, CA 92840, ☎ 714/740–0808 or 800/266–8454, FAX

714/740–0818). **AESU Travel** (✉ 2 Hamill Rd., Suite 248, Baltimore, MD 21210-1807, ☎ 410/323–4416 or 800/638–7640, ℻ 410–323–4498).

➤ Travel Agency: **Usit Voyages** (✉ 12 rue Vivienne, 2ᵉ, ☎ 01–42–44–14–00) for information on hostels, cheap accommodations, and student travel.

T

TAXES

All taxes must be included in affixed prices in France. Prices in **restaurants and hotels must by law include taxes and service charges:** If these appear as additional items on your bill, you should complain. VAT (value added tax, known in France as TVA), at a standard rate of 20.6% (33% for luxury goods), is included in the price of many goods, but **foreigners are often entitled to a refund** (☞ Chapter 6).

TAXIS

Paris **taxis may not have the charm of their London counterparts—there is no standard vehicle or color—but they're cheaper.** Daytime rates (7 AM–7 PM) within Paris are 3.36 francs per kilometer, and nighttime rates are around 5.45 francs. There is a basic hire charge of 13 francs for all rides, and a 6-franc supplement per piece of luggage. Rates outside the city limits are about 40% higher. Waiting time is charged at 130 francs per hour. You are best off asking your hotel or restaurant to call for a taxi or going to the nearest taxi station (you can find one every couple of blocks); cabs with their signs lit can be hailed but are annoyingly difficult to spot. Note that taxis seldom take more than three people at a time. Tip the driver about 10%.

TELEPHONES

The country code for France is 33. All phone numbers in France have a two-digit prefix determined by zone: Paris and the Ile de France, 01; the northwest, 02; the northeast, 03; the southeast, 04; and the southwest, 05. All you need to do to call any region in France is to dial the full 10-digit number.

CALLING FRANCE

To call France from the U.S., dial 011 (for all international calls), then dial 33 (the country code), and the number in France, minus any inital 0. To call France from the United Kingdom, dial 00–33, then dial the number in France minus any initial 0.

LONG-DISTANCE

To make a direct international call out of France, dial 00 and wait for the tone, then dial the country code (1 for the United States and Canada, 44 for the United Kingdom) and the area code (minus any initial 0) and number. Expect to be overcharged if you make calls from your hotel. Approximate daytime rates, per minute, are 5 francs to the United States and Canada (8 AM–9:30 PM), and 4 francs for the United Kingdom (2 PM–8 PM); reduced rates at other time intervals, per minute, are 4 francs to the United States and Canada and 3 francs to the United Kingdom.

Before you go, **find out the local access codes** for your destinations. AT&T, MCI, and Sprint long-distance services make calling home relatively convenient, but you may find the local access number blocked in many hotel rooms. First ask the hotel operator to connect you. If the hotel operator balks, ask for an international operator, or dial the international operator yourself. One way to improve your odds of getting connected to your long-distance carrier is to travel with more than one company's calling card (a hotel may block Sprint, for example, but not MCI). If all else fails, call your phone company collect in the United States or call from a pay phone in the hotel lobby.

➤ To Obtain Access Codes: **AT&T USADirect** (☎ 800/874–4000). **MCI Call USA** (☎ 800/444–4444). **Sprint Express** (☎ 800/793–1153).

OPERATORS & INFORMATION

To find a number in France, **dial 12 for information.** For international inquiries, dial 00–33 plus the country code.

Another source of information is the Minitel, an on-line network similar to the Internet. You can find one—they look like small computer terminals—in most post offices, nearly all hotels, and a vast majority of French homes. One Minitel service—available free in many post offices—is an on-line phone book covering the entire country. To use it, dial 3611. When you hear a screeching sound, hit the *appel* (call) key. Type the name you are looking for and hit *envoi* (return). It is also useful for tracking down services: tap in *piscine* (swimming pool) under *activité* (activity), for example, and it will give you a list of all the pools in Paris. Go to other lines or pages by hitting the *suite* (next) key. Newer models will connect automatically when you hit the book-icon key. To disconnect, hit *fin* (end).

PAY PHONES

Telephone **booths can almost always be found in post offices, métro stations, and in many cafés.** A local call costs 1 franc for every three minutes.

Most French pay phones are now operated by cards (*télécartes*), which you can buy from post offices, tabacs, and métro stations (the cost is 40 francs for 50 units; 96 francs for 120 units). These cards will save you money and hassle. In cafés you can still find pay phones that operate with 1-, 2,- and 5-franc coins (1 franc for local calls). Lift the receiver, place your coin(s) in the appropriate slots, and dial. Unused coins are returned when you hang up.

TIPPING

Bills in bars and restaurants must, by law, include service, but **it is customary to leave some small change unless you're dissatisfied.** The amount of this varies—from 50 centimes or 1 franc for a beer to 10 or 15 francs after a meal. In expensive restaurants, it's common to leave an additional 5% of the bill on the table.

Tip taxi drivers and hairdressers about 10% of the bill. Give theater and cinema ushers a couple of francs. In some theaters and hotels, cloak-room attendants may expect nothing (watch for signs that say *pourboire interdit*—no tip); otherwise, give them 5 francs. Washroom attendants usually get 2–5 francs, though the sum is often posted.

If you stay more than two or three days in a hotel, it is customary to leave something for the chambermaid—about 10 francs per day. Expect to pay about 10 francs (5 francs in a moderately priced hotel) to the person who carries your bags or who hails you a taxi. In hotels providing room service, give 5 francs to the waiter (this does not apply if breakfast is routinely served in your room). If the chambermaid does some pressing or laundering for you, give her 5–10 francs on top of the bill.

Service station attendants get nothing for gas or oil but 5 or 10 francs for checking tires. Train and airport porters get a fixed sum (6–10 francs) per bag. Museum guides should get 5–10 francs after a guided tour. It is standard practice to tip bus drivers about 10 francs after an excursion.

TOUR OPERATORS

Buying **a prepackaged tour or independent vacation can make your trip to Paris less expensive and more hassle-free.** Because everything is prearranged you'll spend less time planning.

Operators that handle several hundred thousand travelers per year can use their purchasing power to give you a good price. Their high volume may also indicate financial stability. But some small companies provide more personalized service; because they tend to specialize, they may also be more knowledgeable about a given area.

A GOOD DEAL?

The more your package or tour includes, the better you can predict the ultimate cost of your vacation. Make sure you know exactly what is covered, and **beware of hidden costs.** Are taxes, tips, and service charges included? Transfers and baggage handling? Entertainment and excursions? These can add up.

If the package or tour you are considering is priced lower than in your wildest dreams, **be skeptical.** Also, **make sure your travel agent knows the accommodations** and other services. Ask about the hotel's location, room size, beds, and whether it has a pool, room service, or programs for children, if you care about these. Has your agent been there in person or sent others you can contact?

BUYER BEWARE

Each year consumers are stranded or lose their money when tour operators—even very large ones with excellent reputations—go out of business. So **check out the operator.** Find out how long the company has been in business, and ask several agents about its reputation. **Don't book unless the firm has a consumer-protection program.**

Members of the National Tour Association and United States Tour Operators Association are required to set aside funds to cover your payments and travel arrangements in case the company defaults. Nonmembers may carry insurance instead. Look for the details, and for the name of an underwriter with a solid reputation, in the operator's brochure. Note: When it comes to tour operators, **don't trust escrow accounts.** Although there are laws governing charter-flight operators, no governmental body prevents tour operators from raiding the till. For more information, *see* Consumer Protection, *above*.

➤ TOUR-OPERATOR RECOMMENDATIONS: **National Tour Association** (✉ NTA, 546 E. Main St., Lexington, KY 40508, ☎ 606/226–4444 or 800/755–8687). **United States Tour Operators Association** (✉ USTOA, 342 Madison Ave., Suite 1522, New York, NY 10173, ☎ 212/599–6599, FAX 212/599–6744).

USING AN AGENT

Travel agents are excellent resources. When shopping for an agent, however, you should **collect brochures from several sources**; some agents' suggestions may be skewed by promotional relationships with tour and package firms that reward them for volume sales. If you have a special interest, **find an agent with expertise in that area** (☞ Travel Agencies, *below*). Don't rely solely on your agent, who may be unaware of small-niche operators. Note that some special-interest travel companies only sell directly to the public and that some large operators only accept bookings made through travel agents.

SINGLE TRAVELERS

Prices for packages and tours are usually quoted per person, based on two sharing a room. If traveling solo, **you may be required to pay the full double-occupancy rate.** Some operators eliminate this surcharge if you agree to be matched with a roommate of the same sex, even if one is not found by departure time.

GROUP TOURS

Among companies that sell tours to Paris, the following are nationally known, have a proven reputation, and offer plenty of options. The classifications used below represent different price categories, and you'll probably encounter these terms when talking to a travel agent or tour operator. The key difference is usually in accommodations, which run from budget to better, and better-yet to best.

➤ SUPER-DELUXE: **Abercrombie & Kent** (✉ 1520 Kensington Rd., Oak Brook, IL 60521-2141, ☎ 630/954–2944 or 800/323–7308, FAX 630/954–3324). **Travcoa** (✉ Box 2630, 2350 S.E. Bristol St., Newport Beach, CA 92660, ☎ 714/476–2800 or 800/992–2003, FAX 714/476–2538).

➤ DELUXE: **Globus** (✉ 5301 S. Federal Circle, Littleton, CO 80123-2980, ☎ 303/797–2800 or 800/221–0090, FAX 303/347–2080). **Maupintour** (✉ 1515 St. Andrews Dr., Lawrence, KS 66047, ☎ 913/843–1211 or 800/255–4266, FAX 913/843–8351). **Tauck Tours** (✉ Box 5027, 276 Post Rd. W, Westport, CT 06881-5027, ☎ 203/226–6911 or 800/468–2825, FAX 203/221–6828).

➤ FIRST-CLASS: **Brendan Tours** (✉ 15137 Califa St., Van Nuys, CA 91411, ☎ 818/785–9696 or 800/421–8446, FAX 818/902–9876). **Collette Tours** (✉ 162 Middle St., Pawtucket, RI 02860, ☎ 401/728–3805 or 800/832–4656, FAX 401/728–1380). **Trafalgar Tours** (✉ 11 E. 26th St., New York, NY 10010, ☎ 212/689–8977 or 800/854–0103, FAX 800/457–6644).

➤ BUDGET: **Cosmos** (☞ Globus, above). **Trafalgar** (☞ above).

➤ FROM THE U.K.: Contact **Paris Travel Service** (✉ Bridge House, High Rd., Broxbourne, Hertfordshire, EN10 7DT, ☎ 01992/456–000), **Travelscene** (✉ Travelscene House, 11–15 St. Ann's Rd., Harrow, Middlesex HA1 1AS, ☎ 0181/427–

8800), or **Sovereign** (✉ First Choice House, Peel Cross Rd., Salford, Manchester M5 2AN, ☎ 0161/742–2244).

PACKAGES

Like group tours, independent vacation packages are available from major tour operators and airlines. The companies listed below offer vacation packages in a broad price range.

➤ AIR/HOTEL: **American Airlines Fly AAway Vacations** (☎ 800/321–2121). **Continental Vacations** (☎ 800/634–5555). **Delta Dream Vacations** (☎ 800/872–7786). **DER Tours** (✉ 11933 Wilshire Blvd., Los Angeles, CA 90025, ☎ 310/479–4140 or 800/937–1235). **United Vacations** (☎ 800/328–6877).

THEME TRIPS

➤ COOKING SCHOOLS: **Le Cordon Bleu** (✉ 404 Airport Executive Park, Nanuet, NY 10954, ☎ 800/457–2433 in U.S.). **Ritz-Escoffier** (☎ 800/966–5758) in Paris's Ritz hotel.

➤ CUSTOMIZED PACKAGES: **Abercrombie & Kent** (☞ Group Tours, above). **Alekx Travel** (✉ 519A S. Andrews Ave., Fort Lauderdale, FL 33301, ☎ 954/462–6767, FAX 954/462–8691). **Five Star Touring** (✉ 60 E. 42nd St., #612, New York, NY 10165, ☎ 212/818–9140 or 800/792–7827, FAX 212/818–9142). **The French Experience** (✉ 370 Lexington Ave., Ste. 812, New York, NY 10017, ☎ 212/986–1115).

➤ SPAS: **Spa-Finders** (✉ 91 5th Ave., #301, New York, NY 10003-3039, ☎ 212/924–6800 or 800/255–7727).

➤ TENNIS: **Championship Tennis Tours** (✉ 7350 E. Stetson Dr., #106, Scottsdale, AZ 85251, ☎ 602/990–8760 or 800/468–3664, FAX 602/990–8744). **Steve Furgal's International Tennis Tours** (✉ 11828 Rancho Bernardo Rd., #123-305, San Diego, CA 92128, ☎ 619/675–3555 or 800/258–3664).

➤ VILLA RENTALS: **Chez Vous** (✉ 1001 Bridgeway, #245, Sausalito, CA 94965 ☎ 415/331–2535, FAX 415/331–5296). **Villas International** (✉ 605 Market St., San Francisco, CA 94105, ☎ 415/281–0910 or 800/221–2260, FAX 415/281–0919).

The SNCF is generally recognized as Europe's best national rail service: It's fast, punctual, comfortable, and comprehensive. The high-speed TGV, or Trains à Grande Vitesse (average 255 kph/160 mph on the Lyon/southeast line, 300 kph/190 mph on the Lille and Bordeaux/southwest lines), are the best domestic trains. They operate between Paris and Lille/Calais, Paris and Lyon/Switzerland/the Riviera, Paris and Angers/Nantes, Paris and Tours/Poitiers/Bordeaux, Paris and Brussels, and Paris and Amsterdam. As with other main-line trains, a small supplement may be assessed at peak hours. You must **always make a seat reservation for the TGV**—easily obtained at the ticket window or from a machine. Seat reservations are reassuring but seldom necessary on other main-line French trains, except at certain busy holiday times.

Paris has six international rail stations: Gare du Nord (northern France, northern Europe, and England via Calais or Boulogne); Gare St-Lazare (Normandy, England via Dieppe); Gare de l'Est (Strasbourg, Luxembourg, Basle, and central Europe); Gare de Lyon (Lyon, Marseille, the Riviera, Geneva, Italy); and Gare d'Austerlitz (Loire Valley, southwest France, Spain). Note that Gare Montparnasse has taken over as the main terminus for trains bound for southwest France since the introduction of the new TGV-Atlantique service.

You can **call for train information from any station or reserve tickets in any Paris station,** irrespective of destination. If you know what station you'll depart from, you can get a free schedule there (while supplies last), or you can access the new multilingual computerized schedule information network at any Paris station. You can also make reservations and buy your ticket while at the computer. Go to the Grandes Lignes counter for travel within France and to the Billets Internationaux desk if you're heading out of the country.

DISCOUNT PASSES

If you plan to travel outside of Paris by train, **consider purchasing a France**

Rail Pass, which allows three days of unlimited train travel in a one-month period. Prices begin at $120 for two adults traveling together in second class and $160 second class for a solo traveler. First-class rates are $198 for two adults and $160 for a solo traveler. Additional days may be added for $30 a day in either class. Other options include the France Rail 'n Drive Pass (combining rail and rental car), France Rail 'n Fly Pass (rail travel and one air travel journey within France), and the France Fly Rail 'n Drive Pass (a rail, air, and rental car program all in one).

France is one of 17 countries in which you can **use EurailPasses,** which provide unlimited first-class rail travel, in all of the participating countries, for the duration of the pass. If you plan to rack up the miles, get a standard pass. These are available for 15 days ($522), 21 days ($678), one month ($838), two months ($1,148), and three months ($1,468). If your plans call for only limited train travel, **look into a Europass,** which costs less money than a EurailPass. Unlike EurailPasses, however, you get a limited number of travel days, in a limited number of countries, during a specified time period. For example, a one-month Europass ($316) allows 5 days of rail travel, but costs $200 less than the least expensive EurailPass. Keep in mind, however, that the Europass is good only in France, Germany, Italy, Spain, and Switzerland, and the number of countries you can visit is further limited by the type of pass you buy.

In addition to standard EurailPasses, **ask about special rail-pass plans.** Among these are the Eurail Youthpass (for those under age 26), the Eurail Saverpass (which gives a discount for two or more people traveling together), a Eurail Flexipass (which allows a certain number of travel days within a set period), the Euraildrive Pass and the Europass Drive (combines travel by train and rental car).

Whichever pass you choose, remember that you must **purchase your pass before you leave** for Europe.

You can also **get reduced fares in France if you are a senior citizen (over 60)** with the Carte Vermeil **or a younger traveler (under 26)** with the Eurodomino and Carrissimo, which carry up to 50% discounts on travel within France. They can be purchased at SNCF stations. The Eurodomino can be bought for a period of 3, 5, and 10 days and entitles you to unlimited travel anywhere in the country for a cost of 943 francs, 1,300 francs, and 1,983 francs, respectively. The Carrissimo costs 189 francs or 295 francs, for four or eight trips respectively. The cost of the Carte Vermeil is 140 francs for four trips and 265 francs for unlimited discount travel for one year. All need proof of identity and two passport photos to purchase.

The reductions are 50% during "blue" periods (most of the time) and 20% during "white" periods (noon Friday through noon Saturday; 3 PM Sunday through noon Monday). Every station can give you a calendar of white/blue periods and sell you the appropriate tickets. Note that there is no reduction for buying an *aller-retour* (round-trip) ticket rather than an *aller simple* (one-way) ticket, with one exception: Rail travelers get a 25% discount for a return ticket (ask for a *billet de séjour*) between stations at least 500 kilometers apart, providing journeys do not take place at peak times and include at least part of a Sunday.

There are also discounts **for children under 16, the Carte Kiwi allows for 50% off** four trips for 285 francs, or for a full year of travel for 444 francs.

Many travelers assume that rail passes guarantee them seats on the trains they wish to ride. Not so. You need to **book seats ahead even if you are using a rail pass;** seat reservations are required on some European trains, particularly high-speed trains, and are a good idea on trains that may be crowded-particularly in summer on popular routes. You will also need a reservation if you purchase sleeping accommodations.

See also Métro, *above,* for more information on discount passes.

➤ SCHEDULE INFORMATION: SNCF (✉ 88 rue St-Lazare, 75009 Paris, ☎ 08–36–35–35–35) can provide you with schedules and other information.

FROM THE U.K.

British Rail has four daily departures from London's Victoria Station, all linking with the Dover-Calais/Boulogne ferry services through to Paris. There is also an overnight service on the Newhaven-Dieppe ferry. Journey time is about eight hours. Credit-card bookings are accepted by phone or in person at a British Rail Travel Centre.

➤ SCHEDULE INFORMATION: **British Rail** (☎ 0171/834–2345).

TRAVEL AGENCIES

A good travel agent puts your needs first. **Look for an agency that specializes in your destination, has been in business at least five years, and emphasizes customer service.** If you're looking for an agency-organized package or tour, your best bet is to choose an agency that's a member of the National Tour Association or the United States Tour Operator's Association (☞ Tour Operators, *above*).

➤ LOCAL AGENT REFERRALS: **American Society of Travel Agents** (✉ ASTA, 1101 King St., Suite 200, Alexandria, VA 22314, ☎ 703/739–2782, FAX 703/684–8319). **Alliance of Canadian Travel Associations** (✉ Suite 201, 1729 Bank St., Ottawa, Ontario K1V 7Z5, ☎ 613/521–0474, FAX 613/521–0805). **Association of British Travel Agents** (✉ 55–57 Newman St., London W1P 4AH, ☎ 0171/637–2444, FAX 0171/637–0713).

TRAVEL GEAR

Travel catalogs specialize in useful items, such as compact alarm clocks and travel irons, that can **save space when packing.** They also offer dual-voltage appliances, currency converters, and foreign-language phrase books.

➤ MAIL-ORDER CATALOGS: **Magellan's** (☎ 800/962–4943, FAX 805/568–5406). **Orvis Travel** (☎ 800/541–3541, FAX 540/343–7053).

TravelSmith (☎ 800/950–1600, FAX 800/950–1656).

U

U.S. GOVERNMENT

The U.S. government can be an excellent source of inexpensive travel information. When planning your trip, **find out what government materials are available.**

➤ ADVISORIES: **U.S. Department of State American Citizens Services Office** (✉ Room 4811, Washington, DC 20520); enclose a self-addressed, stamped envelope. Interactive hot line (☎ 202/647–5225, FAX 202/647–3000). Computer bulletin board (☎ 202/647–9225).

➤ PAMPHLETS: **Consumer Information Center** (✉ Consumer Information Catalogue, Pueblo, CO 81009, ☎ 719/948–3334) for a free catalog that includes travel titles.

V

VISITOR INFORMATION

➤ FRENCH GOVERNMENT TOURIST OFFICE: **U.S. Nationwide:** (☎ 900/990–0040; costs 50¢ per minute). **New York City:** (✉ 444 Madison Ave., New York, NY 10022, ☎ 212/838–7800). **Chicago:** (✉ 676 N. Michigan Ave., Chicago, IL 60611, ☎ 312/751–7800). **Beverly Hills:** (✉ 9454 Wilshire Blvd., Beverly Hills, CA 90212, ☎ 310/271–6665, FAX 310/276–2835). **Canada:** (✉ 1981 Ave. McGill College, Suite 490, Montréal, Québec H3A 2W9, ☎ 514/288–4264, FAX 514/845–4868; ✉ 30 St. Patrick St., Suite 700, Toronto, Ontario M5T 3A3, ☎ 416/491–7622, FAX 416/979–7587). **U.K.:** ✉ 178 Piccadilly, London W1V OAL, ☎ 0891/244–123 (50p per minute charge).

➤ LOCAL TOURIST OFFICE: **Office du Tourisme de la Ville de Paris** (Paris Tourist Office, ✉ 127 av. des Champs-Elysées, ☎ 01–49–52–53–54, ☎ 01–49–52–53–56 for recorded information in English).

W

WHEN TO GO

The major tourist season in France stretches from Easter to mid-September, but **Paris has much to offer in**

every season. Paris in the early spring can be disappointingly damp; June is delightful, with good weather and plenty of cultural and other attractions. July and August can be sultry. Moreover, many theaters and some of the smaller restaurants and shops close for at least four weeks in August. Those undeterred by the hot weather will notice a fairly relaxed atmosphere around the city, as this is the month when most Parisians are on vacation.

September is ideal. Cultural life revives after the summer break, and sunny weather often continues through the first half of October. The ballet and theater are in full swing in November, but the weather is part wet-and-cold, part bright-and-sunny.

December is dominated by the *fêtes de fin d'année* (end-of-year festivities), with splendid displays in food shops and restaurants and a busy theater, ballet, and opera season into January. February and March are the worst months, weatherwise, but with the coming of Easter, Paris starts looking beautiful again.

CLIMATE

➤ FORECASTS: **Weather Channel Connection** (☎ 900/932–8437), 95¢ per minute from a Touch-Tone phone.

What follow are the average daily maximum and minimum temperatures for Paris.

Climate in Paris

Jan.	43F	6C	May	68F	20C	Sept.	70F	21C
	34	1		49	10		53	12
Feb.	45F	7C	June	73F	23C	Oct.	60F	16C
	34	1		55	13		46	8
Mar.	54F	12C	July	76F	25C	Nov.	50F	10C
	39	4		58	14		40	5
Apr.	60F	16C	Aug.	75F	24C	Dec.	44F	7C
	43	6		58	14		36	2

1 Destination: Paris

PARIS À LA PARISIENNE

T IS MIDNIGHT at the neighborhood brasserie. Waiters swathed in starchy white glance discreetly at their watches as a family—mother, son, and wife—sip the last of a bottle of Chiroubles and scrape up the remains of their steak tartare on silverware dexterously poised with arched wrists. They are all wearing scarves: The mother's is a classic silk *carré*, tastefully folded at the throat; the wife's is Indian gauze and glitters; the son's is wool and hangs like a prayer shawl over his black turtleneck. Finished, they stir their coffee without looking. They smoke: the mother, Gitanes; the son, Marlboros; the wife rolls her own from a silver case. Alone, they act out their personal theater, uncontrived and unobserved, their Doisneauesque tableau reflected only in the etched-glass mirrors around them, enhanced by the sobriety of their dress and the pallor of their Gallic skin.

Whoever first said that "God found Paris too perfect, so he invented the Parisians," had it wrong. This extraordinary maquette of a city, with its landscape of mansards and chimneys, its low-slung bridges and vast boulevards, is nothing but a roughsketched stage set that drinks its color from the lifeblood of those infamous Parisians whom everyone claims to hate, but whom everyone loves to emulate.

Mythologized for their arrogance, charm, and savoir faire—as well as their disdain for the foreigners they find genetically incapable of sharing these characteristics—the Parisians continue to mesmerize. For the generations of American and English voyeurs who have ventured curiously, enviously into countless mirrored brasseries, downed numerous bottles of *cuvée maison,* fumbled at nautical knots in newly bought scarves, even suffered squashed berets and unfiltered Gauloises, the Parisian remains inimitable—and infinitely fascinating.

Alternately patronizing and self-effacing, they move through their big-city lives with enviable style and urban grit. They are chronically thin, despite the truckloads of beef stew, pâté, and *tarte tatine* they consume without blushing. They still make the cigarette look glamorous—and a graceful bit of stage business indispensable to good talk—in spite of the gas-mask levels of smoke they generate. They stride over bridges aloof to the monuments framed in every sweeping perspective, yet they discourse—lightly, charmingly—on Racine, NATO, and the latest ruling of the Académie Française. They are proud, practical, often witty and always chic, from the thrift-shop style of the Sorbonne student to the Chanel suit on the thin shoulders of a well-boned *dame d'un certain age.*

Ferociously (with some justice) in love with their own culture—theater, literature, film, art, architecture, haute cuisine, and haute couture—Parisians worship France as ardently as New Yorkers dismiss America. While Manhattanites berate the nonentities west of the Hudson, Parisians romanticize the rest of France, making an art of the weekend foray and the regional vacation: Why should we go *à l'étranger* (abroad) when we have the Dordogne, the Auvergne, and Bretagne?

And for all their vulnerability to what they frame as the "American Assault," for every Disney store, action film, and McDonald's in Paris (not to mention Benetton and Laura Ashley, and France's own Celio, Orcade, and Descamps chains), there is a plethora of unique shops selling all-white blouses, African bracelets, dog jackets, and Art Deco jewelry.

And for every commercial bookstore chain there are five tiny *librairies* selling tooledleather encyclopedias, collections of out-of-print plays, and yellow paperbacks lovingly pressed in waxed paper. The famous *bouquinistes* hover like squatters along the Seine, their folding metal boxes opening to showcase a treasure trove of old magazines, scholarly journals, and hand-colored botanical prints that flap from clothespins in the wind. Yet they are not nomads, these bouquinistes: Dormant through winter, their metal stands are fixtures as permanent and respectable as those of the medieval merchants that built shops along the Pont Neuf. They are determinedly Parisian—individual, independent, and one-of-a-kind.

But in spite of their fierce individuality, Parisians also demand that certain conformities be followed. And here the gap between native and visitor widens. If Parisians treat tourists a bit like occupying forces—disdainfully selling them Beaujolais-Nouveau in July, seating them by the kitchen doors, refusing to understand honest attempts at French—they have formed their opinions based on bitter experience. The waiter who scorches tourists with flared nostrils and firmly turned back was trained to respect his métier—meaning not pouring Coke with fois gras or bringing the check with dessert. The meal is a sacred ritual here and diverging from the norm is tantamount to disgrace.

Doing as the Parisians do, you can go a long way toward closing the gap of disdain. When dining, for example, give yourself over to the meal. Order a kir as an aperitif, instead of a whiskey or beer. Drink wine or mineral water with your meal; more international incidents have occurred over requests for tap water or Coke than over the Suez Canal.

The wine will come chilled, aired, and ready for tasting with the respect usually reserved for a holy relic. Enjoy each course, sipping, discussing, digesting leisurely; the waiter will not be pressed by hurried tourists. When you're done eating, align your silverware on the plate (a sign for the waiter to clear). Cheese can be the climax of the meal, well worth skipping dessert if necessary, and a magnificent way to finish the wine. Have your coffee after dessert and, without exception, black with sugar; a milky froth will not do on a full stomach. The art of stirring *un express* in Paris rivals the art of scarf-tying.

Ask for *l'addition;* the waiter will not commit the gaffe of bringing the check uninvited. And no matter how deeply you enter into your role as Parisian manqué avoid saying "Garcon!" These are rules that apply at the most unassuming corner bistro and the grandest three-star restaurant; following them can thaw the waiterly chill that can render a meal unforgettable—for all the wrong reasons—and can make for meals that are memorable as an evening at the Opéra Bastille, complete with sets and choreography.

It is this fixed attention to experience and detail that sets the Parisians apart. Desk-eaters they are not: When they work, they work without a coffee break. When they eat, business still grinds to a halt. Weekends are sacred. And oh, do they vacation, all of them at once, all of them abandoning Paris in August with a fierceness of purpose that mirrors their commitment to food—an all-night drive, a rental booked months in advance.

By matching that Parisian passion for the complete, the correct, the comme il faut, your own experience will be all the more authentic. Having eaten with proper reverence, keep your sightseeing agenda at the same lofty level. If you go to the Louvre, spend the day; do not lope through the wide corridors in search of *La Joconde* (Mona Lisa). You can leave for a three-hour lunch, if you choose, and come back with the same ticket, even avoiding the lines by reentering via the Passage de Richelieu. If time won't allow an all-day survey, do as the locals do: Choose an era and immerse yourself. Then take a break and plunge into another. Eavesdrop on a guided tour. Go back and look at a painting again. And take the time to stare at the ceilings: The architecture alone of this historic monument merits a day's tour.

As you apply yourself to the Parisian experience in spirit, diverge in fact: Walk. The natives may prefer to sit in a café or even hurry straight home by métro (*"métro, boulot, do-do"*—"métro, work, sleep"— as the saying goes). You, as a visitor, are obliged to wander down tortuous medieval streets; up vast boulevards so overscaled you seem to gain no ground; over bridges that open up broad perspectives on illuminated monuments that outnumber even those in Rome.

They are all there, the clichés of Paris romance: The moon over the Seine reflected in the wake of the bateaux mouches; the steps Leslie Caron blushed down in *An American in Paris;* the lovers kissing under the lime tree pollards. But there are surprises, too: a troop of hunting horns striking unearthly sonorities under a resonant bridge; flocks of wild geese flying low over the towers of Notre-Dame; and a ragged expatriate-writer leaving a well-scraped plat du jour on the table as he bolts away from the bill. (*C'est dommage:* He would have been well-fed by Ragueneau, the baker-writer in *Cyrano de Bergerac* who opened his Paris pastry shop to starving poets.)

The more resourceful you are, the more surprises you will unearth in your Paris wanderings. Follow the strains of Lully into a chamber orchestra rehearsal in St-Julien-le-Pauvre; if you're quiet and still, you may not be asked to leave. Brave the smoking lounge at intermission at the Comédie-Française and you'll find the battered leather chair that the young actor Molière sat in as *L'Invalide Imaginaire*. Take the métro to *L'Armée du Salut* (Salvation Army) in the 13ᵉ arrondissement, and you'll not only find Art Deco percolators and hand-knit stockings, but you'll also be inside the futuristic curves of a 1933 Le Corbusier masterwork.

Tear yourself away from the big-name museums and you'll discover a world of small galleries. Go in: You don't have to press your nose to the glass. The exhibits are constantly changing and you can always find one relevant to Paris—Frank Horvat's photos of Pigalle or a Christo retrospective, including the Pont Neuf wrappings. It is worth buying one of the weekly guides—*Pariscope, Les Officiels des Spectacles, Figaroscope*—and browsing through it over your *café crème* and croissant.

Resourcefulness, after all, is a sign of enthusiasm and appreciation—for when you are well-informed and acutely tuned in to the nuances of the city, you can approach it as a connoisseur. Then you can peacefully coexist with Parisians, partaking, in their passion for this marvelous old city, from the same plate of cultural riches. Hemingway, as usual, put it succinctly: "It was always pleasant crossing bridges in Paris." Cultural bridges, too.

Bon Séjour à Paris.

— Nancy Coons

A frequent contributor to Fodor's, Nancy Coons has written on food and culture for *National Geographic Traveler, Wall Street Journal, Opera News,* and *European Travel & Life.* Based in Luxembourg and France since 1987, she now works out of her 300-year-old farmhouse in Lorraine, which she shares with her husband and two daughters.

WHAT'S WHERE

Paris is divided into 20 *arrondissements* (districts). The last two digits of the zip code (75015) will tell you the arrondissement. Ask a Parisian where she lives and she'll tell you the number ("in the 15th or 15ᵉ"). Arrondissements are subdivided into *quartiers* (neighborhoods), which are often associated with a specific landmark. The following is an overview of Paris quartiers covered in this guide:

From the Eiffel Tower to the Louvre

The Eiffel Tower, rising above the Champ de Mars gardens in the west of the city, has been the unmistakable symbol of Paris ever since it was built in 1889. Facing the Eiffel Tower, from the heights of Trocadéro across the Seine, is the Palais de Chaillot, an Art Deco cultural center. Nearby stands the Arc de Triomphe, at the top of the world's most famous avenue: the Champs-Elysées. From spacious place de la Concorde, at the foot of the Champs-Elysées, the newly restored Tuileries Gardens lead east to the Louvre—the world's largest museum—and its new underground shopping mall.

The Faubourg St-Honoré

The Faubourg St-Honoré, just north of the Champs-Elysées and Tuileries Gardens, is synonymous with style: from the President's "Palace," past the neoclassical Madeleine church, to stately place Vendôme. A little further east, in the very center of the city, once stood the "belly" of Paris: Les Halles, for almost 800 years the site of Paris's main food market. Now a futuristic shopping mall in its place makes a piquant contrast with the colossal medieval church of St-Eustache, the only building to emerge unscathed from the area's redevelopment.

The Grand Boulevards

The Grand Boulevards—in fact, one broad, continuous avenue—stretch in an arc through the Right Bank, from the Madeleine church to place de la République. They are lined with 19th-century buildings, starting with Garnier's bombastic opera house and becoming humbler as you head east. Halfway along are the Porte St-Denis and Porte St-Martin, triumphal arches erected to celebrate the victories of

Louis XIV—victories that enabled the city's medieval walls to be demolished and the boulevards established in their place. Covered *passages* with small shops lead off the boulevards to the bustling financial district around the Bourse (Stock Exchange) and the narrow streets of Sentier, home to the cloth trade.

The Marais and the Bastille

Once a marshy area north of the Seine, the Marais is today perhaps the most sought-after residential district in the city. On its labyrinthine streets you'll find kosher butchers and family storefronts next to trendy clothing boutiques, antiques shops, and sleek cafés. This is also a quartier of museums—including the lovely Musée Picasso and the brash, colorful Centre Pompidou, so popular since it opened in 1977 that major renovation is now in progress to ensure it sees the 21st century. On the eastern fringe of this area is place de la Bastille, site of the fortress-cum-prison stormed on July 14, 1789, at the start of the French Revolution. Since the construction of a new opera house to mark the bicentennial, the Bastille neighborhood has become one of the liveliest in the city, filled with galleries, shops, theaters, jazz clubs, restaurants, and bars.

The Islands and the Latin Quarter

Ile de la Cité, where the earliest inhabitants of Paris settled in about 250 BC, forms the historic heart of Paris and is home to two exquisite Gothic structures: Notre-Dame and the Ste-Chapelle. The smaller, more residential Ile St-Louis is an oasis of calm in the heart of the city. Across the Seine, the Latin Quarter is the geographic and cerebral hub of the Left Bank, populated by Sorbonne students and academics. Here you'll find bookstores, bars, and plenty of cheap restaurants, as well as the Panthéon, whose huge dome dominates the area from the top of the Mont Ste-Geneviève.

From Orsay to St-Germain

The stately 7e arrondissement is peppered with museums, monuments, and ministries, but the highlight is the riverside Musée d'Orsay—once a Belle Epoque train station, now home to the Impressionists. Further back from the river is the majestic Hôtel des Invalides, its gold-leafed dome rising above Napoléon's tomb

to patrol the horizon. The mood becomes livelier as you head further east along the Left Bank. The venerable tower of St-Germain-des-Prés, the oldest church in Paris, anchors a neighborhood of bookstores, publishing houses, galleries, and cafés where the likes of Sartre, Picasso, Camus, and de Beauvoir spent their days and nights.

Montparnasse

Following World War I, Montparnasse was *the* place to be seen. Writers and artists—Hemingway, Stein, Bowles, Braque, Sartre—socialized at La Coupole, La Rotonde, Le Dôme, and La Closerie des Lilas. These cafés still thrive today on boulevard du Montparnasse amid a string of movie houses. The architecture of this business district is dominated by the 59-story Tour Montparnasse—Paris's tallest high-rise; some of the best views of Paris are to be had from its rooftop.

Montmartre

Rising above the city on the highest hill in Paris is Montmartre, site of the Basilique du Sacré-Coeur. The vantage point here provides panoramic views of the city. Venture away from the touristy place du Tertre, where gangs of third-rate portrait painters aggressively ply their craft, to discover quaint gardens and charming cafés frequented by locals. At the bottom of the hill, along a porn strip, the Moulin Rouge attempts to keep the cabaret tradition alive.

PLEASURES AND PASTIMES

Café Culture

Perhaps the most pleasant pastime in Paris is to sit at a table outside a café and watch the world go by. For the price of a café crème, you may linger as long as you like—read the paper, have a meal, or plan your next move while resting your feet. Cafés are found around every bend in Paris—you may prefer a posh perch at a renowned spot such as the Deux Magots on boulevard St-Germain or opt for a tiny *café du coin* (corner café) where you can have a quick cup of coffee at the counter.

Cuisine

Whether your dream meal is savoring truffle-studded foie gras from Limoges china or sharing a baguette, Camembert, and *jambon* (ham) *sur l'herbe* (on the grass), eating in Paris can be a memorable experience. Yes, a dinner of outstanding haute cuisine in formal splendor can be expensive—and well worth splurging. But many famous chefs have also opened bistro annexes where you can sample their cooking for less. Younger chefs are setting up shop in more affordable, outlying parts of Paris, where they are serving their own versions of bistro classics. Some of these locations can mean a long métro or cab ride, but you'll have the opportunity to discover restaurants in neighborhoods that you might not otherwise see. Don't feel guilty if you spend as much of your day in restaurants as in museums, eating is the heart and soul of French culture. Give yourself over to the leisurely meal; two hours for a three-course menu is par, and you may, after relaxing into the routine, feel pressed at less than three.

The Louvre and Beyond

Viewing art at the Louvre could take up all of your time, but don't forget that Paris is filled with an extraordinary number of other excellent museums. Be sure to visit the Musée d'Orsay, with its collection of Impressionist works (including Manet's *Déjeuner sur l'Herbe*), the very manageable Musée Rodin, with its lovely gardens, and the small Musée Picasso in the Marais. The *Lady and the Unicorn* tapestry can be viewed at the Musée National du Moyen-Age (formerly the Musée de Cluny), and Monet's *Water Lilies* are at the Musée de l'Orangerie, off place de la Concorde.

Outdoor Activities and Sports

BICYCLING➤ The **Bois de Boulogne,** on the western edge of Paris, and the **Bois de Vincennes,** on the eastern side, both have wide, leafy avenues, which are good places for biking. There are now also 30 km (18 mi) of **bicycle lanes** through the streets of Paris. Though these lanes have made biking in the city easier, it can still be tricky: Be careful. Cars have been banned altogether on Sunday from certain scenic routes, including the banks of the Seine.

BOATING➤ Rowboats can be rented at the **Lac Inférieur** in the Bois de Boulogne and at **Lac des Minimes** and **Lac Daumesnil** in the Bois de Vincennes.

BOULES➤ The rules of this classic French game (also called *pétanque*), which involves throwing metal balls at a wooden sphere, are fairly fundamental. The elderly men who gather each day for matches in the **Arènes de Lutèce** (a restored Roman amphitheater on rue Navarre in the 5e arrondissement) and in the **Bois de Vincennes** near the château might let you have a go if you demonstrate some enthusiasm. Otherwise, a set of your own costs very little.

CRICKET➤ There are cricket grounds in the **Bois de Vincennes** (Belle Etoile), and at **Château de Thoiry,** with games most weekends in summer.

HEALTH CLUBS➤ If you can't make it through your trip without your workout, the **Club Jean de Beauvais,** the **Club Quartier Latin,** and **Espace Vit Halles** all have temporary passes.

HORSE RACING➤ Paris and its suburbs are remarkably well endowed with racetracks. The most beautiful is **Longchamp** in the Bois de Boulogne, stage for the prestigious (and glamorous) Prix de l'Arc de Triomphe in October. Also in the Bois de Boulogne, and easier to get to (by métro to Porte d'Auteuil), is **Auteuil** racetrack. Other *hippodromes* (grass tracks) near Paris are at **St-Cloud, Maisons-Laffitte, Chantilly, Evry,** and **Enghien-les-Bains. Vincennes** has a cinder track for trotting races. Admission is usually between 10 and 50 francs. Details can be found in the daily press.

ICE-SKATING➤ Every winter from December to March, weather permitting, a small skating rink is erected on the Rivoli side of the **Tuileries Gardens.** A short RER ride away, **Disneyland Paris's Hotel New York** has an outdoor skating rink complete with Disney characters (tickets to the park aren't necessary). Admission is between 30 and 50 francs.

JOGGING➤ The best inner-city running is in the **Champs de Mars,** next to the Eiffel Tower, measuring 2½ km (1½ mi) around the perimeter. Shorter and more crowded routes are found in the **Luxembourg Gardens,** with a 1½-km (1-mi) loop just inside the park's fence; and in the **Tu-**

ileries Gardens, again measuring about 1½ km (1 mi). The **Bois de Boulogne** offers miles of trails through woods, around lakes, and across grassy meadows. The equally bucolic **Bois de Vincennes** offers a 14½-km (9-mi) circuit or a 1½-km (1-mi) loop around the Château de Vincennes itself.

ROLLER-SKATING➤ Paris's unofficial roller-skating venue is the concourse between the two wings of the Palais de Chaillot at Trocadéro. Or try the rink **La Main Jaune** (✉ rue du Caporal-Peugot) at Porte de Champerret. Admission is 50 francs with skate rental.

RUGBY➤ The Paris Université Club plays Sunday afternoons in winter at the futuristic **Stade Charléty** at Porte de Gentilly. The Racing Club de France plays Saturday afternoons at **Colombes,** just north of Paris; trains leave from St-Lazare for Le Stade station.

SOCCER➤ As in most other European countries, soccer is the sport that pulls in the biggest crowds. The main Paris club is Paris St-Germain, which plays at the **Parc des Princes** stadium in southwest Paris; take the métro to Porte de St-Cloud. Matches are usually on Saturday evenings with an 8 PM kickoff. Admission prices vary from 50 to 300 francs.

SWIMMING➤ Every arrondissement has its own public *piscine* (pool); ask for the booklet, *Guide du Sport à Paris,* at the Paris Tourist Office for a list of all the pools in the city. The **Piscine des Halles,** in the Forum des Halles, is one of the best public pools in the city. The best place to take kids is **Aquaboulevard de Paris,** an aquatic park and athletic supercenter that has an enormous indoor wave pool with water slides and a simulated outdoor beach in summer.

TENNIS➤ Tennis courts within Paris are few and far between. Your best bet is to try the public courts in the **Luxembourg Gardens.** There is also a large complex of courts at the Polygone sports ground in the **Bois de Vincennes.** It's a 20-minute walk down route de la Pyramide from Château de Vincennes métro, so you might want to take a taxi. The highlight of the tennis season—in fact the second most important European tennis tournament after Wimbledon—is the **French Open,** held during the last two weeks of May at the

Roland Garros Stadium on the eastern edge of the Bois de Boulogne. (Take the métro to Porte d'Auteuil.) Center-court tickets are difficult to obtain; try your hotel or turn up early in the morning (play starts at 11) and buy a general ground ticket. Tickets range from 100 to 350 francs. The **Bercy Indoor Tournament** in November awards one of the largest prizes in the world and attracts most of the top players.

See Sports *in* the Gold Guide for more information.

Paris by Boat

An hour on the Seine on a bateau mouche or vedette is a fun way to get to know the capital. Boats depart every hour from the Eiffel Tower, Pont de l'Alma, and square du Vert-Galant.

Shopping

If you want to spend some money or just window-shop (the French call it *"lèche-vitrine,"* literally, "window-licking"), try these: the rue du Faubourg-St-Honoré and avenue Montaigne for classic, upscale pret-a-porter; the Marais and place des Victoires for avant-garde designer clothes; place Vendôme for jewelry; the Passy area for secondhand shops; the Louvre des Antiquaires complex for antiques; rue Lepic, rue de Buci, and rue Mouffetard for street markets; and the Bastille area for trendy boutiques. Don't forget the bouquinistes, open-air bookstalls along the Seine.

Strolling

Walking is by far the best way to see Paris; it's hard to get lost, thanks to very visible monuments that serve as your landmarks. Some of our favorite walks are from place St-Michel, through the Latin Quarter to the Panthéon and down rue Mouffetard; along the banks of the Canal St-Martin and Canal de l'Ourcq up to the Parc de la Villette; through the small, winding streets of the Marais from place de la Bastille to the Pompidou Center; along busy rue Faubourg St-Honoré, from the Elysée Palace to the Madeleine, place Vendôme, and the gardens of the Palais-Royal; from the Arc de Triomphe to the Louvre via the Champs-Elysée, place de la Concorde, and the Tuileries Gardens; and along the streets and riverbanks of Ile St-Louis from east to west, ending at Pont

St-Louis for a classic view of the Seine and Notre-Dame.

NEW AND NOTEWORTHY

With work progressing on schedule, the futuristic **Stade de France** now disputes the northern Paris skyline with the nearby Basilica at St-Denis. The 80,000 all-seater stadium will host the Opening Ceremony of the 1998 Soccer World Cup on June 10 and the Final on July 12.

Two of late president François Mitterrand's final legacies to the capital are now up and running: the postmodern **Cité de la Musique** (Music Academy), with its state-of-the-art concert facilities and spectacular museum of musical instruments; and the **Bibliothèque Nationale François-Mitterrand,** or new national library, whose four glass towers, shaped like open books, dominate the city's southeast skyline, anchoring the revamped Bercy-Tolbiac district near Gare d'Austerlitz.

President Jacques Chirac is looking to leave his own cultural stamp on the city by creating a new **Museum of Primal Art** come 1999. Some $180 million has been earmarked to transform one half of the vast Palais de Chaillot at Trocadéro to house the new museum, which will absorb the city's Musée de l'Homme and the African and Oceanic Art Museum. The Marine Museum at Chaillot has been granted $40 million to relocate to a new (as yet unspecified) waterside location in the capital.

The **Centre Pompidou** closed in October 1997 for a $120 million renovation program, and though some exhibits will be staged as resoration allows, it will not fully reopen till the last day of the century—December 31, 1999. The Center was designed for 5,000 visitors a day; instead, 25,000 have been swarming in and extra exhibit space is sorely needed for the Center's huge cache of modern art. In the meantime, the glass-tubed escalator remains open, and so do the nearby IRCAM music academy and the studio of avant-garde sculptor Constantin Brancusi (which reopened in January 1997 after restoration).

Fans of Asian art will be dismayed to learn that the **Musée Guimet** is closed for enlargement and modernization; the date of reopening here, as at the glass-roofed Belle Epoque hall of the **Grand Palais,** remained uncertain at press time (1997). The temporary exhibits formerly housed at the Grand Palais have been transferred to the **Espace Branly,** down the Seine from the Eiffel Tower. Just across from the Grand Palais on Avenue Winston-Churchill, a 10-foot bronze statue of Churchill himself, portrayed as a wartime hero by Frenchman Jean Cardot, was erected in 1997.

There is encouraging news at the Louvre, now fully renovated and cleaned, with the neighboring **Tuileries Gardens** fresh and colorful from a $2 million flower-lift. Emphasizing Parisians' newfound love of ecology, 30 km (18 mi) of **bike lanes** have been painted on the city's roads and a number of boulevards, notably along the Seine, are now closed to cars the first Sunday of each month.

The area around Mitterrand's Grand Library—already being touted as the "Latin Quarter of the next millennium"—is due to be united to central Paris by the express **Météor** métro line by late 1998. Another new subway, **Eole,** is under construction between Gare du Nord and Gare St-Lazare.

GREAT ITINERARIES

A visit to Paris will never be quite as simple as a quick look at a few landmarks. Each quartier has its own treasures, and you should be ready to explore—a very pleasant prospect in this most elegant of cities. Outlined here are the main areas to concentrate on depending on the length of your stay (☞ Chapter 2 for more information about individual sights). Bear in mind that the amount of time spent visiting monuments—and museums in particular—is not something you can, or would want to, predict with any certainty. Also, to see both the city's large museums and its smaller ones, you probably need at least a week.

IF YOU HAVE 3 DAYS➤ On your first day, get your bearings—and an overview of the city's attractive waterfront—by taking a trip along the Seine on a bateau mouche (from place de l'Alma) or on the Vedettes de Pont Neuf (from the Square du Vert-Galant). Visit Notre-Dame Cathedral and, if you enjoy medieval architecture, the nearby Ste-Chapelle on Ile de la Cité, then cross the Seine to the Left Bank and explore the Latin Quarter, using the Panthéon dome as a landmark. End your day in the Luxembourg Gardens, close by. Spend your second day exploring the noble vista between the Arc de Triomphe and the Louvre: Start at the Arc (that way it's all down hill) and work along the Champs-Elysées, across place de la Concorde and the Tuileries Gardens (with the Orangerie and Jeu de Paume museums) to the Louvre. Divide your third day between the Eiffel Tower, the Musée d'Orsay, and Montmartre.

IF YOU HAVE 6 DAYS➤ Follow the three-day itinerary, then spend one day exploring the Marais and Ile St-Louis, and another combining a visit to the Left Bank's St-Germain and the nearby Invalides. For good shopping and a look at Haussmann's 19th-century Paris, walk down the Right Bank's Faubourg St-Honoré and join the Grand Boulevards by the Madeleine church; continue past the Opéra toward place de la République.

IF YOU HAVE 9 DAYS➤ You can attack the city's "other" museums—the Picasso, Rodin, and Marmottan, after following the six-day itinerary. Check out Montparnasse and some of the attractions on the edge of the city, all reachable by métro: Père Lachaise Cemetery and the Parc de La Villette (with, perhaps, a boat ride along the Bassin de la Villette); the Bois de Boulogne to the west, plus the futuristic area of La Défense; or the Bois de Vincennes to the east, with its zoo and medieval fortress. You may also wish to take a day trip to Versailles (☞ Chapter 7).

FODOR'S CHOICE

Churches

★**Basilique de St-Denis.** This cathedral-size Gothic church just north of Paris contains the elaborately carved tombs of the French kings and has a majestic nave and fine stained glass.

★**Église du Dôme.** Under the dome of this magnificently commanding Baroque church, part of Les Invalides, Napoléon rests in imperial splendor.

★**Notre-Dame Cathedral.** This is the most historic and dominant church in the city. Climb to the towers for a glimpse of the gargoyles and for wonderful views of Paris.

★**Ste-Chapelle.** Built by Louis IX (1226–70) to house what he believed to be the Crown of Thorns from Christ's crucifixion and fragments of the True Cross, the Ste-Chapelle shimmers with stained glass.

Dining

★**Guy Savoy, 16ᵉ.** At his handsome luxury restaurant, top chef Guy Savoy creates contemporary classics. $$$$

★**Pierre Gagnaire, 8ᵉ.** Legendary chef Pierre Gagnaire brings together at least three or four different tastes and textures in his sensational dishes. $$$$

★**Jamin, 16ᵉ.** At this intimate, elegant restaurant, where Joel Robuchon made his name, you can find excellent, haute cuisine at almost half the price of what you'd find elsewhere. $$$

★**Chardenoux, 11ᵉ.** This cozy spot with tile floors and a long zinc bar serves traditional bistro fare. $$

★**Philippe Detourbe, 15ᵉ.** Spectacular contemporary French cuisine is served at this unexpectedly glamorous restaurant. $$

★**Le Relais du Parc, 16ᵉ.** This bistro-annex is run by Alain Ducasse, who understands how and what people want to eat today. $$

★**Au Bon Accueil, 7ᵉ.** The excellent, reasonably priced *cuisine du marché* (a menu based on what's in the markets) has made this bistro a hit. $–$$

★**Le Brin de Zinc et Madame, 1ᵉʳ.** Delicious and generously portioned classic bistro dishes are served at this bustling, old-fashioned spot. $–$$

★**Chantairelle, 5ᵉ.** This friendly, good-value restaurant is the place to go for hearty south-central Auvergne cuisine. $

★**La Régalade, 14ᵉ.** This restaurant may be off the beaten path, but Crillon veteran

Yves Camdeborde's feasts make it worth the trip. $

Lodging

⭐**Costes, 1ᵉʳ.** Jean-Louis and Gilbert Costes's eponymous hotel conjures up the palaces of Napoléon III with sumptuous swags and enough brocade and fringe to blanket the Champs-Elysées. $$$$

⭐**Relais Saint-Germain, 6ᵉ.** Rooms in this exquisite hotel are named for French literary heros and are truly enormous—at least twice the size of what you'll find elsewhere at this price level. $$$

⭐**Caron de Beaumarchais, 4ᵉ.** De Beaumarchais's work is the theme of this sumptuously decorated hotel in the heart of the Marais. $$

⭐**Hôtel de Noailles, 2ᵉ.** A star among Paris's new crop of affordable, style-driven boutique hotels, this New Wave place is rife with contemporary details and draws a cosmopolitan crowd. $$

⭐**Le Pavillon Bastille, 12ᵉ.** Ultramodern, colorful, and high-design, this luxury hotel has garnered architectural awards and a fiercely loyal, hip clientele since its transformation from a 19th-century *hôtel particulier.* $$

⭐**Champ de Mars, 7ᵉ.** Near the rue Cler market, the Eiffel Tower, and Invalides, this comfortable two-star hotel is done in attractive, blue and yellow, French country-house style. $

Monuments

⭐**Arc de Triomphe.** Commissioned by Napoléon I as a monument to his military might, this is the largest triumphal arch in the world.

⭐**Eiffel Tower.** The 10,000-ton result of a contest held to design a tower for the 1889 World Exposition, the Eiffel Tower is the most-recognized landmark in Paris.

⭐**July Column.** The bronze column on place de la Bastille, the site of the infamous Bastille prison destroyed on July 14, 1789, commemorates the 1830 and 1848 uprisings.

⭐**The Louvre's glass pyramid.** This modern glass structure was extremely controversial when first unveiled; it was designed by I. M. Pei as a new entrance to the museum.

Views to Remember

⭐**The Champs-Elysées from the Arc de Triomphe.** From here you can admire the vista down the Champs-Elysées toward place de la Concorde and the distant Louvre.

⭐**The Eiffel Tower from Trocadéro.** This view of the Eiffel Tower is unsurpassed and is particularly pretty when the fountains in Trocadéro plaza are on.

⭐**The Ile de la Cité from the Pont des Arts.** The footbridge across the Seine between the Louvre and the Institut de France offers a romantic vantage point of the towers of Notre-Dame climbing above the roofs of Ile de la Cité, with the Hôtel de Ville and Tour St-Jacques piercing the skyline away to the left.

⭐**Notre-Dame from the Pont de l'Archevêché.** Standing on the bridge behind Notre-Dame, you'll have breathtaking views of the east end of the cathedral, ringed by flying buttresses, surmounted by the spire.

⭐**Paris spread out beneath Sacré-Coeur at Montmartre.** The basilica is set on the highest hill in Paris, providing extensive views over the city.

⭐**St-Gervais–St-Protais from the bottom of rue des Barres.** The view of the flying buttresses above the roofs and cobbles of this tumbling pedestrian street has the understated, picturesque charm of quintessential Paris.

FESTIVALS AND SEASONAL EVENTS

Top seasonal events in Paris include the French Open Tennis Championships in May, the Fête de la Musique on June 21, July's Bastille Day, the Festival Estival musical event in the summer, and the Autumn Festival from September through December.

WINTER

LATE NOV.➤ **Salon des Caves Particulières** brings French producers to the exhibition center at Porte de Champerret for a wine-tasting jamboree.

LATE NOV.–LATE DEC.➤ The festive **Christmas Market** features crafts, gifts, and toys from every region of France (✉ place du 11-Novembre-1918, 10ᵉ, métro Gare de l'Est).

EARLY DEC.–EARLY JAN.➤ A **Crèche** is constructed in front of Paris's City Hall (✉ pl. de l'Hôtel-de-Ville, 4ᵉ, métro Hôtel-de-Ville).

LATE DEC.➤ **Christmas** in Paris is highlighted by illuminations throughout the city, particularly on the Champs-Elysées, avenue Montaigne, and boulevard Haussmann. A giant crèche with automatons is set up outside the Hôtel de Ville.

FEB.➤ **Foire à la Feraille de Paris** is an antiques and bric-a-brac fair held in the Parc Floral in the Bois de Vincennes.

SPRING

MAR.➤ **Salon du Livre,** the international book exposition, is held annually at the end of the month.

MAR.–APR.➤ **Foire du Trône** amusement park is in the Bois de Vincennes.

MAR.–APR.➤ The **Prix du Président de la République** takes place at the Auteuil Racecourse.

LATE APR.➤ The **International Marathon of Paris** runs through the city and nearby woods.

EARLY MAY➤ At the **Foire de Paris** hundreds of booths display everything from crafts to wines.

END OF MAY➤ The **Course des Garçons de Café** is an entertaining race through the streets of Paris by waiters bearing full trays of drinks. It begins and ends at the Hôtel de Ville.

MAY–LATE SEPT.➤ **Grandes Eaux Musicales** is a fountain display at the Château de Versailles (Sundays only).

LATE MAY–EARLY JUNE➤ **Festival de Jazz de Boulogne-Billancourt** attracts big names and varied styles of jazz in the suburbs of Boulogne-Billancourt.

LATE MAY–EARLY JUNE➤ **French Open Tennis Championships** take place at Roland Garros Stadium.

SUMMER

MID-JUNE–MID-JULY➤ **Festival du Marais** features everything from music to dance to theater in the churches and historic mansions of the Marais (tickets: ✉ 44 rue François-Miron, 4ᵉ, ☎ 01–48–87–60–08 métro St-Paul). A similar celebration takes place at the **Butte Montmartre Festival** (☎ 01–42–62–46–22).

JUNE➤ The **Paris Air Show,** which takes place in odd-numbered years only, is a display of old and new planes and an update on worldwide technological developments in the aeronautical industry, at Le Bourget Airport.

MID-JUNE➤ **Grand Steeplechase de Paris** is a popular horse race at Auteuil Racecourse.

JUNE 21➤ **Fête de la Musique** celebrates the summer solstice with parades, street theater, and live bands throughout the city.

LAST WEEKEND IN JUNE➤ **Fête du Cinéma** allows you to take in as many movies as you can for the price of a single ticket (check the Tourist Office for details).

LATE JUNE➤ **Grand Prix de Paris,** a major test for three-year-old horses, is held on the flat at Longchamp Racecourse.

MID-JUNE–MID-JULY➤
World Cup Soccer matches take place at Paris's Parc des Princes and St-Denis's new Stade de France throughout the month-long competition.

July 14➤ **Bastille Day** celebrates the storming of the Bastille prison in 1789. There's a military parade along the Champs-Elysées in the morning, fireworks at night at Trocadéro, and (often July 13) local firemen's balls that spill into the streets of every arrondissement.

LATE JULY➤ **Tour de France,** the world's leading bicycle race, speeds to a Sunday finish on the Champs-Elysées.

LATE JULY–END AUG.➤
Fête Musique en l'Ile is a series of concerts held in the picturesque 17th-century Église St-Louis on the Ile St-Louis (☎ 01–45–23–18–25 for details).

MID-JULY–LATE SEPT.➤
Festival Estival features classical music concerts in churches, museums, and concert halls throughout the city (tickets: ✉ 20 rue Geoffroy-l'Asnier, 4e, ☎ 01–48–04–98–01, métro St-Paul).

AUTUMN

SEPT.➤ **Fête à Neu-Neu** amusement park is in the Bois de Boulogne.

LATE SEPT.➤ **Biennale des Antiquaires** (even-numbered years only), the world's swankiest antiques fair, takes place at the Carrousel du Louvre.

LATE SEPT.➤ On the **Journée du Patrimonie,** the third Sunday in September, normally closed historic buildings—such as the state residences of the President and Prime Minister—are open to the public.

MID-SEPT.–DEC.➤ **Fête d'Automne** is a series of concerts, plays, dances, and exhibitions throughout Paris (tickets: ✉ 156 rue de Rivoli, 1er, ☎ 01–42–96–96–94, métro Louvre-Rivoli).

EARLY OCT.➤ **Fêtes des Vendanges,** held the first Saturday of October, marks the grape harvest in the Montmartre Vineyard, at the corner of rue des Saules and rue St-Vincent (and at Suresnes, just west of Paris).

EARLY OCT.➤ **FIAC** (International Fair of Contemporary Art) takes place on quai Branly.

EARLY OCT.➤ **Prix de l'Arc de Triomphe,** Europe's top flat race, takes place the first Sunday of the month at Longchamp Racecourse.

OCT.➤ **Paris Auto Show** (even-numbered years only) at the Porte de Versailles features the latest developments in the international automobile industry.

MID-OCT.–EARLY NOV.➤
Fête de Jazz de Paris is a two-week celebration that includes lots of big-name jazz artists (☎ 01–47–83–33–58 for information).

OCT.–NOV.➤ **Fête d'Art Sacré** features concerts and exhibitions held in churches throughout the city (☎ 01–42–77–92–26 for information).

NOV. 11➤ **Armistice Day** ceremonies at the Arc de Triomphe include a military parade down the Champs-Elysées.

3RD THURS. IN NOV.➤
Beaujolais Nouveau, a light, fruity wine from the Beaujolais region of France, is officially "released" at midnight on Wednesday; its arrival is celebrated on the third Thursday in November in true Dionysian form in cafés and restaurants around the city.

2 Exploring Paris

Bearing the marks of 2,000 years of history and a rich cultural heritage, Paris overwhelms, astonishes, and surprises. From the heights of the Arc de Triomphe the city swaggers with the knowledge that it is at the pinnacle of architectural beauty, artistic development, and culinary delight. On the narrow, winding streets, it invites unhurried exploration rather than awestruck admiration.

CITY OF VAST, NOBLE PERSPECTIVES and winding, hidden streets, Paris remains a combination of the pompous and the intimate. Whether you've come looking for sheer physical beauty, cultural and artistic diversions, world-famous dining and shopping, history, or simply local color, you will find it here in abundance.

Updated by Simon Hewitt

The French capital is also a practical city: It is relatively small as capitals go, with many of its major sites and museums within walking distance of one another. The city's principal tourist axis is less than 6½ km (4 mi) long, running parallel to the north bank of the Seine from the Arc de Triomphe to the Bastille. In fact, the best method of getting to know Paris is on foot, although public transportation—particularly the métro subway system—is excellent. Buy a *Plan de Paris* booklet: a city map-guide with a street-name index that also shows métro stations. Note that all métro stations have a detailed neighborhood map just inside the entrance.

Paris owes both its development and much of its visual appeal to the river Seine, which weaves through its heart. Each bank of the Seine has its own personality; the *Rive Droite* (Right Bank), with its spacious boulevards and formal buildings, generally has a more sober and genteel feeling than the more carefree and bohemian *Rive Gauche* (Left Bank) to the south. The historical and geographical heart of the city is Notre-Dame Cathedral on the Ile de la Cité, the larger of the Seine's two islands (the other is the Ile St-Louis).

Our coverage of Paris is divided into eight neighborhood walks. There are several "musts" that you may not want to miss: the Eiffel Tower, the Champs-Elysées, the Louvre, and Notre-Dame. A few monuments and museums close for lunch, between noon and 2, and many are closed on either Monday or Tuesday. Check before you set off. Admission prices listed are for adults, but often there are special rates for students, children, and senior citizens. Don't forget that cafés in Paris are open all day long. They are a great boon if you are weary and in need of a coffee, a beer, or a sandwich, as are *boulangeries* (bakeries).

It must also be said that a visit to Paris will never be quite as simple as a quick look at a few landmarks. Every *quartier* (neighborhood) has its own treasures, and you should be ready to explore—a very pleasant prospect in this most elegant of cities. Follow our suggested "good walks" or use them as a guide to create your own. Sights that are "off the beaten path" in each neighborhood or "on the fringe" of the city are noted: You might want to make a brief excursion to one of these places in conjunction with a walk or on another day when you have more time.

FROM THE EIFFEL TOWER TO THE LOUVRE

Between the Eiffel Tower and the Louvre lies the grand, opulent Paris of wide avenues and plush hotels. This is an area of dazzling vistas, stellar museums, superb window-shopping, and unbeatable monument-gazing. Fashion shops, jewelers, art galleries, and deluxe hotels proliferate. Local charm is not a feature of this exclusive sector of western Paris; it's beautiful and rich—and a little impersonal. The French moan that it's losing its character, and, as you notice the number of fast-food joints along the Champs-Elysées, you'll know what they mean—though renovation has gone some way to restoring the street's legendary elegance.

The Arc de Triomphe stands foursquare at the top of the most famous street in the city: the Champs-Elysées, site of most French national celebrations. It's the last leg of the Tour de France bicycle race on the third or fourth Sunday in July and the site of vast ceremonies on Bastille Day (July 14) and Armistice Day (November 11). Its trees are often decked with the French *tricolore* and foreign flags to mark visits from heads of state. You'll want to explore both its commercial upper half and its verdant lower section.

Numbers in the text correspond to numbers in the margin and on the Eiffel Tower to Trocadéro and Arc de Triomphe to Louvre maps.

A Good Walk

There is no better place to begin than at that iron symbol of Paris, the **Eiffel Tower** ①. As you get nearer, its colossal bulk (it's far bigger and sturdier than pictures suggest) becomes more evident. Spreading out beyond the Eiffel Tower is the verdant expanse of the **Champ de Mars** ②, once used as a parade ground, then as site of the World Exhibitions. Landscaped at the start of the century, it frames the distant **École Militaire** ③, still in use as a military academy and therefore not open to the public.

Across the Seine from the Eiffel Tower, on the heights of Trocadéro, is the Art Deco **Palais de Chaillot** ④, a cultural center containing numerous museums. In the left wing of the Palais are the **Musée de l'Homme** ⑤, an anthropology museum, and the **Musée de la Marine,** a maritime museum (though there are plans for a new Museum of Primal Art, entailing the departure of the Marine Museum to a new venue). The other wing contains the **Musée des Monuments Français** ⑥, a museum with copies of statues, columns, and archways; and the **Musée du Cinéma Henri-Langlois** ⑦, a museum with motion picture artifacts.

The area around place du Trocadéro is a feast for museum lovers. (If you're in a hurry or have seen enough museums for the day, skip them all and take the métro from here directly to the Arc de Triomphe.) The **Musée Guimet** ⑧, at place d'Iéna, contains three floors of Indo-Chinese and Far Eastern art, but it is closed for renovation until 1999. The **Musée d'Art Moderne de la Ville de Paris** ⑨, farther down the avenue on the other side, has temporary exhibits and a permanent collection of modern art. Across the street in the Palais Galliera is the small, and some would say overpriced, **Musée de la Mode et du Costume** ⑩, where you can see exhibits on clothing design.

Continue down to bustling place de l'Alma. Across the **Pont de l'Alma** is the entrance to **Les Egouts** ⑪, Paris's sewers. If you prefer a less malodorous tour of the city, stay on the Right Bank and head down the sloping side road to the left of the bridge, to the embarkation point of the **Bateaux Mouches** ⑫ and their tours of Paris by water. Stylish avenue Montaigne (☞ Chapter 6), home to many of the leading Paris fashion houses, runs up from place de l'Alma toward the Champs-Elysées. The 1913 facade of the Théâtre des Champs-Elysées (☞ Chapter 5), 100 yards up on the left, is a forerunner of the Art Deco style. Farther along is the plush Hôtel Plaza-Athénée (☞ Chapter 4).

To reach the Arc de Triomphe, you can either walk up avenue Montaigne to the Rond-Point des Champs-Elysées, or take avenue George-V, then turn left after the slender spire of the **American Cathedral of the Holy Trinity** ⑬ to reach avenue Marceau and the church of **St-**

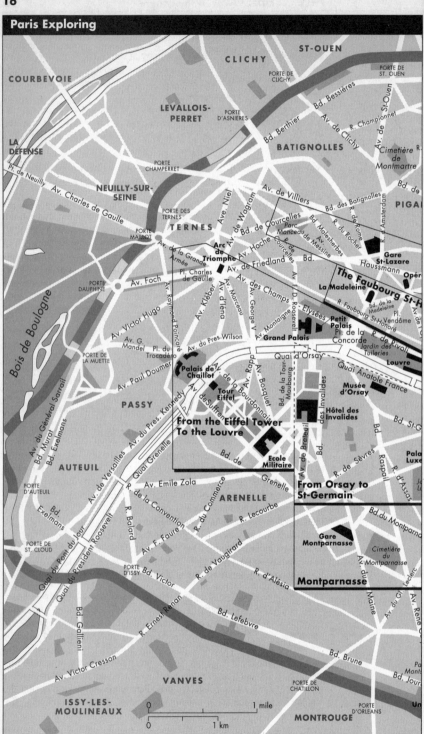

COURBEVOIE

CLICHY

ST-OUEN

LEVALLOIS-
PERRET

PORTE DE
CLICHY

PORTE DE
ST. OUEN

BATIGNOLLES

Cimetière
de
Montmartre

LA
DÉFENSE

PORTE
CHAMPERRET

NEUILLY-SUR-
SEINE

Av. de Villiers

PIGA

Pt. de Neuilly

Av. Charles de Gaulle

PORTE DES
TERNES

TERNES

Parc
Monceau

Bd. des Batignolles

Gare
St-Lazare

PORTE
MAILLOT

Arc
de
Triomphe

Av. de la Grande
Armée

Av. Hoche

Haussmann

Opér

PORTE
DAUPHINE

Av. Foch

Pl. Charles
de Gaulle

Av. de Friedland

The Faubourg St-H

La Madeleine

Av. des Champs

Av. Kléber

Av. d'Iéna

Av. Marceau

Av. George V

Av. des Champs - Elysées

R. Faubourg St-Honoré

Pl.
Vendôme

Bois de Boulogne

Av. Victor Hugo

Av. Raymond Poincaré

Av. du Pres. Wilson

Av. Montaigne

F.D. Roosevelt

Grand Palais

Petit
Palais

Pl. de la
Concorde

Louvre

Av. G.
Mandel

Pl. du
Trocadéro

Palais de
Chaillot

Quai d'Orsay

Quai Anatole France

Musée
d'Orsay

PORTE
DE LA MUETTE

Av. Paul Doumer

Tour
Eiffel

Av. de la Bourdonnais

Rapp

Av. Bosquet

Bd. de la Tour-
Maubourg

Hôtel des
Invalides

Bd. St-G

PASSY

Av. de Suffren

**From the Eiffel Tower
To the Louvre**

Av. de Breteuil

R. de Sèvres

Pala
Luxe

AUTEUIL

Av. du Pres. Kennedy

Quai Grenelle

Ecole
Militaire

Bd. de

Grenelle

**From Orsay to
St-Germain**

Raspail

PORTE
D'AUTEUIL

Av. de Versailles

R. de la Convention

Av. Emile Zola

ARENELLE

R. Lecourbe

Bd. du Montparna

PORTE DE
ST. CLOUD

R. Balard

R. du Commerce

Av. F. Faure

R. de Vaugirard

R. d'Alésia

Gare
Montparnasse

Cimetière
du
Montparnasse

PORTE
D'ISSY

Bd. Victor

Montparnasse

Bd. Galliéni

R. Ernest Renan

Bd. Lefebvre

Bd. Brune

Av. Victor Cresson

VANVES

PORTE DE
CHATILLON

PORTE
D'ORLEANS

MONTROUGE

ISSY-LES-
MOULINEAUX

0   1 mile

0   1 km

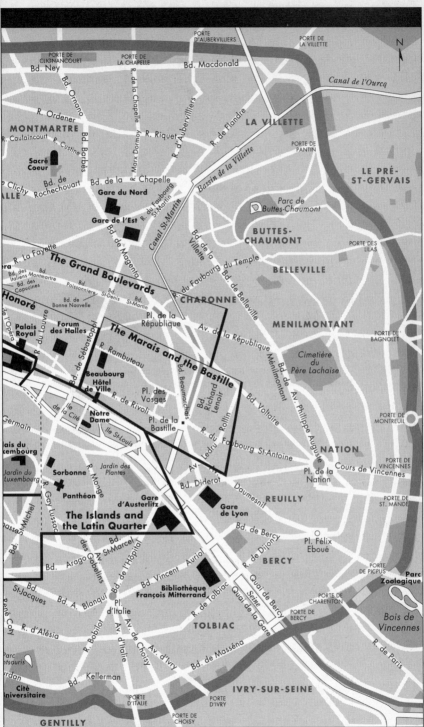

PORTE D'AUBERVILLIERS
PORTE DE LA VILLETTE

Canal de l'Ourcq

PORTE DE CLIGNANCOURT
PORTE DE LA CHAPELLE

Bd. Ney
Bd. Macdonald

R. Ordener
R. Ornano
R. de la Chapelle
R. Riquet
R. d'Aubervilliers
R. de Flandre
LA VILLETTE

MONTMARTRE
R. Caulaincourt
R. Custine
Bd. Barbès
R. Marx Dormoy
Bassin de la Villette

PORTE DE PANTIN

LE PRÉ-ST-GERVAIS

Sacré Coeur
Bd. de Rochechouart
Bd. de la Chapelle
Gare du Nord
Gare de l'Est
R. du Faubourg St-Martin
Canal St-Martin
Bd. de Magenta

Parc de Buttes-Chaumont
PORTE DES LILAS

BUTTES-CHAUMONT

Bd. de la Villette

BELLEVILLE

R. La Fayette
The Grand Boulevards
Bd. des Italiens
Montmartre
Bd. des Capucines
Bd. Poissonnière
Bd. St-Denis
Bd. St-Martin
Bd. de Bonne Nouvelle
Honoré

R. du Faubourg du Temple
Bd. de Belleville
CHARONNE
Av. de la République

MENILMONTANT
PORTE DE BAGNOLET

Palais Royal
Forum des Halles
Bd. de Sébastopol
R. Rambuteau
Pl. de la République
The Marais and the Bastille

Bd. Ménilmontant
Cimetière du Père Lachaise
PORTE DE MONTREUIL

Germain
Beaubourg
Hôtel de Ville
R. de Rivoli
Pl. des Vosges
Bd. Beaumarchais
Bd. Richard Lenoir
Bd. Voltaire
Av. Philippe Auguste

Notre Dame
Île St-Louis
Pl. de la Bastille
R. du Faubourg St-Antoine

NATION
PORTE DE VINCENNES

ais du embourg
Jardin du Luxembourg
Sorbonne
R. Monge
Jardin des Plantes
R. Ledru Rollin
Av. Ledru Rollin
Bd. Diderot
Pl. de la Nation
Cours de Vincennes

Panthéon
R. Gay Lussac
Gare d'Austerlitz
Gare de Lyon
REUILLY
PORTE DE ST-MANDÉ

The Islands and the Latin Quarter
Bd. St-Michel
Bd. Arago
Av. des Gobelins
Bd. St-Marcel
Bd. de l'Hôpital
Daumesnil
Bd. de Bercy
R. de Dijony
Pl. Félix Eboué

BERCY

Bd. St-Jacques
Bd. A. Blanqui
R. Bobillot
Bd. Vincent Auriol
Bibliothèque François Mitterrand
R. de Tolbiac
Quai de Bercy
Quai de la Gare
Seine
PORTE DE CHARENTON
PORTE DE BERCY
PORTE DE PICPUS
Parc Zoologique

Parc ntsouris
R. d'Alésia
Pl. d'Italie
Av. de Choisy
Av. d'Italie
Bd. de Masséna
Bois de Vincennes

R. de Paris
TOLBIAC

Cité Universitaire
Kellerman
IVRY-SUR-SEINE

GENTILLY
PORTE D'ITALIE
PORTE D'IVRY
PORTE DE CHOISY

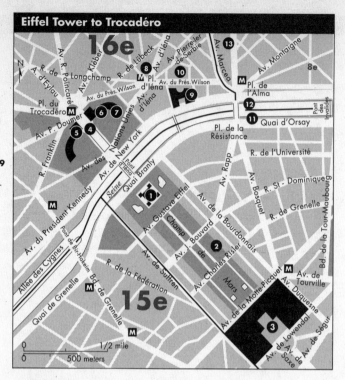

Pierre de Chaillot ⑭. Head up right and, just before the Arc de Triomphe, spin off right along rue de Presbourg to cross the Champs-Elysées.

The colossal, 164-foot **Arc de Triomphe** ⑮, sits on place Charles-de-Gaulle, known to Parisians as L'Etoile, or The Star—a reference to the streets that fan out from it. This is Europe's most chaotic traffic circle: Short of a death-defying dash, your only way of getting to the Arc de Triomphe in the middle is to take an underground passage from the far side of the Champs-Elysées. The view from the top of the Arc de Triomphe illustrates the star effect of the 12 radiating avenues and enables you to admire the vista down the **Champs-Elysées** toward place de la Concorde and the distant Louvre. West of the Champs-Elysées, and visible from the Arc de Triomphe, are the beautiful Bois de Boulogne (☞ On the Fringe, *below*); the posh suburb of Neuilly; and the towering office buildings and ultramodern arch of La Défense (☞ On the Fringe, *below*). Visible to the east is the world's most famous museum: the Louvre. (The Charles de Gaulle–Etoile métro stop, which sprawls underground beneath the Etoile, provides quick access to the western suburbs, if you want to make the excursion now.)

Walk down the Champs-Elysées and stop by the **Office de Tourisme de la Ville de Paris** ⑯ (the main city tourist office) at No. 127, on the right-hand side as you arrive from L'Etoile. Three hundred yards down on the left, at 116 bis, is the famous **Lido** nightclub and the highbrow **Le Fouquet's** restaurant-café, once frequented by Orson Welles and James Joyce (☞ Chapter 3).

Continue to the Rond-Point, home to the **Marionnettes des Champs-Elysées** puppet show, and turn right onto the spacious avenue Franklin-D.-Roosevelt. Some 200 yards down is the **Palais de la Découverte** ⑰, with exhibits on science and technology. It occupies the rear half of the glass-roofed **Grand Palais** ⑱, which forms an attractive duo with the **Petit Palais** ⑲ on the other side of avenue Winston-Churchill. Admire the view from the palaces across the **Pont Alexandre-III,** the exuberant bridge visible in the foreground, toward the gilt-domed Hôtel des Invalides.

The leafy lower reaches of the Champs-Elysées, with well-tended gardens off to the left, lead to the broad, airy **place de la Concorde** ⑳. Across place de la Concorde, facing the Champs-Elysées, two smallish buildings stand sentinel to the Jardin des Tuileries or Tuileries Gardens. Nearest the rue de Rivoli is the **Musée du Jeu de Paume** ㉑, host to outstanding exhibits of contemporary art. An identical building, nearer the Seine, is the **Musée de l'Orangerie** ㉒, containing some early 20th-century paintings by Monet, Renoir, and other Impressionists.

Stroll through the newly landscaped **Jardin des Tuileries** ㉓ and survey the surrounding cityscape. To the north is the disciplined, arcaded rue de Rivoli; to the south, the Seine and the gold-hued Musée d'Orsay with its enormous clocks; to the west, the Champs-Elysées and Arc de Triomphe; to the east, the Arc du Carrousel and the Louvre. Manicured lawns and eccentric diagonal hedges lead on toward the **Arc du Carrousel** ㉔, a small relation of the distant Arc de Triomphe. Steps lead down here to the **Carrousel du Louvre** ㉕, a swanky underground shopping mall, but you'll probably want to stay above ground and cross the paved esplanade, pass Louis XIV on his rearing bronze steed, and reach I. M. Pei's famous glass pyramid entry to the **Louvre** ㉖. Before plunging into the depths of the world's largest museum, pause to admire the newly cleaned, statue-lined 19th-century facades of the giant forecourt, and turn to assess the vista—aligned almost perfectly—that leads through the Arc du Carrousel to the Concorde obelisk, then up the Champs-Elysées to the Arc de Triomphe, with the shadowy towers of La Défense beyond.

TIMING

This 7-km (4½-mi) walk could be done in a morning or afternoon—if you don't stop and visit any of the shops, monuments, and museums that lie in wait along the way. Chances are you'll need a full day to do justice to this spectacular end of the city. It makes sense to do this walk on one of your first few days in Paris: The city's tourist office is here, and the view from the top of the Arc de Triomphe is like a short course in the city's geography. Sunny weather is a must, when the tour's vistas and photogenic moments are best. At night, head elsewhere in search of Parisian ambience and an affordable meal.

Sights to See

⑬ **American Cathedral of the Holy Trinity.** This slender-spired, neo-Gothic church was built by G. S. Street between 1885 and 1888. ⊠ *23 av. George-V,* ☎ *01–47–20–17–92.* ☉ *Weekdays 9–12:30 and 2–5, Sat. 9–noon. Services: weekdays 9 AM, Sun. 9 and 11 AM. Guided tours Sun. and Wed. 12:30. Métro: Alma-Marceau.*

㉔ **Arc du Carrousel.** This small triumphal arch between the Louvre and the Tuileries was erected by Napoléon from 1806 to 1808. The four bronze horses on top were originally the famous gilded horses that Napoléon looted from Venice; when these were returned in 1815, Bosio designed four new ones harnessed to a chariot, driven by a goddess symbolizing the Restoration (of the monarchy). *Métro: Palais-Royal.*

★ ⑮ **Arc de Triomphe.** This colossal, 164-foot Triumphal Arch was planned by Napoléon—who believed himself to be the direct heir to the Roman emperors—to celebrate his military successes. Unfortunately, Napoléon's strategic and architectural visions were not entirely on the same plane, and the Arc de Triomphe proved something of an embarrassment. Al-

Arc de Triomphe to Louvre

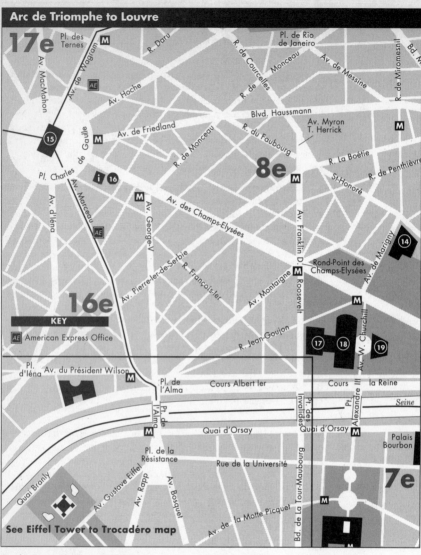

Arc du Carrousel, **24**
Arc de Triomphe, **15**
Carrousel
du Louvre, **25**
Grand Palais, **18**

Jardin des
Tuileries, **23**
Louvre, **26**
Musée du Jeu de
Paume, **21**

Musée de
l'Orangerie, **22**
Office de Tourisme de
la Ville de Paris, **16**
Palais de la
Découverte, **17**

Petit Palais, **19**
Place de la
Concorde, **20**
St-Pierre
de Chaillot, **14**

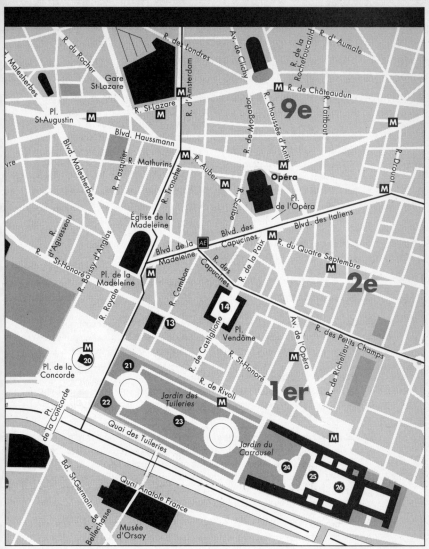

though the emperor wanted the monument completed in time for an 1810 parade in honor of his new bride, Marie-Louise, the arch was still only a few feet high, and a dummy arch of painted canvas was strung up to save face.

Empires come and go, and Napoléon's had been gone for more than 20 years before the Arc de Triomphe was finally finished, in 1836. It has some magnificent sculpture by François Rude, such as the *Departure of the Volunteers*, better known as *La Marseillaise*, situated to the right of the arch when viewed from the Champs-Elysées. After showing alarming signs of decay, the structure received a thorough overhaul in 1989 and is once again neo-Napoléonic in its splendor. There is a small museum halfway up the arch devoted to its history. France's Unknown Soldier is buried beneath the archway; the flame is rekindled every evening at 6:30. ⊠ *pl. Charles-de-Gaulle,* ☎ *01–43–80–31–31.* ▦ *32 frs.* ☉ *Daily 10–5:30; winter, daily 10–5. Métro or RER: Etoile.*

OFF THE   **MUSÉE DAPPER** – Precolonial African art is beautifully displayed in this
BEATEN PATH   tranquil four-story *hôtel particulier* (mansion). It's one métro stop from
L'Etoile or a 10-minute walk down avenue Victor-Hugo. ⊠ *50 av. Victor-Hugo,* ☎ *01–45–00–01–50.* ▦ *20 frs, Wed. free.* ☉ *Daily 11–7. Métro: Victor-Hugo.*

☾ ⑫ **Bateaux Mouches.** These popular motorboats set off on their hour-long tours of Paris waters regularly (every half hour in summer) from place de l'Alma, heading east to the Ile St-Louis and then back west, past the Eiffel Tower, as far as the Allée des Cygnes and its miniature version of the Statue of Liberty. *Bateau mouche* translates, misleadingly, as "fly boat"; the name mouche actually refers to a district of Lyon where the boats were originally manufactured. ⊠ *pl. de l'Alma,* ☎ *01–40–76–99–99.* ▦ *40 frs. Métro: Alma-Marceau.*

㉕ **Carrousel du Louvre.** This smart subterranean shopping complex, part of the early '90s Louvre renovation program, is centered on an inverted glass pyramid and contains a wide range of stores, spaces for fashion shows, an auditorium, and a huge parking garage. At lunchtime, museum visitors rush to the mall-style food court where fast food goes international. *Métro: Palais-Royal.*

☾ ❷ **Champ de Mars.** This long, formal garden, landscaped at the start of the century, lies between the Eiffel Tower and École Militaire. It was previously used as a parade ground and was the site of the World Exhibitions of 1867, 1889 (date of the construction of the Eiffel Tower), and 1900. *Métro: École Militaire; RER: Champ-de-Mars.*

Champs-Elysées. The 2-km (1¼-mi) Champs-Elysées was originally laid out in the 1660s by the landscape gardener Le Nôtre as a garden sweeping away from the Tuileries. You won't see many signs of those pastoral origins as you stroll past the cafés, restaurants, airline offices, car showrooms, movie theaters, and chic arcades that occupy its upper half. In an attempt to reestablish this thoroughfare as one of the world's most beautiful avenues, the city planted extras trees, broadened sidewalks, added coordinated designer street-furniture (everything from benches and lighting to traffic lights, telephone booths and trash cans), refurbished Art Nouveau newsstands, built underground parking to alleviate congestion, and clamped down on garish storefronts. *Métro: George-V, Franklin-D.-Roosevelt.*

❸ École Militaire. This harmonious 18th-century military academy, facing the Eiffel Tower across the Champ de Mars, is still in use and not open to the public. ⌑ *pl. du Maréchal-Joffre. Métro: École Militaire.*

⓫ Les Egouts. Brave the unpleasant—though tolerable—smell of the Paris sewers to follow an underground city of banks, passages, and footbridges. Name signs indicate the streets above you, and detailed panels and displays illuminate the history of waste disposal in Paris, whose sewer system is the largest in the world after Chicago's. ⌑ *pl. de la Résistance,* ☎ *01–47–05–10–29.* ⌑ *25 frs.* ☉ *Sat.–Wed. 11–5. Métro: Alma-Marceau; RER: Pont de l'Alma.*

OFF THE **AMERICAN CHURCH –** This Left Bank neo-Gothic church, built 1927–31,
BEATEN PATH offers help and advice to English-speaking foreigners. ⌑ *65 quai d'Orsay,* ☎ *01-47-05-07-99. Métro: Alma-Marceau; RER: Pont de l'Alma.*

★ ☙ ❶ Eiffel Tower. Known to the French as La Tour Eiffel (pronounced F.L.), Paris's most famous landmark was built by Gustave Eiffel for the World Exhibition of 1889, the centennial of the French Revolution, and was still in good shape to celebrate its own 100th birthday. Such was Eiffel's engineering wizardry that even in the strongest winds his tower never sways more than 4½ inches. Its colossal bulk exudes a feeling of mighty permanence. You may have trouble believing that it nearly became 7,000 tons of scrap iron when its concession expired in 1909. Only its potential use as a radio antenna saved the day; it now bristles with a forest of radio and television transmitters. Restoration in the late 1980s didn't make the elevators any faster (lines are inevitable), but the nocturnal illumination is fantastic—every girder highlighted in glorious detail. If you're full of energy, stride up the stairs as far as the third deck. If you want to go to the top, you'll have to take the elevator. The view at 1,000 feet may not beat that from the Tour Montparnasse (☞ Montparnasse, *below*), but the setting makes it considerably more romantic. ⌑ *quai Branly,* ☎ *01–44–11–23–23.* ⌑ *By elevator: 2nd floor, 20 frs; 3rd floor, 40 frs; 4th floor, 56 frs. By foot: 2nd and 3rd floors only, 12 frs.* ☉ *July–Aug., daily 9 AM–midnight; Sept.–June, daily 9 AM–11 PM. Métro: Bir-Hakeim; RER: Champ-de-Mars.*

Fouquet's. This 1898 restaurant-café has a highbrow clientele; bronze plaques honor faithful patrons past and present, including François Truffaut and Orson Welles. ⌑ *99 av. des Champs-Elysées. Métro: George-V.*

⓲ Grand Palais. With its curved glass roof, the Grand Palais is unmistakable when approached from either the Seine or the Champs-Elysées and forms an attractive duo with the Petit Palais on the other side of avenue Winston-Churchill. Both these stone buildings are adorned with mosaics and sculpted friezes. Both were built for the World Fair of 1900, and, as with the Eiffel Tower, there was never any intention that they would be permanent additions to the city. But once they were up, no one seemed inclined to take them down. Today, the atmospheric iron-and-glass interior of the Grand Palais plays host to major exhibitions but was closed for renovation in 1994 and is unlikely to reopen before 1999. ⌑ *av. Winston-Churchill. Métro: Champs-Elysées–Clemenceau.*

☙ ㉓ Jardin des Tuileries. The recently renovated Tuileries Gardens are typically French: formal and neatly patterned, with statues, rows of trees, and gravel paths. This is a charming place to stroll and survey the surrounding cityscape; you may see a string quartet or jugglers entertaining large crowds on weekends. A fair, with a small skating rink, sets up here between December and February. *Métro: Tuileries.*

Lido. Free-flowing champagne, foot-stomping melodies in French and English, and topless razzmatazz pack in the crowds every night for the show at this famous nightclub, which has been around since 1946. ⊠ *116 av. des Champs-Elysées. Métro: George-V.*

❷⁶ **Louvre.** Though it is now a coherent, unified structure, the Louvre—the world's largest museum and one of its most stunning at night when illuminated by 70,000 discreet lightbulbs—is the product of centuries. Originally built by Philippe-Auguste in the 13th century as a fortress, it was not until the reign of pleasure-loving François I, 300 years later, that today's Louvre gradually began to take shape. Through the years, Henri IV (1589–1610), Louis XIII (1610–43), Louis XIV (1643–1715), Napoléon (1804–14), and Napoléon III (1852–70) all contributed to its construction. Before rampaging revolutionaries burned part of it down during the bloody Paris Commune of 1871, the building was even larger. The open section facing the Tuileries Gardens was originally the Palais des Tuileries, the main Paris residence of the royal family.

The uses to which the building has been put have been almost equally varied. Though Charles V (1364–80) made the Louvre his residence—parts of the original medieval fortress have been excavated and can be seen during your visit—later French kings preferred to live elsewhere, mainly in the Loire Valley. Even after François I decided to make the Louvre his permanent home, and accordingly embarked on an ambitious rebuilding program (most of which came to nothing), the Louvre never became more than a secondary palace.

When, in 1682, Louis XIV decided to move the French court out of the city to Versailles, despite having initiated a major program of rebuilding at the Louvre, it seemed that the Louvre would never be more than a home for minor courtiers. Indeed, during the remainder of Louis's reign, the palace underwent a rapid decline. Its empty apartments were taken over by a rabble of artists; little shacklike shops were set up against the walls; and chimneys projected higgledy-piggledy from the severe lines of the facades. Louis XV (1715–74), thanks in large measure to the financial shrewdness of his chief minister, Marigny, inaugurated long-overdue renovations, though he, too, preferred to live at Versailles.

The Louvre's association with the French crown did not last much longer. It was from the Tuileries Palace that Louis XVI and Marie-Antoinette fled in 1791, two years after the start of the Revolution, only to be arrested and returned to Paris for their executions. The palace was taken over by the Revolutionary leaders—the Convention first, then the Directory. At the very end of the century, Napoléon, initially as first consul, subsequently as emperor, initiated further renovations and made the Louvre into a museum. This did not, however, prevent the three remaining French kings—Louis XVIII (1814–24), who has the dubious distinction of having been the only French monarch to die in the Louvre; Charles X (1824–30); and Louis-Philippe (1830–48)—from making the Louvre their home. The latter two suffered the indignity of expulsion at the hands of the dreaded Paris mob in the uprisings of 1830 and 1848, respectively.

★ The Louvre's recent history centers on I. M. Pei's glass **Pyramid**, surrounded by three smaller pyramids in the Cour Napoléon. Unveiled in March of 1989, it's more than just a grandiloquent gesture, a desire on the part of former president François Mitterrand, who com-

Louvre

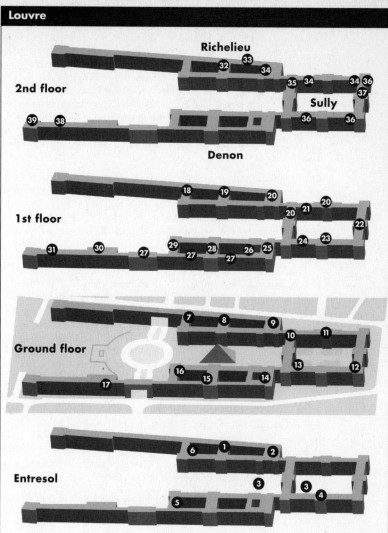

Richelieu

2nd floor

32 33 34

35 34 34 36
37

Sully

36 36

39 38

Denon

1st floor

18 19 20

20 21 20
20
22
24 23

31 30 27 29 28 26 25
27 27

Ground floor

7 8 9
10 11
13
16 12
17 15 14

Entresol

6 1 2

3
3
5 4

Egyptian Antiquities:
Christian Egypt, **12**
Crypt of the
Sphinx, **4**
Pharaonic
Egypt, **12, 22**
French Paintings:
14th–17th cent., **34**
18th–19th cent., **36**
19th cent. (large), **26**
French Sculptures:
17th–18th cent., **1**
17th–19th cent., **8**
Middle Ages,
Renaissance, **7**
**Greek, Etruscan and
Roman Antiquities:**
Bronzes and Precious
Objects, **24**
Ceramics and
Terracotta, **23**

Greek Antiquities, **13**
Etruscan and Roman
Antiquities, **14**
Salle du Manège
(copies of
antiques), **15**
Venus de Milo, **13**
Italian Paintings: 27
Mona Lisa, **28**
Italian Sculptures:
11th–15th cent., **5**
16th–19th cent., **16**
*Michelangelo's
Slaves*, **17**
Medieval Louvre: 3
**Northern School
Paintings:**
Holland, Flanders,
Germany, **32**

Northern Sculptures:
12th–16th cent., **5**
17th–19th cent., **16**
Objets d'Art:
17th–18th cent., **20**
First Empire, **18**
Galerie d'Apollon
(Crown Jewels), **25**
Middle Ages,
Renaissance, **19**
Napoléon III
Apartments, **18**
Restoration, July
Monarchy, **21**
Oriental Antiquities:
Gudéa, **9**
Islamic Art, **2**
Mesopotamia,
Ancient Iran, **10**
Near East, **11**

Prints and Drawings:
Documentation
Room, **31**
French School:
17th century, **35**
18th century, **37**
Italian School, **29**
Northern Schools, **33**
Temporary
Exhibitions, **39**
Spanish Paintings: 30
Thematic Exhibitions:
Sculpture, **6**
Paintings, **38**

missioned it, to make his mark on the city. The pyramid provided a new, and much needed, entrance to the Louvre; it also tops a large museum shop, café, and restaurant. Moreover, it acts as the terminal point for the most celebrated city view in Europe, a majestic vista stretching through the Arc du Carrousel, the Tuileries Gardens, across place de la Concorde, up the Champs-Elysées to the towering Arc de Triomphe, and ending at the giant modern arch at La Défense, 4 km (2½ mi) more to the west. Needless to say, the architectural collision between the classical stone blocks of the courtyard surrounding the pyramid and the pseudo-Egyptian glass panels caused a furor. But, as time has passed, initial outrage has faded—as it once did for the Eiffel Tower.

The pyramids marked only the first phase of the Grand Louvre Project, a plan for the restoration of the museum launched by Mitterrand in 1981 for an estimated $1.3 billion. In November 1993, exactly 200 years after the Louvre first opened its doors to the public, Mitterrand cut the ribbon on the second phase: the renovation of the **Richelieu wing** on the north side of the Cour Napoléon. Built between 1852 and 1857 by Napoléon III and grudgingly vacated in 1989 by the Ministry of Finance, the wing was gutted and reconstructed by Pei and his French associates and reopened to house more than 12,000 artworks, nearly a third from storage. The wing contains principally the Islamic and Mesopotamian art collections, French sculpture and painting, and Napoléon III's sumptuous apartments lovingly restored to their full ostentatious glory. The final phase of the Grand Louvre project, which was finished in 1996, included a much-needed improvement of lighting and air-conditioning throughout the museum; on the exterior the remaining facades have been restored and cleaned.

Don't let the main court and Pei's pyramids tempt you away from the second, architecturally more sophisticated courtyard: Louis XIV's harmoniously imposing **Cour Carrée,** with its assured feel of an Oxford quadrangle, was one of the supreme architectural achievements of his reign. It has been painstakingly restored and thousands of cobblestones laid in place of tarmac. Facing it, on the east side, is a giant colonnade, designed by Claude Perrault in the 1660s.

The Louvre's extraordinary collections encompass paintings, drawings, antiquities, sculpture, furniture, coins, and jewelry—the quality and the sheer variety are overwhelming. The number one attraction is Leonardo da Vinci's enigmatic **Mona Lisa,** *La Joconde* to the French. The picture is smaller than you might expect and kept behind protective glass; it is invariably surrounded by a crowd of worshipers. But there are numerous other works of equal quality. The collections are divided into seven areas: Asian antiquities, Egyptian antiquities, Greek and Roman antiquities, sculpture, objets d'art, paintings, and prints and drawings. What follows is no more than a selection of favorites, chosen to act as key points for your exploration. If you have time for only one visit, they give an idea of the riches of the museum. But try to make repeat visits—the Louvre is half price on Sundays and after 3 PM on other days. Study the plans at the entrance to get your bearings and pick up a map to take with you. ⊠ *Palais du Louvre,* ☎ *01–40–20–53–17 for information.* ⌨ *45 frs; 26 frs after 3 PM and all day Sun.; free 1st Sun. of month.* ☉ *Thurs.–Sun. 9–6, Mon. and Wed. 9 AM–9:45 PM. Some sections open limited days. Métro: Palais-Royal.*

PAINTINGS

French paintings dominate the picture collection. Here are the highlights, in chronological order:

Shepherds in Arcadia, by Poussin (1594–1665), is a sturdy example of the Rome-based painter's fascination with the classical world and of the precision of his draftsmanship. His colors, by contrast, are surprisingly vivid, almost Venetian.

Cleopatra Landing, by Claude (1600–82), presents an altogether more poetic vision of the ancient world as delicately atmospheric, with the emphasis on light and space rather than on the nominal subject matter.

Embarkation for the Island of Cythera, by Watteau (1684–1721), concentrates on creating an equally poetic mood, but there is an extra layer of emotion: The gallant gentlemen and courtly women seem drugged by the pleasures about to be enjoyed but disturbingly aware of their transitory nature, too.

Oath of the Horatii, by David (1748–1825), takes a much sterner view of classical Rome; this is neoclassicism—severe, uncompromising, and austere. The moral content of the painting takes precedence over purely painterly qualities; it also held an important political message for contemporaries, championing the cause of Republicanism.

La Grande Odalisque, by Ingres (1780–1867), is one of the supreme achievements of this habitually staid "academic" artist; sensuous yet remote and controlled. Here, exoticism and the French classical tradition gel to produce a strikingly elegant image.

Raft of the Medusa, by Géricault (1791–1824), conveys a gloomily Romantic view of the human state, nightmarish despite its heroism and grand scale.

Liberty Guiding the People, by Delacroix (1798–1863), in sharp contrast to the conservative classical paintings of the 19th century, celebrates the courageous spirit of revolutionary idealism. While Liberty evokes a classical reference, she symbolizes the heroism of the bloody uprising on July 27–29, 1830.

Among works by non-French painters, pride of place must go to the **Mona Lisa,** if only by virtue of its fame. The Italian Renaissance is also strongly represented by Fra Angelico, Mantegna, Raphael, Titian, and Veronese. Holbein, Van Eyck, Rembrandt, Hals, Brueghel, and Rubens—whose giant Maria de Medici canvases have an entire hall to themselves—underline the achievements of northern European painting. The Spanish painters El Greco, Murillo, and Goya are also represented.

SCULPTURE

Three-dimensional attractions start with marvels of ancient Greek sculpture, such as the soaring *Victory of Samothrace,* from the 3rd century BC and the *Venus de Milo,* from the 2nd century BC. The strikingly realistic *Seated Scribe* dates from around 2000 BC. One of the best-loved exhibits is Michelangelo's *Slaves,* intended for the unfinished tomb of Pope Julius II. These can be admired in the Denon Wing, where the sculpture section is housed partly in the brick-vaulted former imperial stables. Other highlights include a 12th-century Crucifixion from Bavaria, Gregor Erhart's sensuous 15th-century colored wooden statue of *Mary Magdalene,* and a 17th-century walnut *Death of St. Francis* from Spain.

FURNITURE AND OBJETS D'ART

The number one attraction is the French crown jewels, a glittering display of extravagant jewelry, including the 186-karat Regent diamond. Among the collections of French furniture, don't miss the grandiose 17th- and 18th-century productions of Boulle and Riesener, marvels of intricate craftsmanship and elegant luxury. The series of immense Gobelins tapestries are for those with a fondness for opulent decoration.

🕑 **Marionnettes des Champs-Elysées.** Guignol, the French counterpart to Punch and Judy, amuses youngsters at the corner of avenues Matignon and Gabriel halfway down the Champs-Elysées. ✉ *Rond-Point,* ☎ *01–40–35–47–20.* 🎫 *15 frs.* 🕑 *Shows Wed., Sat., and Sun. at 3, 4, and 5. Métro: Champs-Elysées–Clemenceau.*

❾ **Musée d'Art Moderne de la Ville de Paris.** Both temporary exhibits and the permanent collection of top-quality 20th-century art can be found at the City Museum of Modern Art. It takes over, chronologically speaking, where the Musée d'Orsay leaves off: Among the earliest works are Fauve paintings by Vlaminck and Derain, followed by Picasso's early experiments in Cubism. Its vast, unobtrusive, white-walled galleries provide an ideal background for the bold statements of 20th-century art. Loudest and largest are the canvases of Robert Delaunay. Other highlights include works by Braque, Rouault, Gleizes, Da Silva, Gromaire, and Modigliani. There is also a large room devoted to Art Deco furniture and screens, where Jean Dunand's gilt and lacquered panels consume oceans of wall space. There is a pleasant, if expensive, museum café and an excellent bookshop specializing in 19th- and 20th-century art and architecture, with many books in English. ✉ *11 av. du Président-Wilson,* ☎ *01–53–67–40–00.* 🎫 *27 frs.* 🕑 *Tues.–Sun. 10–5:30, Wed. 10–8:30. Métro: Iéna.*

❼ **Musée du Cinéma Henri-Langlois.** This cinema museum, in the basement of the Palais de Chaillot, traces the history of motion pictures since the 1880s. Henri Langlois devoted his life to collecting the memorabilia contained in this museum, which include scripts, photos, costumes, and Louis Lumière's first movie camera, dating from 1895. ✉ *1 pl. du Trocadéro,* ☎ *01–45–53–74–39.* 🎫 *30 frs.* 🕑 *Wed.–Mon; guided tours only, at 10, 11, 2, 3, 4, and 5. Métro: Trocadéro.*

....

NEED A BREAK?   Get a tremendous view of the Eiffel Tower, and a drink or a snack at **Les Monuments** (☎ 01–44–05–90–00), an elegant bar and restaurant in the cinema wing of the Palais de Chaillot.

....

❽ **Musée Guimet.** This Belle Epoque museum was founded by Lyonnais industrialist Emile Guimet, who traveled around the world in the late 19th century amassing priceless Indo-Chinese and Far Eastern objets d'art, plus the largest collection of Cambodian art this side of Cambodia. Trouble is, most of the museum is closed for restoration until 1999; just the Heidelbach-Guimet gallery around the corner (✉ 19 av. d'Iéna), featuring Buddhist art from China and Japan, stays open in the interim. ✉ *6 pl. d'Iéna,* ☎ *01–47–23–61–65.* 🎫 *15 frs.* 🕑 *Wed.–Mon. 9:45–6. Métro: Iéna.*

❺ **Musée de l'Homme.** Artifacts, costumes, and domestic tools from around the world, dating from prehistoric times, make up this earnest anthropological Museum of Mankind on the second and third floors of the Palais de Chaillot. ✉ *17 pl. du Trocadéro,* ☎ *01–44–05–72–72.* 🎫 *30 frs.* 🕑 *Wed.–Mon. 9:45–5. Métro: Trocadéro.*

㉑ **Musée du Jeu de Paume.** France's Impressionist paintings used to be housed at the Jeu de Paume Museum (now they're at the Musée d'Orsay), at the entrance to the Tuileries Gardens. Renovations transformed the museum into an ultramodern, white-walled showcase for excellent temporary exhibits of bold contemporary art. ✉ *pl. de la Concorde,*

☎ *01–42–60–69–69.* ✍ *35 frs.* ☉ *Tues. noon–9:30, Wed.–Fri. noon–7, weekends 10–7. Métro: Concorde.*

Musée de la Marine. The Maritime Museum, on the first floor of the Palais de Chaillot (☞ *below*), contains ship models and seafaring paraphernalia, illustrating French naval history up to the age of the nuclear submarine. At press time (late 1997), there were plans to move the museum to an unspecified new location. ✉ *17 pl. du Trocadéro,* ☎ *01–45–53–31–70.* ✍ *38 frs.* ☉ *Wed.–Mon. 10–6. Métro: Trocadéro.*

⑩ Musée de la Mode et du Costume. The Museum of Fashion and Costume is housed in the stylish, late-19th-century Palais Galliera. Exhibits on costumery and clothing design are held here. ✉ *10 av. Pierre-1er-de-Serbie,* ☎ *01–47–20–85–23.* ✍ *26 frs.* ☉ *Tues.–Sun. 10–5:40. Métro: Iéna.*

❻ Musée des Monuments Français. This museum was founded in 1879 by architect-restorer Viollet-le-Duc (the man mainly responsible for the extensive renovation of Notre-Dame and countless other Gothic cathedrals). Its tribute to French buildings of the Romanesque and Gothic periods (roughly 1000–1500) takes the form of painstaking copies of statues, columns, archways, and frescoes—an excellent introduction to French medieval architecture. It is easy to imagine yourself strolling among ruins as you pass through the first-floor gallery. Substantial sections of a number of French churches and cathedrals are represented here, notably Chartres and Vézelay. Mural and ceiling paintings—copies of works in churches around the country—dominate the other three floors. The value of these paintings has become increasingly evident as many of the originals continue to deteriorate. On the ceiling of a circular room is a reproduction of the painted dome of Cahors cathedral, which gives a more vivid sense of the skills of the original medieval painter than the original itself. ✉ *1 pl. du Trocadéro,* ☎ *01–44–05–39–10.* ✍ *21 frs, Sun. 14 frs.* ☉ *Wed.–Mon. 10–6. Métro: Trocadéro.*

㉒ Musée de l'Orangerie. Several of Claude Monet's *Water Lily* series head the choice array of early 20th-century paintings in the Orangerie Museum in the Tuileries Gardens. Works by Renoir, Cézanne, Matisse, and Marie Laurencin, the "Popess of Cubism," are also on display. ✉ *pl. de la Concorde,* ☎ *01–42–97–48–16.* ✍ *28 frs.* ☉ *Wed.–Mon. 9:45–5:15. Métro: Concorde.*

⑯ Office de Tourisme de la Ville de Paris. The modern, spacious, Paris Tourist Office, near the Arc de Triomphe, is worth a visit at the start of your stay to pick up free maps, leaflets, and information on upcoming events. Most of the uniformed hostesses speak English and can also help book accommodations or tickets for shows. You can also exchange money here and buy métro tickets and souvenirs. ✉ *127 av. des Champs-Elysées,* ☎ *01–49–52–53–54 (01–49–52–53–56 for recorded information in English).* ☉ *Daily 9–8. Métro: Charles de Gaulle–Etoile.*

❹ Palais de Chaillot. This honey-color Art Deco cultural center was built in the 1930s to replace a Moorish-style building constructed for the World Exhibition of 1878. It contains four large museums: the **Musée de l'Homme**, the **Musée de la Marine**, the **Musée des Monuments Français**, and the **Musée du Cinéma Henri-Langlois** (☞ individual museum listings, *above*). The tumbling gardens leading to the Seine contain sculptures and some dramatic fountains. The palace terrace, flanked by gilded statuettes (and often invaded by roller skaters and skateboarders), offers a wonderful, picture-postcard view of the Eiffel Tower. ⊠ *pl. du Trocadéro. Métro: Trocadéro.*

MAISON DE BALZAC – The Paris home of the great French 19th-century novelist, Honoré de Balzac (1799–1850), contains a wide range of exhibits charting his tempestuous life. ⊠ *47 rue Raynouard,* ☎ *01–42–24–56–38.* ⊠ *17 frs.* ☾ *Feb.–Dec., Tues.–Sun. 10–5:40. Métro: Passy.*

MUSÉE MARMOTTAN – Paris's "other" Impressionist museum (after the Musée d'Orsay) is in a 19th-century mansion, only a short métro ride from the Trocadéro. The Marmottan has an extensive collection of works by Claude Monet (including *Impression-Sunrise,* from which the term Impressionist derives). There are also fine works by other Impressionists, including Pissarro, Renoir, and Sisley. Displayed on the first and second floors are some magnificent medieval illuminated manuscripts and the original furnishings of a sumptuous early 19th-century Empire mansion. The Marmottan is one of the most underestimated museums in Paris. ⊠ *2 rue Louis-Boilly,* ☎ *01–42–24–07–02.* ⊠ *40 frs.* ☾ *Tues.–Sun. 10–5:30. Métro: La Muette.*

MUSÉE DU VIN – Housed in the vaulted cellars of a former 13th-century abbey, the small Museum of Wine is devoted to traditional wine-making artifacts. The premises double as a wine bar. ⊠ *5 square Charles-Dickens,* ☎ *01–45–25–63–26.* ⊠ *32 frs, including wine tasting.* ☾ *Daily 10–6. Métro: Passy.*

☾ **⑰ Palais de la Découverte.** Working models, a planetarium, and scientific and technological exhibits make up this Palace of Discovery behind the Grand Palais. ⊠ *av. Franklin-D.-Roosevelt,* ☎ *01–40–74–80–00.* ⊠ *27 frs, 13 frs extra for planetarium.* ☾ *Tues.–Sat. 9:30–6, Sun. 10–7. Métro: Champs-Elysées–Clemenceau.*

⑲ Petit Palais. The smaller counterpart to the Grand Palais, just off the Champs-Elysées, beautifully presents a permanent collection of French painting and furniture, with splendid canvases by Courbet and Bouguereau. Temporary exhibits are often held here, too. The sprawling entrance gallery contains several enormous turn-of-the-century paintings on its walls and ceilings. ⊠ *av. Winston-Churchill,* ☎ *01–42–65–12–73.* ⊠ *27 frs.* ☾ *Tues.–Sun. 10–5:30. Métro: Champs-Elysées–Clemenceau.*

⑳ Place de la Concorde. This majestic square at the foot of the Champs-Elysées was laid out in the 1770s, but there was nothing in the way of peace or concord about its early years. Between 1793 and 1795, it was the scene of more than 1,000 deaths by guillotine; victims included Louis XVI, Marie-Antoinette, Danton, and Robespierre. The Obelisk, a present from the viceroy of Egypt, was erected in 1833. The handsome, symmetrical 18th-century buildings facing the square include the deluxe Crillon hotel (☞ Chapter 4), identified by a discreet marble plaque. At the near end of high-walled rue Royale is the legendary Maxim's restaurant. Unless you choose to eat here, you won't be able to see the inside, a riot of crimson velvets and florid Art Nouveau furniture. *Métro: Concorde.*

Pont Alexandre-III. No other bridge over the Seine epitomizes the fin de siècle frivolity of the Belle Epoque like the exuberant, bronze lamp-lined Pont Alexandre-III. The bridge was built, like the Grand and Petit Palais nearby, for the 1900 World Fair, and ingratiatingly named in honor of the visiting Russian czar. *Métro: Invalides.*

Pont de l'Alma. The Alma Bridge is best known for the chunky stone "Zouave" statue carved into one of the pillars. Zouaves were Algerian infantrymen recruited into the French army who were famous for their bravura and colorful uniforms. (The term came to be used for volunteers in the Union army during the American Civil War.) There is nothing quite so glamorous, or colorful, about the Alma Zouave, however, whose hour of glory comes in times of watery distress: Parisians use him to judge the level of the Seine during heavy rains. As recently as January 1995, the Zouave was submerged up to his waist, and the roads running along the riverbanks were under several feet of water. *Métro: Alma-Marceau.*

 St-Pierre de Chaillot. A sturdy 210-foot tower signals this neo-Romanesque church, built in 1937, between the Seine and the Champs-Elysées. Henri Bouchard's monumental frieze above the entrance depicts scenes from the life of St. Peter. ⊠ *av. Marceau. Métro: Alma-Marceau.*

THE FAUBOURG ST-HONORÉ

The Faubourg St-Honoré—the area just north of the Champs-Elysées and the Tuileries—is synonymous with style, as you will see as you progress from the President's Palace, past a wealth of art galleries and the neo-classical Madeleine church, to stately place Vendôme. Leading names in modern fashion can be found further east on place des Victoires, close to what was, for centuries, the gastronomic heart of Paris: Les Halles (pronounced *lay al*), once the city's main market.

The giant glass-and-iron market halls of Les Halles used to be replenished every night by an army of wagons, then trucks, which caused astounding traffic jams in the city's already congested streets. The market was closed in 1969 and replaced by a park and a modern shopping mall, the Forum des Halles. The surrounding streets underwent a transformation and are now filled with shops, cafés, restaurants, and chic apartment buildings.

The brash modernity of the Forum stands in contrast to the August church of St-Eustache nearby. Similarly, the incongruous black-and-white columns in the classical courtyard of Richelieu's neighboring Palais-Royal present a further case of daring modernity—or architectural vandalism, depending on your point of view. Parisians may delight in their role as custodians of a glorious heritage, but are not content to remain mere guardians of the past.

Numbers in the text correspond to numbers in the margin and on the Faubourg St-Honoré map.

A Good Walk

Start your walk in front of the most important home in France: the **Palais de l'Elysée** ①, or Presidential Palace. Crash barriers and stern policemen keep visitors at bay; in fact, there's more to see in the plethora of art galleries and luxury fashion boutiques that line rue du Faubourg St-Honoré. Pass the British Embassy, then turn left onto rue Boissy-d'Anglas and cut right through an archway into Cité Berryer, a newly restored courtyard with several trendy boutiques. It leads to rue Royale, a classy street lined with jewelry stores. Looming to the left is the **Église de la Madeleine** ②, a sturdy neoclassical edifice.

Cross boulevard de la Madeleine and take rue Duphot down to rue St-Honoré, where you'll find **Notre-Dame de l'Assomption** ③, noted for its huge dome and solemn interior. Continue to rue de Castiglione, then head left to one of the world's most opulent squares, **place Vendôme** ④, ringed with jewelers. That's Napoléon standing at the top of the square's bronze central column—and that's the Ritz, fronted by those Rolls-Royces halfway down on the left. Return to rue St-Honoré and continue to the mighty church of **St-Roch** ⑤. It's worth having a look inside to see the bombastically Baroque altarpiece in the circular lady chapel at the far end.

Take the next right onto rue des Pyramides and cross **place des Pyramides,** with its gilded statue of Joan of Arc on horseback, to the northernmost wing of the Louvre: home to the **Musée des Arts Décoratifs** ⑥, dedicated to French furniture and applied arts. Stay on arcaded rue de Rivoli to place du Palais-Royal. On the far side of the square is the **Louvre des Antiquaires** ⑦, a chic shopping mall housing upscale antiques shops. Opposite, beyond the exuberant fountains of place André-Malraux, the Opéra Garnier (☞ The Grand Boulevards, *below*) beckons at the far end of the avenue of the same name.

On the corner of rue de Richelieu and rue de Rivoli is the **Comédie Française** ⑧, the time-honored setting for performances of classical French drama. To the right of the theater is the unobtrusive entrance to the **Palais-Royal** ⑨; its courtyard is a surprising oasis in the heart of the city, and a study in both classical and contemporary French landscape architecture. Walk down to the far end of the garden and peek into the glassy, Belle Epoque interior of Le Grand Véfour (☞ Chapter 3), one of the swankiest restaurants in the city.

One block north of here, on rue de Richelieu, stands France's national library, the **Bibliothèque Nationale** ⑩. Rue des Petits-Champs heads east to the circular **place des Victoires** ⑪: That's Louis XIV riding the plunging steed in the center of the square. You'll find some of the city's most upscale fashion shops here and on the surrounding streets, along with the 17th-century church of **Notre-Dame des Victoires** ⑫. Head south down rue Croix-des-Petits-Champs, past the nondescript Banque de France on your right, and take the second street on the left to the circular **Bourse du Commerce** ⑬, the Commercial Exchange. Alongside it is a 100-foot-high fluted column, the **Colonne de Ruggieri.**

You don't need to scale Ruggieri's Column to spot the bulky outline of the church of **St-Eustache** ⑭, a curious architectural hybrid of Gothic and classical. The vast site next to St-Eustache once housed Les Halles, the halls of the central Paris food market. Today most of the market area is occupied by a garden, the **Jardin des Halles** ⑮, and a modern, multilevel shopping mall, the **Forum des Halles** ⑯. Rue Berger leads to the square des Innocents, with its handsome 16th-century Renaissance fountain. Further east you can see the futuristic funnels of the Centre Pompidou (☞ The Marais and the Bastille, *below*) jutting above the surrounding buildings.

From the far end of the square des Innocents, rue St-Denis leads to place du Châtelet, with its theaters, fountain, and the **Tour St-Jacques** ⑰ looming up to your left—all that remains of a church that once stood here. Turning right on quai de la Mégisserie, you can divide your attention between the exotic array of caged birds for sale along the sidewalk and the view across the Seine toward the turreted Conciergerie. As you cross rue du Pont-Neuf, the birds give way to the Art Deco Samaritaine department store with its panoramic rooftop café. Turn right on rue de l'Arbre-Sec, then the first left on to rue des Prêtres to reach **St-Germain l'Auxerrois** ⑱, once the French royal family's parish church. Opposite is the colonnaded eastern facade of the Louvre (☞ From the Eiffel Tower to the Louvre, *above*).

TIMING

With brief visits to churches and monuments, this 5½-km (3½-mi) walk should take about three to four hours. On a nice day, linger in the gardens of the Palais-Royal; on a cold day, indulge in an unbelievably thick hot chocolate at the Angélina tearoom.

Sights to See

⑩ Bibliothèque Nationale. France's national library used to contain more than 7 million printed volumes; many have been removed to the giant new Bibliothèque François-Mitterrand (☞ The Islands and the Latin Quarter, *below*). You can admire Robert de Cotte's 18th-century courtyard and peep into the magnificent 19th-century reading room, but you cannot enter (it's only open to researchers). The collections are on exhibit from time to time in the library's galleries. ⊠ *58 rue de Richelieu.* ⊙ *Daily 9–8. Métro: Bourse.*

⑬ Bourse du Commerce. The circular, shallow-domed, 18th-century Commercial Exchange near Les Halles began life as a Corn Exchange; Victor Hugo waggishly likened it to a jockey's cap without the peak. ⊠ *rue de Viarmes. Métro or RER: Les Halles.*

Colonne de Ruggieri. The 100-foot-high fluted column, behind the Bourse du Commerce, is all that remains of a mansion built here in 1572 for Catherine de' Medici. The column is said to have been used as a platform for stargazing by her astrologer, Ruggieri. *Métro: Les Halles.*

⑧ Comédie Française. This theater is the setting for performances of classical French drama, with tragedies by Racine and Corneille and comedies by Molière regularly on the bill. The building itself dates from 1790, but the Comédie Française company was created by that most theatrical of French monarchs, Louis XIV, back in 1680. If you understand French and have a taste for the mannered, declamatory style of French acting—it's a far cry from method acting—you'll appreciate an evening here (☞ Chapter 5). ⊠ *pl. André-Malraux,* ☎ *01–44–58–15–15. Métro: Palais-Royal.*

❷ Église de la Madeleine. With its rows of uncompromising columns, this sturdy neoclassical edifice—designed in 1814 but not consecrated until 1842—looks more like a Greek temple than a Christian church. In fact, La Madeleine, as it is called, was nearly selected as Paris's first train station (the site of the Gare St-Lazare, just up the road, was chosen instead). Inside, the only natural light comes from three shallow domes. The walls are richly and harmoniously decorated; gold glints through the murk. The portico's majestic Corinthian colonnade supports a gigantic pediment with a frieze of the Last Judgment. From the top of the church's steps, you can see down rue Royale across place de la Concorde to the Palais Bourbon (parliament building). From the bottom of the steps, another vista extends up boulevard Malesherbes to the domed church of St-Augustin. ⊠ *pl. de la Madeleine.* ⊙ *Mon.–Sat. 7:30–7, Sun. 8–7. Métro: Madeleine.*

NEED A BREAK?   **L'Ecluse** (⊠ 15 pl. de la Madeleine), a cozy wine bar on the square to the west of the Église de la Madeleine, offers stylish snacks, such as foie gras and carpaccio, and a range of Bordeaux wines.

⑯ Forum des Halles. Les Halles, the iron-and-glass halls of the central Paris food market, were closed in 1969 and replaced in the late '70s by the Forum des Halles, a modern shopping mall. Nothing remains of either the market or the rambunctious atmosphere that led 19th-century novelist Emile Zola to dub Les Halles *"le ventre de Paris"* ("the belly of Paris"), although rue Montorgueil, behind St-Eustache, retains something of its original bustle. Unfortunately, much of the plastic, concrete, glass, and mock-marble facade of the multilevel shopping mall, still referred to as "Les Halles," is already showing signs of wear and

The Faubourg St-Honoré

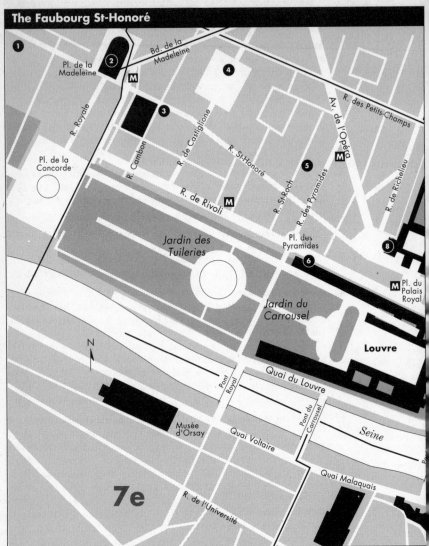

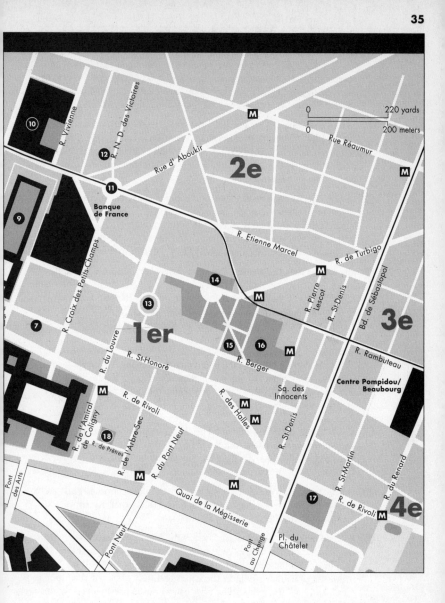

10

R. Vivienne

12

R. N. D. des Victoires

Rue d' Aboukir

M

Rue Réaumur

0   220 yards
0   200 meters

2e

M

11

Banque
de France

9

R. Etienne Marcel

R. de Turbigo

Bd. de Sébastopol

14

R. Croix des Petits-Champs

13

1er

R. Pierre
Lescot

R. St-Denis

3e

7

R. du Louvre

R. St-Honoré

15

16

R. Berger

M

R. Rambuteau

Sq. des
Innocents

Centre Pompidou/
Beaubourg

M

R. de l'Amiral
de Coligny

R. de Rivoli

R. des Halles

M

M

R. St-Denis

R. St-Martin

R. du Renard

18

R. de Prêtres

R. de l'Arbre-Sec

R. du Pont Neuf

M

M

17

R. de Rivoli

4e

Pont
des Arts

Quai de la Mégisserie

M

Pont Neuf

Pont
au Change

Pl. du
Châtelet

tear. This state of affairs is not much helped by the hordes of teenagers and down-and-outs who invade it toward dusk. Nonetheless, if you are a serious shopper, you might want to check out the French chain stores, the few small boutiques, and the weekly fashion shows by up-and-coming young designers held here (☞ Chapter 6). ⊠ *Main entrance on rue Pierre-Lescot. Métro or RER: Châtelet–Les Halles.*

⑮ Jardin des Halles. This garden, crisscrossed with paths and alleyways flanked by bushes, flower beds, and trim little lawns, takes up much of the site once occupied by Les Halles, the city's central market. Children will love the bush shaped like a rhinoceros. *Métro or RER: Châtelet–Les Halles.*

❼ Louvre des Antiquaires. This chic shopping mall, off place du Palais-Royal opposite the Louvre, is a minimuseum in itself. Its stylish, glass-walled corridors, lined with upscale antiques dealers, deserve a browse whether you intend to buy or not. (☞ Chapter 6). ⊠ *Main entrance: pl. du Palais-Royal.* ☉ *Tues.–Sun. 11–7. Métro: Palais-Royal.*

❻ Musée des Arts Décoratifs. The Decorative Arts Museum in the Pavillon de Marsan, the northwestern wing of the Louvre, houses more than 50,000 objects charting the course of French furniture and applied arts through the centuries. ⊠ *107 rue de Rivoli.* 🖃 *20 frs.* ☉ *Wed.–Sat. 12:30–6, Sun. noon–6. Métro: Palais-Royal.*

NEED A BREAK?	Founded in 1903, **Angélina** (⊠ 226 rue de Rivoli, ☎ 01–42–60–82–00) is an elegant *salon de thé* (tea room), famous for "L'Africain"—a cup of hot chocolate so thick you'll need a fork to eat it (irresistible even in the summer). Nonchocoholics can select from a dizzying assortment of pastries and other goodies.

❸ Notre-Dame de l'Assomption. This 1670 church, with its huge dome and solemn interior, was the scene of Lafayette's funeral in 1834. It is now a chapel for Paris's Polish community. ⊠ *rue Cambon. Métro: Concorde.*

⑫ Notre-Dame des Victoires. Visit this central Paris church, built from 1666 to 1740, to see the 30,000 ex-voto tablets that adorn its walls. ⊠ *pl. des Petits-Pères. Métro: Sentier.*

❶ Palais de l'Elysée. This "palace," where the French president lives, works, and receives official visitors, was originally constructed as a private mansion in 1718. (Incidentally, when Parisians talk about "l'Elysée," they mean the president's palace; the Champs-Elysées is known simply as "les Champs," the fields.) The Elysée has housed presidents only since 1873; before then, Madame de Pompadour (Louis XV's influential mistress), Napoléon, Josephine, the Duke of Wellington, and Queen Victoria all stayed here. President Félix Faure died here in 1899 in the arms of his mistress, so it is said. Although you can catch a glimpse of the palace forecourt and facade through the Faubourg St-Honoré gateway, it is difficult to get much idea of the building's size, or of the extensive gardens that stretch back to the Champs-Elysées because it is closed to the public. ⊠ *55 rue du Faubourg-St-Honoré. Métro: Miromesnil.*

OFF THE BEATEN PATH	**ST. MICHAEL'S ENGLISH CHURCH** – Down the street from the Palais de l'Elysée, on rue du Faubourg-St-Honoré, this modern church is an architectural disaster. But it's worth the trip for the warm welcome offered visitors, English-speaking ones in particular. ⊠ 5 rue d'Aguesseau, ☎ 01–47–42–70–88. Services Thurs. 12:45 and Sun. 10:30 (with Sun. school) and 6:30. Métro: Miromesnil.

❾ **Palais-Royal.** The buildings of this former palace—royal only in that all-powerful Cardinal Richelieu (1585–1642) magnanimously bequeathed them to Louis XIII—date from the 1630s. In his early days as king, Louis XIV preferred the relative intimacy of the Palais-Royal to the intimidating splendor of the Louvre. He soon decided, though, that his own intimidating splendor warranted a more majestic setting; hence, of course, Versailles. Today, the Palais-Royal is home to the French Ministry of Culture, and its buildings are not open to the public. They overlook a colonnaded courtyard with black-and-white striped half-columns and revolving silver spheres that slither around in two fountains, the controversial work of architect Daniel Buren. The splendid gardens beyond are bordered by arcades harboring discreet boutiques and divided by rows of perfectly trimmed little trees. This was once the haunt of prostitutes and gamblers: a veritable sink of vice. These days it's hard to imagine anywhere more hoity-toity. ✉ *pl. du Palais-Royal. Métro: Palais-Royal.*

⓫ **Place des Victoires.** This circular square, now home to many of the city's top fashion boutiques, was laid out in 1685 by Jules-Hardouin Mansart in honor of the military victories of Louis XIV, that indefatigable warrior whose nearly continuous battles may have brought much prestige to his country but came perilously close to bringing it to bankruptcy, too. Louis is shown galloping along on a bronze horse in the middle; his statue dates from 1822 and replaced one destroyed during the Revolution. *Métro: Sentier.*

❹ **Place Vendôme.** With its granite pavement and Second Empire street lamps, Mansart's rhythmic, perfectly proportioned example of 17th-century urban architecture shines in all its golden-stoned splendor. The square is a fitting showcase for the deluxe Ritz Hotel and the cluster of jewelry display windows to be found here. Napoléon had the square's central column made from the melted bronze of 1,200 cannons captured at the battle of Austerlitz in 1805. That's him standing vigilantly at the top. Painter Gustave Courbet headed the Revolutionary hooligans who, in 1871, toppled the column and shattered it into thousands of metallic pieces. The Third Republic stuck them together again and sent him the bill. There's parking in an underground lot. *Métro: Opéra.*

⓮ **St-Eustache.** Since the demolition of the 19th-century iron-and-glass market halls at the beginning of the '70s, St-Eustache has reemerged as a dominant element on the central Paris skyline. It is a huge church, the "cathedral" of Les Halles, built as the market people's Right Bank reply to Notre-Dame on the Ile de la Cité. St-Eustache dates from a couple of hundred years later than Notre-Dame. With the exception of the feeble west front, added between 1754 and 1788, construction lasted from 1532 to 1637, spanning the decline of the Gothic style and the emergence of the Renaissance. As a consequence, the church is a curious architectural hybrid. Its exterior flying buttresses are Gothic, but its column orders, rounded arches, and thick, comparatively simple window tracery are unmistakably classical. Few buildings bear such eloquent witness to stylistic transition. St-Eustache also features occasional organ concerts. ✉ *2 rue du Jour,* ☎ *01–46–27–89–21 for concert information.* ⊙ *Daily 8–7. Métro or RER: Châtelet–Les Halles.*

⓲ **St-Germain l'Auxerrois.** Until 1789, this was used by the French royal family as their Paris parish church, in the days when the adjacent Louvre was a palace rather than a museum. The fluid stonework of the facade reveals the influence of 15th-century Flamboyant Gothic style, enjoying its final neurotic shrieks before the classical takeover of the Renaissance. Notice the unusually wide windows in the nave and the equally unusual double aisles. The triumph of classicism is evident, however, in the fluted columns around the choir, the area surrounding the altar. These were added in the 18th century and are characteristic of the desire of 18th-century clerics to dress up medieval buildings in the architectural raiment of their own day. ⊠ *pl. du Louvre. Métro: Louvre-Rivoli.*

⑤ St-Roch. This huge church, designed by Lemercier in 1653 but completed only in the 1730s, is almost as long as Notre-Dame (138 yards) thanks to Hardouin-Mansart's domed Lady Chapel at the far end, with its elaborate Baroque altarpiece. Classical playwright Pierre Corneille (1606–84) is buried here; a commemorative plaque honors him at the left of the entrance. ⊠ *rue St-Honoré. Métro: Tuileries.*

⑰ Tour St-Jacques. This ornate 170-foot stump tower (now used for meteorological purposes and not open to the public) belonged to a 16th-century church destroyed in 1797. ⊠ *pl. du Châtelet. Métro: Châtelet.*

NEED A BREAK?	Twenty different international beers are available on draft, and more than 180 in bottles, at **Le Trappiste** (⊠ 4 rue St-Denis, ☎ 01–42–33–08–50), just north of place du Châtelet. Mussels and french fries are the traditional accompaniment, although various other snacks (hot dogs, sandwiches) are also available. There are tables upstairs and on the pavement.

THE GRAND BOULEVARDS

The focal point of this walk is the uninterrupted avenue that runs in almost a straight line from St-Augustin, the city's grandest Second Empire church, to place de la République, whose very name symbolizes the ultimate downfall of the imperial regime. The avenue's name changes six times along the way, which is why Parisians refer to it, in plural, as the Grand Boulevards.

The makeup of the neighborhoods along the Grand Boulevards changes steadily as you head east from the posh 8ᵉ arrondissement toward working-class east Paris. The *Grands Magasins* (Department Stores) at the start of the walk epitomize upscale Paris shopping. They stand on boulevard Haussmann, named in honor of the regional prefect who oversaw the reconstruction of the city in the 1850s and 1860s. The opulent Opéra Garnier, just past the Grands Magasins, is the architectural showpiece of the period (often termed the Second Empire and corresponding to the rule of Napoléon III).

Haussmann's concept of urban planning proved grand enough to ward off the postwar skyscrapers and property sharks that bedevil so many other European cities (Paris's urban planners relegated them to the outskirts of the city). Though the boulevards are lined with the seven-story blocks typical of Haussmann's time, they date from the 1670s, when the streets were created on the site of the city's medieval fortifications. These were razed when Louis XIV's military triumphs appeared to render their raison d'être obsolete, and replaced by leafy promenades known from the outset as "boulevards."

This walk takes in some of the older sights on both sides of the boulevard, including the city's auction house, the colonnaded stock exchange, and the rambunctious Sentier district with its streetwise fabric traders. It ends on the tranquil banks of the little-known Canal St-Martin.

Numbers in the text correspond to numbers in the margin and on the Grand Boulevards map.

A Good Walk

Step through gold-topped iron gates to enter the **Parc Monceau** ① in the tony 8ᵉ arrondissement. At the middle of the park, head left to avenue Velasquez and past the **Musée Cernuschi** ②—home to Chinese art from Neolithic pottery to contemporary paintings. Continue on to boulevard Malesherbes and turn right, then right again onto rue de Monceau, to reach the **Musée Nissim de Camondo** ③, whose aristocratic interior reflects the upbeat tone of this haughty part of Paris.

Take a left down rue de Téhéran, left along avenue de Messine, and left again on rue de Laborde to reach the innovative iron-and-stone church of **St-Augustin** ④. Cross the square in front and turn left along boulevard Haussmann to get to the leafy, intimate **square Louis XVI** ⑤. Be sure to take a look at the amusing stone carvings on the gleaming 1930s-style facade of the bank at the corner of rue Pasquier and rue Mathurins. Some 300 yards farther down boulevard Haussmann, you'll find the Grands Magasins: Paris's most renowned department stores. First come the cupolas of **Au Printemps** ⑥, then **Galeries Lafayette** ⑦. Marks & Spencer, across the street, provides a brave outpost for British goods like ginger biscuits and bacon rashers. Opposite the Galeries Lafayette is the massive bulk of the **Opéra Garnier** ⑧. Before venturing around to inspect its extravagant facade, you might like to take in a multiscreen overview of Paris and its history at the **Paristoric** ⑨ movie venue at No. 7 rue Scribe.

Boulevard des Capucines, lined with cinemas and restaurants, heads left from the Opera, becoming boulevard des Italiens before colliding with boulevard Haussmann. A left here down rue Drouot will take you to the **Hôtel Drouot** ⑩, Paris's central auction house. Rue Rossini leads from "Drouot" to rue de la Grange-Batelière. Halfway along on the right is the **Passage Jouffroy,** one of the many covered galleries that honeycomb the center of Paris. At the far end of the passage is the **Musée Grévin** ⑪, a waxworks museum. Cross boulevard Montmartre to the passage des Panoramas, leading to rue St-Marc. Turn right, then left down rue Vivienne, to find the foresquare, colonnaded **Bourse** ⑫, the Paris Stock Exchange.

If you wish, you can continue down rue Vivienne from the Bourse and join the Faubourg St-Honoré (☞ *above*) walk at the Bibliothèque Nationale. If you're feeling adventurous, head east along rue Réaumur, once the heart of the French newspaper industry—stationery shops still abound—and cross rue Montmartre. You can catch sight of the St-Eustache church to your right; the distant spires of St-Ambroise emerge on the horizon. Take the second left up rue de Cléry: A narrow street that is the exclusive domain of fabric wholesalers, and often crammed with vans, palettes, and delivery boys creating colorful chaos. The lopsided building at the corner of rue Poissonnière looks as if it is struggling to stay upright on the district's drunken slopes. Continue up rue de Cléry as far as rue des Degrés—not a street at all, but a 14-step stairway—then look for the crooked church tower of **Notre-Dame de Bonne-Nouvelle** ⑬, hemmed in by rickety housing that looks straight out of Balzac. The porticoed entrance is around the corner on rue de la Lune, which leads back to the Grand Boulevards, by now going under the name of boulevard de Bonne-Nouvelle.

The **Porte St-Denis** ⑭, a triumphal arch, looms up ahead and, a little farther on, the smaller but similar **Porte St-Martin** ⑮. From here take the rue St-Martin south to the **Conservatoire National des Techniques** ⑯,

The Grand Boulevards

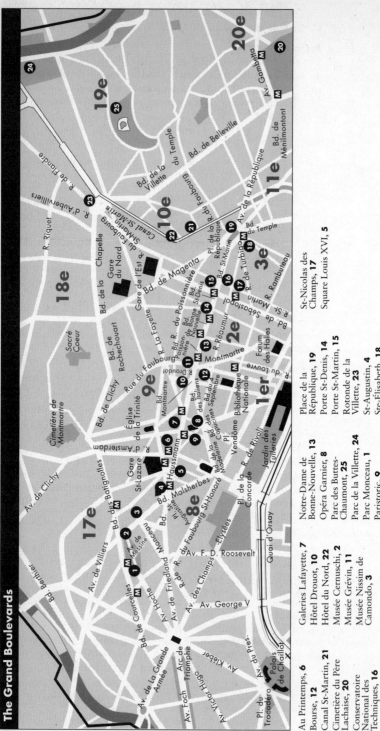

an industrial museum housed partly in the former church of St-Martin. Current restoration may not end before 1999, so console yourself with a glimpse of the solemn domed forecourt and repair to the leafy square opposite, or to the high, narrow, late Gothic church of **St-Nicolas des Champs** ⑰ across rue Réaumur. Head left on rue de Turbigo, past the cloister ruins and Renaissance gateway that embellish the far side of St-Nicolas. Some 400 yards along on the right is the baroque church of **Ste-Elisabeth** ⑱; shortly after you reach **place de la République** ⑲. It's a short métro ride from here to the city's most famous cemetery, the **Cimetière du Père Lachaise** ⑳.

Alternately you could cross the square and take rue du Faubourg-du-Temple to the **Canal St-Martin** ㉑, whose locks and pale-green footbridges conjure up an unexpected flavor of Amsterdam. You arrive as the canal emerges from a 2½-km (1½-mi) tunnel that starts beyond the Bastille; follow it left for 500 yards and cross at the bend to find the unassuming white facade of the famous **Hôtel du Nord** ㉒. The canal continues north to the circular **Rotonde de la Villette** ㉓. It surveys both the airborne métro line and the unruffled sheen of the Bassin de la Villette, where boats leave on a mile-long trip to the **Parc de la Villette** ㉔, with its postmodern science and music museums. Landlubbers may prefer the 10-minute walk to La Villette, as it is known, along the canal or the 10-minute walk along avenue Secrétan to the tumbling **Parc des Buttes-Chaumont** ㉕.

TIMING

The distance between Parc Monceau and the Canal St-Martin is almost 7 km (4½ mi), which will probably take you four hours to walk, including coffee breaks and window-shopping. Allow more time if you include the 1½ km (1 mi) stretch along the Canal St-Martin to the Bassin de la Villette. You may want to allot a whole morning or afternoon to visit Père Lachaise, the Parc des Buttes-Chaumont, or the Parc de la Villette. Or you might return to these on another day.

Sights to See

❻ **Au Printemps.** Founded in 1865 by Jules Jaluzot—former employee of Au Bon Marché, which opened 13 years earlier on the Left Bank—Au Printemps swiftly became the mecca of Right Bank shoppers, enabling the current opulent Belle Epoque buildings, with their domes and gold and green mosaic name signs, to be erected by the turn of the century. The rooftop cafeteria has a splendid view of the Paris skyline. (☞ Chapter 6). ⊠ *64 bd. Haussmann. Métro: Havre-Caumartin.*

OFF THE BEATEN PATH

ÉGLISE DE LA TRINITÉ – This church, a worthy 1860s essay in neo-Renaissance, is fronted by a lawn and fountains, and crowned by a central wedding-cake tower of dubious aesthetic merit that has nonetheless emerged as a landmark feature of the Right Bank skyline. ⊠ *pl. d'Estienne-d'Orves. Métro: Trinité.*

ATELIER DE GUSTAVE MOREAU – This town house and studio of painter Gustave Moreau (1826–98), doyen of the Symbolist movement, is one of the strangest artistic experiences in Paris. The Symbolists strove to convey ideas through images, but many of the ideas Moreau was trying to express were so obscure that the artist had to provide explanatory texts, which rather defeats the point. But it's easy to admire his extravagant colors and flights of fantasy, influenced by Persian and Indian miniatures. ⊠ *14 rue de la Rochefoucauld,* ☎ *01–48–74–38–50.* ⊠ *17 frs.* ☉ *Thurs.–Sun. 10–12:45 and 2–5:15, Mon. and Wed. 11–5:15. Métro: Trinité.*

⑫ Bourse. The Paris Stock Exchange, a serene, colonnaded 19th-century building, is a far cry from Wall Street. Take your passport if you want to tour it. ✉ *rue Vivienne.* 🎟 *30 frs. Guided tours only (in French), weekdays every ½ hr 1:15–4. Métro: Bourse.*

㉑ Canal St-Martin. Place de la République is the gateway to east Paris, a largely residential area often underestimated by tourists. One of its highlights is the Canal St-Martin, which starts just south of place de la Bastille but really comes into its own during the mile-long stretch north of République across the 10ᵉ arrondissement. The canal was built at the behest of Napoléon from 1802 to 1825, with the aim of providing the city with drinking water. It was not assigned to navigable traffic until the 1850s and was partly covered (between Bastille and République) by Haussmann in 1862. With its quiet banks, locks, and footbridges, the canal is much-loved by novelists and film directors; Simenon's famous inspector Maigret solved many a mystery along its deceptively sleepy banks. Major development has transformed the northern end of the Canal, around place de Stalingrad and its 18th-century rotunda, and there are boat trips (✉ Embarkation at 13 quai de la Loire, 🎟 10 francs) along the once industrial Bassin de la Villette to the nearby Parc de la Villette. *Métro: Jacques-Bonsergent, Jaurès.*

⑳ Cimetière du Père Lachaise. The largest, most interesting, and most prestigious of Paris's cemeteries dates from the start of the 19th century. On the eastern fringe of Paris, it is a veritable necropolis whose tombs compete in grandiosity, originality, and often, alas, dilapidation. Cobbled avenues, steep slopes, and lush vegetation create a powerful atmosphere. Named after the Jesuit father—Louis XIV's confessor—who led the reconstruction of the Jesuit Rest House completed here in 1682, the cemetery houses the tombs of the French author Colette; the composer Chopin; the playwright Molière; the writers Honoré Balzac, Marcel Proust, Paul Eluard, Oscar Wilde, and Gertrude Stein; the popular French actress Simone Signoret and her husband, singer-actor Yves Montand; and Edith Piaf. Perhaps the most noticeable shrine is to rock star Jim Morrison, where dozens of faithful come to pay homage to the songwriter. Now, along with the fans, there's a guard who makes sure you don't stay too long. Of less dubious taste is the sculpted tomb of Romantic artist Théodore Géricault, shown brush in hand above a bronze relief plaque replicating his *Raft of the Medusa.* The cemetery was the site of the Paris Commune's final battle, on May 28, 1871, when the rebel troops were rounded up, lined against the Mur des Fédérés (Federalists' Wall) in the southeast corner, and shot. Get hold of a map at the entrance—Père Lachaise is an easy place to get lost in. ✉ *Entrances on rue des Rondeaux, bd. de Ménilmontant, and rue de la Réunion.* ☉ *Daily 8–6; winter, daily 8–dusk. Métro: Gambetta, Philippe-Auguste, Père Lachaise.*

⑯ Conservatoire National des Techniques. The former church and priory of St-Martin des Champs was built between the 11th and 13th centuries. Confiscated during the Revolution, it was used first as an educational institution, then as an arms factory, before becoming, in 1799, the Conservatoire des Arts et Métiers. Today the church forms the south wing of the National Technical Museum, an industrial museum with a varied collection of models (locomotives, vehicles, and agricultural machinery), astronomical instruments, looms, and glass, together with displays on printing, photography, and the history of television. The splendid 13th-century refectory, a large hall supported by central columns, is now used as a library. A major renovation may keep the museum shut until 1999. ✉ *292 rue St-Martin,* ☎ *01–40–27–23–31. Métro: Arts et Métiers.*

❼ Galeries Lafayette. This turn-of-the-century department store has a vast, shimmering, Belle Epoque glass dome that can only be seen if you venture inside. (☞ Chapter 6). ✉ *40 bd. Haussmann. Métro: Chaussée d'Antin; RER: Auber.*

❿ Hôtel Drouot. Hidden away in a grid of narrow streets not far from the Opéra is Paris's central auction house, offering everything from stamps and toy soldiers to Renoirs and 18th-century commodes. The 16 salesrooms make for fascinating browsing, and there's no obligation to bid. The mix of ladies in fur coats with money to burn, penniless art lovers desperate to unearth an unidentified masterpiece, and scruffy dealers trying to look anonymous makes up Drouot's unusually rich social fabric. Sales are held most weekdays, with viewings in the morning; anyone can attend. ✉ *9 rue Drouot,* ☎ *01–48–00–20–00.* ☉ *Viewings Mon.–Sat. 11–noon and 2–6, with auctions starting at 2. Métro: Richelieu-Drouot.*

OFF THE
BEATEN PATH

NOTRE-DAME DE LORETTE – This little-known church was built from 1823 to 1836 in the neoclassical style popular at the time. Of principal interest is the array of religious wall paintings; they are of varying quality but have been successfully restored. ✉ *rue de Châteaudun. Métro: Notre-Dame-de-Lorette.*

㉒ Hôtel du Nord. This hotel, with its unassuming white facade, was so famous in France for its starring role in Marcel Carné's 1938 movie of the same name that plans to demolish it provoked a public outcry. It was restored to former glory (as a café-restaurant) in 1995. ✉ *102 quai de Jemmappes,* ☎ *01–40–40–78–78. Métro: Jacques-Bonsergent.*

❷ Musée Cernuschi. The collection includes Chinese art from Neolithic pottery (3rd century BC) to funeral statuary, painted 8th-century silks, and contemporary paintings, as well as ancient Persian bronze objects. ✉ *7 av. Velasquez,* ☎ *01–45–63–50–75.* 💳 *17 frs.* ☉ *Tues.–Sun. 10–5:40. Métro: Monceau.*

⓫ Musée Grévin. Founded in 1882, this waxworks museum, around the corner from the Hôtel Drouot, ranks in scope and ingenuity with Madame Tussaud's in London. Dozens of wax renderings of historical and contemporary celebrities are on display. ✉ *10 bd. Montmartre,* ☎ *01–42–46–13–26.* 💳 *55 frs.* ☉ *Daily 1–7; during school holidays 10–7. Métro: Rue Montmartre.*

❸ Musée Nissim de Camondo. The elegant decadence of the last days of the regal Ancien Régime (1770–90) is fully reflected in the lavish interior of this aristocratic Parisian mansion, built in the style of Louis XVI. ✉ *63 rue de Monceau,* ☎ *01–45–63–26–32.* 💳 *27 frs.* ☉ *Wed.–Sun. 10–noon and 2–5. Métro: Monceau.*

⓭ Notre-Dame de Bonne-Nouvelle. This wide, soberly neoclassical church is tucked away off the Grand Boulevards. The previous church on the spot (the second) was ransacked during the Revolution, and the current one, built 1823–29 after the restoration of the French monarchy, was ransacked by Communard hooligans in May 1871. The highlight is the semicircular apse behind the altar, featuring some fine 17th-century paintings beneath a three-dimensional, 19th-century grisaille composition by Abel de Pujol. A wide variety of pictures, statues, and works of religious art can be found in the side chapels. ✉ *rue de la Lune. Métro: Bonne-Nouvelle.*

ST-VINCENT DE PAUL – Flanked by two foresquare towers, this early 19th-century church (1824–44) stands out amid the undistinguished streets surrounding the Gare du Nord. The facade is lent drama by the pedimented portico and the majestic flight of steps leading up from a cheerful square. Inside, Hippolyte Flandrin's glittering gold fresco, high up the nave walls, depicts an endless procession of religious worthies. ⊠ *pl. Franz-Liszt. Métro: Poissonnière.*

❽ Opéra Garnier. The original Paris Opera, begun in 1862 by Charles Garnier at the behest of Napoléon III, was not completed until 1875, five years after the emperor's abdication. It is said that it typifies Second Empire architecture, which is to say that it is a pompous hodgepodge of styles, imbued with as much subtlety as the crash of cymbals. After paying the entry fee, you can stroll around at leisure. The monumental foyer and staircase are impressive—a stage in their own right—where, on opening nights, celebrities preen and prance. If the lavishly upholstered auditorium seems small, it is only because the stage is the largest in the world—more than 11,000 square yards, with room for up to 450 performers. Marc Chagall painted the ceiling in 1964. The Opera Museum, containing a few paintings and theatrical mementos, is unremarkable. ⊠ *pl. de l'Opéra,* ☎ *01–40–01–22–63.* ☜ *30 frs.* ☉ *Daily 10–4:30; closed occasionally for rehearsals; call 01–47–42–57–50 to check. Métro: Opéra.*

There are few grander cafés in Paris than the Belle Epoque **Café de la Paix** (⊠ 5 pl. de l'Opéra, ☎ 01–40–07–30–10). Once described as "the center of the civilized world," it was a regular meeting place for the glitterati of 19th- and 20th-century Paris. It's a good place to people-watch; the prices are as grand as the setting.

🐾 **㉕ Parc des Buttes-Chaumont.** This immensely picturesque park, in the unprepossessing 19e arrondissement of northeast Paris, has a lake, waterfall, and cliff-top folly. Until town planner Baron Haussmann got his hands on it in the 1860s, the area was a garbage dump and quarry—hence the steep slopes. ⊠ *rue Botzaris. Métro: Buttes-Chaumont, Botzaris.*

🐾 **❶ Parc Monceau.** The most picturesque gardens on the Right Bank were laid out as a private park in 1778 and retain some of the fanciful elements then in vogue, including mock ruins and a phony pyramid. In 1797 André Garnerin, the world's first-recorded parachutist, staged a landing in the park. The rotunda—known as the Chartres Pavilion—has well-wrought iron gates and was originally a tollhouse. ⊠ *Entrances on bd. de Courcelles, av. Velasquez, av. Ruysdaël, av. van Dyck. Métro: Monceau.*

MUSÉE JEAN-JACQUES HENNER – At this museum, you can see the work of Jean-Jacques Henner (1829–1905), a nearly forgotten Alsatian artist whose obsessive fondness for milky-skinned, auburn-haired female nudes distinguishes his work. ⊠ *43 av. de Villiers,* ☎ *01–47–63–42–73.* ☜ *20 frs, Sun. 15 frs.* ☉ *Tues.–Sun. 10–noon and 2–5. Métro: Malesherbes.*

ST-ALEXANDRE NEVSKY – The gilt onion domes of this Russian Orthodox cathedral erected in neo-Byzantine style in 1860 provide an exotic addition to the city's roof line. Inside, the wall of icons that divides the church in two creates a mystical atmosphere. ⊠ *12 rue Daru. Métro: Courcelles.*

MUSÉE JACQUEMART-ANDRE – Art from the Italian Renaissance and 18th-century France compete for attention in the museum's late-19th-century mansion. ✉ *158 bd. Haussmann,* ☎ *01–42–89–04–91.* 🎫 *45 frs.* ⊘ *Wed.–Sun. 1–6. Métro: St-Philippe-du-Roule.*

STE-ODILE – The colossal, dark-brick tower of this modern church (built 1938–46) surges into the northern Paris skyline like a stumpy rocket, reminiscent of something out of Soviet Russia. The inside smacks more of Scandinavia, with its harmony, simple lines, splendid stained glass, and decorative restraint. Take the métro at Villiers to Porte de Champerret: The church is off place Stuart Merrill on avenue Stéphane-Mallarmé. ✉ *av. Stéphane-Mallarmé. Métro: Porte de Champerret.*

ST-PHILIPPE-DU-ROULE – The best part about this dimly lit church, built by Chalgrin between 1769 and 1784, is the 19th-century fresco by Théodore Chassériau above the altar, featuring the *Descent from the Cross.* ✉ *pl. Chassaigne-Goyonand. Métro: St-Philippe-du-Roule.*

🌀 ㉔ **Parc de la Villette.** Until the 1970s this 130-acre site, in an unfashionable corner of northeast Paris commonly known as "La Villette," was home to a cattle market and slaughterhouse (*abattoir*). Only the slaughterhouse, known as **La Grande Halle,** remains: a magnificent iron-and-glass structure ingeniously transformed into an exhibition-cum-concert center. But everything else here—from the science museum and spherical cinema to the music academy, each interconnected by designer gardens with canopied walkways and red cubical follies—is futuristic.

Although La Villette breathes the architectural panache of the Mitterrand era, the late president only oversaw one project himself: the **Cité de la Musique** (☞ Chapter 5), a giant postmodern musical academy with a state-of-the-art concert hall, designed by Christian de Portzamparc and only completed in 1997 with the opening of a spectacular museum of musical instruments, the **Musée de la Musique.** The museum contains a mind-tingling array of 900 instruments that sound as you pass thanks to infrared headphones. ✉ *221 av. Jean-Jaurès,* ☎ *01–44–84–46–21.* 🎫 *Music Museum 35 frs.* ⊘ *Tues.–Thurs. noon–6, Fri. noon–9:30, Sat. noon–6, Sun. 10–6. Métro: Porte de Pantin.*

The **park,** itself, laid out in the 1980s to the design of Bernard Tschumi, links the academy to the science museum half a mile away. Water and the Grande Halle are the park's focal elements. Two new bridges cross the Canal de l'Ourcq, which bisects the park; one becomes a covered walkway, running parallel to the Canal St-Denis, and continues up to the science museum—itself surrounded by the unruffled sheen of a broad moat, reflecting the spherical outline of the **Géode** (☞ Chapter 5). This looks like a huge silver golf ball but is actually a cinema made of polished steel, with an enormous, 180-degree curved screen.

The pompously styled **Cité des Sciences et de l'Industrie** tries to do for science and industry what the Pompidou Center does for modern art. Adrien Fainsilber's rectangular building, also conceived in the 1970s, even looks like the Pompidou Center, minus the gaudy piping. Inside, displays are bright and thought-provoking, though most are in French only. The brave attempt to render technology fun and easy involves dozens of try-it-yourself contraptions that make you feel more participant than onlooker. Lines (especially during school holidays) can be intimidating. ✉ *30 av. Corentin-Cariou,* ☎ *08–36–68–29–30.* 🎫 *50 frs (planetarium 25 frs), 25 frs after 4pm.* ⊘ *Wed.–Sun. 10–noon and 2–6. Métro: Porte de la Villette.*

❾ **Paristoric.** This 40-minute split-screen presentation of Paris and its history is pricey and sometimes hard to follow, but the spectacular photography and tasteful musical accompaniment, with Saint-Saëns's Organ Symphony employed to majestic effect, are enjoyable. Be sure to get headphones to hear the English translation. ⊠ *11 bis rue Scribe,* ☏ *01–42–66–62–06.* ☑ *50 frs.* ☉ *Sun.–Thurs. 9–6, Fri.–Sat. 9–9. Métro: Opéra.*

Passage Jouffroy. Built in 1846, as its giant clock will tell you, this *passage* (gallery) was one of the first precursors to the modern day shopping mall. ⊠ *Entrance on bd. Montmartre, rue de la Grange-Batelière. Métro: Richelieu-Drouot.*

⑲ Place de la République. This large, oblong square, laid out by Haussmann in 1856–65, is dominated by a matronly, Stalin-size statue symbolizing *The Republic* (1883). The square is often used as a rallying point for demonstrations. République boasts more métro lines than any other station in Paris. *Métro: République.*

⑭ Porte St-Denis. This 76-foot triumphal arch, slightly larger and older than the neighboring Porte St-Martin, was erected by François Blondel in 1672 to celebrate the victories of *Ludovico Magno* (as Louis XIV is here styled) on the Rhine. The bas reliefs by François Girardon include campaign scenes and military attributes stacked on shallow, slender pyramids. The arch faces the Rue St-Denis—formerly the royal processional route into Paris from the north (last so used by Queen Victoria in 1855), but now better known for activity along the sidewalk. ⊠ *rue du Faubourg-St-Denis. Métro: Strasbourg-St-Denis.*

⑮ Porte St-Martin. This 56-foot triumphal arch, slightly smaller and later than the neighboring Porte St-Denis, was designed by Blondel's pupil Pierre Bullet in 1674. Louis XIV's recent victories at Limburg (in Flanders) and Besançon in Franche-Comté get bas-relief coverage from Martin Desjardins. ⊠ *rue du Faubourg-St-Martin. Métro: Strasbourg-St-Denis.*

㉓ Rotonde de la Villette. This strange, circular building was one of the tollhouses built around the edge of Paris by Nicolas Ledoux in the 1780s. Symbols, to the populace, of taxes and oppression, most of these austere, daunting buildings were promptly dismantled during the Revolution. Luckily, the Rotunda survived to remind us of Ledoux's thrilling architecture. Like Mitterrand, Ledoux was fascinated by masonic symbols such as spheres and pyramids. Although the Rotunda is partly obscured by the overground métro as you approach from the south, its clean-cut outlines and honey-color stonework can be admired from the north, where a newly paved courtyard overlooks the Bassin de la Villette and the barges queueing at the lock to reach the Canal St-Martin. ⊠ *pl. de Stalingrad. Métro: Stalingrad.*

④ St-Augustin. This domed church was dexterously constructed in the 1860s within the confines of an awkward, V-shape site. It represented a breakthrough in ecclesiastical engineering, insofar as the use of metal pillars and girders obviated the need for exterior buttressing. The dome is bulky but well proportioned and contains some grimy but competent frescoes by the popular 19th-century French artist William Bouguereau. ⊠ *pl. St-Augustin. Métro: St-Augustin.*

⑱ Ste-Elisabeth. This studied essay in Baroque (1628–46) is pleasantly unpretentious; there's no soaring bombast here. The church has brightly restored wall paintings and a wide, semicircular apse around the choir, where biblical scenes are carved into a stupendous 17th-century wood panel transferred from an abbey at Arras in northern France. ⊠ *rue du Temple. Métro: Temple.*

⑰ **St-Nicolas des Champs.** The rounded-arch, fluted Doric capitals in the chancel of this church date from 1560 to 1587, a full century later than the pointed-arch nave (1420–80). There is a majestic mid-17th-century organ and a fine *Assumption of the Virgin* (1629) by Simon Vouet above the high altar. The south door (1576) on rue au Maire is gloriously carved and surrounded by a small but unexpectedly well-tended lawn complete with rosebushes. ⊠ *rue St-Martin. Métro: Arts et Métiers.*

❺ **Square Louis XVI.** An unkempt mausoleum emerges defiantly from the lush undergrowth of this verdant square off boulevard Haussmann, marking the initial burial site of Louis XVI and Marie-Antoinette after their turns at the guillotine on place de la Concorde. Two stone tablets are inscribed with the last missives of the doomed royals: touching pleas for their Revolutionary enemies to be forgiven. When compared to the pomp and glory of Napoléon's memorial at the Invalides, this tribute to royalty (France was ruled by kings until 1792 and again from 1815 to 1848) seems halfhearted and trite. ⊙ *Daily 10–noon and 2–6; winter, daily 10–4. Métro: St-Augustin.*

THE MARAIS AND THE BASTILLE

The Marais is one of Paris's oldest, most historic, and sought-after residential districts. Renovation is the keynote; well into the '70s this was one of the poorest areas, filled with dilapidated tenements and squalid courtyards. The area's regeneration was sparked by the building of the Centre Pompidou (known to Parisians as Beaubourg), arguably Europe's most architecturally whimsical museum. The gracious architecture of the 17th and early 18th centuries, however, sets the tone for the rest of the Marais. Today, most of the Marais's spectacular *hôtels particuliers*—loosely, "mansions," onetime residences of aristocratic families—have been restored and many are now museums. There are trendy boutiques and cafés among the kosher shops in the formerly run-down streets of the Jewish neighborhood around rue des Rosiers. By crisscrossing the neighborhood on these intimate little streets, you can see it all.

The history of the Marais—the word, incidentally, means marsh or swamp—goes back to when Charles V, king of France in the 14th century, moved his court here from the Ile de la Cité. However, it wasn't until Henri IV laid out place Royale, today the place des Vosges, in the early 17th century, that the Marais became *the* place to live. Aristocratic dwellings began to dot the neighborhood, and their salons filled with the beau monde. But following the French Revolution, the Marais rapidly became one of the most deprived, dissolute areas in Paris. It was spared the attentions of Baron Haussmann, the man who rebuilt so much of Paris in the mid-19th century, so that, though crumbling, its ancient golden-hued buildings and squares remained intact.

On the eastern edge of the Marais, in the Bastille neighborhood, is place de la Bastille, site of the infamous prison stormed on July 14, 1789: an event that came to symbolize the beginning of the French Revolution. Largely in commemoration of the bicentennial of the Revolution, the Bastille area was renovated and became one of the trendiest sections of Paris. Galleries, shops, theaters, cafés, restaurants, and bars fill formerly decrepit buildings and alleys. Southeast of the Bastille are the imposing place de la Nation, the up-and-coming Bercy neighborhood, and the verdant Bois de Vincennes (☞ *On the Fringe, below*).

Numbers in the text correspond to numbers in the margin and on The Marais and the Bastille map.

A Good Walk

Make **place de la Bastille** ①, which is easily accessible by métro, your gateway into the Marais, to the west. Today the square is dominated by the Colonne de Juillet and the curving glass facade of the modern **Opéra de la Bastille** ②. The best view of both is to be had from the start of rue St-Antoine. Walk down past the church of **Ste-Marie** ③, then cross to inspect the **Hôtel de Sully** ④, home to the Caisse Nationale des Monuments Historiques (Historic Monuments Trust) at No. 62. You won't be able to get into many of the historic homes that spangle the Marais—the private hôtels particuliers—but this shouldn't stop you from admiring their handsome facades or pushing through the heavy formal doors (*portes cochères*) to glimpse the discreet courtyards that lurk behind them.

Across rue St-Antoine, pause to admire the mighty Baroque church of **St-Paul–St-Louis** ⑤. Take the left-hand side-door out of the church into narrow passage St-Paul, then turn right onto rue St-Paul, past the grid of courtyards that make up the Village St-Paul antiques-shops complex. Children will enjoy the **Académie de la Magie** ⑥ further down at No. 11. At rue de l'Ave-Maria, turn right to reach the painstakingly restored **Hôtel de Sens** ⑦, a strange mixture of defensive stronghold and fairy-tale château. If you are a photography fan, head up rue Figuier, then right on rue de Fourcy to the beautiful **Maison Européenne de la Photographie** ⑧. Back down rue Figuier, take a left on rue de Jouy past two 17th-century mansions: the Hôtel d'Aumont on your left and the **Hôtel de Beauvais** ⑨ on your right (entry round the corner in rue François-Miron). The next left, rue Geoffroy-l'Asnier leads past the stark **Mémorial du Martyr Inconnu** ⑩: a huge bronze memorial to those who died in Nazi concentration camps.

Turn right along quai de l'Hôtel-de-Ville; *bouquinistes* (book sellers) line the Seine to your left, and you may catch a glimpse of the towers of Notre-Dame through the trees. Pause by the Pont Louis-Philippe to admire the dome of the Panthéon floating above the skyline, then take the next right up picturesque rue des Barres to the church of **St-Gervais–St-Protais** ⑪, one of the last Gothic constructions in the country and a newly cleaned riot of Flamboyant decoration. Beyond the church stands the **Hôtel de Ville** ⑫, the city hall. You can't inspect the lavish interior, but head round left to the traffic-free square, with its fountains and forest of street lamps, to admire the exuberant facade. From the Hôtel de Ville, cross rue de Rivoli and go up rue du Temple. On your right, you'll pass one of the city's most popular department stores, the Bazar de l'Hôtel de Ville, or BHV, as it's known (☞ Chapter 6). Take rue de la Verrerie, the first street on your left, and pause as you cross rue du Renard to take in a poignant clash of architectural styles: to your left, the medieval silhouette of Notre-Dame; to the right, the gaudy colored pipes of the Centre Pompidou.

Cross rue du Renard and take the second right to the ornate 16th-century church of **St-Merri** ⑬. Rue St-Martin, full of stores, restaurants, and galleries, leads past the designer Café Beaubourg, on the next corner on the right, to the **Centre Pompidou** ⑭. Most of the Center is closed for renovation, but you can still ride to the top in the glass-tubed escalator. The plateau Beaubourg, the square in front, is filled in summer with musicians, mimes, dancers, fire-eaters, and acrobats. The adjacent **square Igor-Stravinsky** ⑮ merits a stop for its unusual fountain. On one side of the square is IRCAM, where you can hear performances of contemporary classical music (☞ Chapter 5).

Turn left around the back of the Pompidou Center onto rue Beaubourg, then right along rue Rambuteau and the first left onto rue du Temple. The **Hôtel de St-Aignan** at No. 71 and the **Hôtel de Montmor** at No. 79 are both splendid Renaissance mansions. Take a right onto rue des Haudriettes; just off to the left at the next corner is the **Musée de la Chasse et de la Nature** ⑯, the Museum of Hunting and Nature, housed in one of the Marais's most stately mansions. Head right on rue des Archives, crossing rue des Haudriettes, and admire the medieval gateway with two fairy-tale towers, now part of the **Archives Nationales** ⑰, the archives museum entered from rue des Francs-Bourgeois (Street of the Free Citizens) around to the left.

Continue past the Crédit Municipal (the city's grandiose pawnbroking concern), the Dômarais restaurant (housed in a circular 18th-century chamber originally used for auctions), and the church of **Notre-Dame des Blancs-Manteaux** ⑱, with its superb inlaid pulpit. A corner-turret signals rue Vieille-du-Temple: Turn left past the palatial Hôtel de Rohan (now part of the Archives Nationales), then right onto rue de la Perle to the **Musée Bricard** ⑲, occupying a mansion as impressive as the assembly of locks and keys within. From here it is a step down rue de Thorigny (opposite) to the palatial 17th-century Hôtel Salé, now the **Musée Picasso** ⑳. Church-lovers may wish to detour up rue de Thorigny and along rue du Roi-Doré to admire the severe neoclassical portico of **St-Denis-du-St-Sacrement** ㉑ or the *Deposition* by Delacroix inside.

Backtrack along rue de Thorigny and turn left onto rue du Parc-Royal. Halfway down rue Elzévir is the **Musée Cognacq-Jay** ㉒, a must for fans of 18th-century furniture, porcelain, and paintings. If you cannot face another museum, take the next right, rue Payenne, instead, and tarry in the sunken garden at square Georges-Cain, opposite the 16th-century Hôtel de Marle, now used as a Swedish culture center. Next door you can enjoy a rear view of the steep-roofed Cognacq-Jay building. Rue Payenne becomes rue Pavée as you pass beneath a look-out turret. Peek into the next courtyard on the left at the cheerfully askew facade of the Bibliothèque Historique de la Ville de Paris. Continuing on rue Pavée will take you to rue des Rosiers, with its excellent Jewish bakeries and falafel shops. Back on rue des Francs-Bourgeois is the **Musée Carnavalet** ㉓, the Paris History Museum, in perhaps the swankiest edifice in the Marais. A short walk along rue des Francs-Bourgeois takes you to large, pink-brick **place des Vosges** ㉔, lined with covered arcades. At No. 6, you can visit the **Maison de Victor Hugo** ㉕, where the workaholic French author once lived.

If you want to see more of the Bastille neighborhood, follow rue de Pas-de-la-Mule from the far side of place des Vosges and cross boulevard Beaumarchais. Take rue Pasteur and rue Wagner to cross boulevard Richard-Lenoir: The Bastille Column rises to your right, and the Canal St-Martin (☞ The Grand Boulevards, *above*) flows underneath. Rue Daval leads to rue de la Roquette—a street alive with shops and cafés—and continues into rue de Lappe, a vibrant nocturnal rendezvous lined with bars, clubs, and restaurants. Turn right at the end into rue de Charonne to reach rue du Faubourg-St-Antoine, famous for its cabinetmakers. You'll see why if you take the unevenly cobbled passage du Chantier, just opposite. Its boutiques sell furniture and nothing else.

Turn left along rue de Charenton, then take the third right down avenue Ledru-Rollin past the cool modern church of St-Antoine, to reach avenue Daumesnil. The disused railroad viaduct has been tastefully transformed into a series of designer boutiques, restyled the **Viaduc des Arts** ㉖.

50

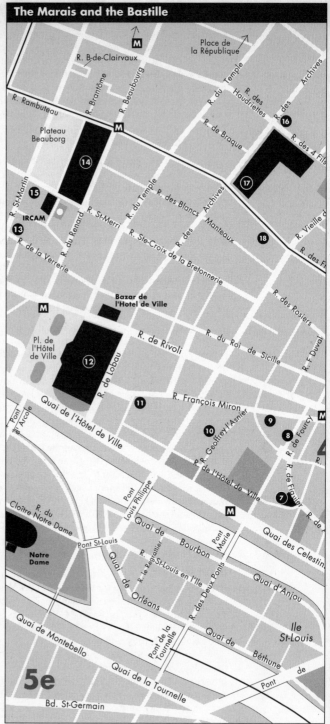

The Marais and the Bastille

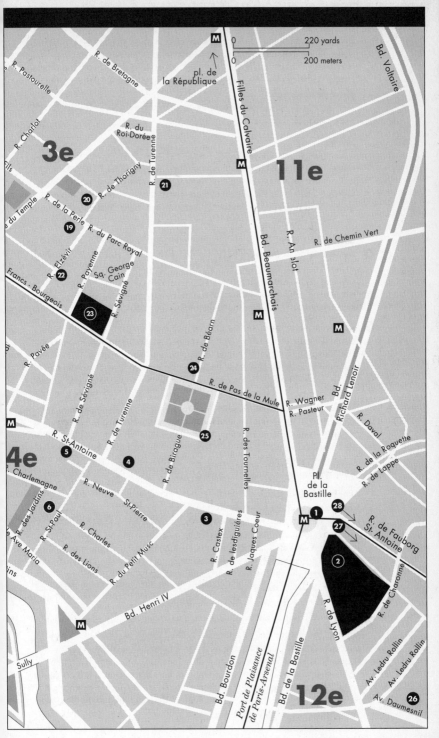

Saunter down as far as rue Hector-Malot, then spin left and mount the stairs to see what's on top of the viaduct: Gone are the tracks, ousted by a walkway lined with trees and flowers. Stay on the walkway for about 300 yards and return to ground level just past rue de Rambouillet. If you've still the energy, you can pursue your exploration of east Paris to the south, at the revamped riverside **Bercy** ㉗ site; to the north, at **place de la Nation** ㉘ with its two giant, statue-topped columns; or further east at the **Bois de Vincennes** (☞ On the Fringe, *below*), a large park with lakes and a zoo.

TIMING

This walk is just over 6½ km (4 mi) long and will comfortably take a morning or an afternoon. If you choose to spend an hour or two in any of the museums along the way, allow a full day. Be prepared to wait in line at the Picasso Museum. Note that some of the museums don't open until the afternoon and that most shops in the Bastille and the Marais don't open until the late morning.

Sights to See

🐌 ❻ **Académie de la Magie.** The Museum of Curiosity and Magic, housed in a 16th-century cellar, contains antique magic paraphernalia, including some from Houdini's bag of tricks. There's a magic show every hour. ⊠ *11 rue St-Paul,* ☎ *01–42–72–13–26.* ⊡ *45 frs.* ☾ *Wed. and weekends 2–7. Métro: St-Paul.*

❶ **Archives Nationales.** If you're a serious history buff, you will be fascinated by the thousands of intricate historical documents, dating from the Merovingian period to the 20th century, at the National Archives (also known as the Musée de l'Histoire de France) in the palatial Hôtel de Soubise. The highlights are the Edict of Nantes (1598), the Treaty of Westphalia (1648), the wills of Louis XIV and Napoléon, and the Declaration of Human Rights (1789). Louis XVI's diary is also in the collection, containing his sadly ignorant entry for July 14, 1789, the day the Bastille was stormed and, for all intents and purposes, the French Revolution began: "*Rien*" ("Nothing"). You can also visit the apartments of the prince and princess de Soubise; don't miss them if you have any interest in the lifestyles of 18th-century French aristocrats.

The buildings housing the Archives have external charm, too: The **Hôtel de Soubise** and the **Hôtel de Rohan** (originally built for the archbishop of Strasbourg), across the lawn facing rue Vieille-du-Temple, both display the cool, column-fronted elegance of the early 18th century; the Porte de Clisson, a turreted gateway on rue des Archives, was erected in 1380 for the Hôtel de Clisson, the Paris base of the Duke of Bedford (regent of France during the English occupation from 1420 to 1435). ⊠ *60 rue des Francs-Bourgeois,* ☎ *01–40–27–62–18.* ⊡ *15 frs.* ☾ *Wed.–Mon. 1:45–5:45. Métro: Rambuteau.*

㉗ **Bercy.** The Bercy neighborhood in east Paris is a testament to the French genius for urban renewal. Tucked away on the Right Bank of the Seine, south of the Gare de Lyon in the 12ᵉ arrondissement, this colorful district was for decades filled with warehouses storing wine from the provinces. Now sport and finance set the tone. The first thing you'll see as you emerge from Bercy métro station is the mighty glass wall of the **Finance Ministry,** which moved—grudgingly—to these new quayside offices from the Louvre. To your left is the ingeniously sloping, grass-walled **Palais Omnisports,** a weird-looking stadium that hosts sports and music events and seats 17,000, approached on all sides by gleaming white steps. The stadium and ministry serve as cornerstones for the stretch of land that has become the Parc de Bercy.

A hundred yards along, facing the charming gardens with their trim lawns, vines, and rose-strewn arbors, is the witty, cubistic, $40 million **American Center,** opened to the public in 1994 but closed in 1996 due to lack of funds. Its architect, California's Frank O. Gehry, described it as "a dancing figure in the park," but now, empty and forlorn, it has as much spring in its step as a rag doll. Across the Seine, dominating the city's southeast skyline, are the four glass towers of architect Dominique Perrault's new national library, the Bibliothèque François Mitterrand (☞ The Islands and the Latin Quarter, *below*). ⊠ *rue de Bercy. Métro: Bercy.*

⑭ **Centre Pompidou.** The Centre National d'Art et de Culture Georges-Pompidou is its full name, although it is known to Parisians simply as Beaubourg (for the district). Georges Pompidou (1911–74) was the president of France who launched the project. Unveiled in 1977, three years after his death, the Pompidou Center was soon attracting over 8 million visitors a year—five times more than intended. Hardly surprising, then, that it was soon showing signs of fatigue: The much-vaunted, gaudily painted service pipes snaking up the exterior (painted the same colors that were used to identify them on the architects' plans) needed continual repainting, while the plastic tubing enclosing the exterior escalators was cracked and grimy. In 1996 the government stepped in and took drastic action: shutting the Center until the end of the century and embarking on top-to-bottom renovation.

It's still worth passing by, of course. You'll approach the center across **Plateau Beaubourg,** a substantial square that slopes gently down toward the main entrance. In summer it's often thronged with musicians, mimes, dancers, fire-eaters, acrobats, and other performers. Although the Center is closed for renovation until December 1999, the escalator up to the roof remains open, with the Parisian skyline unfolding as you are carried through the clear plastic tubes. Inside, some exhibitions will be staged when restoration allows; but the modern art museum will remain closed as it is extended and redesigned to ensure accommodation of a larger proportion of what the French already claim to be the largest collection of modern art in the world. Modern French art, no doubt; American painters and sculptors are conspicuous in their absence. ⊠ *pl. Georges-Pompidou,* ☎ *01–44–78–12–33.* 🏛 *Building and library entry and escalator ride to the roof: free. Exhibitions: prices vary, check at the main ticket booth on the ground floor.* ☉ *Wed.–Mon. noon–10 PM, weekends 10 AM–10 PM; closed Tues. Métro: Rambuteau.*

NEED A BREAK? | Stop in for coffee at the **Café Beaubourg** (⊠ 43 rue St-Merri, ☎ 01–48–87–63–96), on the corner of place Georges-Pompidou. A staircase takes you up from the first floor to a *passerelle,* or footbridge, linking the two sides of a mezzanine. The severe high-tech design is lightened by the little glass-top tables, several of which are covered with artists' paintings.

⑨ **Hôtel de Beauvais.** This is one of the finest hôtels particuliers in the Marais, dating from 1655 and built for Pierre de Beauvais with surprisingly generous funding from the normally parsimonious Louis XIV. The reason for the Sun King's unwonted largesse: a reward for de Beauvais's willingness to turn a blind eye to the activities of his wife, Catherine-Henriette Bellier, in educating the young monarch in matters sexual. Louis, who came to the throne in 1643 at the age of 4, was 14 when Catherine gave him first benefit of her expertise; she was 40. ⊠ *68 rue François-Miron. Métro: St-Paul.*

Hôtel de Montmor. This 17th-century hôtel particulier was once the scene of the Boffins, who founded the Académie des Sciences in 1666. Note the huge windows and intricate ironwork on the second-floor balcony. ⊠ *79 rue de Temple. Métro: Rambuteau.*

Hôtel de St-Aignan. Built in 1640, this hôtel particulier is scheduled to reopen after restoration as a Museum of Jewish Art and History in late 1998 or early 1999. ⊠ *71 rue de Temple. Métro: Rambuteau.*

❼ Hôtel de Sens. This sumptuous Marais mansion, built in 1474 for the archbishop of Sens, is one of a handful of civil buildings in Paris to have survived from the Middle Ages—witness the pointed corner towers, Gothic porch, and richly carved decorative details. Its best-known occupants were Henri IV and his queen, Marguérite, philanderers both. While Henri dallied with his mistresses—he is said to have had 56—at a series of royal palaces, Marguérite entertained her almost equally large number of lovers here. Today the building houses a fine-arts library, the Bibliothèque Forney. ⊠ *1 rue du Figuier,* ☎ *01–42–78–14–60.* ▣ *Free.* ☉ *Tues.–Fri. 1:30–8:30, Sat. 10–8:30. Métro: Pont-Marie.*

❹ Hôtel de Sully. This late-Renaissance mansion, begun in 1624, has a stately garden and a majestic courtyard with statues, richly carved pediments, and dormer windows. It is the headquarters of the **Caisse Nationale des Monuments Historiques,** responsible for administering France's historic monuments. Guided visits to Paris sites and buildings begin here, though all are conducted in French. The excellent bookshop, just inside the gate, has a wide range of publications on Paris, many of them in English. The bookshop is open daily 10–12:45 and 1:45–6. ⊠ *62 rue St-Antoine,* ☎ *01–44–61–20–00. Métro: St-Paul.*

⓬ Hôtel de Ville. The City Hall, overlooking the Seine, is something of a symbol for the regeneration of the surrounding Marais district, since much of the finance and direction for the restoration of the area has been provided by municipal authorities. As the area has been successfully redeveloped, the prestige of the mayor of Paris has grown. In fact, until 1977, Paris was the only city in France without a mayor; with the creation of the post and the election of Jacques Chirac (now president of France), leader of the right-of-center Gaullist party, the position has become pivotal in both Parisian and French politics. It comes as no surprise, therefore, that Chirac oversaw a thorough restoration of the Hôtel de Ville, both inside and out.

The square in front of the Hôtel de Ville was relaid in the 1980s and equipped with fancy lamps and fountains. It was once the site of public executions. Most victims were hanged, drawn, and quartered; the lucky ones were burned at the stake. It was here that Robespierre, the fanatical Revolutionary, came to suffer the fate of his many victims when a furious mob accompanied him to the guillotine in 1794. Following the short-lived restoration of the Bourbon monarchy in 1830, the building became the seat of the French government, a role that came to a sudden end with the uprisings in 1848. During the Commune of 1871, the Hôtel de Ville was burned to the ground. Today's exuberant building, based closely on the 16th-century Renaissance original, went up between 1874 and 1884. In 1944, following the liberation of Paris from Nazi rule, General de Gaulle took over the leadership of France from here. ⊠ *pl. de l'Hôtel-de-Ville.* ☉ *For special exhibitions. Métro: Hôtel-de-Ville.*

❽ Maison Européenne de la Photographie. This beautiful museum, unveiled in 1996, is housed in two hôtels particuliers. Despite its name, the museum has an impressive collection of both European and American works of photography. ⊠ *5 rue Fourcy,* ☎ *01–44–78–75–00.* 🎟 *30 frs. Free Wed. after 5 PM.* ⊘ *Wed.–Sun. 11–8. Métro: St-Paul.*

㉕ **Maison de Victor Hugo.** The workaholic French author, famed for *Les Misérables* and the *Hunchback of Notre-Dame,* lived in a corner of place des Vosges between 1832 and 1848. The memorabilia here includes several of his atmospheric, Gothic-horror-movie ink sketches, tribute to Hugo's unsuspected talent as an artist. ⊠ *6 pl. des Vosges,* ☎ *01–42–72–10–16.* 🎟 *27 frs.* ⊘ *Tues.–Sun. 10–5:45. Métro: St-Paul.*

⑩ **Mémorial du Martyr Inconnu.** In March 1992, this Memorial of the Unknown Jewish Martyr was erected at the **Center for Contemporary Jewish Documentation**—50 years after the first convoy of deportees left France—to honor the memory of the 6 million Jews who died "without graves." The basement crypt has a dramatic, black marble Star of David containing the ashes of victims from Nazi death camps in Poland and Austria. The center has archives, a library, and a gallery that hosts temporary exhibitions. ⊠ *17 rue Geoffroy-l'Asnier,* ☎ *01–42–77–44–72.* 🎟 *12 frs.* ⊘ *Sun.–Fri. 10–1 and 2–6. Métro: Pont-Marie.*

☙ ⑲ **Musée Bricard.** The Lock Museum—also called the Musée de la Serrure—is housed in a sober Baroque mansion designed in 1685 by the architect of Les Invalides, Libéral Bruand, for himself. Anyone with a taste for fine craftsmanship will appreciate the intricacy and ingenuity of many of the older locks displayed here. One represents an early security system—it would shoot anyone who tried to open it with the wrong key. Another was made in the 17th century by a master locksmith who was himself held under lock and key while he labored over it—the task took him four years. ⊠ *1 rue de la Perle,* ☎ *01–42–77–79–62.* 🎟 *30 frs.* ⊘ *Weekdays 2–5. Métro: St-Paul.*

㉓ **Musée Carnavalet.** Two adjacent mansions in the heart of the Marais house the Carnavelet Museum, the Paris history museum. Material dating from the city's origins until 1789 is in the Hôtel Carnavalet, and material from 1789 to the present is in the Hôtel Peletier St-Fargeau. In the late 17th century, the Hôtel Carnavalet was home to the most brilliant salon in Paris, presided over by Madame de Sévigné, best known for the hundreds of letters she wrote to her daughter; they've become one of the most enduring chronicles of French high society in the 17th century. The Hôtel Carnavalet, transformed into a museum in 1880, is full of maps and plans, furniture, and busts and portraits of Parisian worthies down the ages. The section on the Revolution includes riveting models of guillotines and objects associated with the royal family's final days, including the king's razor, and the chess set used by the royal prisoners at the approach of their own endgame. ⊠ *23 rue de Sévigné,* ☎ *01–42–72–21–13.* 🎟 *27 frs.* ⊘ *Tues.–Sun. 10–5:30. Métro: St-Paul.*

NEED A BREAK? **Marais Plus** (⊠ 20 rue des Francs-Bourgeois, ☎ 01-48-87-01-40), on the corner of rue Elzévir and rue des Francs-Bourgeois, is a delightful, artsy gift shop with a cozy salon de thé at the rear. Tarts—*salé* and *sucré* (savory and sweet)—will not disappoint.

⑯ **Musée de la Chasse et de la Nature.** The Museum of Hunting and Nature is housed in the Hôtel de Guénégaud, designed around 1650 by François Mansart and one of the Marais's most stately mansions. There's an extensive collection of hunting paraphernalia, including a series of immense 17th- and 18th-century still lifes (notably by Desportes and Oudry) of dead animals and a wide variety of swords, guns, muskets, and stuffed animals. ✉ *60 rue des Archives,* ☎ *01–42–72–86–43.* 🖅 *25 frs.* ◎ *Wed.–Mon. 10–12:30 and 1:30–5:30. Métro: Rambuteau.*

㉒ **Musée Cognacq-Jay.** This museum, devoted to the arts of the 18th century, contains outstanding furniture, porcelain, and paintings (notably by Watteau, Boucher, and Tiepolo). ✉ *8 rue Elzévir,* ☎ *01–40–27–07–21.* 🖅 *17 frs.* ◎ *Tues.–Sun. 10–5:30. Métro: St-Paul.*

⓴ **Musée Picasso.** The Picasso Museum opened in the fall of 1985 and shows no signs of losing its immense popularity. The building itself, put up between 1656 and 1660 for financier Aubert de Fontenay, quickly became known as the Hôtel Salé—*salé* meaning, literally, salted—as a result of the enormous profits made by de Fontenay as the sole appointed collector of the salt tax. The mansion was luxuriously restored by the French government as a permanent home for the pictures, sculptures, drawings, prints, ceramics, and assorted works of art given to the government by Picasso's heirs after the painter's death in 1973 in lieu of death duties. It's the largest collection of works by Picasso in the world—no masterpieces, but all works kept by Picasso himself; in other words, works that he especially valued. There are pictures from every period of his life: a grand total of 230 paintings, 1,500 drawings, and nearly 1,700 prints, as well as works by Cézanne, Miró, Renoir, Braque, Degas, and Matisse. The palatial surroundings of the Hôtel Salé add to the pleasures of a visit. ✉ *5 rue de Thorigny,* ☎ *01–42–71–25–21.* 🖅 *28 frs, Sun. 18 frs.* ◎ *Thurs.–Mon. 9:30–6. Métro: St-Sébastien.*

⓲ **Notre-Dame des Blancs-Manteaux.** The Blancs Manteaux were white-robed 13th-century mendicant monks whose monastery once stood on this spot. For the last 100 years, this late-17th-century church has had an imposing 18th-century facade that belonged to a now-destroyed church on the Ile de la Cité. Unfortunately, the narrow streets of the Marais leave little room to step back and admire it. The inside has fine woodwork and a Flemish-style Rococo pulpit whose marquetry panels are inlaid with pewter and ivory. ✉ *rue des Blancs-Manteaux. Métro: Rambuteau.*

➋ **Opéra de la Bastille.** The state-of-the-art Bastille Opera was erected on the south side of place de la Bastille. Designed by Argentine-born Carlos Ott, it opened July 14, 1989, the bicentennial of the French Revolution. The steep-climbing auditorium seats more than 3,000 and has earned more plaudits than the curving glass facade, which strikes Parisians as depressingly like that of yet another modern office building. ✉ *pl. de la Bastille,* ☎ *01–44–73–13–00. Métro: Bastille.*

➊ **Place de la Bastille.** Nothing remains of the infamous Bastille prison destroyed at the beginning of the French Revolution. Until 1988, there was little more to see here than a huge traffic circle and the **Colonne de Juillet,** the July Column. As part of the countrywide celebrations for July 1989, the bicentennial of the French Revolution, the Opéra de la Bastille was erected, inspiring substantial redevelopment on the surrounding streets, especially along rue de Lappe—once a haunt of Edith Piaf—and rue de la Roquette. What was formerly a humdrum neighborhood rapidly became one of the most sparkling and attractive in the city. Streamlined art galleries, funky jazz clubs, and Spanish-style tapas bars set the tone.

The Bastille, or, more properly, the Bastille St-Antoine, was a massive building, protected by eight immense towers and a wide moat (its ground plan is marked by paving stones set into the modern square).

It was built by Charles V in the late 14th century. He intended it not as a prison but as a fortress to guard the eastern entrance to the city. By the reign of Louis XIII (1610–43), however, the Bastille was used almost exclusively to house political prisoners. Voltaire, the Marquis de Sade, and the mysterious Man in the Iron Mask were all incarcerated here, along with many other unfortunates. It was this obviously political role—specifically, the fact that the prisoners were nearly always held by order of the king—that led the "furious mob" (in all probability no more than a largely unarmed rabble) to break into the prison on July 14, 1789, kill the governor, steal what firearms they could find, and free the seven remaining prisoners.

Later in 1789, the prison was knocked down. A number of the original stones were carved into facsimiles of the Bastille and sent to each of the provinces as a memento of royal oppression. The key to the prison was given by Lafayette to George Washington, and it has remained at Mount Vernon ever since. The power of legend being what it is, what soon became known as the Storming of the Bastille was elevated to the status of a pivotal event in the course of the French Revolution, demonstrating the newfound power of a long-suffering population. Thus it was that July 14 became the French national day, an event now celebrated with patriotic fervor throughout the country.

The July Column actually commemorates a more substantial political event: the July uprising of 1830 when the repressive Charles X, the Bourbon king about whom it was said that "the Bourbons learnt nothing, and forgot nothing," was overthrown. It's sometimes hard to imagine the turmoil that was a feature of French political life from the Revolution of 1789 through the 19th century (and, arguably, well into the 20th). After the fall of Napoléon in 1815, the restoration of a bone-headed monarchy, personified first by Louis XVIII, then by Charles X, virtually guaranteed that further trouble was in store. Matters came to a head in July 1830 with the St-Cloud Decrees, restricting the franchise—the right to vote—to a handful of landowners. Charles was duly toppled in three days of fighting at the end of the month—the Three Glorious Days—and a new, constitutionally elected monarch, Louis-Philippe, took the throne.

Louis-Philippe's reign was hardly more distinguished, despite attempts to curry favor among the populace. Nor was it noticeably more liberal. Louis-Philippe did, nonetheless, have the July Column built as a memorial, stipulating that 500 of those killed in the fighting of 1830 were to be buried under it. When, in 1848, Louis-Philippe himself was ousted, the names of a handful of the Parisians killed in the fighting of 1848 were then added to those already on the column. Meanwhile Louis-Philippe and his wife, disguised as Mr. and Mrs. William Smith, fled to Britain and threw themselves at the mercy of Queen Victoria. Mr. Smith died in England two years later. *Métro: Bastille.*

㉘ Place de la Nation. The towering, early 19th-century, statue-topped columns on majestic place de la Nation stand sentinel at the Gates of Paris—the eastern sector's equivalent of the Arc de Triomphe, with the bustling but unpretentious Cours de Vincennes providing a down-to-earth echo of the Champs-Elysées. Place de la Nation (known as place du Trône until the Revolution) was the scene of 1,300 executions at the guillotine in 1794. Many victims were buried at the nearby **Cimetière de Picpus** (35 rue Picpus), which also contains the grave of General Lafayette, identified by its U.S. flag. The cemetery is open Tuesday–Sunday 2–6; in winter, Tuesday–Sunday 2–4. *Métro or RER: Nation.*

㉔ Place des Vosges. Laid out by Henri IV at the start of the 17th century, and originally known as place Royale, this square is the oldest in Paris. It stands on the site of a former royal palace, the Palais des Tournelles, which was abandoned by the Italian-born queen of France, Catherine de' Medici, when her husband, Henri II, was killed in a tournament here in 1559. It was always a highly desirable address, reaching a peak of glamour in the early years of Louis XIV's reign, when the nobility were falling over themselves for the privilege of living here. Its buildings have been softened by time, their pale pink brick crumbling slightly in the harsh Parisian air and the darker stone facings pitted with age. The two larger buildings on either side of the square were originally the king's and queen's pavilions. The statue in the center is of Louis XIII. It's not the original; that was melted down in the Revolution, the same period when the square's name was changed in honor of the French département of the Vosges, the first in the country to pay the new revolutionary taxes. With its arcades, symmetrical pink-brick town houses, and trim green garden, bisected in the center by gravel paths and edged with plane trees, the square achieves harmony and balance: It's a charming place to tarry on a sultry summer afternoon. *Métro: Chemin-Vert.*

㉑ St-Denis-du-St-Sacrement. This severely neoclassical edifice (close to the Picasso Museum in the Marais) dates from the 1830s. It is a formidable example of architectural discipline, oozing restraint and monumental dignity (or banality, according to taste). The grisaille frieze and gilt fresco above the semicircular apse have clout if not subtlety; the Delacroix *Deposition* (1844), in the front right-hand chapel as you enter, has both. ⊠ *rue de Turenne. Métro: St-Sébastien.*

⑪ St-Gervais–St-Protais. This imposing church near the Hôtel de Ville is named after two Roman soldiers martyred by the emperor Nero in the 1st century AD. The original church—no trace remains of it now—was built in the 7th century. The present church, a riot of Flamboyant-style decoration, went up between 1494 and 1598, making it one of the last Gothic constructions in the country. Pause to look at the facade, constructed between 1616 and 1621. It's an early example of French architects' use of the classical orders of decoration on the capitals (topmost sections) of the columns. Those on the first floor are plain and sturdy Doric; the more elaborate Ionic is used on the second floor; and the most ornate of all—Corinthian—is used on the third floor. The church hosts occasional organ and choral concerts. ⊠ *pl. St-Gervais,* ☎ *01–47–26–78–38 for concert information.* ⊙ *Tues.–Sun. 6:30 AM–8 PM. Métro: Hôtel-de-Ville.*

⑬ St-Merri. This church near the Pompidou Center, completed in 1552, has a turret containing the oldest bell in Paris (cast in 1331) and an 18th-century pulpit supported on carved palm trees. ⊠ *rue de la Verrerie. Métro: Hôtel-de-Ville.*

⑤ St-Paul–St-Louis. The leading Baroque church in the Marais was begun in 1627 by the Jesuits and partly modeled on their Gesu church in Rome. Look out for Delacroix's dramatic *Christ in the Mount of Olives* high up in the transept, and the two huge shells, used as fonts, presented by Victor Hugo when he lived on nearby place des Vosges. ⊠ *rue St-Antoine. Métro: St-Paul.*

③ Ste-Marie. Constructed 1632–34 by François Mansart as the chapel of the Convent of the Visitation, this is now a Protestant "reformed" church. The large dome above the distinctive nave rotunda is one of the earliest in Paris. ⊠ *rue St-Antoine. Métro: Bastille.*

⓯ Square Igor-Stravinsky. The café-lined square, backed by the church of St-Merri and around the corner from the Pompidou Center, has a fountain animated by the colorful and imaginative sculptures of French artist Niki de St-Phalle, together with the aquatic mechanisms of Jean Tinguely. The fountain (sculptures and all) was erected in 1980. It is not part of the Pompidou Center, but it fits in. *Métro: Rambuteau.*

㉖ Viaduc des Arts. With typical panache, Paris planners have converted this redbrick viaduct—originally, the last mile of the suburban railroad that led to place de la Bastille (the site of the Bastille Opéra was once a station)—into a stylish promenade. Two-story art and crafts boutiques occupy the archways below, and a designer walkway, with shrubs, flowers, and benches, has ousted the tracks up above. The neatly pruned shrubs and designer benches clash provocatively with the dilapidated eye-level rooftops of this seamy sector of the city. (☞ Chapter 6). ✉ *av. Daumesnil. Métro: Gare de Lyon.*

THE ISLANDS AND THE LATIN QUARTER

Of the two islands in the Seine—the Ile St-Louis and the Ile de la Cité—it is the Ile de la Cité that forms the historic heart of Paris. It was here, for obvious reasons of defense, and in the hope of controlling the trade that passed along the Seine, that the earliest inhabitants of Paris, the Gaulish tribe of the Parisii, settled in about 250 BC. They called their little home Lutetia, meaning "settlement surrounded by water." Whereas the Ile St-Louis is today largely residential, the Ile de la Cité remains deeply historic. It has been inhabited for more than 2,000 years and is the site of one of the most beautiful churches in France—the great, brooding cathedral of Notre-Dame. Most of the island's other medieval buildings fell victim to town planner Baron Haussmann's ambitious rebuilding program of the 1860s. Among the rare survivors are the jewel-like Ste-Chapelle, a vision of shimmering stained glass, and the Conciergerie, the former city prison.

South of Ile de la Cité on the Left Bank of the Seine is the bohemian Quartier Latin, with its warren of steep sloping streets, populated largely by Sorbonne students and academics who fill the air of the cafés with their ideas—and tobacco smoke. The name Latin Quarter comes from the university tradition of studying and speaking in Latin, a tradition that disappeared during the Revolution. The university began as a theological school in the Middle Ages and later became the headquarters of the University of Paris; in 1968, the student revolution here had an explosive effect on French politics, resulting in major reforms in the education system.

A grim modern skyscraper at the Jussieu campus, the science division of the University of Paris, reiterates the area's yen for learning, yet fails to outgun the mighty dome of the Panthéon in its challenge for skyline supremacy. Most of the district's appeal is less emphatic: Roman ruins, tumbling street markets, the two oldest trees in Paris, and chance glimpses of Notre-Dame all await your discovery.

Numbers in the text correspond to numbers in the margin and on The Islands and the Latin Quarter map.

A Good Walk

The oldest bridge in Paris, confusingly called the **Pont Neuf** ①, or New Bridge, is built across the western tip of Ile de la Cité. Find your way to the middle of the bridge and the **square du Vert-Galant** ② below, with its proud equestrian statue of Henri IV. On the quayside of the square, Vedette motorboats start their tours along the Seine.

Opposite the square, on the other side of the bridge, is place Dauphine, completed the same year as the Pont Neuf (although much altered since). Cross place Dauphine and head left along quai de l'Horloge, named for the oldest clock (*horloge*) in Paris—marking time since 1370 from high up on the turreted **Conciergerie** ③, the prison where Marie-Antoinette was kept during the French Revolution. Take a left on boulevard du Palais to reach the imposing **Palais de Justice** ④, the 19th-century Law Courts; you can wander around the buildings amongst the black-robed lawyers or attend a court hearing. But the real interest here is the medieval **Ste-Chapelle** ⑤, tucked away to the left of the main courtyard. The chapel walls, consisting mainly of stained glass, constitute a technical tour de force. Rue de Lutèce, opposite the Law Courts, leads to the extensive flower market 150 yards down on the left. Turn right on rue de la Cité to come face to face with the serene, golden facade of **Notre-Dame** ⑥. The cathedral is at the geographic and historic heart of Paris, and its dark, solemn interior feels suitably reverential.

Cross the Seine along the pont au Double to square René-Viviani, where you'll find a battered acacia—which vies with a specimen in the Jardin des Plantes for the title of oldest tree in Paris—and a spectacular view of Notre-Dame. Behind the square lies the church of **St-Julien-le-Pauvre** ⑦, built at the same time as Notre-Dame, and the tiny, elegant streets of the Maubert district. Turn left out of the church and cross rue St-Jacques to the elegantly proportioned church of **St-Séverin** ⑧. The surrounding streets are pedestrians only and crammed with cheap restaurants fronted by suave waiters competing for customers at most hours of the day or night. Take rue St-Séverin, a right on rue Xavier-Privas, and a left on rue de la Huchette—home to Paris's smallest theater and oldest jazz club—to reach **place St-Michel** ⑨. The grandiose fountain, depicting St. Michael slaying the dragon, is a popular meeting spot at the nerve center of the Left Bank.

Turn left up boulevard St-Michel and cross boulevard St-Germain. To your left, behind some forbidding railings, lurks a garden with ruins that date from Roman times. These belong to the **Musée National du Moyen-Age** ⑩, the National Museum of the Middle Ages. The entrance is down rue Sommerard, the next street on the left. Cross place Paul-Painlevé, in front of the museum, up toward **La Sorbonne** ⑪ university, fronted by a small plaza where the Left Bank's student population congregate after classes. Continue uphill until you are confronted, up rue Soufflot on your left, by the menacing domed bulk of the **Panthéon** ⑫, originally built as a church but now a monument to France's most glorious historical figures. On the far left corner of place du Panthéon stands **St-Etienne-du-Mont** ⑬, a church whose facade is a mishmash of architectural styles. Explore the top of quaint rue de la Montagne-Ste-Geneviève alongside, then turn right onto rue Descartes to reach **place de la Contrescarpe** ⑭. This square looks almost provincial during the day as Parisians flock to the daily market on rue Mouffetard.

Duck into the old church of **St-Médard** ⑮ at the foot of rue Mouffetard, then head left for 250 yards along rue Censier and turn left again into rue Georges-Desplas to discover the beautiful white **Mosquée** ⑯, complete with minaret. Blink twice and you'll be convinced you've left Paris behind. On the far side of the Mosque extends the **Jardin des Plantes** ⑰, spacious botanical gardens; the first building you'll come to is the **Grande Galerie de l'Evolution** ⑱, a museum with a startling collection of stuffed animals, many extinct or endangered. The museums of entomology, paleontology, and mineralogy are on the south side of the park along rue Buffon; an old-fashioned zoo is on the other.

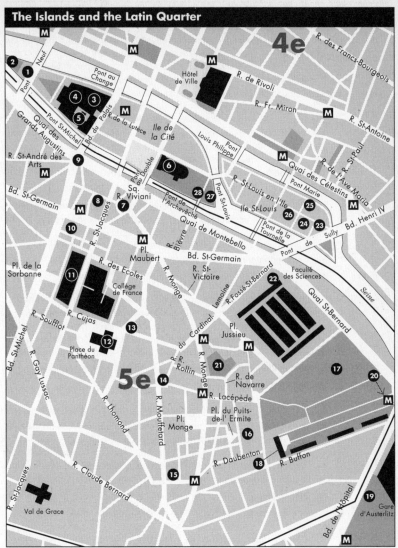

Although it's a bit out of the way, **St-Louis de la Salpêtrière** ⑲, the church of the Salpêtrière Hospital, is in walking distance from the Jardin des Plantes: take boulevard de l'Hôpital, at the east end of the park; the church is between the Gare d'Austerlitz and the hospital. Further up-river, via quai d'Austerlitz and quai de la Gare, is the new **Bibliothèque François Mitterrand** ⑳, the French National Library, with its four huge shiny glass towers. If you forego the distant pleasures of southeast Paris, take the northwest exit from the Jardin des Plantes up rue Lacépède then rue de Navarre to the **Arènes de Lutèce** ㉑, the remains of a Roman amphitheater. Rue des Arènes and rue Limé lead to place Jussieu and its hideous 1960s concrete campus; there's greater refinement around the corner down rue des Fossés-St-Bernard at the glass-facaded **Institut du Monde Arabe** ㉒, a center devoted to Arab culture.

Cross the Seine on Pont de Sully to the **Ile St-Louis** ㉓, the smaller of the city's two islands; it's an ideal place for strolling and window-shopping. The **Hôtel Lambert** ㉔ and the **Hôtel de Lauzun** ㉕ are two of the most majestic mansions on the island. Rue St-Louis-en-l'Ile runs the length of the island, bisecting it in two. Walk down the street and admire the strange, pierced spire of **St-Louis-en-l'Ile** ㉖; stop off for an ice cream at Berthillon at No. 31. Then head down to the Pont St-Louis at the island's western tip to admire the views of Notre-Dame, and the Hôtel de Ville and St-Gervais church on the Right Bank. Just across the bridge on Ile de la Cité lies the **Mémorial de la Déportation** ㉗, a starkly moving modern crypt dedicated to the French people who died in Nazi concentration camps. You may wish to linger in the quiet garden above before savoring the view of Notre-Dame from the **Pont de l'Archevêché** ㉘ that links the island to the Left Bank.

TIMING

At just under 6 km (about 3½ mi), this walk can be fitted into a morning or afternoon or serve as the basis for a leisurely day's exploring—given that several sites, notably Notre-Dame and the Musée de Cluny—deserve a lengthy visit. If you're with children, try and do this tour on a Thursday, when the enchanting Grande Galerie d'Evolution stays open till 10 PM. You can easily make a brief excursion to St-Louis de la Salpêtrière and the Bibliothèque François Mitterrand.

Sights to See

🐾 ㉑ **Arènes de Lutèce.** This Roman arena was only discovered in 1869 and has since been excavated and landscaped to reveal parts of the original amphitheater. Designed as a theater and circus, the arena was almost totally destroyed by the barbarians in AD 280, although you can still see part of the stage and tiered seating. Along with the remains of the baths at the Cluny, this constitutes rare evidence of the powerful Roman city of Lutetia that flourished on the Left Bank in the 3rd century. ⊠ *Enter by rue Monge or rue de Navarre.* ☉ *Daily 8–sunset. Métro: Monge.*

㉟ **Bibliothèque François Mitterrand.** As the last of former president Mitterrand's *grands travaux* (grand building projects) before he left office, the *Très Grande Bibliothèque* (Very Big Library, as some facetiously call it) opened in early 1997. The new library subsumes the majority of the collections in the old Bibliothèque Nationale and, with some 11 million volumes between its walls, surpasses the Library of Congress as the largest library in the world. Architect Dominique Perrault's controversial design features four soaring 24-story towers that house most of the books; readers and visitors are relegated to underground reading rooms. A vast interior courtyard—resembling a sunken garden—provides breathing space. As for the area surrounding the library, plans are underway to create new housing and schools, and the neighborhood is due to be served by the new high-speed Météor subway, which will run from Tolbiac to La Madeleine. ✉ *11 quai François-Mauriac,* ☎ *01–53–79–53–79. Métro: Quai de la Gare.*

❸ Conciergerie. This turreted medieval building by the Seine was originally part of the royal palace on Ile de la Cité. Most people know it, however, as a prison, the place of confinement for Danton, Robespierre, and, most famously, Marie-Antoinette during the French Revolution. From here, all three—and countless others who fell foul of the Revolutionary leaders—were bundled off to the guillotine. Marie-Antoinette's cell can still be seen, as well as objects connected with the ill-fated queen. A chapel, embellished with the initials M. A., occupies the true site of her confinement. You can also visit the guardroom, complete with hefty Gothic vaulting and intricately carved columns, and the monumental Salle des Gens d'Armes, where a short corridor leads to the kitchen, with its four vast fireplaces. The building's name derives from the governor, or *concierge,* of the palace, whose considerable income was swollen by the privilege he enjoyed of renting out shops and workshops. ✉ *Entrance on quai de l'Horloge.* 🎟 *28 frs.* ☉ *Daily 9:30–6:30; winter, daily 10–5. Métro: Cité.*

⓲ Grande Galerie de l'Evolution. This vast, handsome glass-and-iron structure in the Jardin des Plantes (☞ *below*) was built, as was the Eiffel Tower, in 1889 but abandoned in the 1960s. It reopened amid popular acclaim in 1994 and now contains one of the world's finest collections of stuffed animals, including a section devoted to extinct and endangered species. There's a reconstituted dodo—only a foot actually remains of this clumsy, flightless bird from Madagascar—and a miniature South African zebra, the quagga, which disappeared earlier this century. Stunning lighting effects include push-button spotlighting and a roof that changes color to suggest storms, twilight, or hot savannah sun. ✉ *36 rue Geoffroy-St-Hilaire,* ☎ *01–40–79–39–39.* 🎟 *40 frs, 30 frs before 1 PM.* ☉ *Wed.–Mon. 10–6, Thurs. 10–10. Métro: Monge.*

㉔ Hôtel Lambert. Louis Le Vau (1612–70) designed this majestic mansion on the eastern end of the Ile St-Louis. The interior decor is by Eustache Le Sueur and Charles Le Brun. Voltaire was its most illustrious inhabitant. ✉ *2 rue St-Louis-en-l'Ile. Métro: Pont-Marie.*

㉕ Hôtel de Lauzun. There is rich history to this Ile St-Louis mansion, built in about 1650 for Charles Gruyn, a supplier of goods to the French army who accumulated an immense fortune, then landed in jail before the house was even completed. In the 19th century, the revolutionary critic and visionary poet Charles Baudelaire (1821–67) had an apartment here, where he kept a cache of stuffed snakes and crocodiles. In 1848, the poet Théophile Gautier (1811–72) moved in, making it the meeting place of the Club des Haschischines, the Hashish Eaters' Club; novelist Alexander Dumas and painter Eugène Delacroix were both members. The club came to represent more than just a den of drug takers and gossips, for these men believed passionately in the purity of art and the crucial role of the artist as sole interpreter of the chaos of life. Art for Art's Sake—the more refined and exotic the better—was their creed. Anything that helped the artist reach heightened states of perception was applauded. Now the building is used for more decorous receptions by the mayor of Paris. ✉ *17 quai d'Anjou,* ☎ *01–43–54–27–14.* 🎟 *25 frs.* ☉ *Easter–Oct., weekends 10–5:30. Métro: Pont-Marie.*

㉓ Ile St-Louis. The smaller of the two Paris islands is linked to the Ile de la Cité by Pont St-Louis. The contrast between the islands is striking:

Whereas the Ile de la Cité is steeped in history and dotted with digni-
fied public buildings, the Ile St-Louis is a discreet residential district.
The island's most striking feature is its architectural unity, which stems
from the efforts of a group of early 17th-century property speculators.
At that time, there were two islands here, the Ile Notre-Dame and Ile
aux Vaches—Cow Island, a reference to its use as grazing land. The
speculators, led by an energetic engineer named Christophe Marie
(after whom the Pont Marie was named), bought the two islands,
joined them together, and divided the newly formed Ile St-Louis into
building plots. Leading Baroque architect Louis Le Vau (1612–70) was
commissioned to erect a series of imposing town houses, and by 1664
the project was largely complete. People still talk about the quaint, vil-
lage-street feel of rue St-Louis-en-l'Ile, which runs the length of the island, bisecting it neatly in two. From quai de Bourbon at the western
end, facing the Ile de la Cité, there are attractive views of Notre-Dame,
the Hôtel de Ville, and the church of St-Gervais. In summer, rows of
baking bodies attest to the quai's enduring popularity as the city's favorite sunbathing spot. *Métro: Pont-Marie.*

㉒ Institut du Monde Arabe. Jean Nouvel's striking glass-and-steel edifice,
the Institute of the Arab World, adroitly fuses Arabic and European
styles and was greeted with enthusiasm when it opened in 1988. Note
the 240 shutterlike apertures that open and close to regulate light exposure. Inside, the Institute tries to do for Arab culture what Beaubourg
does for modern art, with the help of a sound-and-image center; a vast
library and documentation center; and an art museum containing an
array of Arab-Islamic art, textiles, and ceramics, plus exhibits on Arabic mathematics, astronomy, and medicine. Glass elevators whisk you
to the ninth floor, where you can sip mint tea on the roof and enjoy a
memorable view of the Seine and Notre-Dame. ⊠ *1 rue des Fossés-St-
Bernard,* ☎ *01–40–51–38–38.* ☑ *25 frs.* ⊙ *Tues.–Sun. 10–6. Métro:
Cardinal-Lemoine.*

㉗ Jardin des Plantes. Bordered by the Seine, the drab Gare d'Austerlitz,
and the utilitarian Jussieu (a branch of the Paris University system),
this enormous swath of greenery contains botanical gardens, the
Grande Galerie de l'Evolution, and three other natural history museums. The **Grande Galerie de l'Evolution** (☞ *above*) is devoted to
stuffed animals; the **Musée Entomologique** to insects; the **Musée
Paléontologique** to fossils and prehistoric animals; and the **Musée
Minéralogique** to rocks and minerals. The stock of plants in the botanical gardens, dating from the first collections from the 17th century,
has been enhanced by subsequent generations of devoted French
botanists. The garden is claimed to shelter Paris's oldest tree, an *acacia robinia,* planted in 1636. There is also an alpine garden; an aquarium; a maze; a number of hothouses; and a small, old-fashioned zoo
that is open daily 9–5. ⊠ *Entrances on rue Geoffroy-St-Hilaire, rue
Buffon.* ☑ *Museums and zoo 12–25 frs.* ⊙ *Museums Mon. and
Wed.–Fri. 9–11:45 and 1–4:45, weekends 2–4:45; garden daily 7:30–
sunset. Métro: Monge.*

㉗ Mémorial de la Déportation. On the eastern tip of the Ile de la Cité, in
what was once the city morgue, lies a starkly moving modern crypt,
dedicated to those French men, women, and children who died in
Nazi concentration camps. ☑ *Free.* ⊙ *Daily 9–6; winter, daily 9–dusk.
Métro: Maubert-Mutualité.*

㉖ Mosquée. This beautiful white mosque was built from 1922 to 1925,
complete with arcades and minaret, and decorated in the style of
Moorish Spain. Students from the nearby Jussieu and Censier universities pack themselves into the Muslim restaurant here, which serves

copious quantities of couscous. The sunken garden and tiled patios are open to the public (the prayer rooms are not) and so are the *hammams,* or Turkish baths. Venture in and sip a restorative cup of sweet mint tea at the café. ⊠ *2 pl. du Puits-de-l'Ermite,* ☎ *01–45–35–97–33.* 🎫 *15 frs for guided tour, 65 frs for Turkish baths.* ☉ *Baths daily 11* AM*–8* PM*; Fri. and Sun. men only; Mon., Wed., Thurs., and Sat. women only. Guided tours of mosque Sat.–Thurs. 10–noon and 2–5:30. Métro: Monge.*

OFF THE BEATEN PATH
CHINATOWN – If China, rather than Arabia, is your cup of tea, take the métro at nearby Censier-Daubenton to Paris's Chinatown. Although not as ornamental as San Francisco's or New York's, Paris's Chinatown nevertheless offers myriad electronics and clothing stores and dozens of restaurants with an exciting array of Chinese *comestibles* (foods). **Tang-Frères Chinese supermarket** (⊠ 48 av. d'Ivry) packs in a serious crowd of shoppers on weekends. The **Temple de l'Association des Résidents d'Origine Chinoise** (⊠ 37 rue du Disque) is a small Buddhist temple that looks like a cross between a school cafeteria and an exotic Asian enclave filled with Buddha figures, fruit, and incense. For a more upscale version of Chinatown, head out to the eastern suburb of **Chinagora** (☞ Alfortville *in* On the Fringe, *below). Métro: Tolbiac.*

🔟 **Musée National du Moyen-Age.** The National Museum of the Middle Ages is housed in the 15th-century Hôtel de Cluny. The mansion has an intricately vaulted chapel and a cloistered courtyard with mullioned windows that originally belonged to monks of the Cluny Abbey in Burgundy, hence the museum's former name, the Musée de Cluny. A stunning array of tapestries heads its vast exhibition of medieval decorative arts; don't miss the graceful *Dame à la Licorne* (Lady and the Unicorn), woven in the 15th or 16th century, probably in the southern Netherlands. Alongside the mansion are the city's Roman baths—both hot (*Caldarium*) and cold (*Frigidarium*), the latter containing the *Boatmen's Pillar,* Paris's oldest sculpture. ⊠ *6 pl. Paul-Painlevé,* ☎ *01–43–25–62–00.* 🎫 *28 frs, Sun. 18 frs.* ☉ *Wed.–Mon. 9:45–5:45. Métro: Cluny–La Sorbonne.*

★ 6️⃣ **Notre-Dame.** Looming above the large, pedestrian place du Parvis on the Ile de la Cité is the Cathédrale de Notre-Dame, the most enduring symbol of Paris. The square (*kilomètre zéro* to the French, the spot from which all distances to and from the city are officially measured) is the perfect place to assess the facade. The cathedral was begun in 1163, with an army of stonemasons, carpenters, and sculptors working on a site that had previously seen a Roman temple, an early Christian basilica, and a Romanesque church. The chancel and altar were consecrated in 1182, but the magnificent sculptures surrounding the main doors were not put into position until 1240. The north tower was finished 10 years later.

Despite various changes in the 17th century, principally the removal of the rose windows, the cathedral remained substantially unaltered until the French Revolution. Then, the statues of the kings of Israel were hacked down by the mob, chiefly because they were thought to represent the despised royal line of France, and everything inside and out that was deemed "anti-Republican" was stripped away. An interesting postscript to this destruction occurred in 1977, when some of the heads of these statues were discovered salted away in a bank vault on boulevard Haussmann. They'd apparently been hidden there by an ardent royalist who owned the small mansion that now forms part of the bank. (The restored heads are now on display in the Musée National du Moyen-Age.)

By the early 19th century, the excesses of the Revolution were over, and the cathedral went back to fulfilling its religious functions again. Napoléon crowned himself emperor here in May 1804 (David's heroic painting of the lavish ceremony can be seen in the Louvre). Full-scale restoration started in the middle of the century, the most conspicuous result of which was the reconstruction of the spire. It was then, too, that Haussmann demolished the warren of little buildings in front of the cathedral, creating place du Parvis.

The facade divides neatly into three levels. At the first-floor level are the three main entrances, or portals: the Portal of the Virgin on the left, the Portal of the Last Judgment in the center, and the Portal of St. Anne on the right. All three are surmounted by magnificent carvings—most of them 19th-century copies of the originals—of figures, foliage, and biblical scenes. Above these are the restored statues of the kings of Israel, the Galerie des Rois. Above the gallery is the great rose window and, above that, the Grand Galerie, at the base of the twin towers. The south tower houses the great bell of Notre-Dame, as tolled by Quasimodo, Victor Hugo's fictional hunchback. The 387-step climb to the top of the towers is worth the effort for a close-up of the famous gargoyles—most of them added in the 19th century—and the expansive view of the city.

The cathedral interior, with its vast proportions, soaring nave, and soft, multicolor light filtering through the stained-glass windows, inspires awe, despite the inevitable throngs of tourists. Visit early in the morning, when the cathedral is at its lightest and least crowded. At the entrance are the massive 12th-century columns supporting the twin towers. Look down the nave to the transepts—the arms of the church—where, at the south (right) entrance to the chancel, you'll glimpse the haunting 12th-century statue of Notre-Dame de Paris, Our Lady of Paris. The chancel itself owes parts of its decoration to a vow taken by Louis XIII in 1638. Still without an heir after 23 years of marriage, he promised to dedicate the entire country to the Virgin Mary if his queen produced a son. When the longed-for event came to pass, Louis set about redecorating the chancel and choir. On the south side of the chancel is the **Trésor** (treasury), with a collection of garments, reliquaries, and silver and gold plate. ⊠ *pl. du Parvis.* 🖾 *Tower 28 frs; treasury 15 frs.* ☉ *Cathedral 8–7; tower daily (summer) 9:30–12:15 and 2–6, daily (winter) 10–5; treasury weekdays 9:30–6. Métro: Cité.*

Under the square in front of the cathedral is the **Crypte Archéologique,** Notre-Dame's archaeological museum. It contains remains of previous churches on the site, scale models charting the district's development, and relics and artifacts dating from the Parisii who lived here 2000 years ago, unearthed during excavations here in the 1960s. Slides and models detail the history of the Ile de la Cité. The foundations of the 3rd-century Gallo-Roman rampart and of the 6th-century Merovingian church can also be seen. 🖾 *28 frs.* ☉ *Daily 10–6:30; winter, daily 10–5.*

If your interest in the cathedral is not yet sated, duck into the **Musée Notre-Dame,** across the street opposite the North Door. Paintings, engravings, medallions, and other objects and documents chart the history of Notre-Dame cathedral. ⊠ *10 rue du Cloître-Notre-Dame.* 🖾 *15 frs.* ☉ *Wed. and weekends 2:30–6.*

❹ **Palais de Justice.** The city Law Courts were built by Baron Haussmann in his characteristically weighty neoclassical style in about 1860. You can wander around the buildings, watch the bustle of the lawyers, or attend a court hearing. But the real interest here is the medieval part

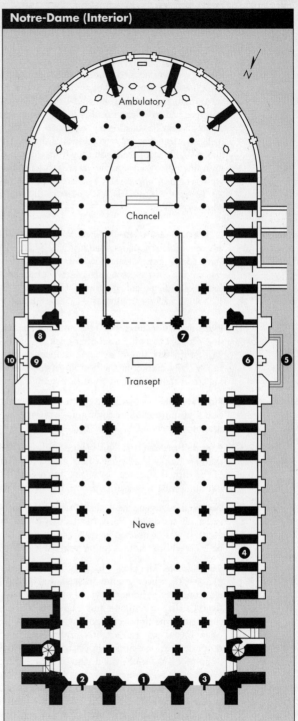

Notre-Dame (Interior)

Ambulatory

Chancel

Transept

Nave

of the complex, spared by Haussmann: the Conciergerie and Ste-Chapelle (☞ *above* and *below*). ⊠ *bd. du Palais. Métro: Cité.*

⑫ Panthéon. Originally commissioned as a church by Louis XV, as a mark of gratitude for his recovery from a grave illness in 1744, the Panthéon is now a monument to France's most glorious historical figures. The crypt holds the remains of Voltaire, Zola, Rousseau, and dozens of French statesmen, military heroes, and other thinkers. Germain Soufflot's building was not begun until 1764, or completed until 1790, whereupon godless Revolutionary supremos had its windows blocked and ordered it transformed into a national shrine. The dome, which weighs about 10,000 tons, needs admiring from a distance. Puvis de Chavannes's monumental frescoes in the nave, retracing the life of St-Geneviève, warrant closer appraisal. ⊠ *pl. du Panthéon,* ☎ *01–43–54–34–51.* 🎟 *32 frs.* ☉ *Daily 10–5:30. Métro: Cardinal-Lemoine; RER: Luxembourg.*

OFF THE
BEATEN PATH

LYCÉE LOUIS-LE-GRAND – Molière, Voltaire, and Robespierre studied at this venerable school, founded in 1530 by François I as the College of Three Languages. Students learned High Latin, Greek, and Hebrew as well as any other subjects eschewed by academics at the Sorbonne. Today's buildings, dating from the 17th century, are still part of a school. ⊠ *123 rue St-Jacques. RER: Luxembourg.*

---

⑭ Place de la Contrescarpe. This intimate square behind the Panthéon doesn't start to swing until after dusk, when its cafés and bars fill up. During the day, the square looks almost provincial as Parisians flock to the daily market at the bottom of rue Mouffetard, a steeply sloping street that retains much of its bygone charm. *Métro: Monge.*

⑨ Place St-Michel. This square on the Seine was named for Gabriel Davioud's grandiose 1860 fountain, depicting St. Michael slaying the dragon. *Métro, RER: St-Michel.*

㉘ Pont de l'Archevêché. This bridge, built in 1828, links Ile St-Louis to the Left Bank. The bridge offers a breathtaking view of the east end of the cathedral, ringed by flying buttresses, floating above the Seine like some vast stone ship. *Métro: Maubert-Mutualité.*

❶ Pont Neuf. Crossing the Ile de la Cité, just behind square du Vert-Galant, is the oldest bridge in Paris, confusingly called the New Bridge, or Pont Neuf. It was completed in 1607 and was the first bridge in the city to be built without houses lining either side. *Métro: Pont-Neuf.*

★ **❺ Ste-Chapelle.** The Holy Chapel built by the genial and pious Louis IX (1226–70), whose good works ensured his subsequent canonization, was conceived as home for what Louis believed to be the crown of thorns from Christ's crucifixion and fragments of the true cross; he acquired these from the impoverished Emperor Baldwin of Constantinople at phenomenal expense. Architecturally, for all its delicate and ornate exterior decoration—notice the open latticework of the pencil-like *flèche,* or spire, on the roof—the design of the building is simplicity itself. In essence, it's no more than a thin, rectangular box, much taller than it is wide. But think of it first and foremost as an oversize reliquary, an ornate medieval casket designed to house holy relics. The building is actually two chapels in one. The plainer, first-floor chapel, made gloomy by insensitive mid-19th-century restorations (which could do with restoration themselves), was for servants and lowly members of the court. The infinitely more spectacular upper chapel, up a dark spiral staircase, was for the king and important members of the court. Here, again, some clumsy 19th-century work has added a deadening touch, but the glory of the chapel—the stained glass—is spectacularly intact. The chapel is airy and diaphanous, the walls glowing and sparkling as light plays on the windows. Notice how the walls, in fact, consist of at least twice as much glass as masonry: The entire aim of the architects was to provide the maximum amount of window space. Ste-Chapelle is one of the supreme achievements of the Middle Ages and will be a highlight of your visit to Paris. Come early in the day to avoid the dutiful crowds that trudge around it. Better still, try to attend one of the regular, candle-lit concerts given here. ⊠ *In the Palais de Justice,* ☎ *01–43–54–30–09 for concert information.* ☎ *32 frs.* ☉ *Daily 9:30–6:30; winter, daily 10–6. Métro: Cité.*

⓭ **St-Etienne-du-Mont.** The ornate facade of this mainly 16th-century church combines Gothic, Baroque, and Renaissance elements. Inside, the curly, carved rood screen (1525–35), separating nave and chancel, is the only one of its kind in Paris. Note the uneven-floored chapel behind the choir, which can be reached via a cloister containing exquisite 17th-century stained glass. ⊠ *pl. de l'Abbé-Basset. Métro: Cardinal-Lemoine.*

❼ **St-Julien-le-Pauvre.** This tiny church was built at the same time as Notre-Dame (1165–1220), on a site where a succession of chapels once stood. The church belongs to a Greek Orthodox order today, but was originally named for St. Julian, bishop of Le Mans, who was nicknamed Le Pauvre after he gave all his money away. ⊠ *rue St-Julien-le-Pauvre. Métro: St-Michel.*

OFF THE BEATEN PATH | **ST-NICOLAS DU CHARDONNET –** The first church on the site was apparently built in a field of *chardons* (thistles), and, more recently, St-Nicolas has been a thorn in the side of the Catholic Church by refusing to abandon Latin mass. Stubborn priests are not, however, the most visible attraction of this pleasant Baroque edifice (1656–1709) just off place Maubert. There is a Corot study for the *Baptism of Christ* in the first chapel on the right and a *Crucifixion* by Brueghel the Younger in the sacristy. ⊠ *square de la Mutualité. Métro: Maubert-Mutualité.*

⓳ **St-Louis de la Salpêtrière.** The church of the Salpêtrière Hospital stands next to the Gare d'Austerlitz, which it dominates with its unmistakable, lantern-topped octagonal dome. It was built (1670–77) in the shape of a Greek cross from the designs of Libéral Bruant. ⊠ *bd. de l'Hôpital. Métro: Gare d'Austerlitz.*

㉖ **St-Louis-en-l'Ile.** The only church on the Ile St-Louis, built from 1664 to 1726 to the Baroque designs of Louis Le Vau, is lavishly furnished and has two unusual exterior features: its original pierced spire, holy in every sense, and an iron clock added in 1741. ⊠ *rue St-Louis-en-l'Ile. Métro: Pont-Marie.*

NEED A BREAK? | Cafés all over sell **Berthillon,** but the place to come for this haute couture of ice cream is still this little Ile St-Louis shop (⊠ 31 rue St-Louis-en-l'Ile, ☎ 01–43–54–31–61), where more than 30 flavors are offered. Expect to wait in line. This shop is open Wednesday–Sunday.

⓯ **St-Médard.** This church at the bottom of rue Mouffetard contains a painting of *St. Joseph with the Christ Child* by Spanish master Zurburan. The nave and facade, with its large late-Gothic window, date from the late 15th century. The 17th-century choir is in contrasting classical style. ⊠ *rue Mouffetard. Métro: Censier-Daubenton.*

❽ **St-Séverin.** This unusually wide, Flamboyant Gothic church dominates a Left Bank neighborhood filled with squares and pedestrian streets.

In the 11th century, the church that stood here was the parish church for the entire Left Bank. Louis XIV's cousin, a capricious woman known simply as the Grande Mademoiselle, adopted St-Séverin when she tired of St-Sulpice; she then spent vast sums getting court decorator Le Brun to modernize the chancel in the 16th century. Note the splendidly deviant spiraling column in the forest of pillars behind the altar. ⊠ *rue des Prêtres St-Séverin.* ☉ *Weekdays 11–5:30, Sat. 11–10. Métro: St-Michel.*

⓫   **La Sorbonne.** Named after Robert de Sorbon, a medieval canon who founded a theological college here in 1253 for 16 students, the Sorbonne is one of the oldest universities in Europe. For centuries it has been one of France's principal institutions of higher learning, as well as the hub of the Latin Quarter and nerve center of Paris's student population. The church and university buildings were restored by Cardinal Richelieu in the 17th century, and the maze of amphitheaters, lecture rooms, and laboratories, and the surrounding courtyards and narrow streets, retain a hallowed air. You can visit the main courtyard on rue de la Sorbonne and peek into the main lecture hall, a major meeting point during the tumultuous student upheavals of 1968 and also of interest for a giant mural by Puvis de Chavannes, the *Sacred Wood* (1880–89). The square is dominated by the university church, the noble **Église de la Sorbonne,** whose outstanding exterior features are its cupola and Corinthian columns. Inside is the white marble tomb of that ultimate crafty cleric, Cardinal Richelieu himself. ⊠ *rue de la Sorbonne. Métro: Cluny–La Sorbonne.*

OFF THE   **CENTRE DE LA MER ET DES EAUX –** A spell of fish-gazing is a soothing,
BEATEN PATH   mesmerizing experience for young and old alike. This center of sea and waters is one of the principal aquariums in Paris. ⊠ *195 rue St-Jacques.* 🎫 *30 frs.* ☉ *Tues.–Fri. 10–12:30 and 1:15–5:30, weekends 10–5:30. RER: Luxembourg.*

➋   **Square du Vert-Galant.** The equine statue of the Vert Galant himself—amorous adventurer Henri IV—surveys this leafy square at the western end of the Ile de la Cité. Henri, king of France from 1589 until his assassination in 1610, was something of a dashing figure, by turns ruthless and charming, a stern upholder of the absolute rights of monarchy, and a notorious womanizer. He is probably best remembered for his cynical remark that *"Paris vaut bien une messe"* ("Paris is worth a mass"), a reference to his readiness to renounce Protestantism to gain the throne of predominantly Catholic France and, indeed, be allowed to enter the city. To ease his conscience he issued the Edict of Nantes in 1598, according French Protestants (almost) equal rights with their Catholic counterparts. It was Louis XIV's renunciation of the edict nearly 100 years later that led to the massive Huguenot exodus from France—an economic catastrophe for the country. The square itself is a fine spot to linger on a sunny afternoon, and is the departure point for the glass-topped vedette tour boats on the Seine (at the bottom of the steps to the right). *Métro: Pont-Neuf.*

FROM ORSAY TO ST-GERMAIN

This walk covers the western half of the Left Bank, from the Musée d'Orsay in the stately 7ᵉ arrondissement, to the Faubourg St-Germain, a lively and colorful area in the 6ᵉ arrondissement. The Musée d'Orsay houses one of the world's most spectacular arrays of Impressionist paintings in a daringly converted Belle Epoque rail station on the Seine. Further along the river, the 18th-century Palais Bourbon, home to the National Assembly, sets the tone. Luxurious ministries and embassies—including the Hôtel Matignon, residence of the French prime minister—line the surrounding streets, their majestic scale in total keeping with the Hôtel des Invalides, whose gold-leafed dome climbs heavenward above the regal tomb of Napoléon. The splendid Rodin Museum is only a short walk away.

To the east, the boulevard St-Michel slices the Left Bank in two: on one side, the Latin Quarter (☞ The Islands and the Latin Quarter, *above*); on the other, the Faubourg St-Germain, named for St-Germain-des-Prés, the oldest church in Paris. The venerable church tower has long acted as a beacon for intellectuals, most famously during the 1950s when Albert Camus, Jean-Paul Sartre, and Simone de Beauvoir ate and drank existentialism in the neighborhood cafés. Today most of the philosophizing is done by tourists, yet a wealth of bookshops, art stores, and antiques galleries ensure that "St-Germain" (as the area is commonly known) retains its highbrow appeal. A highlight of St-Germain is the Jardin du Luxembourg, the city's most famous and colorful park. The 17th-century palace overlooking the gardens houses the French Senate.

Numbers in the text correspond to numbers in the margin and on the Orsay to St-Germain map.

A Good Walk

Arrive at the **Musée d'Orsay** ① early to avoid the crowds that flock to see the museum's outstanding works of art, all created between 1848 and 1914. A good meeting point is the pedestrian square outside the museum, where huge bronze statues of an elephant and a rhinoceros disprove the notion that the French take their art *too* seriously. Across the square stands the **Musée de la Légion d'Honneur** ②, where you can find an array of French and foreign decorations. From here, if you're short on time, you can cut south down rue de Bellechasse to Hôtel Matignon (☞ *below*). Otherwise, head west along rue de Lille to the **Palais Bourbon** ③, home of the Assemblée Nationale (French Parliament). There's a fine view across the Seine to place de la Concorde and the church of the Madeleine.

Rue de l'Université leads from the Assemblée to the grassy Esplanade des Invalides and an encounter with the **Hôtel des Invalides** ④, founded by Louis XIV to house wounded (or "invalid") veterans. The most impressive dome in Paris towers over the church at the Invalides—the Église du Dôme. From the church, double back along boulevard des Invalides and take rue de Varenne to the Hôtel Biron, better known as the **Musée Rodin** ⑤, where you can see a fine collection of Auguste Rodin's emotionally charged statues. The quiet, distinguished 18th-century streets between the Rodin Museum and the Parliament are filled with embassies and ministries. The most famous, further along rue de Varenne, is the **Hôtel Matignon** ⑥, residence of the French prime minister. Just before, at No. 51, is one of Paris's handful of private cul-de-sacs. Next door at No. 53 you can pay your respects to American novelist Edith Wharton, who lived and worked here from 1910 to 1920.

Carry on to rue du Bac, turn left, then right onto rue de Grenelle, past the **Musée Maillol** ⑦, dedicated to the work of sculptor Aristide Maillol, and Bouchardon's **Fontaine des Quatre Saisons.** Continue on rue de Grenelle to the Carrefour de la Croix-Rouge, with its mighty bronze Centaur by the contemporary sculptor César. Take rue du Vieux-Colombier to place St-Sulpice, a spacious square ringed with cafés; Yves St-Laurent's famous Rive Gauche store is at No. 6. Looming over the square is the enormous church of **St-Sulpice** ⑧.

72

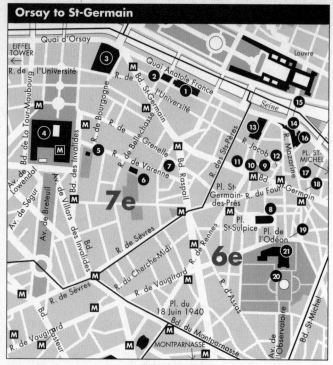

Exit the church, head back across the square, and turn right on rue Bonaparte to reach **St-Germain-des-Prés** ⑨, Paris's oldest church. Across the cobbled place St-Germain-des-Prés stands **Les Deux Magots** ⑩ café, one of the principal haunts of the intelligentsia after World War II. Another popular spot, two doors down boulevard St-Germain, is the **Café de Flore** ⑪. Politicians and showbiz types still wine and dine at the pricey Brasserie Lipp (☞ Chapter 3).

Follow rue de l'Abbaye, alongside the far side of the church, to rue de Furstemberg. The street opens out into a quiet square, bedecked with white globe lamps and catalpa trees, where you'll find Eugène Delacroix's studio, the **Atelier Delacroix** ⑫. Take a left on rue Jacob and turn right down rue Bonaparte to the **École Nationale des Beaux-Arts** ⑬, whose students can often be seen painting and sketching on the nearby quays and bridges. Wander into the courtyard and galleries of the school to see the casts and copies of the statues stored here for safekeeping during the Revolution. Continue down to the Seine and turn right along the quai, past the **Institut de France** ⑭. With its distinctive dome and commanding position overlooking the **Pont des Arts** ⑮—a footbridge affording delightful views of the Louvre and Ile de la Cité—the Institute is one of the city's most impressive waterside sights. Further along, on quai de Conti, you will pass the **Hôtel des Monnaies** ⑯, the national mint.

Head up rue Dauphine, the street that singer Juliet Greco put on the map when she opened the Tabou jazz club here in the '50s. It's linked 150 yards up by the open-air passage Dauphine to rue Mazarine, which leads left to the **Carrefour de Buci** ⑰. This crossroads once contained a gallows, an execution stake, and an iron collar for punishing troublemakers. Fanning out from the Carrefour are lively rue de Buci, with one of the best morning food markets in Paris; rue de l'Ancienne-Comédie, so named because it was the first home of the legendary Comédie Française, cutting through to the busy place de l'Odéon; and rue St-André des Arts, which leads swiftly to the historic **Cour du Commerce St-André** (opposite No. 66), a cobbled pedestrian street. Halfway down on the left—opposite the oldest café in Paris, **Le Procope** ⑱— stands one of the few remaining towers of the 12th-century fortress wall built by Philippe-Auguste, overlooking a cute, tiny courtyard, the **Cour de Rohan.** (From here it's a short walk to place St-Michel; ☞ The Islands and the Latin Quarter, *above*.)

Head to the end of Cour du Commerce St-André, cross boulevard St-Germain, and climb rue de l'Odéon to the colonnaded **Théâtre de l'Odéon** ⑲. Behind the theater lies the spacious **Jardin du Luxembourg** ⑳, one of the most stylish parks in the city. The large pond, usually animated by an armada of toy boats that can be hired alongside, enjoys the scenic backdrop of the rusticated **Palais du Luxembourg** ㉑. Today the palace houses the French Senate and is not open to the public. If you wish to now explore Montparnasse (☞ *below*), walk south to the Vavin métro station or return to St-Sulpice (☞ *above*) and take the métro three stops to Vavin.

TIMING

This 6½-km (4-mi) walk could take four hours to a couple of days, depending on how long you spend in the plethora of museums along the way. Aim for an early start—that way you can hit the Musée d'Orsay early, when crowds are smaller, then get to the rue de Buci street market in full swing, in the late afternoon (the stalls are generally closed for lunch until 3 PM). Note that the Hôtel des Invalides is open daily, but Orsay is closed Monday. You might consider returning to one or more museums on another day or night—Orsay is open late on Thursday evenings.

Sights to See

⑫ **Atelier Delacroix.** The studio of artist Eugène Delacroix (1798–1863) contains only a small collection of his sketches and drawings. But those who feel the need to pay homage to France's foremost Romantic painter will want to visit, especially as the atelier has been recently renovated. ⊠ *6 rue Furstemberg,* ☎ *01–43–54–04–87.* 🎫 *15 frs, Sun. 10 frs.* 🕑 *Wed.–Mon. 9:45–5:15. Métro: St-Germain-des-Prés.*

⑪ **Café de Flore.** In the postwar years, Jean-Paul Sartre and Simone de Beauvoir would meet their friends and followers at this popular café (☞ Chapter 3). ⊠ *172 bd. St-Germain. Métro: St-Germain-des-Prés.*

⑰ **Carrefour de Buci.** This crossroads was once a notorious Left Bank landmark; during the 18th century, it contained a gallows and an execution stake. In September 1792 the revolutionary army used this daunting site to enroll its first volunteers, and many Royalists and priests lost their heads here during the bloody course of the Revolution. There's nothing sinister, however, about the carrefour today, as brightly colored flowers spill onto the sidewalk at the flower shop on the corner of rue Grégoire-de-Tours. A couple of the small streets fanning out from the carrefour are of interest: **Rue de Buci** has a very good outdoor food market; **Rue de l'Ancienne-Comédie** got its name because it was the first home of the Comédie Française. 🕑 *rue de Buci market: Tues.–Sat. 8–1 and 4–7, Sun. 9–1. Métro: Mabillon.*

<table>
<tr><td>NEED A
BREAK?</td><td>If you happen to arrive when the market on rue de Buci is closed, **La Vieille France** patisserie may help fill the gap. ⊠ 14 rue de Buci, ☎ 01–43–26–55–13.</td></tr>
</table>

Cour du Commerce St-André. Revolutionary Jean-Paul Marat printed his newspaper, *L'Ami du Peuple,* at No. 8; and at No. 9, Dr. Guillotin conceived the idea for a new, "humane" method of execution—it was rumored that he practiced it on sheep first—that remained in force for murderers until 1981. *Métro: Odéon.*

Cour de Rohan. This series of three cloistered courtyards was once part of the hôtel of the archbishops of Rouen, established in the 15th century. Over the years the name was transformed into Rohan. ⊠ *Entrance on cour du Commerce St-André. Métro: Odéon.*

❿ **Les Deux Magots.** This old-fashioned St-Germain café, named after the two Chinese figures, or *magots,* inside, still thrives on its post–World War II reputation as one of the Left Bank's prime meeting places for the intelligentsia. It remains crowded day and night, but these days you're more likely to rub shoulders with tourists than with philosophers. Still, if your are in search of the mysterious glamour of the Left Bank you can do no better than to station yourself at one of the sidewalk tables—or at a window table on a wintry day—to watch the passing parade of acrobats, fire-eaters, and street musicians who perform in front of the church. ⊠ *6 pl. St-Germain-des-Prés,* ☎ *01–45–48–55–25. Métro: St-Germain-des-Prés.*

⓭ **École Nationale des Beaux-Arts.** The National Fine Arts College occupies three large mansions near the Seine. The school—today the breeding ground for painters, sculptors, and architects—was once the site of a convent, founded in 1608 by Marguerite de Valois, the first wife of Henri IV. During the Revolution, the convent was turned into a depot for works of art salvaged from the monuments that were under threat of destruction by impassioned mobs. Only the church and cloister remained by the time the Beaux-Arts school was established in 1816. ⊠ *14 rue Bonaparte.* ⊘ *Daily 1–7. Métro: St-Germain-des-Prés.*

<table>
<tr><td>NEED A
BREAK?</td><td>The popular **La Palette** café (⊠ 43 rue de Seine, ☎ 01-43-26-68-15), on the corner of rue de Seine and rue Callot, has long been a favorite haunt of Beaux-Arts students. One of them painted the ungainly portrait of the patron, François, that presides with mock authority over the shaggy gathering of clients.</td></tr>
</table>

Fontaine des Quatre Saisons. This allegorical fountain, designed by Edme Bouchardon in 1739 to help boost the district's water supply, has a wealth of sculpted detail. Bas-reliefs peopled by industrious cupids represent the *Seasons;* the seated figure of *Paris,* framed by Ionic columns, surveys the rivers *Seine* and *Marne* at her feet. ⊠ *57–59 rue de Grenelle. Métro: Rue du Bac.*

❹ **Hôtel des Invalides.** Les Invalides, as it is widely known, is an outstanding monumental Baroque ensemble, designed by Libéral Bruand in the 1670s at the behest of Louis XIV to house wounded, or "invalid," soldiers. Although no more than a handful of old soldiers live at the Invalides today, the military link remains in the form of the **Musée de l'Armée,** one of the world's foremost military museums, with a vast, albeit musty, collection of arms, armor, uniforms, banners, and military pictures down through the ages. The **Musée des Plans-Reliefs** contains a fascinating collection of old scale models of French towns; the largest and most impressive is Strasbourg, which takes up an entire room. The main, cobbled courtyard is a fitting scene for the parades and ceremonies still occasionally held at the Invalides.

The 17th-century **Église St-Louis des Invalides,** the Invalides's original church, was the site of the first performance of Berlioz's *Requiem,* in 1837. The most impressive dome in Paris towers over Jules Hardouin-

★ Mansart's **Église du Dôme,** built onto the end of Église St-Louis but blocked off from it in 1793—no great pity, perhaps, as the two buildings are vastly different in style and scale. The remains of Napoléon are here, in a series of no fewer than six coffins, one inside the next, within a bombastic tomb of red porphyry, ringed by low reliefs and a dozen statues symbolizing Napoléon's campaigns. Among others commemorated in the church are French World War I hero Marshal Foch; Napoléon's brother Joseph, erstwhile king of Spain; and fortification builder Vauban. ⊠ *Esplanade des Invalides,* ☎ *01–44–42–37–67.* ⊠ *35 frs.* ☉ *Daily 10–6; winter, daily 10–5.*

Some 200 display cabinets in the west wing of the Invalides, at the **Musée de l'Ordre de la Libération,** evoke various episodes of the war: De Gaulle's Free France organization, the Resistance, the Deportation, and the 1944 Liberation. The Order of the Liberation was created by General de Gaulle after the fall of France in 1940 to honor those who made outstanding contributions to the Allied victory in World War II (Churchill and Eisenhower figure among the rare foreign recipients). ⊠ *51 bis bd. de La Tour-Maubourg,* ☎ *01–47–05–35–15.* ⊠ *10 frs.* ☉ *Mon.–Sat. 2–5. Métro: La Tour–Maubourg.*

NEED A BREAK?
A short trek down boulevard des Invalides to rue de Babylone is the **Pagode** (⊠ 57 bis rue de Babylone), a movie theater and small tearoom, which offers an exotic environment for sipping hot tea and cooling your heels. It is open Monday to Saturday 4–10 and Sunday 2–8.

❻ Hôtel Matignon. The residence of the French prime minister is the Left Bank counterpart to the president's Elysée Palace. "Matignon" was built in 1721, but only since 1958 has it housed heads of state. From 1888 to 1914, it was the embassy of the Austro-Hungarian Empire. ⊠ *57 rue de Varenne. Not open to the public. Métro: Varenne.*

⓰ Hôtel des Monnaies. Louis XVI transferred the Royal Mint to this imposing mansion in the late 18th century. Although the mint was moved again, to Pessac, near Bordeaux, in 1973, weights and measures, medals, and limited-edition coins are still made here. The **Musée de la Monnaie** (Coin Museum) has an extensive collection of coins, documents, engravings, and paintings. On Tuesday and Friday at 2 PM you can catch the coin metal craftsmen at work in their ateliers overlooking the Seine. ⊠ *11 quai de Conti.* ⊠ *20 frs, Sun. 15 frs.* ☉ *Tues., Thurs.–Sun. 1–6, Wed. 1–9. Métro: Pont-Neuf.*

⓮ Institut de France. The Institute is one of France's most revered cultural institutions, and its curved, dome-topped facade is one of the Left Bank's most impressive waterside sights. The Tour de Nesle, which formed part of Philippe-Auguste's wall fortifications along the Seine, used to stand here and, in its time, had many royal occupants, including Henry V of England. The French novelist Alexandre Dumas (1824–95) featured the stormy history of the Tour de Nesle—during which the lovers of a number of French queens were tossed from its windows—in a melodrama of the same name. In 1661 the wealthy Cardinal Mazarin left 2 million French *livres* (books) in his will for construction of a college that would be dedicated to educating students from Piedmont, Alsace, Artois, and Roussillon, provinces that had been annexed to France during the years of his ministry. Mazarin's coat of arms is sculpted on the dome, and the public library in the east wing, which holds more than 350,000 volumes, still bears his name.

At the beginning of the 19th century, Napoléon stipulated that the Institute be transferred here from the Louvre. The Académie Française, the oldest of the five academies that compose the Institute, was created by Cardinal Richelieu in 1635. Its first major task was to edit the definitive French dictionary (which still isn't finished); it is also charged with safeguarding the purity of the French language. Election to its ranks, subject to approval by the French head of state, is the highest literary honor in the land—there can only be 40 "immortal" lifelong members at any one time. The appointment of historian and author Marguerite Yourcenar to the Académie in 1986 broke the centuries-old tradition of the academy as a male bastion. The Institute also embraces the Académie des Beaux-Arts, the Académie des Sciences, the Académie des Inscriptions et Belles Lettres, and the Académie des Sciences Morales et Politiques. ⊠ *pl. de l'Institut. Guided visits reserved for cultural associations only. Métro: Pont-Neuf.*

🐾 ⓴ **Jardin du Luxembourg.** The Luxembourg Garden is one of the prettiest of Paris's few large parks. The fountains, ponds, trim hedges, precisely planted rows of trees, and gravel walks are typical of the French fondness for formal gardens. The 17th-century Palais du Luxembourg provides an imposing backdrop. *Métro: Odéon; RER: Luxembourg.*

❷ **Musée de la Légion d'Honneur.** French and foreign decorations are displayed in this elegant mansion by the Seine (officially known as the Hôtel de Salm). The original building, constructed in 1786, burned down during the Commune in 1871 and was rebuilt in 1878. ⊠ *2 rue de Bellechasse,* ☎ *01–45–55–95–16.* 🎫 *10 frs.* ☉ *Tues.–Sun. 2–5. Métro: Solférino; RER: Musée d'Orsay.*

❼ **Musée Maillol.** Plaster casts and bronzes by Art Deco sculptor Aristide Maillol (1861–1944), whose sleek, stylized nudes adorn the Tuileries, can be admired at this handsome town house lovingly restored by his former muse Dina Vierny. ⊠ *61 rue de Grenelle,* ☎ *01–42–22–59–58.* 🎫 *40 frs.* ☉ *Wed.–Mon. 11–6. Métro: Rue du Bac.*

❶ **Musée d'Orsay.** Since opening in December 1986, the Musée d'Orsay—devoted to the arts (mainly French) spanning the period 1848–1914—has become one of the city's most popular museums. Beginning in 1900, the building was used as a train station for routes between Paris and the southwest of France. By 1939, the Gare d'Orsay had become too small for mainline travel, and intercity trains were transferred to the Gare d'Austerlitz. Gare d'Orsay became a suburban terminus until it closed in the 1960s. The building was temporarily used as a theater, an auction house, and a setting for Orson Welles's movie *The Trial,* based on Kafka's novel, before it was finally slated for demolition. However, the destruction of the 19th-century Les Halles (market halls) across the Seine provoked a furor among conservationists, and in the late 1970s, former president Giscard d'Estaing ordered Orsay to be transformed into a museum. The architects Pierre Colboc, Renaud Bardou, and Jean-Paul Philippon were commissioned to remodel the building; Gae Aulenti, known for her renovation of the Palazzo Grassi in Venice, was hired to reshape the interior. Aulenti's modern design in a building almost a century old provoked much controversy, but the museum's attributes soon outweighed any criticism.

The museum sets out to form a bridge between the classical collections of the Louvre and the modern collections of the Pompidou Center. Exhibits take up three floors, but the immediate impression is of a single, vast, stationlike hall. The chief artistic attraction is the Impressionists,

Musée d'Orsay

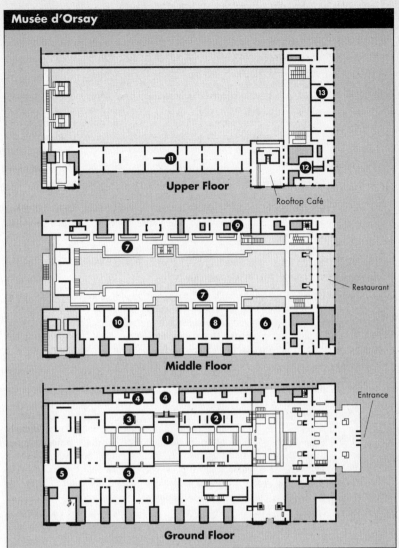

Upper Floor

Rooftop Café

Restaurant

Middle Floor

Entrance

Ground Floor

Architecture
1850-1900, **5**

Art Noveau, **10**

Decorative Arts
1850-1880, **4**

Decorative Arts and
Interiors of the Third
Republic, **6**

History of Painting
and the Portrait
1850-1880, **2**

Impressionism
and Post-
Impressionism, **11**

Neo-
Impressionism, **12**

Painting before
1870, **3**

Painting
1880-1900, **8**

Painting after 1900, **9**

Rousseau; the
Pont-Aven School;
the Nabis, **13**

Sculpture, **7**

Sculpture
1850-1870, **1**

whose works are displayed under the roof. Renoir, Sisley, Pissarro, and Monet are all well represented. Highlights include Monet's *Poppy Field* and Renoir's *Le Moulin de la Galette,* which differs from many other Impressionist paintings in that Renoir worked from numerous studies and completed it in his studio rather than painting it in the open air. Nonetheless, its focus on the activities of a group of ordinary Parisians amusing themselves in the sun on a Montmartre afternoon is typical of the spontaneity and fleeting sense of moment that are the essence of Impressionism. Whereas Monet, the only one of the group to adhere faithfully to the tenets of Impressionism throughout his career, strove to catch the effects of light, Renoir was more interested in the human figure.

The post-Impressionists—Cézanne, van Gogh, Gauguin, and Toulouse-Lautrec—are also represented on the top floor. Some may find the intense, almost classical serenity of Cézanne the dominant presence here; witness his magnificent Mont Ste-Victoire series, in which he paints and repaints the same subject, in the process dissolving form until the step to cubism and abstract painting seems an inevitability. Others will be drawn by the vivid simplicity and passion of van Gogh or by the bold, colorful rhythms of Gauguin.

On the first floor, you'll find the work of Manet and the delicate nuances of Degas. Be sure to see Manet's *Déjeuner sur l'Herbe,* the painting that scandalized Paris in 1863 at the Salon des Refusés, an exhibit organized by artists refused permission to show their work at the Academy's official annual salon. The painting shows a nude woman and two clothed men picnicking in a park. In the background, another naked girl bathes in a stream. Manet took the subject, poses and all, from a little-known Renaissance print in the Louvre but updated the clothing to mid-19th century France. What would otherwise have been thought a respectable "academic" painting thus became deeply shocking: two clothed men with two naked women in 19th-century France! The loose, bold brushwork, a far cry from the polished styles of the Renaissance, added insult to artistic injury. Another reworking by Manet of a classical motif is his reclining nude, *Olympia.* Gazing boldly out from the canvas, she was more than respectable 19th-century Parisian proprieties could stand.

If you prefer more academic paintings, look at Puvis de Chavannes's larger-than-life classical canvases. The pale, limpid beauty of his figures is enjoying considerable attention after years of neglect. If you are excited by more modern developments, look for the early 20th-century Fauves (meaning wild beasts, the name given them by an outraged critic in 1905)—particularly Matisse, Derain, and Vlaminck.

Thought-provoking sculptures litter the museum at every turn. Two further highlights are the faithfully restored Belle Epoque restaurant and the model of the entire Opéra quarter, displayed beneath a glass floor. ⊠ *1 rue de Bellechasse,* ☎ *01–40–49–48–84.* ⊡ *36 frs, Sun. 24 frs.* ☉ *Tues.–Sat. 10–6, Thurs. 10–9:30, Sun. 9–6. Métro: Solférino; RER: Musée d'Orsay.*

NEED A BREAK?　Find respite from the overwhelming collection of art in the **Musée d'Orsay Café,** behind one of the giant station clocks, close to the Impressionist galleries on the top floor. From the rooftop terrace alongside there is a panoramic view across the Seine toward Montmartre and Sacré-Coeur.

❺ **Musée Rodin.** The splendid Hôtel Biron, with its spacious vestibule, broad staircase, and light, airy rooms, retains much of its 18th-century atmosphere and makes a gracious setting for the sculpture of Auguste Rodin (1840–1917). You'll doubtless recognize the seated *Thinker,* with his elbow resting on his knee, and the passionate *Kiss.* There is also an outstanding white marble bust of Austrian composer Gustav Mahler, as well as numerous examples of Rodin's obsession with hands and erotic subjects. From the second-floor rooms, which contain some fine paintings by Rodin's friend Eugène Carrière (1849–1906), you can see the large garden behind the house. Don't go without visiting the garden: It is exceptional both for its rosebushes (more than 2,000 of them, representing 100 varieties) and for its sculpture, including a powerful statue of the novelist Balzac and the despairing group of medieval city fathers known as the *Burghers of Calais.* ⊠ *77 rue de Varenne,* ☎ *01–44–18–61–10.* 🎫 *28 frs, Sun. 18 frs.* ☉ *Easter–Oct., Tues.–Sun. 10–6; Nov.–Easter, Tues.–Sun. 10–5. Métro: Varenne.*

❸ Palais Bourbon. The most prominent feature of the home of the Assemblée Nationale (French Parliament) is its colonnaded facade, commissioned by Napoléon. It was cleaned at the start of the decade (although jeopardized at one stage by political squabbles as to whether cleaning should begin from the left or the right) and is now a sparkling sight. ⊠ *pl. du Palais-Bourbon.* ☉ *During temporary exhibits only. Métro: Assemblée Nationale.*

OFF THE BEATEN PATH **STE-CLOTILDE –** This neo-Gothic church (1846–58) is notable for its imposing twin spires, visible from across the Seine. French classical composer César Franck was organist here from 1858 to 1890. ⊠ *rue Las-Cases. Métro: Solférino.*

㉑ Palais du Luxembourg. The gray, imposing, rusticated Luxembourg Palace was built, like the surrounding Luxembourg Garden, for Maria de' Medici, widow of Henri IV, at the beginning of the 17th century. Maria was born and raised in Florence's Pitti Palace, and, having languished in the Louvre after the death of her husband, she was eager to build herself a new palace, where she could recapture something of the lively, carefree atmosphere of her childhood. In 1612, she bought the Paris mansion of the Duke of Luxembourg, tore it down, and built her palace. It was not completed until 1627, and Marie was to live there for just five years. In 1632, Cardinal Richelieu had her expelled from France, and she saw out her declining years in Cologne, Germany, dying there almost penniless in 1642. The palace remained royal property until the Revolution, when the state took it over and used it as a prison. Danton, the painter David, and Thomas Paine were all detained here. Today the French Senate meets here, so the building is not open to the public. ⊠ *15 rue de Vaugirard,* ☎ *01–42–34–20–00. Métro: Odéon; RER: Luxembourg.*

⑮ Pont des Arts. This elegant iron-and-wood footbridge linking the Louvre to the Institut de France is a favorite with painters, art students, and misty-eyed romantics moved by the delightful views of the Ile de la Cité. *Métro: Pont-Neuf.*

⑱ Le Procope. The oldest café in Paris was opened in 1686 by an Italian named Francesco Procopio. Many of Paris's most famous literary sons and daughters have imbibed here through the centuries, ranging from erudite academics like Denis Diderot to debauchees like Oscar Wilde, as well as Voltaire, Balzac, George Sand, Victor Hugo, and even Benjamin Franklin, who popped in whenever business brought him to Paris. The fomenters of the French Revolution met at the Procope, too, so old Ben may have rubbed shoulders with Marat, Danton, Robespierre and company. In 1988 a large restaurant group bought the Procope, aiming to give it a "new lease on life and a renewed literary and cultural vocation." They have succeeded in resuscitating it as a restaurant, but it's now filled with tourists, not writers. ⊠ *13 rue de l'Ancienne-Comédie,* ☎ *01–43–26–99–20. Métro: Odéon.*

❾ **St-Germain-des-Prés.** Paris's oldest church was first built to shelter a relic of the true cross, brought back from Spain in AD 542. The chancel was enlarged and the church then consecrated by Pope Alexander III in 1163; the tall, sturdy tower—a Left Bank landmark—dates from this period. The colorful 19th-century frescoes in the nave by Hippolyte Flandrin, a pupil of the classical painter Ingres, depict vivid scenes from the Old Testament. The church stages superb organ concerts and recitals. ⊠ *pl. St-Germain-des-Prés.* ☉ *Weekdays 8–7:30; weekends 8–9. Métro: St-Germain-des-Prés.*

❽ **St-Sulpice.** Dubbed the Cathedral of the Left Bank, this enormous 17th-century church has entertained some unlikely christenings—the Marquis de Sade's and Charles Baudelaire's, for instance—and the nuptials of irreverent wordsmith Victor Hugo. The 18th-century facade was never finished, and its unequal towers add a playful touch to an otherwise sober design. The interior is baldly impersonal, despite the magnificent Delacroix frescoes—notably *Jacob Wrestling with the Angel*—in the first chapel on your right. ⊠ *pl. St-Sulpice. Métro: St-Sulpice.*

❿ **Théâtre de l'Odéon.** At the north end of the Luxembourg Gardens, on place de l'Odéon, sits the colonnaded Odéon theater. It was established in 1792 to house the Comédie Français troupe; the original building was destroyed by fire in 1807. Since World War II it has specialized in 20th-century productions and was the base for Jean-Louis Barrault's and Madeleine Renaud's theater company, the Théâtre de France, until they fell out of favor with the authorities for their alleged role in spurring on student revolutionaries in May 1968. Today, the Théâtre de l'Odéon is the French home of the Theater of Europe and stages excellent productions by major foreign companies, sometimes in English (☞ Chapter 5). ⊠ *pl. de l'Odéon,* ☎ *01–44–41–36–36. Métro: Odéon.*

MONTPARNASSE

A mile to the south of the Seine lies the district of Montparnasse, named after Mount Parnassus, the Greek mountain associated with the worship of Apollo and the Muses. Montparnasse's cultural heyday came in the first four decades of the 20th century, when it replaced Montmartre as *the* place for painters and poets to live. Pablo Picasso, Amedeo Modigliani, Ernest Hemingway, Jean Cocteau, and Trotsky were among the luminaries who spawned an intellectual café society—later to be found at St-Germain (☞ *above*)—and prompted the launch of a string of arty brasseries along the district's main thoroughfare, the broad boulevard du Montparnasse.

The boulevard may lack poetic charm these days, but nightlife stays the pace as bars, clubs, restaurants, and cinemas crackle with energy beneath continental Europe's tallest high-rise: the 59-story Tour Montparnasse. While the Tower itself is a typically bland product of the early 1970s, of note only for the view from the top, several more adventurous buildings have risen in its wake. Ricardo Bofil's semicircular Amphithéâtre housing complex, with its whimsical postmodernist quotations of classical detail, is the most famous. The glass-cubed Cartier center for contemporary art, and the Montparnasse train station with its giant glass facade and designer garden above the tracks, are other outstanding examples.

If you have a deeper feel for history, you may prefer the sumptuous Baroque church of Val-de-Grâce or the quiet earth of Montparnasse cemetery, where Baudelaire, Sartre, Bartholdi (who designed the *Statue of Liberty*), and actress Jean Seberg slumber. The Paris underground had its headquarters nearby—in the Roman catacombs—during the Nazi occupation. After ignoring Hitler's orders to blow up the city, it was in Montparnasse that Governor von Choltitz signed the German surrender in August 1944.

Numbers in the text correspond to numbers in the margin and on the Montparnasse map.

A Good Walk

Walk or take the métro to the Vavin station (only three stops from St-Sulpice; ☞ From Orsay to St-Germain, *above*), beneath Rodin's 10-foot statue of Balzac, at the corner of boulevards Raspail and Montparnasse. Four cafés, famous since Montparnasse's interwar heyday, are all within a stone's throw on boulevard du Montparnasse. The Café du Dôme is at No. 108 and **La Coupole** ①, one of Montparnasse's most famous brasseries, is at No. 102. Across the street are two other famous cafés, La Rotonde at No. 105 and Le Sélect at No. 99 (☞ Chapter 3). Head west along boulevard du Montparnasse to the historic **place du 18-Juin-1940** ②. Towering above the square is the **Tour Montparnasse** ③. Behind the tower is the huge, gleaming glass facade of the Gare Montparnasse, home to the 200-mph *TGV Atlantique,* which serves the west of France. Take boulevard Edgar-Quinet to the side of the tower and turn right onto rue de la Gaîté; take note of the ornate facade of the **Théâtre Montparnasse** at No. 31.

Cross avenue du Maine and follow rue Vercingétorix to **place de Catalogne** ④, dominated by the monumental curves of the postmodern **Amphithéâtre** housing complex. Explore its arcades and circular forecourts, and compare its impersonal grandeur with the cozy charm of **Notre-Dame du Travail.** As you reemerge from the Amphithéâtre, Pont des Cinq-Martyres leads left over the rail tracks of Montparnasse station. The tracks are hidden beneath a small park, the **Jardin Atlantique** ⑤. Rue Jean-Zay leads from place de Catalogne to the corner of the high-walled **Cimetière de Montparnasse** ⑥. Enter the cemetery down rue Froidevaux if you wish to pay homage to local and foreign worthies. Rue Froidevaux continues to place Denfert-Rochereau, where you can admire the huge bronze *Lion of Belfort* by Frédéric-Auguste Bartholdi, the sculptor of the Statue of Liberty (he, too, is buried in Montparnasse cemetery), and visit the extensive underground labyrinth of the **Catacombs** ⑦, which tunnel under much of the Left Bank and the suburbs.

Walk up boulevard Raspail, past the eye-catching glass cubicle that houses the **Fondation Cartier** ⑧. Take the third right onto rue Campagne-Première, a handsome street once inhabited by Picasso, Miró, Kandinsky, and Modigliani. Note the tiled facade on the artists' residence at No. 31. Turn right at the bottom of the street onto boulevard du Montparnasse. At avenue de l'Observatoire stands perhaps the most famous bastion of Left Bank café culture, the **Closerie des Lilas** ⑨. Down avenue de l'Observatoire is the **Observatoire de Paris** ⑩, Louis XIV's astronomical observatory. In the other direction, the tree-lined avenue sweeps past the **Fontaine de l'Observatoire** ⑪. To the right of the fountain, along rue du Val-de-Grâce, is the imposing Baroque dome of **Val**

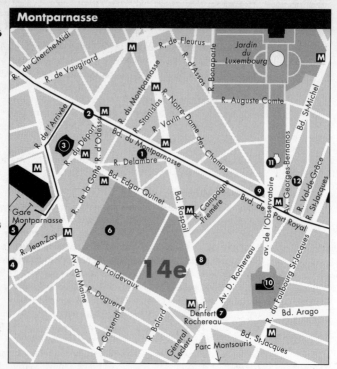

de Grâce ⑫. Straight ahead is the Jardin du Luxembourg (☞ From Orsay to St-Germain, *above*).

TIMING

The walk around Montparnasse is just under 5 km (3 mi) long and will comfortably take a morning or an afternoon if you choose to check out one of the historic cafés, the cemetery, and the catacombs along the way.

Sights to See

Amphithéâtre. Ricardo Boffil's monumental Amphitheater housing complex dominates the top side of the circular place de Catalogne. Its chunky reinvention of classical detail will strike some as witty, others as overkill. Be sure to explore its arcades and circular forecourts. *Métro: Gaîté.*

⑦ Catacombs. Enter the Paris catacombs, originally built by the Romans to quarry stone, from aptly named place Denfert-Rochereau: *denfert* is a corruption of the French for hell, *enfer*. The catacombs, which tunnel under much of the Left Bank, were used to store millions of skeletons from disused graveyards; during World War II, they were the headquarters of the French Resistance. Take a flashlight. ✉ *1 pl. Denfert-Rochereau,* ☎ *01–43–22–47–63.* 🎟 *27 frs.* 🕐 *Tues.–Fri. 2–4, weekends 9–11 and 2–4. Guided tours on Wed. at 2:45; 20 frs extra. Métro and RER: Denfert-Rochereau.*

⑥ Cimetière de Montparnasse. High walls encircle Montparnasse Cemetery, a haven of peace in one of Paris's busiest shopping and business areas. It is not a picturesque cemetery (with the exception of the towered rump of an old windmill that used to be a student tavern) but contains many of the quarter's most illustrious residents, buried only a stone's throw away from where they lived and loved: Charles Baudelaire, Augustè Bartholdi (who designed the Statue of Liberty), Alfred Dreyfus, Guy de Maupassant, Camille Saint-Saëns, Jean-Paul Sartre, Tristan Tzara, and, more recently, photographer Man Ray, playwright Samuel Beckett, actress Jean Seberg, and singer-songwriter Serge Gainsbourg. ⊠ *Entrances: rue Froidevaux, bd. Edgar-Quinet. Métro: Raspail, Gaîté.*

❾ Closerie des Lilas. Now a pricey bar-restaurant, the Closerie remains a staple of all literary tours of Paris. Commemorative plaques fastened to the bar mark the places where litterati like Baudelaire, Verlaine, Hemingway, and Apollinaire used to station themselves. Although the lilacs (*lilas*) have gone from the terrace, it still opens onto a garden wall of luxuriant evergreen foliage, and is as crowded in the summer as it ever was in the '30s. ⊠ *171 bd. du Montparnasse,* ☏ *01–43–26–70–50. Métro: Vavin; RER: Port-Royal.*

OFF THE
BEATEN PATH
MUSÉE ZADKINE – Russian-born sculptor Ossip Zadkine (1890–1967) trained in London before setting up in Paris in 1909. The works on exhibit here, in Zadkine's former house and studio, reveal the influences of Rodin, African art, and Cubism. ⊠ *100 bis rue d'Assas,* ☏ *01–43–26–91–90.* 🎟 *17 frs, Sun. free.* ☼ *Tues.–Sun. 10–5:40. Métro: Vavin.*

❶ La Coupole. One of Montparnasse's most famous brasseries, La Coupole opened in 1927 as a bar–restaurant–dance hall and soon became a home-away-from-home for Apollinaire, Max Jacob, Cocteau, Satie, Stravisnky, and Hemingway. It may not be quite the same mecca these days, but it still pulls in a classy crowd. The columns painted by Chagall and Brancusi, which lend La Coupole its Art Deco panache, were tellingly restored in the late '80s. For more information, *see* Chapter 3. ⊠ *102 bd. du Montparnasse,* ☏ *01–43–20–14–20. Métro: Vavin.*

❽ Fondation Cartier. Architect Jean Nouvel's eye-catching giant glass cubicle is a suitable setting for the temporary, thought-provoking shows of contemporary art organized here by jewelry giant Cartier. ⊠ *261 bd. Raspail,* ☏ *01–42–18–56–50.* 🎟 *30 frs.* ☼ *Tues.–Sun. noon–8. Métro: Raspail.*

⓫ Fontaine de l'Observatoire. Gabriel Davioud's fountain, built in 1873, is topped by Jean-Baptiste Carpeaux's four bronze statues of female nudes holding a globe, representing Les Quatre Parties du Monde (The Four Continents). ⊠ *av. de l'Observatoire. RER: Port-Royal.*

❺ Jardin Atlantique. The Atlantic Garden, which opened in 1994, is a small park built over the tracks of Gare Montparnasse, featuring an assortment of trees and plants from countries on the Atlantic Ocean. ⊠ *Pont des Cinq-Martyrs-du-Lycée-Buffon. Métro: Gaîté.*

Notre-Dame du Travail. The turn-of-the-century church made a powerful statement when it was built: Its riveted iron-and-steel framework was meant to symbolize the work ethos enshrouded in the church's name. The Sebastopol Bell above the facade is a trophy from the Crimean War. *Métro: Gaîté.*

❿ Observatoire de Paris. The Paris Observatory was built in 1667 for Louis XIV by architect Claude Perrault. Its four facades are aligned with the four cardinal points—north, south, east, and west—and its southern wall is the determining point for Paris's official latitude, 48° 50′11″N. French time was based on this Paris meridian until 1911, when the country decided to adopt the international Greenwich Meridian. ⊠ *av. de l'Observatoire. RER: Port-Royal.*

❹ Place de Catalogne. This square is dominated by the monumental Amphithéâtre and the church of Notre-Dame du Travail. *Métro: Gaîté.*

❷ **Place du 18-Juin-1940.** This square beneath the Tour Montparnasse is significant in World War II history. It is named for the date of the radio speech Charles de Gaulle broadcast from London, urging the French to resist the Germans after the Nazi invasion of May 1940. And it was here that German military governor Dietrich von Choltitz surrendered to the Allies in August 1944, ignoring Hitler's orders to destroy the city as he withdrew. A plaque on the wall of what is now a shopping center—originally the Montparnasse train station extended this far—commemorates the event. *Métro: Montparnasse-Bienvenue.*

OFF THE
BEATEN PATH
MUSÉE DE LA POSTE – This multistory museum of postal history has displays of international and French stamps (as far back as 1849), postmen's uniforms and postboxes, sorting and stamp-printing machines, and the balloon used to send mail out of Paris during the Prussian siege of 1870. ✉ *34 bd. de Vaugirard,* ☎ *01-42-79-23-45.* ✆ *25 frs.* ☉ *Mon.–Sat. 10–6. Métro: Falguière.*

Théâtre Montparnasse. The ornate facade of this theater recalls the halcyon days when this dingy little street was the heart of the Paris theater district. ✉ *31 rue de la Gaîté.*

❸ **Tour Montparnasse.** As continental Europe's tallest skyscraper, completed in 1973, this 685-foot tower offers a stupendous view of Paris from its open-air roof terrace. It attracts 800,000 visitors each year; on a clear day, you can see for 40 km (25 mi). If you go to the top-floor bar for drinks, the ride up is free. (A glossy brochure, *Paris Vu d'en Haut,* explains just what to look for.) It is also supposed to have the fastest elevator in Europe! Fifty-two of the 59 stories are taken up by offices, and a vast commercial complex, including a Galeries Lafayette department store, spreads over the first floor. Banal by day, the tower becomes Montparnasse's neon-lit beacon at night. ✉ *33 av. du Maine.* ✆ *42 frs.* ☉ *Apr.–Sept., daily 9:30 AM–11:30 PM; Oct.–Mar., Sun.–Thurs. 9:30 AM–10:30 PM, Fri.–Sat. 9:30 AM–11 PM. Métro: Montparnasse-Bienvenue.*

OFF THE
BEATEN PATH
MUSÉE BOURDELLE – A bust of his teacher, Rodin, by Antoine Bourdelle (1861–1929) heads the collection of works displayed in Bourdelle's house, garden, and studio. There is also a notable series of portraits of Beethoven. ✉ *16 rue Antoine-Bourdelle,* ☎ *01-45-48-67-27.* ✆ *27 frs.* ☉ *Tues.–Sun. 10–5:30. Métro: Falguière.*

⓬ **Val de Grâce.** This imposing 17th-century Left Bank church, extensively restored in the early 1990s, was commissioned by Anne of Austria and designed by François Mansart. Its powerfully rhythmic two-story facade rivals the Dôme Church at the Invalides as the city's most striking example of Italianate Baroque. Pierre Mignard's 1663 cupola fresco features more than 200 sky-climbing figures. ✉ *1 pl. Alphonse-Laveran. RER: Port-Royal.*

MONTMARTRE

On a dramatic rise above the city is Montmartre, site of the Sacré-Coeur basilica and home to a once-thriving artistic community. Although the fabled nightlife of old Montmartre has fizzled down to some glitzy nightclubs and porn shows, Montmartre still exudes a sense of history, a timeless quality infused with that hard-to-define Gallic charm.

Windmills once dotted Montmartre (often referred to by Parisians as *La Butte,* meaning "the mound"). They were set up here not just because the hill was a good place to catch the wind—at more than 300 feet, it's the highest point in the city—but because Montmartre was covered with wheat fields and quarries right up to the end of the 19th century. Today, only two of the original 20 windmills remain.

Visiting Montmartre means negotiating a lot of steep streets and flights of steps. The crown atop this urban peak, Sacré-Coeur, is something of an architectural oddity. It has been called everything from grotesque to sublime; its silhouette, viewed from afar at dusk or sunrise, looks more like a mosque than a cathedral.

There is a disputed story of how Montmartre got its name. Some say the name comes from the Roman temple to Mercury that was once here, called the Mound of Mercury, or *Mons Mercurii*. Others contend that it was an adaptation of *Mons Martyrum,* a name inspired by the burial here of Paris's first bishop, St. Denis. The popular version of his martyrdom is that he was beheaded by the Romans in AD 250 but arose to carry his severed head from rue Yvonne-Le-Tac to a place 6½ km (4 mi) to the north, an area now known as St-Denis. A final twist on the name controversy is that Montmartre briefly came to be known as Mont-Marat during the French Revolution. Marat was a leading Revolutionary figure who was stabbed to death in his bath.

Numbers in the text correspond to numbers in the margin and on the Montmartre map.

A Good Walk

Set off from **place Blanche** ①, on boulevard de Clichy, is the **Moulin Rouge** ②, the windmill-turned-dance-hall, immortalized by Toulouse-Lautrec. The Café Cyrano, next door to the Moulin Rouge, was once the haunt of Salvador Dali and his fellow Surrealists. If you want to visit the **Cimetière de Montmartre** ③, continue down boulevard de Clichy to avenue Rachel: The entrance to the cemetery is on your right.

If you want to skip the cemetery, or return to it later, walk up rue Lepic. You'll pass the tiny Lux Bar at No. 12: Inspect its 1910 mosaic showing place Blanche at the beginning of the century. Wind your way up to the **Moulin de la Galette** ④, on your left, atop its leafy hillock opposite rue Tholozé, once a path over the hill. Then turn right down rue Tholozé, past **Studio 28** ⑤, the first cinema built expressly for experimental films.

Continue down rue Tholozé to rue des Abbesses, and turn left toward the triangular **place des Abbesses** ⑥. Note the austere, redbrick **St-Jean l'Evangéliste** ⑦ on the square. Tiny rue André-Antoine, to the right of the popular Café St-Jean, leads to what was originally the **Théâtre Libre** ⑧, or Free Theater, at No. 37. Return to the square and take rue Yvonne-Le-Tac, off to the right. Paris's first bishop, St-Denis, is commemorated by the 19th-century **Chapelle du Martyre** ⑨ at No. 9, built on the spot where he is said to have been beheaded.

Return to the square and follow rue Ravignan as it climbs, via place Emile-Goudeau, an enchanting little cobbled square, to the **Bateau-Lavoir** ⑩, or Boat Wash House, at its northern edge. Painters Picasso and Braque had studios in the original building; this drab concrete building was built in its place. Continue up the hill via rue de la Mire to **place Jean-Baptiste Clément** ⑪, where Modigliani had a studio.

The upper reaches of rue Lepic lead to rue Norvins, formerly rue des Moulins (Windmill Street). At the end of the street, to the left, is stylish avenue Junot, site of the Cité Internationale des Arts (International Residence of the Arts), where the city authorities rent out studios to artists from all over the world. Continue right past the bars and tourist shops

Montmartre

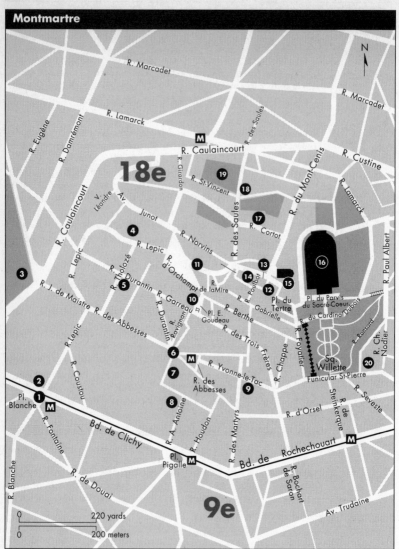

Bateau-Lavoir, **10**
Chapelle du
Martyre, **9**
Cimetière de
Montmartre, **3**
Cimitière
St-Vincent, **19**
Espace Dali, **14**

Halle St-Pierre, **20**
Lapin Agile, **18**
La Mère
Catherine, **13**
Moulin de la
Galette, **4**
Moulin Rouge, **2**

Musée du Vieux
Montmartre, **17**
Place des Abbesses, **6**
Place Blanche, **1**
Place Jean-Baptiste
Clément, **11**
Place du Tertre, **12**
Sacré-Coeur, **16**

St-Jean
l'Evangéliste, **7**
St-Pierre de
Montmartre, **15**
Studio 28, **5**
Théâtre Libre, **8**

until you reach famous **place du Tertre** ⑫. Check out the restaurant **La Mère Catherine** ⑬, a favorite with the Russian Cossacks when they occupied Paris. Fight your way through to the southern end of the square for a breathtaking view of the city. Around the corner on rue Poulbot, the **Espace Dali** ⑭ houses works by Salvador Dali, who once had a studio in the area.

Return to place du Tertre. Just off the square is the tiny church of **St-Pierre de Montmartre** ⑮. Looming menacingly behind is the scaly white dome of the Basilique du **Sacré-Coeur** ⑯. The cavernous interior is worth visiting for its golden mosaics; climb to the top of the dome for the view of Paris.

Walk back toward place du Tertre. Turn right onto rue du Mont-Cenis and left onto rue Cortot, site of the **Musée du Vieux Montmartre** ⑰, which, like the Bateau-Lavoir, once sheltered an illustrious group of painters, writers, and assorted cabaret artists. One of the best things about the museum, however, is its view of the tiny vineyard on neighboring rue des Saules. Another famous Montmartre landmark is at No. 22: the bar-cabaret **Lapin Agile** ⑱, originally one of the raunchiest haunts in Montmartre. Opposite the Lapin Agile is the tiny **Cimetière St-Vincent** ⑲.

Return to Sacré-Coeur and head down the cascading staircases to place St-Pierre. On the corner to the left is the **Halle St-Pierre** ⑳, site of the Museum of Naive Art. The neighboring streets teem with fabric shops and are the perfect place to rummage for cheap clothes and materials. From the top of rue de Steinkerque, one of the busiest shopping streets, you can take in the archetypal view of Sacré-Coeur soaring skyward atop its grassy mound, with the funicular railway to the left. Turn right at the bottom of rue de Steinkerque and head toward place Pigalle, notorious as a center of sleazy nightlife, although recently smarter bars and nightclubs have been springing up.

If, after you've walked around Montmartre, you still have the energy to see another illustrious church, make the excursion to the Gothic Basilique de St-Denis (☞ On the Fringe, *below*) in the nearby suburb of St-Denis. Take the métro at place de Clichy to St-Denis Basilique. Or get on at Anvers (near the Halle St-Pierre) and transfer at place de Clichy.

TIMING

Reserve four to five hours for this 4-km (2½-mi) walk: Many of the streets are steep and slow. Include half an hour each at Sacré-Coeur and the museums (the Dali museum is open daily, but the Montmartre museum is closed Monday). Leave about 1½ hours for the excursion to St-Denis Basilique, including the métro ride there.

From Easter through September, Montmartre is besieged by tourists. Two hints to avoid the worst of the rush: Come on a gray day, when Montmartre's sullen-tone facades suffer less than most in the city; or during the afternoon, and return to place du Tertre (maybe via the funicular) by the early evening, once the tourist buses have departed. More festive times of the year are June 24, when fireworks and street concerts are staged around Montmartre, or on the first weekend of October for the revelry that accompanies the wine harvest at the vineyard on rue des Saules.

Sights to See

❿ **Bateau-Lavoir.** Montmartre poet Max Jacob coined the name, meaning Boat Wash House, for the original building on this site, which burned down in 1970. He said it resembled a boat and that the warren of artists' studios within was perpetually paint-splattered and in need of a good hosing down. It was in the original Bateau-Lavoir that, early this century, Pablo Picasso and Georges Braque made their first bold stabs at the concept of Cubism—a move that paved the way for abstract painting. The poet Guillaume Apollinaire also had a studio here; his book *Les Peintures du Cubisme* (1913) set the seal on the movement's historical acceptance. The new building also contains art studios, but, if you didn't know its history, you'd probably walk right past it; it is the epitome of poured concrete drabness. ⊠ *13 pl. Emile-Goudeau. Métro: Abbesses.*

⑨ Chapelle du Martyre. It was in the crypt of the original chapel—built over the spot where St-Denis is said to have been martyred around AD 250—that Ignatius of Loyola, Francis Xavier, and five other companions swore an oath of poverty, chastity, and service to the Church. This led to the founding of the Society of Jesus (the Jesuits) in Rome six years later: a decisive step in the efforts of the Catholic Church to reassert its authority in the face of the Protestant Reformation. ⊠ *9 rue Yvonne-Le-Tac. Métro: Abbesses.*

❸ Cimetière de Montmartre. Montmartre Cemetery is not as romantic or as large as the better-known Père Lachaise, but it contains the graves of many prominent French men and women, including Edgar Degas; the 18th-century painters Jean-Baptiste Greuze and Honoré Fragonard; and Adolphe Sax, inventor of the saxophone. The Russian ballet dancer Nijinsky is also buried here. ⊠ *av. Rachel. Métro: Place de Clichy.*

⑲ Cimetière St-Vincent. It's a small graveyard, but serious students of Montmartre may want to visit painter Maurice Utrillo's burial place. ⊠ *Entrance on rue Lucien-Gaulard (via rue St-Vincent), behind the Lapin Agile. Métro: Abbesses, Lamarck-Caulaincourt.*

⑭ Espace Dali. Some of Salvador Dali's less familiar works are among the 25 sculptures and 300 prints housed in this museum. The atmosphere is meant to approximate the surreal experience, with black walls, low lighting, and a New Agey musical score—punctuated by recordings of Dali's own voice. ⊠ *11 rue Poulbot,* ☎ *01–42–64–40–10.* ▦ *35 frs.* ◷ *Daily 10–6; summer, daily 10–8. Métro: Abbesses.*

Ⓒ ⑳ Halle St-Pierre. This elegant iron-and-glass 19th-century market hall, at the foot of Sacré-Coeur, houses a children's play area, a café, and the **Musée de l'Art Naïf Max-Fourn** (Museum of Naive Art) with its psychedelic collection of contemporary international Naive painters. ⊠ *2 rue Ronsard,* ☎ *01–42–58–72–89.* ▦ *40 frs.* ◷ *Daily 10–6. Métro: Anvers.*

⑱ Lapin Agile. This bar-cabaret was originally one of the raunchiest haunts in Montmartre. It got its curious name—the Nimble Rabbit—when the owner, André Gill, hung up a sign (now in the Musée du Vieux Montmartre) of a laughing rabbit jumping out of a saucepan clutching a bottle of wine. In those days, the place was still tamely called La Campagne (The Countryside). Once the sign went up, locals rechristened it the Lapin à Gill, meaning Gill's Rabbit. When, in 1886, it was sold to cabaret singer Jules Jouy, he called it the Lapin Agile, which has the same pronunciation in French as Lapin à Gill. In 1903, the premises were bought by the most celebrated cabaret entrepreneur of them all, Aristide Bruand, portrayed by Toulouse-Lautrec in a series of famous posters. Today, it manages to preserve at least something of its earlier flavor, unlike the Moulin Rouge. ⊠ *22 rue des Saules,* ☎ *01–46–06–85–87. Métro: Lamarck-Caulaincourt.*

In case you want to see the world.

At American Express, we're here to make your journey a smooth one. So we have over 1,700 travel service locations in over 120 countries ready to help. What else would you expect from the world's largest travel agency?

do more

AMERICAN
EXPRESS

http://www.americanexpress.com/travel

Travel

In case you want to be welcomed there.

We're here to see that you're always welcomed at establishments everywhere. That's why millions of people carry the American Express® Card – for peace of mind, confidence, and security, around the world or just around the corner.

do more

AMERICAN EXPRESS

Cards

Fodor's Travel Publications

Available at bookstores everywhere, or call 1–800–533–6478, 24 hours a day.

Gold Guides

U.S.

Alaska	Florida	New Orleans	Seattle & Vancouver
Arizona	Hawai'i	New York City	The South
Boston	Las Vegas, Reno, Tahoe	Pacific North Coast	U.S. & British Virgin Islands
California		Philadelphia & the Pennsylvania Dutch Country	USA
Cape Cod, Martha's Vineyard, Nantucket	Los Angeles		Virginia & Maryland
	Maine, Vermont, New Hampshire	The Rockies	Walt Disney World, Universal Studios and Orlando
The Carolinas & Georgia	Maui & Lāna'i	San Diego	
Chicago	Miami & the Keys	San Francisco	Washington, D.C.
Colorado	New England	Santa Fe, Taos, Albuquerque	

Foreign

Australia	Europe	Montréal & Québec City	Scotland
Austria	Florence, Tuscany & Umbria	Moscow, St. Petersburg, Kiev	Singapore
The Bahamas			South Africa
Belize & Guatemala	France	The Netherlands, Belgium & Luxembourg	South America
Bermuda	Germany		Southeast Asia
Canada	Great Britain	New Zealand	Spain
Cancún, Cozumel, Yucatán Peninsula	Greece	Norway	Sweden
	Hong Kong	Nova Scotia, New Brunswick, Prince Edward Island	Switzerland
Caribbean	India		Thailand
China	Ireland	Paris	Toronto
Costa Rica	Israel	Portugal	Turkey
Cuba	Italy	Provence & the Riviera	Vienna & the Danube
The Czech Republic & Slovakia	Japan	Scandinavia	
	London		
Eastern & Central Europe	Madrid & Barcelona		
	Mexico		

Special-Interest Guides

Adventures to Imagine	Fodor's Gay Guide to the USA	Halliday's New Orleans Food Explorer	Rock & Roll Traveler USA
Alaska Ports of Call			
Ballpark Vacations	Fodor's How to Pack	Healthy Escapes	Sunday in San Francisco
Caribbean Ports of Call	Great American Learning Vacations	Kodak Guide to Shooting Great Travel Pictures	Walt Disney World for Adults
The Official Guide to America's National Parks	Great American Sports & Adventure Vacations		Weekends in New York
		National Parks and Seashores of the East	
Disney Like a Pro	Great American Vacations	National Parks of the West	Wendy Perrin's Secrets Every Smart Traveler Should Know
Europe Ports of Call	Great American Vacations for Travelers with Disabilities	Nights to Imagine	
Family Adventures		Rock & Roll Traveler Great Britain and Ireland	

WHEREVER YOU TRAVEL, *H*ELP IS NEVER FAR AWAY.

From planning your trip to providing travel assistance along the way, American Express® Travel Service Offices are always there to help.

Paris

American Express Bureau de Change
14 Bd. de la Madeleine
1/53 30 50 94

American Express Bureau de Change
26 Avenue de l'Opéra
1/53 29 40 39

American Express TFS Bureau de Change
5 rue St. Eleuthère
1/42 23 93 52

American Express Travel Service
11 rue Scribe
1/47 77 77 07

Travel

http://www.americanexpress.com/travel

American Express Travel Service Offices are found in central locations throughout France.

And just in case.

We're here with American Express® Travelers Cheques
and Cheques *for Two*® They're the safest way to carry
money on your vacation and the surest way to get a
refund, practically anywhere, anytime.
Another way we help you...

do more ®

AMERICAN
EXPRESS

Travelers
Cheques

13 **La Mère Catherine** was a favorite with the Russian Cossacks who occupied Paris in 1814. Little did they know that when they banged on the tables and shouted "*bistro*," the Russian word for "quick," they were inventing a new breed of French restaurant. *Métro: Abbesses.*

OFF THE
BEATEN PATH

MUSÉE D'ART JUIF – Montmartre's Museum of Jewish Art contains devotional items, models of synagogues, and works by Camille Pissarro and Marc Chagall. ⊠ *42 rue des Saules,* ☎ *01-42-57-84-15.* ⊠ *30 frs.* ☉ *Sept.–July, Sun.–Thurs. 3–6. Métro: Lamarck-Caulaincourt.*

4 **Moulin de la Galette.** This windmill, on a hillock shrouded by shrubbery, is one of two remaining windmills in Montmartre. It was once the focal point of an open-air cabaret (made famous in a painting by Renoir), and rumor has it that the miller, Debray, was strung up on its sails and spun to death after striving vainly to defend it against invading Cossacks in 1814. Unfortunately, it is now privately owned and can only be admired from the street below. ⊠ *rue Tholozé. Métro: Abbesses.*

2 **Moulin Rouge.** This world-famous cabaret was built in 1885 as a windmill, then transformed into a dance hall in 1900. Those wild, early days were immortalized by Toulouse-Lautrec in his posters and paintings. It still trades shamelessly on the notion of Paris as a city of sin: If you fancy a Vegas-style night out, with computerized light shows and troupes of bare-breasted women sporting feather headdresses, this is the place to go (☞ Chapter 5). The cancan, by the way—still a regular feature here—was considerably more raunchy when Toulouse-Lautrec was around. ⊠ *82 bd. de Clichy,* ☎ *01–46–06–00–19. Métro: Blanche.*

17 **Musée du Vieux Montmartre.** In its turn-of-the-century heyday, Montmartre's historical museum was home to an illustrious group of painters, writers, and assorted cabaret artists. Foremost among them were Renoir—he painted the *Moulin de la Galette,* an archetypal Parisian scene of sun-drenched revelers, while he lived here—and Maurice Utrillo, Montmartre painter par excellence. Utrillo was encouraged to paint by his mother, Suzanne Valadon, a model of Renoir's and a major painter in her own right. Utrillo's life was anything but happy, despite the considerable success his paintings enjoyed. He was an alcoholic continually in trouble with the police and spent most of his declining years in hospitals. He took the gray, crumbling streets of Montmartre as his subject matter, working more effectively from postcards than from the streets themselves. For all that, almost all his best works—from his "White Period"—were produced before 1916 (he died in 1955). They evoke the atmosphere of old Montmartre hauntingly: To help convey the decaying buildings of the area, he mixed plaster and sand with his paints. The museum also provides a view of the tiny vineyard—the only one in Paris—on neighboring rue des Saules. A symbolic 125 gallons of wine are still produced every year. It's hardly vintage stuff, but there are predictably bacchanalian celebrations during the harvest on the first weekend of October. ⊠ *12 rue Cortot,* ☎ *01–46–06–61–11.* ⊠ *25 frs.* ☉ *Tues.–Sun. 11–6. Métro: Lamarck-Caulaincourt.*

6 **Place des Abbesses.** This triangular square is typical of the picturesque, slightly countrified style that has made Montmartre famous. The entrance to the Abbesses métro station, a curving, sensuous mass of delicate iron, is one of the two original Art Nouveau entrance canopies left in Paris. *Métro: Abbesses.*

❶ Place Blanche. The name—White Square—comes from the clouds of chalky dust that used to be churned up by the carts that carried wheat and crushed flour from the nearby windmills, including the Moulin Rouge. *Métro: Blanche.*

OFF THE BEATEN PATH

MUSÉE DE LA VIE ROMANTIQUE – For many years the Romantic Museum at the foot of Montmartre was the site of Friday-evening salons hosted by painter Ary Schiffer and including the likes of Ingres, Delacroix, Turgenev, Chopin, and Sand. The memory of author George Sand (1804–76)—real name Aurore Dudevant—haunts the museum. Portraits, furniture, and household possessions, right down to her cigarette box, have been moved here from her house at Nohant in the Loire Valley. ⊠ *16 rue Chaptal,* ☎ *01-48-74-95-38.* 🎟 *27 frs.* ☉ *Tues.–Sun. 10–5:30. Métro: St-Georges.*

⓫ Place Jean-Baptiste Clément. Painter Amedeo Modigliani (1884–1920) had a studio here at No. 7. Some say he was the greatest Italian artist of the 20th century, fusing the genius of the Renaissance with the modernity of Cézanne and Picasso. He claimed that he would drink himself to death—he eventually did—and chose the right part of town to do it in. Look for the octagonal tower at the north end of the square; it's all that's left of Montmartre's first water tower, built around 1840 to boost the area's feeble water supply. ⊠ *pl. Jean-Baptiste Clément. Métro: Abbesses.*

⓬ Place du Tertre. This tumbling square (*tertre* means hillock) regains its village atmosphere only in the winter, when the branches of the planetrees sketch traceries against the sky. At any other time of year you'll be confronted by a swarm of artists clamoring to do your portrait and crowds of tourists. If one produces a picture of you without your permission, you're under no obligation to buy. *Métro: Abbesses.*

NEED A BREAK?

Patachou (⊠ 9 pl. du Tertre, ☎ 01-42-51-06-06) sounds the one classy note on place du Tertre, offering exquisite, if expensive, cakes and teas.

⓰ Sacré-Coeur. The white domes of the Sacred Heart Basilica patrol the Paris skyline from the top of Montmartre. The French government decided to erect Sacré-Coeur in 1873, as a sort of national guilt offering in expiation for the blood shed during the Commune and Franco-Prussian War in 1870–71. It was to symbolize the return of self-confidence to late-19th-century Paris. Even so, the building was to some extent a reflection of political divisions within the country: It was largely financed by French Catholics fearful of an anticlerical backlash and determined to make a grandiloquent statement on behalf of the Church.

Building lasted until World War I; the basilica was not consecrated until 1919. Stylistically, the Sacré-Coeur borrows elements from Romanesque and Byzantine models. Built on a grand scale, the effect is strangely disjointed and unsettling; architect Paul Abadie (who died in 1884, long before the church was finished) had made his name by sticking similar scaly, pointed domes onto the medieval cathedrals of Angoulême and Périgueux in southern France. The gloomy, cavernous interior is worth visiting for its golden mosaics; climb to the top of the dome for the view of Paris. ⊠ *pl. du Parvis-du-Sacré-Coeur. Métro: Anvers.*

❼ St-Jean l'Évangéliste. This austere, redbrick church, built in 1904, was one of the first concrete buildings in France; the bricks were added later to soothe offended locals. ⊠ *pl. des Abbesses. Métro: Abbesses.*

NEED A
BREAK? **Le St-Jean** (✉ 23 rue des Abbesses) is an intimate, large-windowed café, popular with locals on account of its authentic 1950s decor—neon lighting, vast bar, and mosaic-tile floor. The tables outside on the narrow sidewalk offer a good vantage point over bustling place des Abbesses.

⑮ St-Pierre de Montmartre. Sitting awkwardly beneath the brooding silhouette of Sacré-Coeur, just off place du Tertre, is this church—one of the oldest in Paris. Built in the 12th century as the abbey church of a substantial Benedictine monastery, it's been remodeled on a number of occasions through the years; thus the 18th-century facade, built under Louis XIV, clashes with the mostly medieval interior. ✉ *Off pl. du Tertre. Métro: Anvers.*

⑤ Studio 28. What looks like no more than a generic little movie theater has a distinguished dramatic history: When it opened in 1928, it was the first purposely built for *art et essai,* or experimental theater, in the world. Over the years, the movies of directors like Jean Cocteau, François Truffaut, and Orson Welles have been shown here before their official premieres. ✉ *10 rue Tholozé,* ☎ *01–46–06–36–07. Métro: Abbesses.*

⑧ Théâtre Libre. The Free Theater was founded in 1887 by André Antoine and was immensely influential in popularizing the work of iconoclastic young playwrights such as Ibsen and Strindberg. ✉ *37 rue André-Antoine. Métro: Abbesses.*

ON THE FRINGE

If you are in search of wide open green spaces, skyscrapers, unique museums, or the church where Gothic architecture made its first appearance, then make a brief excursion to the city's peripheries. Unlike New York or London, most large parks in Paris (with the notable exception of the Tuileries and Luxembourg Gardens) are found on the fringes of the city and in its nearby *banlieus* (suburbs). Soaring steel and glass have been banished to the outskirts at La Défense; the Gothic Basilique de St-Denis is in a suburb just north of Montmartre; and small, specialized museums are scattered throughout.

TIMING

Though none of these fringe sights is more than 25 minutes from central Paris on the métro or RER (with a 10-minute walk from the station in some instances), set aside at least a couple hours, if not a whole morning or afternoon to visit them. Late spring is a particularly good time to explore any of the parks, especially the Bois de Vincennes and the Bois de Boulogne whose gardens are most colorful between April and June.

Sights to See

Alfortville. In the near eastern suburb of Alfortville, at the confluence of the Marne and Seine rivers, the Chinese village of Chinagora offers an upscale look at Chinese culture. Hong Kong architect Liang Kunhao's glitzy $90 million complex includes everything from restaurants and a hotel to an emporium, an exhibition center, and a tearoom. Some 400,000 green-and-ochre glazed tiles, imported from China, make up the pagoda roofscape. Stop off nearby at the high-towered church of **Ste-Agathe** (✉ 1 pl. du Confluent, Alfortville, ☎ 01–43–96–37–38), an Art Deco bijou from the 1930s. *Métro: Alfort–École Vétérinaire.*

★ **Basilique de St-Denis.** Although today St-Denis is a dowdy northern suburb, not far from Montmartre, its history—exemplified by its huge green-roofed cathedral—is illustrious. Built between 1136 and 1286, the Basilique is in some ways the most important Gothic church in the Paris region. It was here, under dynamic prelate Abbé Suger, that Gothic architecture (typified by pointed arches and rib vaults) arguably made its first appearance. Suger's writings also show the medieval fascination with the bright, shiny colors that appear in stained glass. The kings of France soon chose St-Denis as their final resting place, and their richly sculpted tombs—along with what remains of Suger's church—can be seen in the choir area at the east end of the church. The vast 13th-century nave is a brilliant example of structural logic; its columns, capitals, and vault are a model of architectural harmony. The facade, retaining the rounded arches of the Romanesque style that preceded the Gothic style, is set off by a small rose window, reputedly the earliest in France. There was originally a left tower, with spire, as well as a right one; there is currently talk of reconstructing it. ⊠ *1 rue de la Légion d'Honneur.* ✆ *Choir: 27 frs.* ⊘ *Mon.–Sat. 10–7, Sun. noon–7; winter, Mon.–Sat. 10–5, Sun. noon–5. Guided tours daily at 3. Métro: St-Denis-Basilique.*

Ⓒ **Bois de Boulogne.** "Le Bois," as it is known, starts at the bottom of avenue Foch, connecting it to the Champs-Elysées. Avenue Foch used to be known as avenue de l'Impératrice in honor of the empress Eugénie (wife of Napoléon III); Paris's widest boulevard, it is 330 yards across. The sprawling, 2,200-acre wood, crisscrossed by broad, leafy roads, lies on the west side of Paris, surrounded by the wealthy residential districts of Neuilly, Auteuil, and Passy. Class and style have been associated with the park ever since it was landscaped into an upper-class playground by Baron Haussmann in the 1850s. Here you will discover rowers, joggers, strollers, riders, *pétanque* players, picnickers, and lovers. Horse races at **Longchamp** and **Auteuil** are high up the social calendar and re-create something of a Belle Epoque atmosphere. The French Open tennis tournament at the beautiful **Roland Garros Stadium** in late May is another occasion when Parisian style and elegance are on full display.

The manifold attractions of these woods include cafés, restaurants, lakes, waterfalls, gardens, and museums. Rowboats can be rented at the two largest lakes, the **Lac Inférieur** and **Lac Supérieur.** A cheap and frequent ferry crosses to the idyllic island in the middle of Lac Inférieur. The **Fête à Neu-Neu,** a giant fair, takes place every September and October around the two lakes. Buses traverse the Bois de Boulogne during the day (service 244 from Porte Maillot), but Le Bois becomes a distinctly adult playground after dark, when prostitutes come here looking for clients. The métro goes only to the fringe: Alight at Les Sablons (north), Porte d'Auteuil (south), or Porte Dauphine (east), which retains its original Art Nouveau iron-and-glass entrance canopy, designed by métro architect Hector Guimard.

The **Jardin d'Acclimatation,** a delightful children's amusement park on the northern edge of the Bois de Boulogne, offers boat trips along an "enchanted river," a zoo with a refreshing mix of exotic and familiar animals, a miniature railway, a high-towered folly, and various fairground booths to keep young and old entertained. The zoo and amusement park can be reached via the miniature railway—a surefire hit with children—that runs from Porte Maillot on Wednesdays and weekends, beginning at 1:30; tickets cost 5 francs. Many of the attractions have separate entry fees (except the zoo, which is spread throughout the park), notably the child-oriented art museum and workshop center, the **Musée en Herbe** (literally, "green museum"); admission is 16 francs and 25 francs with a workshop. ⊠ *bd. des Sablons,* ☎ *01–40–67–90–82.* 🖼 *12 frs.* ☉ *Daily 10–6. Métro: Les Sablons.*

The **Musée des Arts et Traditions Populaires,** in a nondescript modern building next to the Jardin d'Acclimatation, contains an impressive variety of artifacts related principally to preindustrial rural life. Many exhibits have buttons to press and knobs to twirl; however, there are no descriptions in English. The museum is a favorite destination for school field trips, so avoid weekday afternoons. ⊠ *6 rte. du Mahatma-Gandhi,* ☎ *01–44–17–60–00.* 🖼 *20 frs, Sun. 13 frs.* ☉ *Wed.–Mon. 10–5:15. Métro: Les Sablons.*

The **Pré Catalan** garden, in the heart of the Bois de Boulogne, includes one of Paris's largest trees: a copper beech more than 200 years old. The **Shakespeare Garden** contains flowers, herbs, and trees mentioned in Shakespeare's plays. ⊠ *rte. de la Grande Cascade.* ☉ *Guided tours at 11, 1:30, 3, 5, and 5:30. Métro: Porte Dauphine.*

The beautiful floral **Parc de Bagatelle** counts irises, roses, tulips, and water lilies among its showstoppers; it is at its most colorful between April and June. The velvet green lawns and majestic 18th-century buildings (often hosts to art exhibitions) are fronted by a terrace with attractive views of the Seine. ⊠ *rte. de Sèvres à Neuilly.* 🖼 *10 frs gardens only; 35 frs park and château buildings.* ☉ *Daily 9–5. Métro: Pont de Neuilly.*

At the **Serres d'Auteuil,** on the southern fringe of the Bois de Boulogne, tropical and exotic plants sweat it out in the mighty hothouses. A bewildering variety of plants and flowers are grown here for use in Paris's municipal parks and for displays on official occasions. The surrounding gardens' leafy paths and well-tended lawns offer cooler places to admire floral virtuosity. ⊠ *3 av. de la Porte d'Auteuil.* 🖼 *3 frs.* ☉ *Daily 10–5:30. Métro: Porte d'Auteuil.*

✪ **Bois de Vincennes.** Sandwiched between the unexciting suburb of Charenton and the working-class district of Fontenay-sous-Bois, to the southeast of Paris, the Bois de Vincennes is often considered a poor man's Bois de Boulogne. But the comparison is unfair: The Bois de Vincennes is no more difficult to get to (métro to Porte Dorée; Bus 46) and has equally illustrious origins. It, too, was landscaped under Napoléon III, although a park had already been created here by Louis XV in 1731. The park has several lakes, notably Lac Daumesnil, with two islands, and Lac des Minimes, with three; rowboats can be hired at both. In addition, the park is home to a zoo, an African art museum, a cinder-track racecourse (Hippodrome de Vincennes), a castle, a flower garden, and several cafés. In the spring there's an amusement park, the Foire du Trône. Bikes can be rented from Château de Vincennes métro station (☎ 01–47–66–55–92; 25 francs an hour or 100 francs a day).

Some 600 mammals and 200 species of birds can be seen at the Bois de Vincenne's **Zoo de Vincennes,** the largest in France. One of the most striking features is an artificial rock 236 feet high, inhabited by wild mountain sheep and penguins. The rock, built in 1934 of reinforced concrete, reopened in 1996 after a $16 million restoration program that added a new elevator to the top. ⊠ *53 av. de St-Maurice,* ☎ *01–44–75–20–10.* 🖼 *40 frs.* ☉ *Apr.–Oct., daily 9–6; Nov.–Mar., daily 9–5. Métro: Porte Dorée.*

The **Musée des Arts d'Afrique et d'Océanie** (Museum of the Arts of Africa and Oceania), at the Porte Dorée entrance to the Bois de Vincennes, is housed in an Art Deco building whose awesome facade is covered with a sculpted frieze depicting sites and attractions of France's erstwhile overseas empire. Inside, headdresses, bronzes, jewelry, masks, statues, and pottery from former French colonies are spaciously displayed under subtle spotlighting. Look out for the ominous Hakenkreuz set in the patterned mosaic floor of the huge reception hall; the sinister overtones it was soon to acquire, as the Nazi swastika emblem, were unsuspected when the building opened for the Colonial Exhibition in 1931. There is also a tropical aquarium (open from 10 weekends) in the basement, with rows of tanks with colorful tropical fish. ✉ *293 av. Daumesnil,* ☎ *01–44–74–84–80.* ✇ *28 frs, Sun. 18 frs.* ⊙ *Mon. and Wed.–Fri. 10–noon and 1:30–5:30, weekends 12:30– 6. Métro: Porte Dorée.*

The historic **Château de Vincennes,** on the northern edge of the Bois de Vincennes, is France's medieval Versailles, an imposing, high-walled castle surrounded by a dry moat and dominated by a 170-foot keep. The sprawling castle grounds also contain a replica of Ste-Chapelle (1379–1552) on the Ile de la Cité and two elegant, classical wings designed by Louis Le Vau in the mid-17th century, now used for naval-military administration and closed to the public. ✉ *av. de Paris,* ☎ *01–43–28–15–48.* ✇ *32 frs.* ⊙ *Daily 10–6; winter, daily 10–5. Guided tours of chapel every 45 mins. Métro: Château de Vincennes.*

The **Parc Floral de Paris,** the 70-acre Bois de Vincennes Paris Flower Garden, includes a lake and water garden and is renowned for its seasonal displays of blooms. It also contains a miniature train, a game area, and an "exotarium" with tropical fish and reptiles. ✉ *rte. de la Pyramide.* ✇ *5 frs.* ⊙ *Daily 9:30–8; winter, daily 9:30–5:30. Métro: Château de Vincennes.*

La Défense. You may be pleasantly surprised by the absence of high-rise buildings and concrete towers in central Paris; one of the reasons for this is that French planners, with their usual desire to rationalize, ordained that modern high-rise development be expelled to the outskirts. Over the last 20 years, La Défense, just west of Paris across the Seine from Neuilly, has been transformed into a futuristic showcase for state-of-the-art engineering and architectural design. Few people actually live amid all this glass and concrete; most just come to work. The soaring high-rises are mainly taken up by offices—often the French headquarters of multinational companies—with no expense spared in the pursuit of visual ingenuity. Outlines, shadows, reflections, plays of light, and swirling underpasses make for a stimulating, but slightly terrifying, cityscape. Highlights include the spherical IMAX cinema, **Musée de l'Automobile** for car fans, and, crowning the plaza, the **Grande Arche de La Défense,** aligned with avenue de la Grande-Armée, the Arc de Triomphe, the Champs-Elysées, and the Louvre. Tubular glass elevators whisk you to the top. ✉ *Parvis de La Défense,* ☎ *01– 49–07–27–57.* ✇ *Arch 40 frs; auto museum 30 frs.* ⊙ *Arch daily 10– 7; auto museum daily 12:15–7. Métro: Grande Arche de La Défense; RER: La Défense.*

☾ **Musée de la Femme et Collection d'Automates.** The museum, housed in a stately 18th-century mansion once owned by Latin-American millionaire Arturo Lopez in the tony northwest suburb of Neuilly, has two distinct sections. The automatons—ingenious 19th-century clockwork toys—burst into life every day at 3 PM. The Musée de la Femme (Women's Museum) takes up four cozy rooms but is not worth a separate visit. The collection ranges from Marie-Antoinette's corset to a naive portrait of newly betrothed Prince Charles and Lady Di to a tart missive from Margaret Thatcher declaring she has nothing to donate.

Although the eclectic array of artifacts conveys a conventional, even patronizing, view of womanhood, some may find it intriguing from a cultural point of view. The museum is a 10-minute walk from the métro station. ⊠ *12 rue du Centre, Neuilly,* ☎ *01–47–45–29–40.* ⌨ *20 frs.* ⊘ *Wed.–Mon. 2:30–5. Métro: Pont de Neuilly.*

Musée National de la Céramique. Hundreds of the world-famous Sèvres porcelain factory's finest creations are displayed "on premises" in the National Ceramics Museum, at the southern end of the tumbling, wooded Parc de St-Cloud in the southwest suburbs. ⊠ *pl. de la Manufacture, Sèvres,* ☎ *01–41–14–04–20.* ⌨ *17 frs, Sun. 9 frs.* ⊘ *Wed.–Mon. 10–5:15. Métro: Pont de Sèvres.*

♺ **Musée du Sport.** The Sports Museum at the top of the Parc des Princes—France's national stadium, in the southwest fringes of Paris—features posters, trophies, equipment, and an intriguing selection of historic sporting paraphernalia. Fans of cycling and the Olympics will have a field day. The museum is a 10-minute walk from the station. ⊠ *24 rue du Commandant-Guilbaud,* ☎ *01–40–45–99–12.* ⌨ *20 frs.* ⊘ *Sun.–Tues., Thurs., and Fri. 9:30–12:30 and 2–5. Métro: Porte de St-Cloud.*

♺ **Parc Andre-Citroën.** This innovative and lovely park on the eastern edge of Paris was built on the site of the former Citroën automobile factory. Now it has lawns, Japanese rock gardens, rambling wildflowers, and elegant greenhouses full of exotic plants and flowers. To the delight of grownups and children alike there is also a computer-programmed "dancing fountain." On a sunny day, it's a great place to take a break from sightseeing. ⊠ *Entrances on rue St-Charles, rue de la Montagne de l'Esperou. Métro, RER: Javel.*

♺ **Parc Montsouris and Cité Universitaire.** The picturesque, English-style Montsouris Park and the University "City," or campus, are in the residential 14e arrondissement, south of Montparnasse. Parc Montsouris has cascades, a lake, and a meteorological observatory disguised as a Tunisian Palace. Cité Universitaire, opposite Parc Montsouris, houses 5,000 international students in buildings that date mainly from the 1930s and reflect the architecture of different countries. Le Corbusier designed the Swiss and Brazilian houses; John D. Rockefeller funded the Maison Internationale; and the Sacré-Coeur church recalls the simple, muscular confidence of buildings erected in Mussolini's Italy. ⊠ *Parc Montsouris: entrances on av. Reille, bd. Jourdan, and rue Gazan; Cité Universitaire: entrance at 19 bd. Jourdan,* ☎ *01–44–16–64–00. RER: Cité Universitaire.*

3 Dining

Whether your dream meal is savoring truffle-studded foie gras from Limoges china or breaking the crust of a steaming cassoulet in a thick crockery bowl, you can find it in Paris. Despite rumblings about lower standards and increasingly bland fare, Paris remains one of the world's great food capitals. For most, the prospect of eating here is exciting; for many, it's the main reason for a trip.

Updated by
Alexander
Lobrano

PARIS REMAINS THE ULTIMATE gourmet destination. Nonetheless, if you are coming from New York, London, or Los Angeles, where innovative restaurants abound, you may find the French capital a little staid. In fact, there is currently a battle being waged between the traditionalists and a remarkable new generation of chefs who are modernizing French cuisine. The upshot is lighter fare with vegetables and fish alongside the French classics.

Parisians now insist that you can dine just as well at one of the new breed of bistro run by young, upstart chefs as you can at a fancier, more established, more expensive place. The new bistros are very popular, so make reservations as soon as you arrive. Because many places serve a market menu, meaning that the chef shops daily and buys according to what's in season or well-priced, many of the dishes mentioned in our reviews are cited more to give you an idea of a restaurant's cooking style than as specific recommendations.

Facing a penny-wise public, many Paris restaurateurs now offer prix-fixe (fixed-price) dining and bistro fare at the best prices in years. Still, it's not unusual to hear tales of outrageous prices, mediocre food, and haughty service. It's certainly possible to have a bad meal here. Yet the city's restaurants exist principally for the demanding Parisians themselves, for whom every meal is, if not a way of life, certainly an event worthy of their undivided attention. To dine well, therefore, look for restaurants where the French go—even if they are off the beaten path. Keep in mind, however, that world-famous restaurants are bound to be frequented by foreigners as well as Parisians and that an American at the next table is not always a bad sign.

Included in this listing are a variety of restaurants and price ranges, from formal dining rooms serving haute cuisine to cheery bistros offering hearty French cooking. More than half are in the 1er–8^e arrondissements, within easy reach of hotels and sights; many others are in the 14^e and 16^e, also popular visitor areas; and some are in the 11^e–20^e, outlying, often residential neighborhoods where the rents are cheaper and young chefs can afford to strike out on their own. Recognizing that even in Paris many people might not want to eat French food at every meal, several ethnic restaurants are listed.

Restaurant Types

What's the difference between a bistro and a brasserie? Can you order food at a café? Do you go to a restaurant just for a snack? The following definitions should help.

A **restaurant** traditionally serves a three-course meal (first, main, and dessert) at both lunch and dinner. Although this category includes the most formal, three-star establishments, it also applies to humble neighborhood spots. Don't expect to grab a quick snack. In general, restaurants are what you choose when you want a complete meal and when you have the time to linger over it. Wine is typical with restaurant meals. Hours are fairly consistent (☞ Mealtimes, *below*).

Many say that **bistros** served the world's first fast food. After the fall of Napoléon, the Russian soldiers who occupied Paris were known to bang on zinc-topped café bars, crying "bistro"—"hurry" in Russian. In the past, bistros were simple places with minimum decor and service. Although many nowadays are quite upscale, with beautiful interiors and chic clientele, most remain cozy establishments serving straightforward, frequently gutsy cooking, a wide variety of meats, and long-simmered dishes such as pot-au-feu and veal blanquette.

Brasseries—ideal places for quick, one-dish meals—originated when Alsatians fleeing German occupiers after the Franco-Prussian War came to Paris and opened restaurants serving specialties from home. Pork-based dishes, *choucroute* (sauerkraut and sausages), and beer (brasserie) were—and still are—mainstays here. The typical brasserie is convivial and keeps late hours. Some are open 24 hours a day—a good thing to know, since many restaurants stop serving at 10:30 PM.

Like bistros and brasseries, **cafés** come in a confusing variety. Usually informal neighborhood hangouts, cafés may also be veritable showplaces attracting chic, well-heeled crowds. At most cafés, regulars congregate at the bar, where coffee and drinks are cheaper than at tables. At lunch, tables are set and a limited menu is served. Sandwiches, usually with *jambon* (ham), *fromage* (cheese, often Gruyère or Camembert), or *mixte* (ham and cheese), are served throughout the day. Cafés are for lingering, for people-watching, and for daydreaming. Cafés are listed separately below.

Wine bars, or bistros *à vins,* are a newer phenomenon. These informal places serve very limited menus, often no more than open-face sandwiches (*tartines*) and selections of cheeses and cold cuts (*charcuterie*). Owners concentrate on their wine lists, which often include less well-known, regional selections, many of them available by the glass. Like today's bistros and brasseries, some wine bars are very fancy indeed, with costly wine lists and full menus. Most remain friendly and unassuming places for sampling wines you might otherwise never try (☞ Chapter 5, for a more comprehensive list of wine bars).

If you're not very hungry or want to eat at an odd hour, consider putting together a meal at one of Paris's *épiceries* (food shops). Today's *charcuteries* (French delis) are virtually restaurants (though without waiter service); the pâtés and meat products that once filled the shelves have moved over to make room for prepared salads, quiches, breads, and desserts. Choose what appeals to you most and take it to one of the city's green spaces for your own *déjeuner sur l'herbe* (picnic or, literally, "eating on the grass"). Or you can put together your picnic by visiting a number of shops, including *boulangeries* (bakeries), *pâtisseries* (pastry shops), *fromageries* (cheese shops), and *supermarchés* (supermarkets).

Mealtimes

Generally, Paris restaurants are open from noon to about 2 and from 7:30 or 8 to 10 or 10:30. Brasseries have longer hours and often serve all day and late into the evening; some are open 24 hours. The iconoclastic wine bars do as they want, frequently serving hot food only through lunch and cold assortments of charcuterie and cheese until a late-afternoon or early evening close. Assume a restaurant is open every day unless otherwise indicated. Surprisingly, many prestigious restaurants close on Saturday as well as Sunday. July and August are the most common months for annual closings, but Paris in August is no longer the wasteland it used to be.

In the reviews below, we have only indicated where reservations are essential (and when booking weeks or months in advance is necessary) and where reservations are not accepted. Because restaurants are open for only a few hours for lunch and dinner, and because meals are long affairs here, we urge you to make reservations. Most wine bars do not take reservations; reservations are also unnecessary for brasserie and café meals at odd hours. If you want to sit in a no-smoking section, make this clear; the mandatory no-smoking area is sometimes limited to a very few tables and often not strictly enforced.

Menus

All establishments must post their menus outside, so study them carefully before deciding to enter. Most restaurants offer two basic types of menu: à la carte and fixed price (prix fixe, or *un menu*). The prix-fixe menu will usually offer the best value, though choices are limited. Most menus begin with a first course (*une entrée*), often subdivided into cold and hot starters, followed by fish and poultry, then meat; it's rare today that anyone orders something from all three. However, outside of brasseries, wine bars, and other simple places, it's inappropriate to order just one dish, as you'll understand when you see the waiter's expression. In recent years, the *menu dégustation* has become popular; consisting of numerous small courses, it allows for a wide sampling of the chef's offerings. In general, consider the season when ordering. Daily specials are usually based on what's freshest in the market that day.

See the Menu Guide at the end of the book for guidance with menu items that appear frequently on French menus and throughout the reviews that follow.

Wine

The wine that suits your meal is the wine you like. The traditional rule of white with fish and red with meat no longer applies. If the restaurant has a sommelier, let him help you. Most sommeliers are knowledgeable about their lists and will suggest what is appropriate after you've made your tastes and budget known. In addition to the wine list, informal restaurants will have a *vin de la maison* (house wine) that is less expensive. Simpler spots will have wines *en carafe* or *en pichet* (in a pitcher). Except for wine bars and brasseries, most restaurants do not sell wine by the glass. If you'd like something before the meal, consider ordering your wine for the meal ahead of time, or sample a typical French *apéritif,* such as a *kir,* chilled white wine dosed with black-currant liqueur.

What to Wear

Perhaps surprisingly, casual dress is acceptable at all but the fanciest restaurants. Be aware that in Paris, casual does not mean without style. When in doubt, leave the blue jeans behind, and unless you want to be instantly identified as a tourist, don't wear sneakers. Use your judgment. In the reviews below, we have indicated where a jacket and/or tie are required.

Prices

Although prices are high, we have made an effort to include a number of lower-priced establishments. Prices include tax and tip (*service compris* or *prix nets*), but pocket change left on the table in basic places, or an additional 5% in better restaurants, is appreciated.

CATEGORY	COST*
$$$$	over 550 frs
$$$	300 frs–550 frs
$$	175 frs–300 frs
$	under 175 frs

per person for a three-course meal, including tax and service but not drinks

Right Bank Dining

KEY

$\boxed{AE}$ American Express Office

0 _____ 1 mile

0 _____ 1 km

A. Beauvilliers, **58**

A la Cloche
des Halles, **42**

A la Courtille, **67**

Alain Ducasse, **6**

Les Allobroges, **76**

Les Ambassadeurs, **28**

L'Ambroisie, **79**

Amphyclès, **14**

Androuet, **55**

Apicius, **15**

L'Astor, **31**

Astier, **73**

Au Bascou, **70**

Au Bourguignon du
Marais, **91**

Au Camelot, **77**

Au Petit
Colombier, **12**

Au Pied
de Cochon, **43**

Au Pressoir, **86**

Au Trou Gascon, **88**

Au Vieux Bistrot, **61**

Aux Crus de
Bourgogne, **46**

Aux Négotiants, **57**

Baracane, **80**

Batifol, **45**

Bistrot des Deux
Théâtres, **54**

Le Bistrot du
Cochon d'Or, **64**

Le Bistrot du
Sommelier, **30**

Bofinger, **81**

Brasserie Flo, **62**

Le Brin de Zinc et
Madame, **47**

La Butte Chaillot, **7**

Café Marly, **37**

Café Runtz, **51**

Le Cercle
Ledoyen, **27**

Chardenoux, **82**

Chartier, **52**

Chez Georges, **49**

Chez Géraud, **1**

Chez Janou, **78**

Chez Jean, **59**

Chez Jenny, **72**

Chez Michel, **60**

Chez Omar, **71**

Chez Pauline, **34**

Chez Philippe/
Pyrénées-
Cévennes, **69**

Fellini, **97**

La Ferme
St-Hubert, **33**

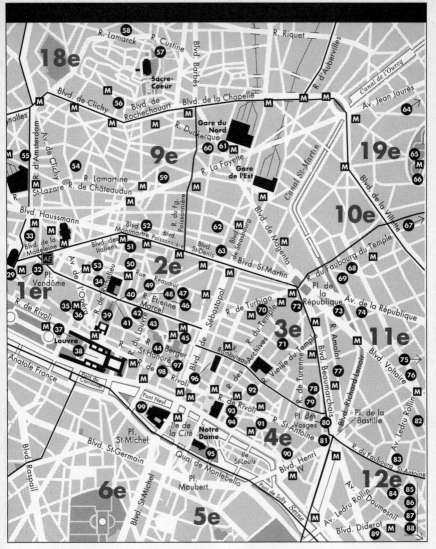

La Fermette Marbeuf, **22**
Les Fernandises, **68**
Gaya, **32**
Gérard Besson, **48**
Le Graindorge, **11**
Le Grand Louvre, **38**
Le Grand Véfour, **39**
Le Grizzli, **96**
Guy Savoy, **18**
L'Huitrier, **17**
Jacques Mélac, **75**
Jamin, **8**
Julien, **63**
Ledoyen, **26**

Lucas-Carton, **29**
Le Maraîcher, **90**
Le Moi, **53**
L'Oulette, **87**
Le Passage, **83**
Le Pavillon Puebla, **65**
Le Petit Rétro, **4**
Le Petit Yvan, **25**
Pierre Gagnaire, **23**
Port Alma, **20**
Le Pré Catalan, **3**
Prunier, **9**
Le Relais du Parc, **5**
Le Restaurant, **56**

Restaurant du Palais-Royal, **40**
Il Ristorantino, **36**
La Rôtisserie d'Armaillé, **13**
Le Rubis, **35**
Saudade, **98**
Savy, **24**
Sébillon, **21**
Le Square Trousseau, **84**
La Table de Pierre, **16**
Taillevent, **19**
La Taverne Henri IV, **99**

Le Timgad, **10**
La Tour du Montlhéry, **44**
Le Train Bleu, **89**
La Truffe, **92**
Trumilou, **94**
Le Vaudeville, **50**
La Verriere, **66**
Il Vicolo, **93**
Le Vieux Bistro, **95**
Le Villaret, **74**
Le Vivarois, **2**
Willi's Wine Bar, **41**
Les Zygomates, **85**

Left Bank Dining

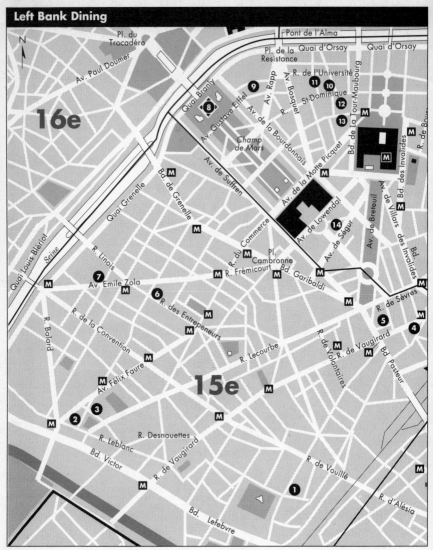

L'Affriole, **10**
Anacreon, **33**
L'Armoise, **6**
L'Arpège, **16**
Au Bon Accueil, **9**
Au Petit
Marguéry, **34**

Le Bambouche, **17**
Le Barrail, **4**
La Bastide Odéon, **25**
Bistro Mazarin, **21**
Les Bookinistes, **23**
Le Bouillon Racine, **22**

Campagne et
Provence, **28**
Chantairelle, **32**
Chez l'Ami Jean, **11**
Chez Dumonet-
Josephine, **42**
Chez René, **29**

Chez Toutoune, **27**
Claude Sainlouis, **19**
Le Clos Morillons, **1**
Contre-Allée, **38**
La Coupole, **40**
Le Comptoir des
Sports, **24**

La Dinée, **2**
L'Epi Dupin, **18**
Jules Verne, **8**
Mirama, **26**
Montparnasse 25, **41**
L'Oeillade, **15**

Les Olivades, **14**
L'Os à Moëlle, **3**
Paul Minchelli, **13**
Le Pavillon
Montsouris, **37**
Le Petit Plat, **7**

Le Petit Zinc, **20**
Philippe Detourbe, **5**
La Régalade, **39**
Thoumieux, **12**
Le Terroir, **36**
La Timonerie, **31**

La Tour d'Argent, **30**
Vin & Marée, **35**

Restaurants

1ᵉʳ Arrondissement (Louvre/Les Halles)
See Right Bank Dining map.

$$$$ ✕ **Gérard Besson.** Chef Besson has mastered a superb classical repertoire, subtly enlivened by his creative touches. The "marble" of beef
and the foie gras in a port aspic are delicious. In season, experience
the *lièvre à la royale,* braised hare in a luscious brown sauce. For
dessert, sample the unusual confit of fennel with vanilla ice cream. The
setting is attractive and intimate, with pale pink fabrics and carved wood
panels. There is an excellent wine cellar and a good-value 260-franc
lunch menu. ⊠ *5 rue du Coq-Héron,* ☎ *01–42–33–14–74. AE, DC,
MC, V. Closed Sun. No lunch Sat. Jan.–Sept. Métro: Les Halles.*

$$$$ ✕ **Le Grand Véfour.** Luminaries from Napoléon to Colette to Jean
Cocteau frequented this intimate address under the arcades of the
Palais-Royal; you can request to be seated at their preferred tables. A
sumptuously decorated restaurant, with mirrored ceiling and painted
glass panels, it is perhaps the prettiest in Paris, and its 18th-century
origins make it one of the oldest. Chef Guy Martin impresses with his
unique blend of sophisticated yet rustic dishes, including roast lamb
in a juice of herbs. ⊠ *17 rue Beaujolais,* ☎ *01–42–96–56–27. Reservations essential 1 wk in advance. Jacket and tie. AE, DC, MC, V. Closed
weekends and Aug. Métro: Palais-Royal.*

$$–$$$ ✕ **Chez Pauline.** For a dressy night out in a chic but comfortable
restaurant where irreproachable traditional French food is served,
head to this venerable bistro. The doorman in livery sets the tone—
service is solicitous and unfailingly correct. Indulge in classic luxury
foods like foie gras, truffles, and fine seafood. Fans of crème brûlée
take note of Chez Pauline's version: four different individual portions
in little china ramekins. ⊠ *5 rue Villedo,* ☎ *01–42–96–20–70. Reservations essential. AE, DC, MC, V. Closed Sun. No lunch Sat. Métro:
Pyramides.*

$$ ✕ **Au Pied de Cochon.** The menu at this lively 24-hour brasserie is clas-
sic French—shellfish, onion soup, *steak frites* (steak and fries), and, of
course, the eponymous pig's feet. The decor is Busby Berkleyesque—
with wall sconces adorned with giant bunches of frosted glass grapes.
Popular since its founding in 1946, this landmark in the former Les
Halles district is today mostly filled with tourists. But a frisky crowd
of noctambulists can be found here, and the terrace is a good spot for
people-watching in fine weather. ⊠ *6 rue Coquillière,* ☎ *01–42–36–
11–75. AE, DC, MC, V. Métro: Les Halles.*

$$ ✕ **Gaya.** Come here for seafood in all its guises, from marinated an-
chovies to fish soup to grilled sole—much of it with a Mediterranean
accent. The colorful Portuguese *azulejos* (tiles) on the ground floor are
delightful; upstairs is less attractive. ⊠ *17 rue Duphot,* ☎ *01–42–60–
43–03. AE, MC, V. Closed Sun. Métro: Madeleine.*

$$ ✕ **Le Grand Louvre.** The austere metal-and-wood decor is in keeping
with this restaurant's location under the pyramid of the Louvre. Cui-
sine from southwest France predominates and includes foie gras with
raisins, pigeon terrine with walnuts, and prune ice cream with Armagnac.
After dinner, the hushed, illuminated pyramid will seem to belong to
you alone. ⊠ *Louvre,* ☎ *01–40–20–53–41. Reservations 48 hrs in
advance essential. AE, DC, MC, V. Closed Tues. Métro: Palais-Royal.*

$$ ✕ **Il Ristorantino.** Chef Ciro Polge serves some of the best Italian food
in Paris at this small place done in minimalist Milanese style. His three
course, 140-franc dinner menu is an excellent value. The fettucine
with a ragu of shellfish in a rich tomato sauce and the *fritto misto* (vegetables dipped in a delicate batter and fried) are particularly good. The

wine list is excellent, if short on affordable bottles. ⊠ *6 rue d'Argenteuil,* ☎ *01–42–60–56–22. AE, DC, MC, V. Closed Sun. No lunch Sat. Métro: Louvre.*

$$ ✕ **Restaurant du Palais-Royal.** Tucked away in the northern corner of the magnificent Palais-Royal garden, this pleasant bistro has a charming terrace and good food. A salad of baby scallops and mushrooms in a balsamic vinaigrette are among the interesting contemporary dishes. Find a perfect wine to match from the appealing list. It's a wonderful spot for a romantic tête-à-tête. ⊠ *Jardins du Palais-Royal, 110 Galerie Valois,* ☎ *01–40–20–00–27. AE, MC, V. Closed Sun. No lunch Sat. Métro: Palais-Royal.*

$$ ✕ **Saudade.** This charming Portuguese restaurant, with fado (traditional music) tapes and compositions of *azuelos* (decorative tiles), serves superb caldo verde, a delicate soup of bouillon, potatoes, kale, and chorizo sausage. You can also choose from 20 different cod dishes: The *bacalhau a bras,* for example, is a delicious combination of salt cod, potatoes, onions, and eggs. Or try the roast suckling pig with a spicy vinaigrette. The Portuguese wines are excellent, as is the service. ⊠ *34 rue des Bourdonnais,* ☎ *01–42–36–30–71. AE, DC, MC, V. Closed Sun. Métro: Les Halles.*

$–$$ ✕ **Aux Crus de Bourgogne.** The din of a happy crowd fills this delightful, old-fashioned bistro with bright lights and red-checker tablecloths. It opened in 1932 and quickly became popular by serving two luxury items—foie gras and cold lobster with homemade mayonnaise—at surprisingly low prices, a tradition that happily continues. Among the bistro classics on the menu, the *boeuf au gros sel* (beef boiled in bouillon with vegetables and garnished with rock salt) and *confit de canard* (duck confit) are very satisfying. Tempting desserts include fruit tarts, flan, and chocolate mousse. ⊠ *3 rue Bachaumont,* ☎ *01–42–33–48–24. V. Closed weekends and Aug. Métro: Sentier.*

$–$$ ✕ **Fellini.** Come to this friendly Italian restaurant with exposed stone walls and pink napery for a salad and pasta. The antipasto buffet is wonderfully varied and the spaghetti with baby clams delicious. The veal dishes are good, too. Offbeat wines from Sardinia or Ischia complete the meal. ⊠ *47 rue de l'Arbre Sec,* ☎ *01–42–60–90–66, métro: Louvre;* ⊠ *58 rue de la Croix-Nivert,* ☎ *01–45–77–40–77, métro: Commerce. MC, V. Closed Sun. No lunch Sat. at Croix-Nivert.*

$–$$ ✕ **La Tour du Montlhéry.** When the centuries-old Les Halles marketplace became an aseptic shopping mall, many neighborhood bistros closed or went upscale. The Montlhéry managed to hang on to the old-market feel, with its sagging wood-beamed ceilings, red-checker tablecloths, and exposed brick walls lined with imaginative portraits. If you don't mind passing under hanging samples of your future meal (sausages, etc.) on your way into the dining room, jovial waiters will serve you simple grilled food. Choose the *côte de boeuf* (prime rib) and wash it down with a good Beaujolais. ⊠ *5 rue des Prouvaires,* ☎ *01–42–36–21–82. MC, V. Closed weekends and July 14–Aug. 15. Métro: Les Halles.*

$–$$ ✕ **Willi's Wine Bar.** This English-owned wine bar, a renowned haunt for Anglophiles as well as chic Parisians, is a phenomenon. The simple, often original menu changes to reflect the market's offerings and might include chicken liver terrine, sea trout with lemon butter, and crème brûlée. The wine list includes more than 250 listings with an emphasis on Rhônes. The quality of the service can vary. ⊠ *13 rue des Petits-Champs,* ☎ *01–42–61–05–09. MC, V. Closed Sun. Métro: Bourse.*

$ ✗ **A la Cloche des Halles.** Forgive the tacky decor and enjoy quiches, omelets, and assortments of high-quality cheeses and charcuterie at this small, popular wine bar. Served by the glass or bottle, wines include some good Beaujolais. Get here by 12:30 PM for lunch—even better, make a reservation. The simple menu is served until 10 PM. ⊠ *28 rue Coquillière,* ☎ *01–42–36–93–89. No credit cards. Closed Sun. Métro: Les Halles.*

$ ✗ **Batifol.** Tourists and businesspeople come together comfortably in the bright, spacious original of what is now a popular Parisian chain. "Batifol" refers to a musical bistro: This modern interpretation carries on the tradition with brass instruments and music-theme prints on the walls. This is an agreeable place for solo diners, who can have a full meal or snack at the counter, in the company of the friendly bartenders. The food is nothing spectacular, but it's a good value and a trusty standby. ⊠ *14 rue Montédour,* ☎ *01–42–36–85–50. AE, DC, MC, V. Métro: Etienne-Marcel.*

$ ✗ **Café Marly.** The latest venture of the Costes brothers, owners of the famous, now closed Café Costes, is one of the chicest places in Paris for a drink or a light meal—perhaps an omelet or a salad. The splendid view of the Louvre Pyramid and—depending on where you're sitting—the Eiffel Tower makes this one of the best fresh-air venues in Paris. Inside, the ebonized moldings and crimson walls create a dramatic mood at night. ⊠ *Musée du Louvre, Cour Napoléon, 93 rue de Rivoli,* ☎ *01–49–26–06–60. MC, V. Reservations not accepted. Métro: Palais-Royal.*

$ ✗ **Le Moi.** At this superb Vietnamese restaurant, you can sample *nems* (deep-fried mini spring rolls), steamed dumplings. The poultry, beef, or seafood salads are enlivened with fresh Asian herbs like lemongrass and lemon basil. Service is prompt and friendly. ⊠ *5 rue Danou,* ☎ *01–47–03–92–05. MC, V. Closed Sun. No lunch Sat. Métro: Opéra.*

$ ✗ **Le Rubis.** This humble neighborhood wine bar enjoys tremendous popularity with everyone from executives to laborers. One or two hearty plats du jour, such as *petit salé* (salted, slow-cooked pork ribs) with lentils and *boudin noir* (blood sausage), plus omelets, cheeses, and charcuterie make up the menu. There's an eclectic selection of adequate wines by the glass or bottle. ⊠ *10 rue du Marché St-Honoré,* ☎ *01–42–61–03–34. Reservations not accepted. No credit cards. Closed Sun. and mid-Aug. No dinner Sat. Métro: Tuileries.*

$ ✗ **La Taverne Henri IV.** An excellent choice for a quick lunch or snack, this informal wine bar with rustic charm is near the Pont Neuf, on the tip of the Ile de la Cité. No full meals are served, but a selection of openface sandwiches on Poilâne bread (from the celebrated bakery), cheese and charcuterie plates, and varied wines by the glass or bottle make for a satisfying meal. Reservations are advised for lunch. ⊠ *13 pl. du Pont Neuf,* ☎ *01–43–54–27–90. No credit cards. Closed Sun. and Aug. No dinner Sat. Métro: Pont-Neuf.*

2ᵉ Arrondissement (Le Bourse)
See Right Bank Dining map.

$$ ✗ **Chez Georges.** The food isn't bad, but the atmosphere is better. A wood-paneled entry leads you to an elegant and unpretentious dining room. One long, white-clothed stretch of table lines the mirrored walls, and attentive waiters sweep efficiently along the entire length. Enjoy the herring, sole, kidneys, and frites. ⊠ *1 rue du Mail,* ☎ *01–42–60–07–11. AE, DC, MC, V. Closed Sun. and Aug. Métro: Sentier.*

$$ ✗ **Le Vaudeville.** One of Jean-Paul Bucher's six Parisian brasseries, the Vaudeville has a good-looking clientele (many of them from the Stock Exchange across the street) and is an excellent value, thanks to its assortment of prix-fixe menus. Shellfish, house-smoked salmon, and

desserts such as profiteroles are particularly fine. You can enjoy the handsome 1930s decor and joyful din until 2 AM daily. ⊠ *29 rue Vivienne,* ☎ *01–40–20–04–62. AE, DC, MC, V. Closed Dec. 24. Métro: Bourse.*

$–$$ ✕ **Le Brin de Zinc et Madame.** A bustling old-fashioned place with a
★ diverse, lively crowd of regulars, this spot is ideal for an easygoing night on the town when you're hungry but don't want to spend too much money. The decor and the service are a bit rough-and-tumble, but the food is delicious and generously portioned. Salads are huge, fresh, and interesting. Main dishes, such as grilled salmon or roast chicken, are served with sautéed potatoes and vegetables. The excellent tarts are homemade. ⊠ *50 rue Montorgueil,* ☎ *01–42–21–10–80. AE, MC, V. No lunch Sun. Métro: Etienne-Marcel.*

$ ✕ **Café Runtz.** Next to the Salle Favart, in a neighborhood once filled with theaters, this friendly bistro with rich *boiseries* (woodwork) and photos of customers from the entertainment industry serves Alsatian cuisine. Tasty, hearty dishes include Gruyère salad, onion tart, choucroute, and fresh fruit tarts. Order a *pichet* (pitcher) of Riesling or other Alsatian wine. ⊠ *16 rue Favart,* ☎ *01–42–96–69–86. AE, MC, V. Closed weekends and Aug. Métro: Richelieu-Drouot.*

3e Arrondissement (Beaubourg/Marais)
See Right Bank Dining map.

$$ ✕ **Chez Janou.** With its pretty art-nouveau tiles and potted plants, this tiny place is the very definition of a neighborhood bistro. Check the daily specials—in season, try the sautéed wild mushrooms—or homey classics, like confit de canard or hearty braised veal shank. The house foie gras and salads are quite good, too. Soothing homemade desserts and a lovely quiet terrace in summer complete the picture. ⊠ *2 rue Roger-Verlomme,* ☎ *01–42–72–28–41. MC, V. Closed weekends. Métro: Bastille.*

$ ✕ **Au Bascou.** Gregarious proprietor Jean-Guy Lousteau enthusiastically shares his knowledge of the wines of southwest France at this fashionable little bistro with mosaics made of broken mirrors. The sturdy, savory cuisine of the Basque country stars on the menu, and the country ham, cod with broccoli puree, and sautéed baby squid are particularly flavorful. ⊠ *38 rue Reaumur,* ☎ *01–42–72–69–25. MC, V. Closed weekends. Métro: Arts et Métiers.*

$ ✕ **Chez Jenny.** Since the installation of a rotisserie grill, this place is home to what is probably the most delicious choucroute *garnie* (with sausage) in the capital. The sauerkraut, delivered weekly by a private supplier in Alsace, is garnished with a variety of Alsatian charcuterie and a big grilled ham knuckle. For dessert, the perfectly aged Muenster cheese or homemade blueberry tart are good choices. The ambience is lively. ⊠ *39 bd. du Temple,* ☎ *01–42–74–75–75. AE, DC, MC, V. Métro: République.*

$ ✕ **Chez Omar.** Whether you're a die-hard couscous fan or have never tried it before, this is the place for this signature North African dish. Order it with grilled skewered lamb, spicy *merguez* sausage, a lamb shank, or chicken—portions are generous. For dessert, try a North African pastry. The restaurant, in a former turn-of-the-century bistro, is popular with a fashionable crowd. Proprietor Omar Guerida is famously friendly and speaks English. ⊠ *47 rue de Bretagne,* ☎ *01–42–72–36–26. MC, V. No lunch Sun. Métro: Filles du Calvaire.*

4e Arrondissement (Marais/Ile St-Louis)
See Right Bank Dining map.

$$$$ ✕ **L'Ambroisie.** This tiny, romantic restaurant on the patrician place des Vosges is one of the best in Paris. Chef-owner Bernard Pacaud's refined, oft-imitated cuisine, including such dishes as mousse of red bell peppers and braised oxtail, is served in a jewel-like Italianate setting of flowers, tapestries, and subdued lighting. ⊠ *9 pl. des Vosges,* ☎ *01–42–78–51–45. Reservations 1 month in advance essential. MC, V. Closed Sun., Mon., Aug., and mid-Feb. Métro: St-Paul.*

$$ ✕ **Au Bourguignon du Marais.** The handsome, contemporary decor of
★ this Marais bistro and wine bar offers a perfect backdrop for the good, traditional fare and excellent Burgundies served by the glass and bottle. Excellent choices are the smoked salmon, the fricasee of cèpe and girolles mushrooms, the reasonably priced escargots, and the nicely seasoned steak tartare. ⊠ *19 rue de Jouy,* ☎ *01–48–87–15–40. MC, V. Closed Sun. Métro: St-Paul.*

$$ ✕ **Le Grizzli.** It's said that this turn-of-the-century bistro used to have dancing bears—thus the name. The owner gets many of his ingredients—especially the wonderful ham and cheeses—from his native Auvergne. Several dishes are cooked on a hot slate, including the salmon and the lamb. There's an interesting selection of wines from southwest France. ⊠ *7 rue St-Martin,* ☎ *01–48–87–77–56. MC, V. Closed Sun. Métro: Châtelet.*

$$ ✕ **Il Vicolo.** Low-key but stylish, with a trendy, young crowd, this restaurant serves authentic and very good contemporary Italian cuisine. It's ideal for a night off from French food. The spicy chickpea soup is delicious, as is the Livorno-style red mullet, which is served in a sauce of wine and herbs. Good desserts and a nice Italian wine list finish off the evening. ⊠ *8 rue de Jouy,* ☎ *01–42–78–38–85. MC, V. Closed Sun., Mon. Métro: St-Paul.*

$$ ✕ **Le Maraîcher.** With its exposed stone walls and wood beams, this intimate restaurant on a quiet street in the Marais is very *vieux Paris.* The owner worked at the renowned Lucas-Carton, which may account for the table settings and service, which are surprisingly refined considering the reasonable prices. Roasted lamb fillet with eggplant and coquilles St-Jacques with potato pulp in a balsamic vinaigrette are good choices. For dessert, go for the caramelized apple mille-feuille or the bittersweet chocolate mousse. ⊠ *5 rue Beautreillis,* ☎ *01–42–71–42–49. MC, V. Closed Sun., late July–early Aug. No lunch Sat. Métro: Sully-Morland.*

$$ ✕ **Le Vieux Bistro.** Overlook the touristy location next to Notre-Dame and the corny name, "the old bistro." This place really *is* generations old, and its menu is full of bistro classics, such as beef fillet with marrow, éclairs, and tart tatine. The decor is nondescript, but the frequently fancy crowd doesn't seem to notice. ⊠ *14 rue du Cloître-Notre-Dame,* ☎ *01–43–54–18–95. MC, V. Métro: Hôtel de Ville.*

$–$$ ✕ **Bofinger.** One of the oldest, most beautiful, and most popular brasseries in Paris has been much improved since brasserie maestro Jean-Paul Bucher took over. Settle in to one of the tables dressed in crisp white linens, under the gorgeous art-nouveau glass cupola, and enjoy fine classic brasserie fare, such as oysters, grilled sole, or fillet of lamb. The house Muscadet is a good white wine, the Fleurie is a pleasant red. Note that the no-smoking section here is not only enforced, but is also in the prettiest part of the restaurant. ⊠ *5–7 rue de la Bastille,* ☎ *01–42–72–87–82. AE, DC, MC, V. Métro: Bastille.*

$ ✕ **Baracane.** The owner of this small, simple place oversees the menu of robust specialties of his native southwest France, including rabbit confit, veal tongue, and pear poached in wine and cassis. A reasonable dinner menu and cheaper menu at lunch keep the Baracane solidly affordable and one of the best values in the Marais. Service is friendly. ⊠ *38 rue des Tournelles,* ☎ *01–42–71–43–33. MC, V. Closed Sun. No lunch Sat. Métro: Bastille.*

$ ✕ **La Truffe.** In this attractive open-space restaurant with a mezzanine, you can find organic, vegetarian food that is prepared without fat or steaming—they use special cooking equipment so that the grains, mushrooms, and vegetables conserve their taste and vitamins. Smoking is not allowed. ⊠ *31 rue Vieille-du-Temple,* ☎ *01–42–71–08– 39. MC, V. Métro: St-Paul.*

$ ✕ **Trumilou.** The Trumilou is unremarkable. Yet the crowds of students, artist types, and others on a budget come to eat bistro cuisine, such as leg of lamb and apple tart. The homely nondecor is somehow homey, the staff is friendly, and the location facing the Seine and the Ile St-Louis is especially pleasant in nice weather, when you can sit on the narrow terrace under the trees. ⊠ *84 quai de l'Hôtel de Ville,* ☎ *01– 42–77–63–98. MC, V. Closed Mon. Métro: Pont-Marie.*

5e Arrondissement (Latin Quarter)
See Left Bank Dining map.

$$$$ ✕ **La Tour d'Argent.** Dining at this temple to haute cuisine is an event— from apéritifs in the ground-floor bar to dinner in the top-floor dining room, with its breathtaking view of Notre-Dame. The food, unfortunately, does not reach the same heights as the setting. La Tour classics such as *caneton Tour d'Argent* (pressed duck) and *filets de sole Cardinal* have been lightened and contemporary creations added, including scallop salad with truffles. The wine list is one of the greatest in the world—visit the cellars before or after your meal. The lunch menu is relatively affordable. ⊠ *15 quai de la Tournelle,* ☎ *01–43–54–23– 31. Reservations essential at least 1 wk in advance. Jacket and tie at dinner. AE, DC, MC, V. Closed Mon. Métro: Cardinal Lemoine.*

$$–$$$ ✕ **La Timonerie.** Only a few steps along the quai from La Tour d'Argent, this small, elegant restaurant has fine cooking and no theatrics. Philippe de Givenchy works with a small staff, and his creations are consistently interesting and well executed. In his hands, a simple dish such as rosemary and lemon mackerel reaches new levels of refinement. ⊠ *35 quai de la Tournelle,* ☎ *01–43–25–44–42. Jacket and tie. MC, V. Closed Sun., Mon. Métro: Maubert-Mutualité.*

$$ ✕ **Campagne et Provence.** On the quai across from Notre-Dame, this very pleasant little restaurant with rustic Provençal fabrics and blue grass-cloth wallpaper has a Provençal menu that includes grilled John Dory with preserved fennel, and peppers stuffed with cod and eggplant. In season, have the roasted figs with shortbread and black-currant sauce, an outstanding dessert. The interesting, well-priced list of regional wines adds to the dining experience. ⊠ *25 quai de la Tournelle,* ☎ *01– 43–54–05–17. MC, V. Closed Sun. No lunch Sat., Mon. Métro: Maubert-Mutualité.*

$$ ✕ **Chez René.** This reliable address at the eastern end of boulevard St-Germain has satisfied three generations of Parisians, who count on finding dishes from Burgundy, such as *boeuf Bourguignon* (beef stewed in wine) and coq au vin, along with the wines of the Mâconnais and Beaujolais. The dining rooms are cozy, with red leatherette banquettes and white honeycomb tile floors. ⊠ *14 bd. St-Germain,* ☎ *01–43–54– 30–23. MC, V. Closed weekends, Aug., and late Dec.–early Jan. Métro: Cardinal Lemoine.*

$ ✕ **Chantairelle.** Delicious south-central Auvergne cuisine is offered at
★ this friendly, good-value restaurant. The owners want you to fully experience the region, hence the decor: recycled barn timbers and a little stone fountain, along with a selection of essential oils diffusing local scents. This is hearty, rustic food, so only order an appetizer if you're really hungry. The copious main courses include stuffed cabbage and *potée,* a casserole of pork and vegetables in broth. Try a bottle of

Châteauguy, a regional red, and finish up with blueberry tart. ✉ *17 rue Laplace,* ☎ *01–46–33–18–59. MC, V. Closed Sun. No lunch Sat. Métro: Maubert-Mutualité.*

$ ✕ **Chez Toutoune.** This spacious restaurant with a cheery Provençal theme is owned and run by Colette Toutoune, one of the most respected female chefs in Paris. All meals begin with complimentary soup—usually vegetable. Appetizers include tabbouleh garnished with plump shrimp and fresh herbs. The main course may be roasted salmon with tomato confit or veal kidneys with bacon and spinach. For dessert, the chocolate tart is superb. Consider splurging on a bottle of velvety, red Domaine de la Bernarde 1991 from the admirable wine list. The prix-fixe menu is an excellent value. ✉ *5 rue de Pontoise,* ☎ *01–43–26–56–81. AE, MC, V. Closed Sun., Mon., and Aug. Métro: Maubert-Mutualité.*

$ ✕ **Mirama.** Regulars at this popular and rather chaotic Chinese restaurant order the soup, a rich broth with a nest of thick noodles garnished with dumplings, barbecued pork, or smoked duck. Main courses are generous, and the best are made with shellfish; the Peking duck is also excellent. It's a good place for someone eating alone. Service is brisk, so plan on coffee in a nearby café. ✉ *17 rue St-Jacques,* ☎ *01–43–29–66–58. V. Métro: St-Michel.*

6ᵉ Arrondissement (St-Germain-des-Prés)
See Left Bank Dining map.

$$ ✕ **La Bastide Odéon.** This little corner of Provence in Paris is just a
★ few steps from the Luxembourg Gardens. A sunny yellow restaurant with old oak tables and chairs, it is one of the best places to sample Mediterranean cuisine. Chef Gilles Ajuelos cooks fine fish dishes; wonderful pastas, such as tagliatelle in *pistou* (basil and pine nuts) with wild mushrooms; and delightful main courses, like peppered tuna steak with ratatouille and roast cod with capers. The best bet on the slightly pricey wine list is the red Côteaux du Tricastin. ✉ *7 rue Corneille,* ☎ *01–43–26–03–65. MC, V. Closed weekends. Métro: Odéon; RER: Luxembourg.*

$$ ✕ **Les Bookinistes.** Talented chef Guy Savoy's fifth bistro is a big success with locals. The cheery postmodern dining room, painted peach, with red, blue, and yellow wall sconces, looks out on the Seine. The French country menu changes seasonally and might include a mussel and pumpkin soup or baby chicken roasted in a casserole with root vegetables. The somewhat pricey wine list contrasts with the reasonable food prices. Service is friendly and efficient. ✉ *53 quai des Grands-Augustins,* ☎ *01–43–25–45–94. AE, DC, MC, V. Closed Sun. No lunch Sat. Métro: St-Michel.*

$$ ✕ **Chez Dumonet–Josephine.** Stylish and bursting with conviviality, this venerable bistro with amber walls, moleskin banquettes, and frosted glass lamps offers generous portions of classic cuisine: The very good boeuf Bourguignon and roasted saddle of lamb with artichokes are typical. The wine list is excellent but expensive. French theater people and politicians are frequent clientele. ✉ *117 rue du Cherche-Midi,* ☎ *01–45–48–52–40. AE, DC, MC, V. Closed weekends. Métro: Duroc.*

$$ ✕ **L'Epi Dupin.** Half-timbered walls, sisal carpeting, and crisp white table linens are the backdrop for this bistro that draws a loyal business crowd at noon and chic locals at night. The menu of delicious and reasonably priced French classics is revised regularly and might include mixed green salad garnished with foie gras and fillet of lamb with ratatouille. Bread and pastries are baked on the premises. The prix-fixe menu is an excellent option, and the waiters are friendly. ✉ *11 rue Dupin,* ☎ *01–42–22–64–56. Reservations essential. MC, V. Closed Sun. Métro: Sèvres-Babylone.*

$$ ✕ **Le Petit Zinc.** The extravagant fin-de-siècle style of this restaurant, just around the corner from two of the most famous cafés in St-Germain, makes the ambience festive. The kitchen does a creditable job with shellfish, veal liver, and duck confit. Careful ordering will lessen the cost of your meal. ⊠ *11 rue St-Benoît,* ☎ *01–42–61–20–60. AE, DC, MC, V. Métro: St-Germain-des-Prés.*

$–$$ ✕ **Le Bouillon Racine.** Originally a *bouillon,* a Parisian soup restaurant popular at the turn of the century, this two-story place is now a delightfully renovated Belle Epoque oasis with a good Belgian menu. The terrine of leeks and the ham mousse are fine starters; the *waterzooie,* Belgian stewed chicken and vegetables, and the roast cod with white beans, are excellent main dishes. The moka-beer mousse with malt sauce is one of the many superb desserts. In honor of Belgium's some 400 different brews, there's a wonderful selection of beers. ⊠ *3 rue Racine,* ☎ *01–44–32–15–60. Reservations essential. AE, MC, V. Closed Sun. Métro: Odéon.*

$–$$ ✕ **Le Comptoir des Sports.** If you took an American-style sports bar and Frenchified it, you might end up with something like this small, pleasant, good-value bistro with sports memorabilia decorating the exposed-stone walls. The short menu changes regularly, but might include lentil soup, salmon tartare, or steak with chorizo-sausage sauce. Chocolate fondant and a mille-feuille of spice bread are typical desserts. ⊠ *3 rue Hautefeuille,* ☎ *01–43–26–93–78. Reservations essential. MC, V. Closed Sat., Sun. Métro: Odéon.*

$ ✕ **Bistro Mazarin.** Leave the tourists on boulevard St-Germain and join the locals at this casual, bustling bistro for good house wines and sturdy food that's especially satisfying given the prices. Lentil salad, a steak with frites, and a pitcher of the house red make for a pleasant meal. When the weather is good, food is served on the terrace. ⊠ *42 rue Mazarine,* ☎ *01–43–29–99–01. MC, V. Closed Sun. Métro: Mabillon.*

$ ✕ **Claude Sainlouis.** Claude Piau has served the same dependable food for a very long time: inexpensive steak, fries, and salad. There's not much variety, but all of Paris—professionals, tourists, lovers—crowds boisterously into the dark, red dining room for lunch and dinner. ⊠ *27 rue du Dragon,* ☎ *01–45–48–29–68. No credit cards. Closed Sun., Aug., and 15 days at Easter and Christmas. No dinner Sat. Métro: St-Germain-des-Prés.*

7ᵉ Arrondissement (Invalides)
See Left Bank Dining map.

$$$$ ✕ **L'Arpège.** It's one block from the Rodin Museum and has an unusually minimalist decor of curving, handcrafted wood panels and wrought-iron window frames. Chef-owner Alain Passard's cuisine is both original (lobster-turnip starter in a sweet-sour vinaigrette, stuffed sweet tomato) and classic (beef Burgundy, pressed duck). Passard is a very talented chef, but this restaurant doesn't quite deliver the same streamlined haute cuisine experience found elsewhere, mainly because the service is often cold and bumbling. Brave it, though, for some splendid food. The prix-fixe lunch is a bargain at 320 francs. ⊠ *84 rue de Varenne,* ☎ *01–45–51–47–33. AE, DC, MC, V. Closed Aug. No lunch weekends. Métro: Varenne.*

$$$$ ✕ **Jules Verne.** Distinctive all-black decor, stylish service, and top-ranked chef Alain Reix's cuisine—not to mention a location at 400 feet, on the second level of the Eiffel Tower—make the Jules Verne one of the hardest dinner reservations to get in Paris. Soufflé of giant crab and lobster tournedos in a veal and butter sauce are examples of Reix's colorful, flavorful dishes. Come for lunch—a table is easier to snag. ⊠

Eiffel Tower, ☎ *01–45–55–61–44. Reservations essential (reserve 2 months in advance for dinner at window table). Jacket and tie. AE, DC, MC, V. Métro: Bir-Hakeim.*

$$$–$$$$ ✕ **Paul Minchelli.** Don't come to this very sleek restaurant expecting elaborate sauces—Minchelli is a minimalist who believes that seasonings should not distract from the taste of his impeccably fresh catch-of-the-day. The baby clams with garlic and fiery espelette peppers as well as the sea bass drizzled with lemon and olive oil are just a few of his wonderful dishes. The dressy dining room with gentle lighting and witty trompe l'oeil "views" out of "portholes" is the backdrop for a very stylish crowd, often sprinkled with celebrities like actress Catherine Deneuve. ✉ *54 bd. de La Tour-Maubourg,* ☎ *01–47–05–89–86. MC, V. Closed Sun., Mon. Métro: École Militaire.*

$$ ✕ **L'Affriole.** At this bustling bistro, friendly service and attractive decor—elaborate Belle Epoque plaster moldings, mirrors, and deco-style chandeliers—create an appealing atmosphere in which to sample good, contemporary bistro cooking. The menu changes weekly, but dishes like fricasee of langoustines with swiss chard, and baby cabbage stuffed with veal and herbs show the chef's style. Wine by the glass is served, as is an admirable assortment of reasonably priced bottles (the best is the red Coteaux de Tricastin for 80 francs). ✉ *17 rue Malar,* ☎ *01–44–18–31–33. MC, V. Closed Sun. Métro: La Tour Maubourg.*

$–$$ ✕ **Au Bon Accueil.** If you want to see what well-heeled Parisians like
★   to eat these days, book a table at this extremely popular bistro as soon as you get to town. The excellent, reasonably priced *cuisine du marché* (daily menu based on what's in the markets) has made it a hit. Desserts are homemade and delicious, from the fruit tarts to the superb *pistache,* a pastry curl filled with homemade pistachio ice cream. The Château Mont Redon Côtes du Rhône is a standout on the wine list. ✉ *14 rue de Montessuy,* ☎ *01–47–05–46–11. Reservations essential. MC, V. Closed Sun. Métro, RER: Pont l'Alma.*

$–$$ ✕ **Le Bambouche.** Ocher walls, chairs skirted in cinnamon-color cotton, and contemporary flower arrangements create the ambience for this chic and cozy restaurant. The menu changes at the start of every season; good examples of chef David Van Laer's innovative bistro cooking are sweet-and-sour duck foie gras and codfish in a crust of spices. Don't skip the well-chosen wine list or the cheese, which comes from Barthelemy, one of the best fromageries in Paris. ✉ *15 rue de Babylone,* ☎ *01–45–49–14–40. AE, MC, V. Closed Fri., Sat. Métro: Sèvres-Babylone.*

$–$$ ✕ **L'Oeillade.** Sample the avocado beignets and the coquilles St-Jacques with endive fondue at this restaurant with generally good food at good prices. Watch out for the wines—they will intoxicate your bill. The decor of blond-wood paneling and interesting 20th-century paintings is unpretentious—the same cannot always be said about the clientele. ✉ *10 rue de St-Simon,* ☎ *01–42–22–01–60. MC, V. Closed Sun. No lunch Sat. Métro: Rue du Bac.*

$–$$ ✕ **Les Olivades.** Excellent Provençal dishes are served in this brightly decorated former storefront café with a cheerful staff. Start with the ravioli stuffed with goat cheese; follow with the scallops with vegetables. The *pain perdu* (French toast) drizzled with chestnut-blossom honey makes a fine finale. The three-course dinner and two-course lunch menus offer good value. ✉ *41 av. Segur,* ☎ *01–47–83–70–09. Reservations essential. MC, V. Closed Sun. No lunch Sat. Métro: Ségur, École Militaire.*

$ ✕ **Chez l'Ami Jean.** It's easy to see why neighborhood families compose a large portion of the clientele at this welcoming, homey Basque restaurant. The haphazard decor includes banners, baskets, and photos of the staff and regulars. Enjoy the *piperade* (eggs with ham, tomatoes, and green peppers), duck or goose confits, and the nutty *gâteau Basque* for dessert. ✉ *27 rue Malar,* ☎ *01–47–05–86–89. MC, V. Closed Sun. and Aug. Métro: La Tour–Maubourg.*

$ ✕ **Thoumieux.** Foie gras, rillettes, duck confit, cassoulet, and superb desserts are all made on the premises at this third-generation restaurant. The red velour banquettes, yellow walls, and bustling waiters in long, white aprons are delightfully Parisian. ✉ *79 rue St-Dominique,* ☎ *01–47–05–49–75. MC, V. Métro: Invalides.*

8ᵉ Arrondissement (Champs-Elysées)

See Right Bank Dining map.

$$$$ ✕ **Les Ambassadeurs.** This hotel restaurant in the opulent Crillon hotel is undoubtedly the finest in Paris. Respected chef Christian Constant is a master at giving even the humblest ingredients sophistication, as exemplified by his petit salé of cod, rabbit with marjoram, and pork with spider crab. Some find the all-marble dining room, with its crystal chandeliers, mirrors, and heavy blue draperies, stiff and inhospitable. But no one can fault the view onto place de la Concorde, the distinguished service, or the memorable wine list. Lunch is more affordable, though still expensive; there's also a good brunch. ✉ *10 pl. de la Concorde,* ☎ *01–44–71–16–16. Reservations essential. Jacket and tie at dinner. AE, DC, MC, V. Métro: Concorde.*

$$$$ ✕ **Ledoyen.** Chef Ghislaine Arabian has set gastronomic fashion by concentrating on northern French cuisine and creating specialties with beer sauces, such as coquilles St-Jacques *à la bière* (cooked in beer). The elegant restaurant has gilded ceilings and walls, plush armchairs, and tables with candelabra. It's off the Champs-Elysées near place de la Concorde. ✉ *1 av. du Tuit, on the Carré des Champs-Elysées,* ☎ *01–47–42–23–23. Reservations essential. AE, DC, MC, V. Closed weekends. Métro: Place de la Concorde or Champs-Elysées–Clemenceau.*

$$$$ ✕ **Lucas-Carton.** Foie gras wrapped in cabbage, a spicy duck Apicius, and pastille of rabbit are examples of chef Alain Senderens's provocative blend of nouvelle and classic cuisine. For wine lovers, Senderens has created a special menu: Each course is accompanied by a precisely chosen wine. The beautiful dining rooms glow with Belle Epoque splendor, and the international crowd is one of the dressiest in Paris. ✉ *9 pl. de la Madeleine,* ☎ *01–42–65–22–90. Reservations at least 3 wks in advance essential. Jacket and tie at dinner. MC, V. Closed Sun., Christmas wk, and Aug. No lunch Sat. Métro: Madeleine.*

$$$$ ✕ **Pierre Gagnaire.** Legendary chef Pierre Gagnaire's cooking is at once
★ intellectual and poetic—in a single dish at least three or four often unexpected tastes and textures are brought together in a sensational experience. Two intriguing dishes from a recent menu—it changes seasonally—included duck foie gras wrapped in bacon and lacquered like a Chinese duck, and sea bass smothered in herbs with tiny clams. The *Grand Dessert*, a five course presentation of different desserts, is not to be missed. The only drawback is the amateurish service and the puzzlingly brief wine list. ✉ *6 rue de Balzac,* ☎ *01–44–35–18–25. Reservations essential. AE, DC, MC, V. Closed Sun. Métro: Charles-de-Gaulle–Etoile.*

$$$$ ✕ **Taillevent.** Many say it's the best restaurant in Paris. Dining in the paneled rooms of this mid-19th-century mansion is certainly a sublime experience. Service is exceptional, the wine list stellar, and the classical French cuisine perfect. Among the signature dishes are cream of watercress soup with caviar and truffled tart of game. Desserts are also superb, especially the creamy chocolate tart served with thyme ice cream. ✉ *15 rue Lamennais,* ☎ *01–45–63–39–94. Reservations 3–*

*4 wks in advance essential. Jacket and tie. AE, MC, V. Closed week-
ends and Aug. Métro: Charles de Gaulle–Etoile.*

$$$ ✕ **L'Astor.** Chef Eric Lecerf pays hommage to his mentor, Joel Robu-
chon by offering some classic Robuchon dishes like cauliflower cream
with caviar and spiced roasted lobster. But he also shows his own tal-
ent with sophisticated offerings like cod steak with cumin. The service
and wine list are superb. Trendy interior designer Frederique Mechiche
is responsible for the look of the spacious and attractive dining room,
which takes a cue from the '30s with star appliqués on the walls and
a checkerboard carpet. ✉ *Hôtel Astor, 11 rue d'Astor,* ☎ *01–53–05–
05–20. AE, DC, MC, V. Métro: Madeleine.*

$$$ ✕ **Le Cercle Ledoyen.** This luxury brasserie is below the landmark
restaurant Ledoyen (☞ *above*). For about $50 a dinner—wine in-
cluded—you can sample chef Ghislaine Arabian's cooking, including
the specials served at Ledoyen. The handsome, curved dining room with
a view of the surrounding park is a pleasure year-round, and the terrace is a special treat in warm weather. ✉ *1 av. Dutuit,* ☎ *01–47–
42–23–23. AE, DC, MC, V. Closed Sun. Métro: Champs-Elysées–
Clemenceau.*

$$–$$$ ✕ **Le Bistrot du Sommelier.** The 30-page wine list is the chief attrac-
tion at this restaurant owned by jolly Philippe Faure-Brac, the world's
Best Sommelier in 1992. He will recommend selections from the Rhône
Valley. Harvest-theme tapestries and frescoes create the backdrop for
the dishes of ravioli with fresh herbs and cheese as well as the fattened
pullet in yellow wine. ✉ *97 bd. Haussmann,* ☎ *01–42–65–24–85.
Reservations essential. AE, DC, MC, V. Closed weekends and Aug.
Métro: St-Augustin.*

$$ ✕ **Androuet.** Ignore the airline-office decor and feast on the vast as-
sortment of beautifully aged fromages at this famous temple to the cheeses
of France. If you really love cheese, or just want to learn more about
it, order the tasting menu, which will take you through the seven main
French types. Also available are a variety of good dishes like lobster
with Roquefort and Camembert croquettes. ✉ *41 rue d'Amsterdam,*
☎ *01–48–74–26–93. AE, DC, MC, V. Closed Sun. Métro: St-Lazare.*

$$ ✕ **La Fermette Marbeuf.** It's a favorite haunt of French TV and movie
stars who like the spectacular Belle Epoque mosaics and stained glass
and appreciate the solid, updated classic cuisine. Try gâteau of chicken
livers and sweetbreads, lamb *navarin* (stew with turnips and potatoes),
and bitter chocolate fondant. Prices here are exceptional, considering
the quality of the food, the surroundings, and the neighborhood. La
Fermette becomes animated around 9 PM. ✉ *5 rue Marbeuf,* ☎ *01–
47–20–63–53. AE, DC, MC, V. Métro: Franklin-D.-Roosevelt.*

$$ ✕ **Savy.** This restaurant still wears an honest, homey face, despite its
rarified location near avenue Montaigne. Expect 1950s decor and sub-
stantial cuisine of central France, such as stuffed cabbage, roast lamb
shoulder, and apple tart. ✉ *23 rue Bayard,* ☎ *01–47–23–46–98. MC,
V. Closed weekends and Aug. Métro: Franklin-D.-Roosevelt.*

$$ ✕ **Sébillon.** The original Sébillon has nurtured chic residents of the fashionable suburb of Neuilly for generations; this elegant, polished branch
off the Champs-Elysées continues the tradition. The menu includes lobster salad, lots of shellfish, and—the specialty—roast leg of lamb sliced
table-side and served in unlimited quantity. Service is notably friendly.
✉ *66 rue Pierre Charron,* ☎ *01–43–59–28–15. AE, DC, MC, V.
Métro: Franklin-D.-Roosevelt.*

$ ✕ **La Ferme St-Hubert.** The owner has a cheese shop next door—one
of the best in the city—and from its shelves come the main ingredients
for fondue, raclette, and the best *croque St-Hubert* (toasted cheese sandwich) in Paris. House wines are decent. Reserve ahead for lunch, when

this unpretentious spot is mobbed. ✉ *21 rue Vignon,* ☎ *01–47–42–79–20. Reservations essential at lunch. AE, MC, V. Closed Sun. Métro: Madeleine.*

$ ✕ **Le Petit Yvan.** Yvan's annex near his eponymous restaurant is a stylish spot for lunch. The decor and the menu are simpler than at Yvan's star-studded outpost. But the cuisine is also very good: The best option is the reasonable prix-fixe menu, which might include lemon-marinated salmon or steak tartare. ✉ *1 bis rue Jean-Mermoz,* ☎ *01–42–89–49–65. MC, V. Closed Sun. No lunch Sat. Métro: St-Philippe-du-Roule.*

9ᵉ Arrondissement (Opéra)
See Right Bank Dining map.

$$ ✕ **Chez Jean.** This tiny, relaxed off-the-beaten-path place has been
★ booked solid ever since it opened, as young, stylish Parisians delight in the creativity of the talented chef and take advantage of his remarkably good-value, 165-franc menu. Some recent selections were a delicious cream of cèpes, John Dory in a crust of potato, and luscious chocolate-and-tea quenelles. ✉ *52 rue Lamartine,* ☎ *01–48–78–62–73. Reservations essential. MC, V. Closed Sun. No lunch Sat. Métro: Cadet.*

$ ✕ **Bistrot des Deux Théâtres.** Quality is high and prices are low at this well-run restaurant in the Pigalle-Clichy area. The prix-fixe menu includes apéritif, first and main dishes, a cheese or dessert course, half a bottle of wine, and coffee. The food—such as foie gras salad, steak with morels, and apple tart flambéed with Calvados—is far from banal. ✉ *18 rue Blanche,* ☎ *01–45–26–41–43. MC, V. Métro: Trinité.*

$ ✕ **Chartier.** People come here more for the bonhomie than the food, which is often rather ordinary. This cavernous turn-of-the-century restaurant enjoys a huge following among budget-minded students, solitary bachelors, and tourists. You may find yourself sharing a table with strangers as you study the long, old-fashioned menu of such favorites as hard-boiled eggs with mayonnaise, steak tartar, and roast chicken with fries. ✉ *7 rue du Faubourg-Montmartre,* ☎ *01–47–70–86–29. Reservations not accepted. No credit cards. Métro: Rue Montmartre.*

10ᵉ Arrondissement (République/Gare du Nord)
See Right Bank Dining map.

$$ ✕ **Brasserie Flo.** The first of brasserie king Jean-Paul Bucher's seven Paris addresses is hard to find down its passageway near Gare de l'Est, but it's worth the effort. The rich wood and stained glass is typically Alsatian, service is enthusiastic, and brasserie standards such as shellfish, steak tartare, and choucroute are savory. Order a carafe of Alsatian wine to go with your meal. It's open until 1:30 AM, with a special night-owl menu from 11 PM. ✉ *7 cour des Petites Ecuries,* ☎ *01–47–70–13–59. AE, DC, MC, V. Métro: Château d'Eau.*

$$ ✕ **Julien.** Another Bucher brasserie, with dazzling Belle Epoque decor, this one is a kind of poor man's Maxim's. Fare includes smoked salmon, foie gras, cassoulet, and sherbets. Diners are ebullient and lots of fun; this place has a strong following with the fashion crowd, so it's mobbed during the biannual fashion and fabric shows. There's service until 1:30 AM, with a special late-night menu from 11 PM. ✉ *16 rue du Faubourg St-Denis,* ☎ *01–47–70–12–06. AE, DC, MC, V. Métro: Strasbourg–St-Denis.*

$–$$ ✕ **Chez Michel.** If you're gastronomically intrepid—willing to go out
★ of your way for excellent food at fair prices even if the decor and the out-of-the-way neighborhood are drab—then this place is for you. Chef Thierry Breton pulls a stylish crowd of Parisians with his wonderful

cuisine du marché and dishes from his native Brittany. Typical of Breton's kitchen are the lasagna stuffed with chèvre cheese and the artichokes and tuna steak with pureed peas. ☒ *10 rue Belzunce,* ☎
*01–44–53–06–20. Reservations essential. MC, V. Closed Sun., Mon.
No lunch Sat. Métro: Gare du Nord.*

$ ✕ **Au Vieux Bistrot.** If you're staying near the Gare du Nord or look-
ing for a meal in the area before taking the train, this pleasant, old-
fashioned neighborhood bistro is a good bet. From the big zinc bar to
the steak with mushroom sauce and veal in cream, this place delivers
a traditional bistro experience. Finish up with the fruit tart. Service is
friendly. ☒ *30 rue Dunkerque,* ☎ *01–48–78–48–01. MC, V. Closed
Sun. No dinner Sat. Métro: Gare du Nord.*

11ᵉ Arrondissement (Bastille/République)
See Right Bank Dining map.

$$ ✕ **Chardenoux.** A bit off the beaten track but well worth the effort,
this cozy neighborhood bistro with etched-glass windows, dark bent-
wood furniture, and a long zinc bar attracts a cross section of savvy
Parisians. The traditional cooking is first-rate: Start with one of the
delicious salads, such as the green beans and foie gras, and then sam-
ple the veal chop with morels or a game dish. Savory desserts and a
nicely chosen wine list with several excellent Côtes du Rhônes com-
plete the meal. ☒ *1 rue Jules-Valles,* ☎ *01–43–71–49–52. AE, V. Closed
weekends and Aug. Métro: Charonne.*

$$ ✕ **Chez Philippe/Pyrénées-Cévennes.** Old-timers still refer to this comfortable bistro by its original name—Pyrénées-Cévennes—while others
know it as Chez Philippe. The eclectic menu combines the cooking of
Burgundy, central France, and Spain in such dishes as snails in garlic
butter, cassoulet, and paella. An attentive staff bustles amid the cozy
surroundings of beamed ceilings and polished copper. ☒ *106 rue de
la Folie-Méricourt,* ☎ *01–43–57–33–78. MC, V. Closed weekends
and Aug. Métro: République.*

$$ ✕ **Les Fernandises.** The chef-owner of this neighborhood spot near place
de la République is more concerned with his Normandy-inspired cui-
sine than with his restaurant's inconsequential decor. Fresh foie gras
sautéed in cider, and scallops in cream sauce are examples of his var-
ied style. Try the selection of Camemberts. ☒ *17 rue Fontaine-au-Roi,*
☎ *01–43–57–46–25. MC, V. Closed Sun., Mon., and Aug. Métro:
République.*

$ ✕ **Astier.** The prix-fixe menu (there's no à la carte) at this pleasant restau-
rant is a remarkable value. Among the high-quality seasonal dishes are
mussel soup with saffron, fricassee of beef cheeks, and plum *clafoutis*
(a creamy cake). Service can be rushed, but the enthusiastic crowd does
not seem to mind. Study the excellent wine list, which has some sur-
prising buys. ☒ *44 rue Jean-Pierre Timbaud,* ☎ *01–43–57–16–35.
AE, MC, V. Closed weekends and Aug. Métro: Parmentier.*

$ ✕ **Au Camelot.** Make a reservation the moment you get to town if you
★ want to be treated to chef Anne Desplanques's excellent, home-style
cooking. A single, five-course menu is served daily at this tiny 20-seat
restaurant; it usually begins with a generous serving of soup, followed
by a fish course, a main dish, cheese, and dessert. Desplanques trained
with Christian Constant at the Crillon Hotel, so expect creative dishes
like crab lasagna alongside classics like chicken in mushroom cream
sauce. Service is friendly, and the house Bordeaux is a treat. ☒ *50 rue
Amelot,* ☎ *01–43–55–54–04. Reservations essential. No credit cards.
Closed Sun. No lunch Mon., Sat. Métro: République.*

$ ✕ **Jacques Mélac.** Robust cuisine matches noisy camaraderie at this
popular wine bar–restaurant, owned by mustachioed Jacques Mélac.
Charcuterie, a salad of preserved duck gizzards, braised beef, and

cheeses from central France are good choices. Monsieur Mélac, who has a miniature vineyard out front, hosts a jolly party at harvest time. ✉ *42 rue Léon Frot,* ☎ *01–43–70–59–27. MC, V. Closed weekends Aug. No dinner Mon. Métro: Charonne.*

$ ✗ **Le Passage.** Not far from place de la Bastille, in the obscure Passage de la Bonne Graine, discover the friendly Passage, with its homey ambience and exposed brick walls. Though it bills itself as a wine bar, it has a full menu, including five kinds of *andouillette* (chitterling sausage). The wine list is excellent. ✉ *18 Passage de la Bonne Graine (enter by 108 av. Ledru-Rollin),* ☎ *01–47–00–73–30. AE, MC, V. Closed Sun. No lunch Sat. Métro: Ledru-Rollin.*

$ ✗ **Le Villaret.** The owner of this restaurant once ran the Astier (☞ *above*), and his experience shows. Salmon tart, hot foie gras salad, duck confit, and seasonal fruit clafoutis are some of the interesting and well-prepared dishes. The decor of exposed stone and half-timbering combines traditional and modern styles. There's no lunch service; dinner runs until 1 AM. ✉ *13 rue Ternaux,* ☎ *01–43–57–89–76. MC, V. Closed Sun. and Aug. No lunch. Métro: Parmentier.*

12ᵉ Arrondissement (Bastille/Gare de Lyon)
See Right Bank Dining map.

$$$ ✗ **Au Pressoir.** Chef-owner Henri Séguin's excellent restaurant in the eastern part of Paris deserves more attention than it receives. His menu has such original, exciting choices as fricassee of lobster with morels, pigeon with eggplant blinis, and chocolate soup with brioche. The wine list is tops, and service is friendly and professional. ✉ *257 av. Daumesnil,* ☎ *01–43–44–38–21. MC, V. Closed weekends, mid-Feb., and Aug. Métro: Michel-Bizot.*

$$$ ✗ **Au Trou Gascon.** At this successful Belle Epoque establishment off the place Daumesnil, owner Alain Dutournier serves his version of the cuisine of Gascony—a region of outstanding ham, foie gras, lamb, and poultry—and his classic white chocolate mousse. ✉ *40 rue Taine,* ☎ *01–43–44–34–26. AE, DC, MC, V. Closed weekends, Christmas wk, and Aug. Métro: Daumesnil.*

$$$ ✗ **L'Oulette.** Chef-owner Marcel Baudis's take on the cuisine of his na-
★ tive southwest France is original and delicious. Recommended dishes include oxtail with foie gras, fresh cod with celeriac and walnuts, and *pain d'épices* (spice cake). The restaurant, in the rebuilt Bercy district, is a bit hard to find, so bring your map. ✉ *15 pl. Lachambeaudie,* ☎ *01–40–02–02–12. AE, MC, V. Closed Sun. No lunch Sat. Métro: Dugommier.*

$$$ ✗ **Le Train Bleu.** This historic brasserie in the Gare de Lyon has gorgeous 19th-century frescoes. Chef Michel Comby turns out standard brasserie fare, such as herring in cream, and hot sausage. Prices are high, but if you come to the station to catch a train, consider stopping here, even for a drink. ✉ *Gare de Lyon,* ☎ *01–43–43–09–06. AE, DC, MC, V. Métro: Gare de Lyon.*

$$ ✗ **Le Square Trousseau.** Since fashion designer Jean-Paul Gaultier moved his headquarters nearby, this charming turn-of-the-century bistro has become very chic. You might see a supermodel or two while dining on the homemade foie gras and the tender baby chicken with mustard and bread-crumb crust. The house wine is a good value, especially the Morgon, a fruity red. ✉ *1 rue Antoine Vollon,* ☎ *01–43–43–06–00. MC, V. Métro: Ledru-Rollin.*

$ ✗ **Les Zygomates.** This handsome old butcher's shop converted into a bistro is popular with young locals. Since it's in a part of the city few tourists venture to, it's mostly filled with Parisians. Experience delicious modern bistro food, like a terrine of rabbit with tarragon, chicken in cream with chives, and a very fairly priced catch-of-the-day selection. ⊠ *7 rue Capri,* ☎ *01–40–19–93–04. V. Closed Sun., Sat. June–Sept., 1st 3 wks of Aug. No lunch Sat. Oct.–May. Métro: Michel-Bizot, Daumesnil.*

13ᵉ Arrondissement (Les Gobelins)

See Left Bank Dining map.

$$$ ✕ **Au Petit Marguéry.** Both staff and diners seem to be having a good time in this warm, convivial place run by three brothers. The menu goes beyond the usual bistro classics to include such dishes as cold lobster, cod fillet with spices, and excellent lamb of the Pyrénées. Prices are at the low end of this category. ⊠ *9 bd. de Port Royal,* ☎ *01–43–31–58–59. AE, DC, MC, V. Closed Sun., Mon., Christmas wk, and Aug. Métro: Les Gobelins.*

$$ ✕ **Anacreon.** A former chef from the Tour d'Argent has transformed a neighborhood café into a pleasant new-wave bistro serving inventive dishes such as pumpkin soup garnished with bacon and chorizo sausage and snails in a watercress cream sauce. Note, though, that the menu changes regularly. Desserts are good, too, and the St-Joseph is a good choice from the wine list. ⊠ *53 bd. St-Marcel,* ☎ *01–43–31–71–18. Reservations essential. MC, V. Closed Sat., Sun. Métro: Les Gobelins.*

$ ✕ **Le Terroir.** A jolly crowd of regulars makes this little bistro festive. The solidly classical menu, based on first-rate ingredients from all over France, offers salads with chicken livers or fresh marinated anchovies, and calves' liver or monkfish with saffron. The pears marinated in wine and cherry is an excellent dessert. Choose a wine from the well-balanced list. ⊠ *11 bd. Arago,* ☎ *01–47–07–36–99. AE, MC, V. Closed Sun. No lunch Sat. Métro: Les Gobelins.*

14ᵉ Arrondissement (Montparnasse)

See Left Bank Dining map.

$$$$ ✕ **Montparnasse 25.** Chef Jean-Yves Guého's stint in Hong Kong gave him a mastery of Chinese cuisine, which he has applied to classical French cooking with intriguing results. Frogs' legs in tempura, turbot in a sauce of Arbois wine, and spectacular roast piglet, served in two courses—the rack and haunch rolled in sesame seeds, and the ribs and shoulder with Asian vegetables—are some of his superb, remarkably original dishes. Don't miss the cheese course—there are more than 150 to choose from, all explained by a *maître fromager.* To conclude the meal, enjoy one of 50 herbal teas. ⊠ *19 rue Commandant-Mouchotte,* ☎ *01–44–36–44–25. AE, DC, MC, V. Closed weekends. Métro: Montparnasse.*

$$ ✕ **Contre-Allée.** Left Bank students and professors crowd this large restaurant, simply decorated with bullfighting posters. The menu includes original selections such as squid salad with mussels and roast cod with Parmesan; homemade fresh pasta accompanies many dishes. A sidewalk terrace enlivens shady avenue Denfert-Rochereau in summer. The restaurant serves until 11:30 PM. ⊠ *83 av. Denfert-Rochereau,* ☎ *01–43–54–99–86. AE, DC, MC, V. No lunch Sat. Métro: Denfert-Rochereau.*

$$ ✕ **La Coupole.** This world-renowned, cavernous address in Montparnasse practically defines the term brasserie (it's owned by Jean-Paul Bucher). Many find it too large, too noisy, and too expensive, and no one likes the long wait at the bar before being seated. Still, it has been popular with everyone from Left Bank intellectuals (Jean-Paul Sartre and Simone de Beauvoir were regulars) to bourgeois grandmothers. Expect the usual brasserie menu, including perhaps the largest shellfish presentation in Paris, choucroute, and a wide range of desserts. The buffet breakfast from 7:30 to 10:30 daily is an excellent value. Note the famous murals. ⊠ *102 bd. du Montparnasse,* ☎ *01–43–20–14–20. AE, DC, MC, V. Métro: Vavin.*

$$ ✕ **Le Pavillon Montsouris.** This bucolic building on the edge of Parc Montsouris has a pretty pastel interior. A multichoice, prix-fixe menu is a real bargain. Dishes are fresh, interesting, and rarely repeated; try the lamb sweetbreads with cucumber. Service can slow down during peak hours; go when you have time for a leisurely meal. The large terrace facing the park is a charming spot on a sunny day. ⊠ *20 rue Gazan,* ☎ *01–45–88–38–52. AE, DC, MC, V. RER: Cité-Universitaire.*

$–$$ ✕ **Vin & Marée.** The third, lower-priced annex of the fancy Right Bank fish house, La Luna, is a welcome addition to Montparnasse. Begin with a tasty bowl of baby clams in a creamy lemon-butter sauce, offered as an hors d'oeuvre, then have a generous plate of fresh red shrimps sautéed in thyme, followed by white tuna in shallot sauce or sautéed red mullets if available—the menu changes with the market. Nicely chosen wines come by the bottle, carafe, or glass. ⊠ *108 av. du Maine, 01–43–20–29–50. AE, MC, V. Métro: Montparnasse, Gaité.*

$ ✕ **La Régalade.** Although it's in a remote, colorless residential neighborhood, which is a nuisance, Yves Camdeborde's cooking is worth the trip. A veteran of the Crillon, he has, remarkably, kept prices low—$37 for a three-course feast. Tables need to be booked at least one month in advance, but service continues until midnight, and you can often sneak in late in the evening. ⊠ *49 av. Jean-Moulin,* ☎ *01–45–45–68–58. MC, V. Closed Sun., Mon., and Aug. No lunch Sat. Métro: Alesia.*

15ᵉ Arrondissement (Motte-Picquet/Balard)
See Left Bank Dining map.

$$ ✕ **Le Barrail.** A favorite with staff from nearby *Le Monde,* this neighborhood spot offers hospitable service in an unassuming setting. Enjoy such dishes as foie gras *aux pommes* (with apples) and the increasingly hard-to-find potatoes *Dauphine,* pureed potatoes added to cabbage pastry, shaped into balls, and deep-fried. Ordering the prix-fixe menu here will lessen the cost of your meal. ⊠ *17 rue Falguière,* ☎ *01–43–22–42–61. AE, MC, V. Closed weekends and early Aug. Métro: Pasteur.*

$$ ✕ **Le Clos Morillons.** The chef's many trips to the Far East have influenced his cuisine. Still, the menu of potato terrine with foie gras, roast guinea fowl, and the all-chocolate dessert (several kinds of chocolate desserts on one plate) is unmistakably French. Loire wines are emphasized on the interesting list. Added pluses are the professional service in the quiet dining room and the less-expensive prix-fixe menus at lunch and dinner. ⊠ *50 rue Morillons,* ☎ *01–48–28–04–37. MC, V. Closed Sun. and 2 wks mid-Aug. No lunch Sat. Métro: Convention.*

$$ ✕ **La Dinée.** Up-and-coming chef Christophe Chabanel's restaurant in this rather remote location is filled noon and night by a crowd of stylish regulars who come to be surprised by his culinary creativity. Signature dishes include fillet of sole with baby shrimp and chicken medallions with peppers in a corn vinaigrette. The dining room, with blue print fabrics and wooden tub chairs, is simple; service is very professional. ⊠ *85 rue Leblanc,* ☎ *01–45–54–20–49. V. Closed weekends. Métro: Balard.*

$$ ✕ **Philippe Detourbe.** With its black-lacquer trim, mirrors, and Bur-
★ gundy velvet upholstery, this place is unexpectedly glamorous. It also serves spectacular food for remarkably good prices, so book several days in advance. Detourbe, a self-taught chef, is extremely gifted and very ambitious—his menu of contemporary French cooking changes with every meal. Dishes may include smoked salmon filled with cabbage *rémoulade* (creamy dressing) or cod steak with white beans and

caramelized endives. Desserts are fantastic. The wine list is brief but well chosen and service is friendly and efficient. ⊠ *8 rue Nicholas Charlet,* ☎ *01–42–19–08–59. Reservations essential. MC, V. Closed Sun. No lunch Sat. Métro: Pasteur.*

$ ✕ **L'Armoise.** At this quiet neighborhood restaurant near the Front de Seine development, chef-owner Georges Outhier prepares one of the best veal livers in Paris, along with such treats as a delicious duck breast with honey and pot-au-feu *de la mer* (seafood stew). Madame Outhier is an attentive hostess in the salmon-pink dining rooms. ⊠ *67 rue des Entrepreneurs,* ☎ *01–45–79–03–31. MC, V. Closed Sun., mid-Feb., and Aug. No lunch Sat. Métro: Charles-Michel.*

$ ✕ **L'Os à Moëlle.** This small, popular bistro offers a very good value six-course dinner menu (there's no à la carte) that changes daily; portions are generous. A sample meal might include white-bean soup, a country terrine of pork with peppers, *rouget* (red mullet fish), sautéed veal, cheese with a small salad, and a delicious apple and rhubarb clafoutis. At lunchtime, the à la carte menu is similarly good. With an excellent list of fairly priced wines, your bill will stay comfortably low. ⊠ *3 rue Vasco-de-Gama,* ☎ *01–45–57–27–27. Reservations essential. MC, V. Closed Sun., Mon. Métro: Balard.*

$ ✕ **Le Petit Plat.** This popular neighborhood bistro is tiny, out of the way, and the service can be a bit off-handed but the food is generally very good. It specializes in the generous portions of urbanized French country cooking that Parisians are currently mad about: terrine of rabbit in tarragon aspic, sausage with potato salad in shallot vinaigrette, and roast chicken with sautéed mushrooms. The excellent wine list was selected by Henri Gault of Gault-Millau, the famous French food guide (his daughter is one of the three owners). ⊠ *45 av. Emile-Zola,* ☎ *01–45–78–24–20. V. Closed Mon. No lunch Tues. Métro: Charles-Michel.*

16e Arrondissement (Trocadéro/Bois de Boulogne)
See Right Bank Dining map.

$$$$ ✕ **Alain Ducasse.** Since he took over from Joel Robuchon, Ducasse has
★ surprised everyone by serving resolutely classical French dishes. Aside from the addition of a bar with an impressive selection of cigars, the handsome, richly decorated town house setting has not changed. One does not feel, however, that this is the pinnacle of French dining, as one did with Joel Robuchon. Ducasse is a marvelous cook, but dishes like a pastry case filled with mushrooms, shrimps, and frog's legs or duckling steamed with anise, satisfy rather than excite. Still you can get a solidly luxurious meal, though you'll have to forgive the robot-like service and the staggeringly expensive menu; the 480-franc lunch menu is your best bet. ⊠ *59 av. Raymond-Poincare,* ☎ *01–47–27–12–27. Reservations several months in advance essential. AE, DC, MC, V. Closed Sat., Sun. Métro: Victor Hugo.*

$$$$ ✕ **Port Alma.** Madame Canal's charming welcome and the nautical-blue and pastel decor make this place festive. Look forward to attentive, polite service. Monsieur Canal, the chef, is from southwest France, near Spain, and his cuisine is bursting with full, sunny flavors. Try turbot with thyme, sea bass in a salt crust with fennel gratin, or bouillabaisse (order ahead). ⊠ *10 av. de New York,* ☎ *01–47–23–75–11. AE, DC, MC, V. Closed Sun. and Aug. Métro: Alma-Marceau.*

$$$$ ✕ **Le Pré Catalan.** Dining beneath the chestnut trees on the terrace of this fanciful palace restaurant in the Bois de Boulogne is a Belle Epoque fantasy. Chef Roland Durand has brought new life to the cuisine of this venerable establishment, with elegant dishes such as risotto with langoustines, sweetbreads with morels and asparagus tips, and chocolate and pistachio cake. The lunch menu is more reasonably priced. ⊠

We'll give you a $20 tip for driving.

See the real Europe with Hertz.

It's time to see Europe from a new perspective. From behind the wheel of a Hertz car. And we'd like to save you $20 on your prepaid Affordable Europe Weekly Rental. Our low rates are guaranteed in U.S. dollars and English is spoken at all of our European locations. Computerized driving directions are available at many locations, and Free Unlimited Mileage and 24-Hour Emergency Roadside Assistance are standard in our European packages. For complete details call 1-800-654-3001. Mention PC #95384 So, discover Europe with Hertz.

Offer is valid at participating airport locations in Europe from Jan.1 – Dec.15,1998, on Economy through Full size cars. Reservations must be made at least 8 hours prior to departure. $20 will be deducted at time of booking. Standard rental qualifications, significant restrictions and blackout periods apply.

Pick up the phone.

Pick up the miles.

MCI Calling Card

415 555 1234 2244
J.D. SMITH

WorldPhone

Use your MCI Card® to make an international call from virtually anywhere in the world and earn frequent flyer miles on one of seven major airlines.

Enroll in an MCI Airline Partner Program today. In the U.S., call **1-800-FLY-FREE.** Overseas, call MCI collect at **1-916-567-5151.**

1. To use your MCI Card, just dial the WorldPhone access number of the country you're calling from.
   (For a complete listing of codes, visit www.mci.com.)
2. Dial or give the operator your MCI Card number.
3. Dial or give the number you're calling.

# Austria (CC) ♦	022-903-012
# Belarus (CC)	
From Brest, Vitebsk, Grodno, Minsk	8-800-103
From Gomel and Mogilev regions	8-10-800-103
# Belgium (CC) ♦	0800-10012
# Bulgaria	00800-0001
# Croatia (CC) ★	99-385-0112
# Czech Republic (CC) ♦	00-42-000112
# Denmark (CC) ♦	8001-0022
# Finland (CC) ♦	08001-102-80
# France (CC) ♦	0-800-99-0019
# Germany (CC)	0130-0012
# Greece (CC) ♦	00-800-1211
# Hungary (CC) ♦	00▼800-01411
# Iceland (CC) ♦	800-9002
# Ireland (CC)	1-800-55-1001
# Italy (CC) ♦	172-1022
# Kazakhstan (CC)	8-800-131-4321
# Liechtenstein (CC) ♦	0800-89-0222
# Luxembourg	0800-0112
# Monaco (CC) ♦	800-90-019

# Netherlands (CC) ♦	0800-022-91-22
# Norway (CC) ♦	800-19912
# Poland (CC) ÷	00-800-111-21-22
# Portugal (CC) ÷	05-017-1234
Romania (CC) ÷	01-800-1800
# Russia (CC) ÷ ♦	
To call using ROSTELCOM ■	747-3322
For a Russian-speaking operator	747-3320
To call using SOVINTEL ■	960-2222
# San Marino (CC) ♦	172-1022
# Slovak Republic (CC)	00-421-00112
# Slovenia	080-8808
# Spain (CC)	900-99-0014
# Sweden (CC) ♦	020-795-922
# Switzerland (CC) ♦	0800-89-0222
# Turkey (CC) ♦	00-8001-1177
# Ukraine (CC) ÷	8▼10-013
# United Kingdom (CC)	
To call using BT ■	0800-89-0222
To call using MERCURY ■	0500-89-0222
# Vatican City (CC)	172-1022

Is this a great time, or what? :-)

MCI

Bois de Boulogne, rte. de Surèsnes, ☎ *01–45–24–55–58. Reservations essential. Jacket and tie. AE, DC, MC, V. Closed Mon. and mid-Feb. No dinner Sun. Métro: Porte Dauphine.*

$$$$ ✕ **Le Vivarois.** Chef-owner Claude Peyrot is one of the most inspired and creative contemporary French chefs, though his cooking can be uneven. He is a master with fish and puff pastry; his *bavarois* of red bell pepper (a creamy, molded concoction) is oft imitated, and his original dishes shine: scallops with sesame and ginger, *rissole* (small meat patty) of lamb's feet with artichokes and basil, and chocolate soufflé with chicory ice cream. Service is not always up to par. ⊠ *192 av. Victor Hugo,* ☎ *01–45–04–04–31. AE, DC, MC, V. Closed weekends and Aug. Métro: Rue de la Pompe.*

$$$ ✕ **Jamin.** At this intimate, elegant restaurant, where Joel Robuchon
★ made his name, you can find excellent, haute cuisine at almost half the price of what you'd find elsewhere. Benoit Guichard, Robuchon's second for many years, is a subtle and accomplished chef and a particularly brilliant *saucier* (sauce maker). The menu changes regularly, but Guichard tends toward dishes like ginger-spiked salad with squid and crayfish, and braised beef with cumin-scented carrots. The poached pears with spice-bread ice cream makes an excellent dessert. ⊠ *32 rue de Longchamp,* ☎ *01–45–53–00–07. Reservations essential. AE, DC, MC, V. Closed Sat., Sun. Métro: Iéna.*

$$–$$$ ✕ **Prunier.** Founded in 1925, this seafood restaurant is one of the best—and surely the prettiest—in Paris. The famous Art Deco mosaics glitter and the white marble counters shine with the impeccably fresh shellfish displayed like precious jewels. The kitchen not only excels at classic French fish cooking but has added some interesting dishes, like a *Saintongeaise* plate—raw oysters with grilled sausages—eaten in Bordeaux. Accompany your meal with wine from the well-balanced list. No reservations are needed for the raw bar on the main level, but book for lunch or dinner in the upstairs dining room. ⊠ *16 av. Victor Hugo,* ☎ *01–44–17–35–85. Jacket and tie. AE, DC, MC, V. Closed Sun., Mon. Métro: Etoile.*

$$ ✕ **La Butte Chaillot.** A dramatic iron staircase connects two levels decorated in turquoise and earth colors at the latest, largest, and most impressive of star chef Guy Savoy's fashionable bistros. Dining here is part theater, as the à la mode clientele will attest, but it's not all show: The very good food includes tasty ravioli from the town of Royans, roast chicken with mashed potatoes, and stuffed veal breast with rosemary. A wide sidewalk terrace fronts tree-shaded avenue Kléber. ⊠ *112 av. Kléber,* ☎ *01–47–27–88–88. AE, MC, V. Métro: Trocadéro.*

$$ ✕ **Chez Géraud.** Cherubic, jolly Géraud Rongier runs this pleasant bistro in the chic Passy district. Dishes such as salad of preserved duck gizzards, roast pigeon with port sauce, and bitter chocolate cake exemplify the robust cuisine. Rongier's knowledge of wine is vast; his eclectic list has everything from great châteaux to little-known regional bottles. Notice the pretty tile mural at the back of the dining room. ⊠ *31 rue Vital,* ☎ *01–45–20–33–00. AE, MC, V. Closed weekends and Aug. Métro: Passy.*

$$ ✕ **Le Relais du Parc.** This bistro-annex is now run by Alain Ducasse,
★ who has instituted a wonderful, new menu. Ducasse understands the way that people want to eat today, and his menu allows you to eat as large or light as you like. Two delicious starters—the lobster salad and the baby potatoes with black truffles in a creamy oxtail-stock sauce—make good meals, followed by cheese or dessert. Main courses, such as the lamb chops with vegetable lasagna, are excellent. The cheese plate is good, too, but the desserts could be better and the wine list is overpriced. ⊠ *55 av. Raymond-Poincare,* ☎ *01–44–05–66–10. Reservations essential. AE, DC, MC, V. Métro: Victor Hugo.*

$ ✕ **Le Petit Rétro.** Two different clienteles—men in expensive suits at noon and well-dressed local couples in the evening—frequent this immaculate little bistro with art nouveau tiles and bentwood furniture. You can't go wrong with the daily special, which is written on a chalkboard presented by one of the friendly waitresses. Come in some night when you want a good solid meal, like the perfect *pavé de boeuf* (thick steak) in a ruddy red-wine and stock sauce, accompanied by potatoes au gratin and caramelized braised endive. ⊠ *5 rue Mesnil,* ☎ *01–44–05–06–05. MC, V. Closed Sun. No lunch Mon. Métro: Victor Hugo.*

17ᵉ Arrondissement (Monceau/Clichy)

See Right Bank Dining map.

$$$$ ✕ **Amphyclès.** Before opening this much-anticipated restaurant, chef-owner Philippe Groult had already made a name for himself. Since then Groult, who trained under Joel Robuchon, has not disappointed. His exciting menu includes cauliflower soup with caviar, herb salad, and duck with coriander and orange. Amphyclès is one of the few grand Parisian restaurants still to proffer desserts from a pastry trolley. Service is excellent. ⊠ *78 av. des Ternes,* ☎ *01–40–68–01–01. AE, DC, MC, V. Reservations essential 1 wk in advance. Closed Sun. No lunch Sat. Métro: Ternes.*

$$$$ ✕ **Apicius.** Chef-owner Jean-Pierre Vigato excels at mixing the humble with the rarified, as he does in dishes from duck *tourte* (pie) and pig's foot to roasted sweetbreads and Bresse chicken cooked in salt. A good-looking crowd occupies the airy, flower-filled dining rooms. ⊠ *122 av. de Villiers,* ☎ *01–43–80–19–66. AE, DC, MC, V. Closed weekends and Aug. Métro: Péreire.*

$$$$ ✕ **Guy Savoy.** Top chef Guy Savoy's other five bistros have not dis-
★ tracted him too much from his handsome luxury restaurant near the Arc de Triomphe. The oysters in aspic, sea bass with spices, and poached and grilled pigeon reveal the magnitude of his talent. His mille-feuille is a contemporary classic. ⊠ *18 rue Troyon,* ☎ *01–43–80–40–61. AE, MC, V. Closed Sun. No lunch Sat. Métro: Charles de Gaulle–Etoile.*

$$–$$$ ✕ **Au Petit Colombier.** It's a perennial favorite among Parisians, who come to eat comforting *cuisine bourgeoise* in the warm dining rooms accented with wood and bright copper. Menu standards include milk-fed lamb chop *en cocotte* (in a small, enameled casserole) and coq au vin. Service is friendly and unpretentious. It's open for Sunday dinner. ⊠ *42 rue des Acacias,* ☎ *01–43–80–28–54. AE, MC, V. Closed Sat. No lunch Sun. Métro: Charles de Gaulle–Etoile.*

$$–$$$ ✕ **Le Graindorge.** Formerly at the immensely popular Au Trou Gascon, chef-owner Bernard Broux has thrived since he opened his own establishment. He prepares an original mix of the cuisines of southwest France and his native Flanders: Experience the succulent eel terrine in a delicious herb aspic (seasonal), pork cheeks with juniper, and caramelized brioche *galette* (buckwheat pancake). Madame Broux oversees the pleasant dining rooms and can help you select one of the fine beers. ⊠ *15 rue de l'Arc-de-Triomphe,* ☎ *01–47–54–00–28. AE, MC, V. Closed Sun. No lunch Sat. Métro: Charles de Gaulle–Etoile.*

$$ ✕ **Le Timgad.** For a stylish evening out and a night off from French food, head to this elegant, beautifully decorated North African restaurant. Start with a savory *brick* (crispy parchment pastry filled with meat, eggs, or seafood), followed by tasty couscous or succulent *tagine* (meat or poultry that's slowly braised inside a domed pottery casserole). Lamb tagine with artichokes is especially good. ⊠ *21 rue de Brunel,* ☎ *01–45–74–23–70. MC, V. Métro: Argentine.*

$ ✕ **L'Huitrier.** If you share the Parisians' craving for oysters, this is the place for you. Owner Alain Bunel will describe the different kinds available; you can follow these with any of several fish specials offered daily. The excellent cheeses are from the outstanding shop of Roger Alléosse. Blond wood and cream colors prevail. ✉ *16 rue Saussier-Leroy,* ☎ *01–40–54–83–44. AE, MC, V. Métro: Ternes.*

$ ✕ **La Rôtisserie d'Armaillé.** Admire the handsome oak paneling, cranberry and green upholstery, and the *très* Parisian crowd at star chef Jacques Cagna's third restaurant. The prix-fixe menu has many tempting choices, among them *pastilla* (pastry layers) of guinea hen and a terrific chocolate cake. Wines are a little pricey. ✉ *6 rue d'Armaillé,* ☎ *01–42–27–19–20. AE, MC, V. Closed Sun. No lunch Sat. Métro: Argentine.*

$ ✕ **La Table de Pierre.** The Louis XVI–style setting is somewhat surprising in one of the best Basque restaurants in Paris. Such dishes as peppers stuffed with *brandade* (salt cod casserole), *émincé* (thin slices) of squid, duck confit, and gâteau Basque are full of the colors and flavors of the Pays Basque. Owner Pierre Darrieumerlou is an agreeable host. ✉ *116 bd. Péreire,* ☎ *01–43–80–88–68. AE, MC, V. Closed Sun. No lunch Sat. Métro: Péreire.*

18e Arrondissement (Montmartre)
See Right Bank Dining map.

$$$$ ✕ **A. Beauvilliers.** Pickwickian owner Edouard Carlier is a born partygiver, and his flower-filled, lavishly decorated restaurant is one of the most festive in Paris. The three dining rooms are filled with his personal collections of paintings and valuable *bibelots* (trinkets). A tiny, vine-covered terrace makes for delightful summer dining. Chefs here come and go, but Monsieur Carlier maintains quality, serving both original creations and reinterpreted classics. Recommended are the red mullet *en escabèche* (in a peppery marinade) and foie gras, lobster, and sweetbread tourte. The mouth-puckering lemon tart is not to be missed. One drawback: Service can be distant. ✉ *52 rue Lamarck,* ☎ *01–42–54–54–42. Reservations essential. Jacket required. AE, MC, V. Closed Sun. No lunch Mon. Métro: Lamarck-Caulaincourt.*

$ ✕ **Aux Négotiants.** This wine bar in Montmartre has zero decor, but the neighborhood regulars and well-heeled clientele find it welcoming. One or two hot plates are offered daily; otherwise, enjoy the terrines, cheeses, and other simple choices, served with affordable wines by the glass or bottle. ✉ *27 rue Lambert,* ☎ *01–46–06–15–11. No credit cards. Closed weekends and Mon. No dinner Fri. Métro: Château Rouge.*

$ ✕ **Le Restaurant.** This pleasant little restaurant remains an oasis in a neighborhood where it's not easy to find a good meal. In tune with the times, chef Yves Pelardeau offers a very good value prix-fixe menu. It features his inventive approach to bistro cooking, using Asian and African seasoning to brighten up classical dishes. The menu changes regularly, but dishes like guinea hen with preserved lemon and duckling with figs express his style. Order the less expensive wine of the week. ✉ *32 rue Veron,* ☎ *01–42–23–06–22. AE, MC, V. Closed Mon. Métro: Abbesses.*

19e Arrondissement (Buttes Chaumont/La Villette)
See Right Bank Dining map.

$$$ ✕ **Le Pavillon Puebla.** Chef Vergès prepares original, flavorful cuisine, such as oyster ravioli with curry, lamb tournedos with truffle juice, and gâteau of crepes and apples at this turn-of-the-century building in the spectacular Parc des Buttes-Chaumont. Madame Vergès oversees the

elegant dining rooms and large terrace. The restaurant feels wonderfully removed from the bustle of the city, but it's a bit hard to find. ⊠ *Parc Buttes-Chaumont (entrance on rue Botzaris)*, ☎ *01–42–08–92–62. MC, V. Closed Sun., Mon., and mid-Aug. Métro: Buttes-Chaumont.*

$$ ✕ **Le Bistrot du Cochon d'Or.** A best bet for real carnivores, this bistro annex is more appealing than the venerable steak house of the same name, which has become absurdly expensive. If you're visiting the Cité de la Musique or La Villette, take a trip across the street for first-rate French specialty cuts, including *pied du cochon* (pig's feet) and *tête de veau* (calf's head). ⊠ *192 av. Jean Jaurès*, ☎ *01–42–45–46–46. AE, DC, MC, V. Métro: Porte de Pantin.*

$$ ✕ **La Verriere.** This simply-decorated little place is a sterling example
★ of a price-conscious, market-menu bistro. Chef Eric Frechon worked with Christian Constant at the Crillon, which means his cooking is more adventurous and elegant than most bistro fare. Examples of his dishes include mackerel stuffed with celery rémoulade and thick slabs of bacon "lacquered" with spices and served on a bed of pickled turnips. Desserts are equally creative. ⊠ *10 rue du Général-Brunet*, ☎ *01–40–40–03–30. V. Closed Sat., Sun. Métro: Danube.*

20ᵉ Arrondissement (Père Lachaise)
See Right Bank Dining map.

$ ✕ **A la Courtille.** A trendy crowd frequents this large wine bar–restaurant with a spectacular view of Paris and the Parc de Belleville. (Notice the black-and-white photos of the quaint old Belleville neighborhood before the wrecking ball.) The kitchen prepares modernized versions of bistro classics and fresh, light creations, such as marinated salmon with dill, roast cod with zucchini, and veal liver. An excellent wine list offers many selections by the glass. There's a large terrace, and service until 11 PM. ⊠ *1 rue des Envierges*, ☎ *01–46–36–51–59. DC, MC, V. Métro: Pyrénées.*

$ ✕ **Les Allobroges.** Intrepid types will be rewarded by this charming, chic restaurant in one of the city's more remote neighborhoods. Chef Olivier Pateyron offers several excellent prix-fixe menus at prices that would be nearly impossible in a city-center location. Surrounded by wood-print wallpaper, framed prints of farm animals, and arrangements of dried flowers, diners feast on delicious langoustines served on ratatouille along with lamb braised with garlic and flambéed plums. ⊠ *71 rue des Grand-Champs*, ☎ *01–43–73–40–00. AE, MC, V. Closed Sun., Mon. Métro: Maraîchers.*

Cafés

Cafés are found at every bend in Paris—you may prefer a posh perch at a renowned *café littéraire* (literary cafés), where *intellectuels* such as Hemingway, de Beauvoir, and Sartre wrote some of their greatest works, or opt for a seat at a tiny *café de quartier* (neighborhood café), where locals come to discuss politics and gossip. Following is a list of cafés that will give you a feel for Paris's best (*see* Chapter 2 for more cafés, listed as suggested spots to take a break).

1ᵉʳ Arrondissement (Les Halles/Palais-Royal)
Au Père Tranquille. One of the best places in Paris for people-watching, this café also offers free entertainment from street artists and local performers. ⊠ *16 rue Pierre Lescot*, ☎ *01–45–08–00–34. Métro: Les Halles.*

Le Ruc Univers. Actors from the Comédie Française hang out at this elegant and rather pricey brasserie dating from 1925. ⊠ *1 pl. André Malraux*, ☎ *01–42–60–31–57. Métro: Palais-Royal.*

Salon de Thé du Palais Royal. Have tea here on a terrace overlooking the gardens of the Palais Royal. ⊠ *Jardins du Palais Royal, 110 Galérie de Valois,* ☎ *01–40–20–00–27. Métro: Palais-Royal.*

4ᵉ Arrondissement (Marais/Beaubourg/Ile St-Louis)

Brasserie de l'Ile St-Louis. This brasserie serves good food on a great terrace in one of the most picturesque parts of the city. ⊠ *55 quai de Bourbon,* ☎ *01–43–54–02–59. Métro: Pont Marie.*

Dame Tartine. Enjoy a delicious tartine as you watch the moving sculptures in the Stravinsky fountain next to the Pompidou Center. ⊠ *2 rue Brisemiche,* ☎ *01–42–77–32–22. Métro: Rambuteau, Les Halles.*

Le Flore en l'Ile. At this café on the Ile St-Louis you can find renowned Berthillon ice cream and a magnificent view of the Seine. ⊠ *42 quai d'Orléans,* ☎ *01–43–29–88–27. Métro: Pont Marie.*

Le Loir dans la Théière. This wonderful tea shop in the heart of the Marais has comfortable armchairs and delicious patisseries. ⊠ *3 rue des Rosiers,* ☎ *01–42–72–90–61. Métro: St-Paul.*

Ma Bourgogne. On the exquisite place des Vosges, this is a calm oasis for a coffee or a light lunch away from the noisy streets. ⊠ *19 pl. des Vosges,* ☎ *01–42–78–44–64. Métro: St-Paul.*

Mariage Frères. London isn't the only city with outstanding tea shops: This elegant place serves 500 kinds of tea, along with delicious tarts. ⊠ *30 rue du Bourg-Tibourg,* ☎ *01–42–72–28–11. Métro: Hôtel-de-Ville.*

Petit Fer à Cheval. Great coffee is served in the perfect setting for watching the fashionable Marais locals saunter by. ⊠ *30 rue Vieille-du-Temple,* ☎ *01–42–72–47–47. Métro: St-Paul.*

6ᵉ Arrondissement (St-Germain/Montparnasse)

Brasserie Lipp. This brasserie, with its turn-of-the-century decor, was a favorite spot of Hemingway's; today television celebrities, journalists, and politicians come here regularly. ⊠ *151 bd. St-Germain,* ☎ *01–45–48–53–91. Métro: St-Germain-des-Prés.*

Café de Flore. Picasso, Chagall, Sartre, and de Beauvoir, attracted by the luxury of a heated café, worked and wrote here in the early 20th century. Today you'll find more tourists than intellectuals, but its outdoor terrace is still a popular spot. (☞ Chapter 2.) ⊠ *172 bd. St-Germain,* ☎ *01–45–48–55–26. Métro: St-Germain-des-Prés.*

Café de la Mairie. Preferred by Henry Miller and Saul Bellow to those on the noisy boulevard St-Germain, this place still retains the quiet and unpretentious air of a local café. ⊠ *8 pl. St-Sulpice,* ☎ *01–43–26–67–82. Métro: St-Sulpice.*

La Rotonde. Once a second home to foreign artists and political exiles in the '20s and '30s, the café's clientele isn't as exotic today. But it's still a pleasant place to have a coffee on the sunny terrace. ⊠ *105 bd. Montparnasse,* ☎ *01–43–26–68–84. Métro: Montparnasse.*

Le Sélect. Isadora Duncan and Hart Crane used to hang out here; now it's a popular spot for a post-cinema beer. ⊠ *99 bd. Montparnasse,* ☎ *01–45–48–38–24. Métro: Vavin.*

Le Vieux Colombier. Take a seat on the lovely wicker furniture in front of one of the big windows in this café just around the corner from St-Sulpice and the Vieux Colombier theater. ⊠ *65 rue de Rennes,* ☎ *01–45–48–53–81. Métro: St-Sulpice.*

Les Deux Magots. Dubbed the second home of the "*élite intellectuelle,*" this café counted Rimbaud, Verlaine, Mallarmé, Wilde, and the Surrealists among its regulars. (☞ Chapter 2.) ⊠ *170 bd. St-Germain,* ☎ *01–45–48–55–25. Métro: St-Germain-des-Prés.*

8ᵉ Arrondissement (Champs-Elysées)

Le Fouquet's. At one of James Joyce's and Orson Welles's favorite cafés, brass plaques bear their names, as well as those of other famous patrons. ⊠ *99 av. des Champs-Elysées,* ☎ *01–47–23–70–60. Métro: George-V.*

11ᵉ Arrondissement (Bastille)

Café de L'Industrie. Have a late afternoon coffee or beer beneath the warm yellow walls covered with photos of movies at this Bastille hangout. ⊠ *16 rue St-Sabin,* ☎ *01–47–00–13–53. Métro: Bastille.*

14ᵉ Arrondissement (Montparnasse)

Café du Dôme. Now a fancy brasserie, this place began as a dingy meeting place for exiled artists and intellectuals such as Lenin, Picasso, and Chaim Soutine. ⊠ *108 bd. Montparnasse,* ☎ *01–43–35–25–81. Métro: Vavin.*

Café de la Place. This café is a charming, wood-paneled spot that is perfect for watching the activity inside and out. ⊠ *23 rue d'Odessa,* ☎ *01–42–18–01–55. Métro: Montparnasse.*

18ᵉ Arrondissement (Montmartre)

La Crémaillère. Alphonse Mucha frescoes decorate the walls at this veritable monument to fin-de-siècle art. ⊠ *15 pl. du Tertre,* ☎ *01–46–06–58–59. Métro: Anvers.*

Le Sancerre. Here you can sit on the terrace sipping coffee or beer and watching artists, hipsters, and tourists pass by. ⊠ *35 rue des Abbesses,* ☎ *01–45–58–08–20. Métro: Abbesses.*

4 Lodging

Whether you favor palatial grandeur or homespun hospitality, there are wonderful hotels for every taste and budget in Paris. Splurge, and you could find yourself in sumptuous digs in a luxurious Right Bank mansion. Search, and you could land a room in one of the city's growing number of stylish good-value hotels.

WINDING STAIRCASES, flower-filled window boxes, concierges who seem to have stepped from a 19th-century novel—all of these still exist in abundance in Paris hotels. So do grand rooms with marble baths, Belle Epoque lobbies, and a polished staff at your beck and call. In Paris there are wonderful hotels for every taste and budget. The Paris Tourist Office's annual lodging guide lists 1,498 member hotels in the city's 20 arrondissements. The true count, though, is closer to 2,000—some 80,000 rooms in all.

Updated by
Suzanne
Rowan
Kelleher

Our criteria when selecting the hotels reviewed below were quality, location, and character. Few chain hotels are listed, since they frequently lack the charm and authenticity found in typical Parisian lodgings. (Best Western is a notable exception.) Similarly, we list fewer hotels in outlying arrondissements (the 10ᵉ to the 20ᵉ) because these are farther from the major sites. Generally, there are more Right Bank hotels offering luxury—or at any rate formality—than there are on the Left Bank, where hotels are frequently smaller and richer in old-fashioned charm. The Right Bank's 1ᵉʳ and 8ᵉ arrondissements are still the most exclusive and prices here reflect this. Less-expensive alternatives on the Right Bank are the fashionable Marais quarter (3ᵉ and 4ᵉ arrondissements) and the 11ᵉ and 12ᵉ, near the Opéra Bastille.

Despite the huge choice of hotels, you should always reserve well in advance, especially if you're determined to stay in a specific place. You can do this by telephoning ahead, then writing or faxing for confirmation. As you will probably be asked to send a deposit, be sure to discuss refund policies before releasing your credit card number or mailing your check or money order. During peak seasons, some hotels require total prepayment. Always demand written confirmation of your reservation, detailing the duration of your stay, the price, the location and the type of your room (single or double, twin beds or double), and the bathroom (☞ *below*).

As part of a general upgrade of the city's hotels in recent years, scores of lackluster, shabby Paris lodgings have been replaced by good-value establishments in the lower to middle price ranges. Despite widespread improvements, however, many Paris hotels still have idiosyncrasies—some charming, others less so. Hotel rooms in Paris's oldest quarters are generally much smaller than their American counterparts. The standard French double bed is slightly smaller than the American version. Although air-conditioning has become de rigueur in middle- to higher-priced hotels, it is generally not a prerequisite for comfort. (Paris's hot-weather season doesn't last long.) Reviews indicate the number of rooms with full bath facilities, including *baignoire* (tub) or *douche* (shower); any exceptions are noted. It's increasingly rare to find moderately priced places that offer shared toilets or bathrooms down the hall, but make sure you know what you are getting when you book.

Almost all Paris hotels charge extra for breakfast, with prices ranging from 30 francs to more than 195 francs per person in luxury establishments. Though hotels may not automatically add the breakfast charge to your bill, it's wise to inform the desk staff if you don't plan to have breakfast there. For anything more than the standard Continental breakfast of café au lait and baguette or croissants, the price will be higher. Some hotels have especially pleasant breakfast areas, and we have noted this where applicable. Luxury hotels often have restaurants, but finding a restaurant is rarely a problem in Paris.

You'll notice that stars appear on a shield on the facade of most hotels. The French government grades hotels on a scale from one star to four-star deluxe based on a notoriously complicated evaluation of amenities and services. At the bottom end of the scale are the one-star hotels, where you might have to share a bathroom and do without an elevator. You can expect two- and three-star hotels to have private bathrooms, elevators, and in-room televisions. At the high end are the luxurious four-star hotels, which have excellent amenities and prices to match. The ratings are sometimes misleading, however, since many hotels prefer to be under starred for tax reasons.

We list hotels by price. Over the past few years luxury hotel prices have risen faster than their more moderate counterparts. Often a hotel in a certain price category will have a few rooms that are less expensive; it's worth asking. Many two- and three-star establishments offer excellent price-to-quality ratios. Rates must be posted in all rooms (usually on the backs of doors), with all extra charges clearly shown. There is a nominal *séjour* tax of 7 francs per person, per night.

Unless otherwise stated, the hotels reviewed below have elevators, rooms have TVs (many with cable, including CNN), minibars, and telephones, and English is spoken. Additional facilities, such as restaurants and health clubs, are listed at the end of each review.

CATEGORY	COST*
$$$$	over 1,750 frs
$$$	1,000 frs–1,750 frs
$$	600 frs–1,000 frs
$	under 600 frs

All prices are for a standard double room, including tax and service.

1ᵉʳ Arrondissement (Louvre)

See Right Bank Lodging map.

$$$$ **🖫 Costes.** Jean-Louis and Gilbert Costes's eponymous hotel is easily
★ their most ambitious project to date. The first surprise is the departure from postmodernism that has been their hallmark. Instead, this sumptuous hotel, converted from an intimate town house, conjures up the palaces of Napoléon III. Every room is swathed in rich garnet and bronze tones and contains a luxurious mélange of patterned fabrics, heavy swags, and enough brocade and fringe to blanket the Champs-Élysées. The bathrooms are truly marvelous affairs. ⊠ *239 rue St-Honoré, 75001,* ☏ *01–42–44–50–50,* 𝖥𝖠𝖷 *01–42–44–50–01. 85 rooms with bath. Restaurant, bar, air-conditioning, in-room modem lines, in-room safes, no-smoking rooms, room service, indoor pool, sauna, exercise room, laundry service. AE, DC, MC, V. Métro: Tuileries.*

$$$$ **🖫 Inter-Continental.** This exquisite late-19th-century hotel has just completed an ambitious restoration. The building was designed by the architect of the Paris Opéra, Charles Garnier, and three of its gilt and stuccoed public rooms are official historic monuments. Spacious guest rooms overlook quiet inner courtyards. In summer, breakfast on the patio is a delicious experience. Service is impeccable. ⊠ *3 rue de Castiglione, 75001,* ☏ *01–44–77–11–11, 800/327–0200 in the U.S.,* 𝖥𝖠𝖷 *01–44–77–10–10. 450 rooms and 75 suites, all with bath. Restaurant, bar, air-conditioning, in-room safes, no-smoking rooms, room service, laundry service, meeting rooms. AE, DC, MC, V. Métro: Concorde.*

$$$$ **🖫 Meurice.** The Meurice, owned by the Italian CIGA chain, is one of the finest hotels in the city. The Louis XVI–style first-floor salons are sumptuous and the bedrooms, adorned with Persian carpets, opulent. Most bathrooms are done in Florentine marble. Book well in advance

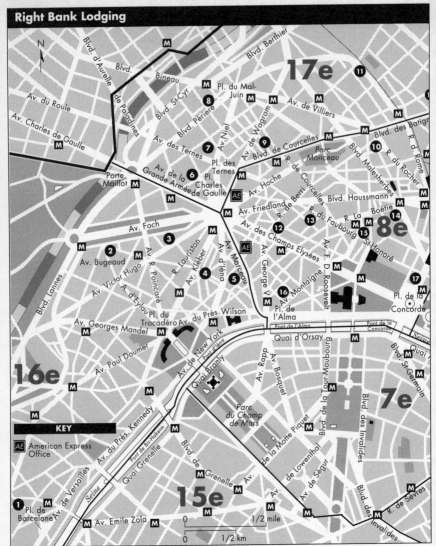

Right Bank Lodging

KEY

AE American Express Office

0   1/2 mile
0   1/2 km

Alexander, **3**

L'Astor, **14**

Axial Beaubourg, **38**

Bradford–Elysées, **13**

Bretonnerie, **40**

Le Bristol, **15**

Britannique, **37**

Caron de
Beaumarchais, **41**

Castex, **47**

Costes, **29**

Crillon, **17**

Deux-Iles, **44**

Eber–Monceau, **9**

Ermitage, **21**

Etoile-Péreire, **8**

Excelsior, **18**

Gaillon-Opéra, **24**

Garden Hotel, **36**

Grand Hôtel de
Besançon, **33**

Grand Hôtel
Inter-Continental, **22**

Hôtel de Noailles, **23**

Hôtel du 7ᵉ Art, **45**

Inter-Continental, **27**

Jules-César, **49**

Keppler, **5**

Kléber, **4**

Lancaster, **12**

Le Laumière, **34**

Londres
St-Honoré, **30**

Louvre Forum, **32**

Meurice, **28**

Modern Hôtel-
Lyon, **50**

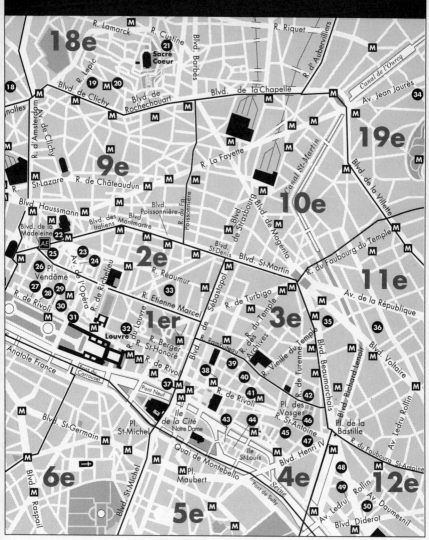

L'Ouest, **11**
Palma, **6**
Le Pavillon
Bastille, **48**
Pavillon de la
Reine, **42**
Place des Vosges, **46**
Plaza-Athénée, **16**

Queen's Hotel, **1**
Regent's Garden, **7**
Régina Paris, **31**
Regyn's
Montmartre, **20**
Résidence
Alhambra, **35**
Résidence
Monceau, **10**

Ritz, **26**
Saint James Paris, **2**
St-Louis, **43**
Utrillo, **19**
Vieux Marais, **39**
Westminster, **25**

Left Bank Lodging

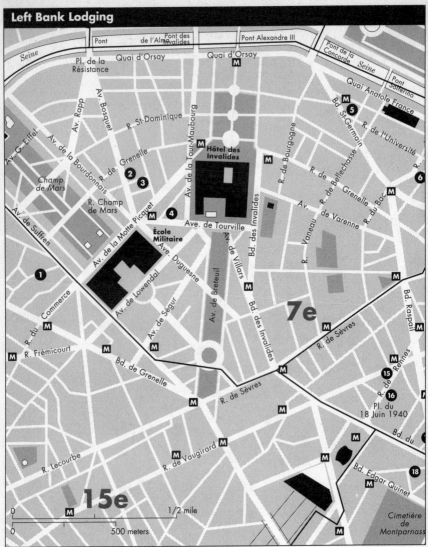

Louvre

1er

4e

R. de Rivoli

Pont Royal

Pont du Carrousel

Pont des Arts

Pont Neuf

du Bac

R. des Sts-Pères

R. Jacob

R. Mazarine

Bd. St-Germain

R. du Four

R. de Rennes

R. St-André des Arts

Pl. St-Michel

Ile de la Cité

Notre Dame

Pont d'Arcade

Quai des Célestins

Ile St-Louis

Quai de Montebello

Pont de la Tournelle

Pl. Maubert

R. St-Jacques

R. des Ecoles

R. Monge

Quai St-Bernard

Pont de Sully

R. Beaubourg

R. de Rivoli

Bd. Sébastopol

Pl. St. Sulpice

R. de Vaugirard

R. Cassette

R. d'Assas

R. Guynemer

R. Vavin

Pl. de l'Odéon

Jardin du Luxembourg

Sorbonne

R. Cujas

R. Soufflot

Pl. du Panthéon

Pl. de la Contrescarpe

Pl. Monge

R. Mouffetard

R. Monge

5e

Jardin des Plantes

6e

Montparnasse

R. Campagne Première

Bd. Raspail

R. Gay Lussac

Bd. St-Michel

R. Claude Bernard

14e

Bd. St-Marcel

7 8 9 10 11 12 13 14 17 19 20 21 22 23 24 25 26 27 28 29 30 31

Raspail-
Montparnasse, **19**
Relais Christine, **9**
Relais St-Germain, **12**
Relais St-Sulpice, **13**
Résidence les
Gobelins, **23**
Solférino, **5**

Sorbonne, **30**
Le Tourville, **4**
Timhotel Jardin des
Plantes, **24**
Tour Eiffel Dupleix, **1**

to land a room or a suite overlooking the Tuileries Gardens. The hotel's restaurant is fabled. ✉ *228 rue de Rivoli, 75001,* ☎ *01–44–58–10–10,* FAX *01–44–58–10–15. 152 rooms and 28 suites, all with bath. Restaurant, bar, air-conditioning, no-smoking rooms, room service, laundry service, business services. AE, DC, MC, V. Métro: Tuileries, Concorde.*

$$$$ 🏨 **Ritz.** Surrounded by the city's finest jewelers, the Ritz is the crowning gem of the sparkling place Vendôme. Festooned with gilt and ormolu, dripping with crystal chandeliers, and swathed in heavy silk and tapestries, this dazzling hotel, which opened in 1896, is the epitome of fin-de-siècle Paris. Yet it's surprisingly intimate. The lack of a lobby discourages paparazzi and sightseers who might annoy the privileged clientele. Legendary suites are named after former residents, such as Marcel Proust and Coco Chanel. Don't miss the famous Hemingway Bar (which the writer claimed to have "liberated" in 1944). ✉ *15 pl. Vendôme, 75001,* ☎ *01–43–16–30–30,* FAX *01–43–16–36–68. 142 rooms and 45 suites, all with bath. 3 restaurants, 2 bars, air-conditioning, in-room safes, room service, indoor pool, beauty salon, health club, shops, laundry service, meeting rooms, parking (fee). AE, DC, MC, V. Métro: Opéra.*

$$$–$$$$ 🏨 **Régina Paris.** In the handsome place des Pyramides, this Art Nouveau gem stuffed with fine antiques oozes old-fashioned grandeur. There's a sublime Belle Epoque lounge and a brand-new health center. Request a room on rue de Rivoli facing the Louvre and the Tuileries Gardens. ✉ *2 rue des Pyramides, 75001,* ☎ *01–42–60–31–10,* FAX *01–40–15–95–16. 129 rooms and 15 suites, all with bath. Restaurant, bar, air-conditioning, in-room safes, no-smoking rooms, room service, massage, sauna, exercise room, laundry service, meeting rooms. AE, DC, MC, V. Métro: Tuileries.*

$$ 🏨 **Britannique.** Open since 1870, the three-star Britannique blends courteous English service with old-fashioned French elegance. It has retained its handsome winding staircase and offers well-appointed, soundproof rooms done in chic, warm tones. During World War I, the hotel served as headquarters for a Quaker mission. ✉ *20 av. Victoria, 75001,* ☎ *01–42–33–74–59,* FAX *01–42–33–82–65. 31 rooms with bath, 9 with shower. Bar, in-room safes. AE, DC, MC, V. Métro: Châtelet.*

$ 🏨 **Londres St-Honoré.** An appealing combination of character and comfort distinguishes this small hotel, a five-minute walk from the Louvre. Exposed oak beams, statues in niches, and rustic stone walls give this place old-fashioned charm, while modern pluses include satellite TV. The elevator doesn't go to the ground floor. ✉ *13 rue St-Roch, 75001,* ☎ *01–42–60–15–62,* FAX *01–42–60–16–00. 23 rooms with bath, 6 with shower. AE, MC, V. Métro: Pyramides.*

$ 🏨 **Louvre Forum.** This friendly two-star hotel is a find: Smack in the ★ center of town, it offers clean, comfortable, well-equipped rooms (with satellite TV) at extremely reasonable prices. The inexpensive breakfast is served in a homey vaulted cellar. ✉ *25 rue du Bouloi, 75001,* ☎ *01–42–36–54–19,* FAX *01–42–33–66–31. 11 rooms with bath, 16 with shower. Bar. AE, DC, MC, V. Métro: Louvre.*

2ᵉ Arrondissement (Le Bourse)

See Right Bank Lodging map.

$$$–$$$$ 🏨 **Westminster.** This former private mansion on an elegant street between the Opéra and place Vendôme was built in the mid-19th century. With marble fireplaces, crystal chandeliers, and parquet floors, it preserves its gracious atmosphere. The pleasant piano bar is a popular rendezvous, and the hotel's restaurant, Le Céladon, offers excellent French cuisine. ✉ *13 rue de la Paix, 75002,* ☎ *01–42–61–57–46,*

FAX 01–42–60–30–66. *83 rooms and 18 suites, all with bath. Restaurant, bar, air-conditioning, in-room safes, no-smoking rooms, room service, baby-sitting, laundry service, meeting rooms, parking (fee). AE, DC, MC, V. Métro: Opéra.*

$$ 🏨 **Gaillon-Opéra.** One of the most charming in the Opéra neighborhood, this hotel has so much character that you would never guess that it's part of a chain. But Best Western has wonderfully preserved the building's original atmosphere: It still has its old oak beams, stone walls, marble tiles, and leafy patio. ✉ *9 rue Gaillon, 75002,* ☎ *01–47–42– 47–74, 800/528–1234 in the U.S.,* FAX *01–47–42–01–23. 26 rooms and 2 suites, all with bath. Bar, air-conditioning, in-room modem lines, in-room safes, no-smoking rooms, room service, baby-sitting, laundry service. AE, DC, MC, V. Métro: Opéra.*

$$ 🏨 **Hôtel de Noailles.** With a nod to the work of postmodern design-
★ ers like André Putnam and Philippe Starck, this new-wave inn is a star among Paris's new crop of well-priced, style-driven boutique hotels. Rooms are individually decorated with funky furnishings and contemporary details; the look is fun and very hip. Breakfast is included in the rate. A young, cosmopolitan clientele has made this one their own. ✉ *9 rue de Michodière, 75002,* ☎ *01–47–42–92–90,* FAX *01– 49–24–92–71. 48 rooms with bath, 5 with shower. In-room safes, no-smoking rooms, laundry service. AE, MC, V. Métro: Opéra.*

$–$$ 🏨 **Grand Hôtel de Besançon.** This superb hotel has it all—intimacy, comfort, affordability, and a location on a delightful, pedestrian market street near Les Halles, the Pompidou Center, and the Marais. The tasteful rooms are quiet, despite the busy area nearby. ✉ *56 rue Montorgueil, 75002,* ☎ *01–42–36–41–08,* FAX *01–45–08–08–79. 11 rooms with bath, 9 rooms with shower. No-smoking rooms. AE, DC, MC, V. Métro: Etienne-Marcel, Les Halles.*

3e Arrondissement (Marais)

See Right Bank Lodging map.

$$$$ 🏨 **Pavillon de la Reine.** This magnificent mansion, reconstructed from
★ original plans, is on the 17th-century place des Vosges. It's filled with Louis XIII–style fireplaces and antiques. Ask for a duplex with French windows overlooking the first of two flower-filled courtyards behind the historic Queen's Pavilion. Breakfast is served in a vaulted cellar. ✉ *28 pl. des Vosges, 75003,* ☎ *01–42–77–96–40, 800/447–7462 in the U.S.,* FAX *01–42–77–63–06. 30 rooms and 25 suites, all with bath. Bar, breakfast room, air-conditioning, room service, laundry service, free parking. AE, DC, MC, V. Métro: Bastille, St-Paul, Chemin Vert.*

4e Arrondissement (Marais/Ile St-Louis)

See Right Bank Lodging map.

$$ 🏨 **Bretonnerie.** This small three-star hotel is in a 17th-century *hôtel particulier* (town house) on a tiny street in the Marais, a few minutes' walk from Beaubourg. Rooms are decorated in Louis XIII style but vary considerably in size from spacious to cramped. Some have antiques, beamed ceilings, four-poster beds, and marble-clad bathrooms. Breakfast is served in the vaulted cellar. ✉ *22 rue Ste-Croix-de-la-Bretonnerie, 75004,* ☎ *01–48–87–77–63,* FAX *01–42–77–26–78. 27 rooms and 3 suites, all with bath. In-room safes. MC, V. Métro: Hôtel de Ville.*

$$ 🏨 **Caron de Beaumarchais.** The theme of this intimate three-star jewel
★ is the work of Caron de Beaumarchais, who wrote the *Marriage of Figaro* in 1778. First-edition copies of his books adorn the public spaces. Rooms are faithfully decorated to reflect the taste of 18th-century

French nobility, right down to the reproduction wallpapers and up-holsteries. Ubiquitous fresh flowers and fluffy bathrobes are a bonus for the price. Bathrooms feature heavy antique mirrors and hand-painted tiles. The fifth- and sixth-floor rooms with balconies are the largest and have beguiling views across Right Bank rooftops. ⊠ *12 rue Vieille-du-Temple, 75004,* ☎ *01–42–72–34–12,* 🆁🅰🆇 *01–42–72–34–63. 17 rooms with bath, 2 with shower. Air-conditioning, in-room safes, laundry service. AE, DC, MC, V. Métro: Hôtel de Ville.*

$$ 🛏 **Deux-Iles.** This converted 17th-century mansion on the Ile St-Louis has long won plaudits for charm and comfort. Flowers and plants are scattered around the stunning main hall. The delightful rooms, blessed with exposed beams, are small but fresh and airy. Ask for one over-looking the little garden courtyard. In winter, a roaring fire warms the lounge. ⊠ *59 rue St-Louis-en-l'Ile, 75004,* ☎ *01–43–26–13–35,* 🆁🅰🆇 *01–43–29–60–25. 8· rooms with bath, 9 with shower. Air-condi-tioning, in-room safes, no-smoking rooms, laundry service, meeting rooms. AE, MC, V. Métro: Pont-Marie.*

$$ 🛏 **St-Louis.** The public areas and bedrooms in this 17th-century town house have been recently refurbished. You'll find Louis XIII–style fur-niture and oil paintings on the ground floor. The bedrooms are ele-gantly simple, with exposed beams and stone walls. Breakfast is served in the atmospheric cellar. ⊠ *75 rue St-Louis-en-l'Ile, 75004,* ☎ *01–46–34–04–80,* 🆁🅰🆇 *01–46–34–02–13. 11 rooms with bath, 10 with shower. In-room safes. MC, V. Métro: Pont-Marie.*

$–$$ 🛏 **Axial Beaubourg.** One of the better deals in the Marais, this three-star hotel in a 16th-century building has beamed ceilings in the lobby and in the six first-floor rooms; the other rooms have functional decor. The Pompidou Center and the Picasso Museum are five minutes away. ⊠ *11 rue du Temple, 75004,* ☎ *01–42–72–72–22,* 🆁🅰🆇 *01–42–72–03–53. 34 rooms with bath, 5 with shower. In-room safes. AE, DC, MC, V. Métro: Hôtel de Ville.*

$ 🛏 **Castex.** This two-star Marais hotel in a Revolution-era building is
★ a bargain-hunter's dream. Rooms are low on frills but squeaky clean, the owners are extremely friendly, and the prices are rock-bottom, which ensures that the hotel is often booked months ahead by a largely Amer-ican clientele. There's no elevator, and the only TV is in the ground-floor salon. ⊠ *5 rue Castex, 75004,* ☎ *01–42–72–31–52,* 🆁🅰🆇 *01–42–72–57–91. 4 rooms with bath, 23 with shower. MC, V. Métro: Bastille.*

$ 🛏 **Hôtel du 7ᵉ Art.** The theme of this hip Marais hotel fits its name ("Seventh Art" is what the French call filmmaking): Hollywood from the '40s to the '60s. Posters of Cagney, Marilyn, Chaplin, and their contemporaries cover the walls. Rooms are small and spartan, but clean, quiet, and equipped with cable TV. There's no elevator. Breakfast is served in the handsome lounge or in the rustic cellar room; there's also a pleasant bar. The clientele is young, trendy, and primarily American. ⊠ *20 rue St-Paul, 75004,* ☎ *01–42–77–04–03,* 🆁🅰🆇 *01–42–77–69–10. 9 rooms with bath, 14 with shower. Bar, breakfast room, in-room safes. AE, DC, MC, V. Métro: St-Paul.*

$ 🛏 **Place des Vosges.** A loyal eclectic clientele swears by this small, his-toric two-star hotel on a charming street just off the exquisite place des Vosges. The Louis XIII–style reception area and rooms with oak-beamed ceilings and rough-hewn stone evoke the old Marais. Ask for the top-floor room, the hotel's largest, for its view over Right Bank rooftops; others are the size of walk-in closets and are less expensive. There's a welcoming little breakfast room. ⊠ *12 rue de Birague, 75004,* ☎ *01–42–72–60–46,* 🆁🅰🆇 *01–42–72–02–64. 11 rooms with bath, 5 with shower. DC, MC, V. Métro: Bastille.*

$ ⊞ **Vieux Marais.** This charming two-star hotel with a turn-of-the-century facade is on a quiet street in the heart of the Marais. Rooms are impeccably clean and are newly equipped with satellite TV; try to get one overlooking the courtyard. Breakfast is served in a pretty lounge, and the staff is exceptionally courteous. ⊠ *8 rue du Plâtre, 75004,* ☏ *01–42–78–47–22,* 𝖥𝖠𝖷 *01–42–78–34–32. 21 rooms with bath, 9 with shower. Air-conditioning, in-room safes. MC, V. Métro: Hôtel de Ville.*

5e Arrondissement (Latin Quarter)

See Left Bank Lodging map.

$$ ⊞ **Elysa Luxembourg.** The Elysa is what the French call *"un hôtel de charme."* Most rooms in this three-star hotel are surprisingly spacious; all are individually decorated and refurbished regularly. Continental and buffet breakfasts are served in the lounge. ⊠ *6 rue Guy-Lussac, 75005,* ☏ *01–43–25–31–74,* 𝖥𝖠𝖷 *01–46–34–56–27. 24 rooms with bath, 6 with shower. No-smoking rooms, laundry service. AE, MC, V. Métro: Luxembourg.*

$$ ⊞ **Jardin du Luxembourg.** Blessed with a charming staff and a smart,
★   stylish look, this hotel, on a calm side street just a block from the Luxembourg Gardens, is one of the most sought-after in the Latin Quarter. Rooms are a bit small (common for this neighborhood) but intelligently furnished and warmly decorated in ocher, rust, and indigo à la provençale. Ask for one with a balcony overlooking the street; the best, No. 25, has dormer windows and a peekaboo view of the Eiffel Tower. ⊠ *5 Impasse Royer-Collard, 75005,* ☏ *01–40–46–08–88,* 𝖥𝖠𝖷 *01–40–46–02–28. 23 rooms with bath, 2 with shower. Bar, air-conditioning, in-room safes. AE, DC, MC, V. Métro: Luxembourg.*

$$ ⊞ **Panthéon.** This three-star hotel occupies a handsome 18th-century building facing the Panthéon. Rooms have rustic charm, with exposed beams and balconies; those on the sixth floor have stunning views of Sacré-Coeur. The vaulted breakfast room and the helpful desk staff are added attractions. ⊠ *19 pl. du Panthéon, 75005,* ☏ *01–43–54–32–95,* 𝖥𝖠𝖷 *01–43–26–64–65. 33 rooms with bath, 1 with shower. Air-conditioning, baby-sitting, laundry service. AE, DC, MC, V. Métro: Luxembourg.*

$ ⊞ **Familia.** The hospitable Gaucheron family bend over backward for
★   their guests and it's hard to beat this level of homespun comfort for the price. Some rooms feature romantic sepia frescoes of celebrated Paris scenes that were painted by an artist from the Beaux Arts; others are appointed with exquisite Louis XV–style furnishings. Those overlooking the animated Latin Quarter street have double-glazed windows; book ahead for one with a walk-out balcony on the second or fifth floor. ⊠ *11 rue des Ecoles, 75005,* ☏ *01–43–54–55–27,* 𝖥𝖠𝖷 *01–43–29–61–77. 14 rooms with bath, 16 with shower. AE, MC, V. Métro: Cardinal Lemoine.*

$ ⊞ **Grandes Ecoles.** This delightfully intimate two-star place looks and feels like a country cottage dropped smack in the middle of the Latin Quarter. It is off the street and occupies three buildings on a beautiful leafy garden, where breakfast is served in summer. Parquet floors, Louis-Philippe furnishings, lace bedspreads, and the absence of TV all add to the rustic ambience. ⊠ *75 rue du Cardinal Lemoine, 75005,* ☏ *01–43–26–79–23,* 𝖥𝖠𝖷 *01–43–25–28–15. 45 rooms with bath, 6 with shower. No-smoking rooms. MC, V. Métro: Cardinal Lemoine.*

$ ⊞ **Sorbonne.** The interior of this pretty, early 18th-century Latin Quarter hotel retains a slightly scruffy, academic ambience well suited to its location. Rooms are small but comfortable and brightened with fresh flowers; try to get one overlooking the little garden. Double-glazed windows ensure tranquility. ⊠ *6 rue Victor-Cousin, 75005,* ☎ *01–43–54–58–08,* FAX *01–40–51–05–18. 11 rooms with bath, 26 with shower. AE, MC, V. Métro: Cluny–La Sorbonne.*

$ ⊞ **Timhotel Jardin des Plantes.** Across the street from the lovely Jardin des Plantes, this pleasant two-star hotel has very reasonable prices and newly updated decor. There's a fifth-floor terrace where you can breakfast or sunbathe in summer, and a sauna in the cellar. ⊠ *5 rue Linné, 75005,* ☎ *01–47–07–06–20,* FAX *01–47–07–62–74. 29 rooms with bath, 4 with shower. Restaurant, bar, sauna. AE, DC, MC, V. Métro: Jussieu.*

6ᵉ Arrondissement (St-Germain/Montparnasse)

See Left Bank Lodging map.

$$$$ ⊞ **Relais Christine.** On a quiet street between the Seine and boulevard St-Germain, this luxurious and popular Left Bank hotel, occupying 16th-century abbey cloisters, oozes romantic ambience. Rooms are spacious (particularly the duplexes on the upper floors) and well appointed in the old Parisian style; the best have exposed beams and overlook the garden. The breakfast room is an erstwhile stone chapel. ⊠ *3 rue Christine, 75006,* ☎ *01–43–26–71–80,* FAX *01–43–26–89–38. 35 rooms and 16 suites, all with bath. Bar, air-conditioning, room service, babysitting, laundry service, meeting rooms, free parking. AE, DC, MC, V. Métro: Odéon.*

$$$–$$$$ ⊞ **L'Hôtel.** Rock idols and movie stars adore this expensive and eccentric Left Bank hotel. Oscar Wilde died here in Room 16. The decor is over the top at times; one small double is decorated entirely in leopard skin; another handsome suite features the mirrored, Art Deco boudoir furniture of vaudeville star Mistinguett. Many rooms are extremely small. The hotel has a fine restaurant, Le Bélier; its decor includes a fountain and a live tree. The piano bar, open until 1 AM, is popular with a well-heeled international crowd. ⊠ *13 rue des Beaux-Arts, 75006,* ☎ *01–44–41–99–00,* FAX *01–43–25–64–81. 14 rooms and 2 suites with bath, 10 rooms with shower. Bar, air-conditioning, in-room safes, laundry service. AE, DC, MC, V. Métro: St-Germain-des-Prés.*

$$$ ⊞ **Relais St-Germain.** The interior-designer owners of this outstanding four-star hotel in the heart of St-Germain-des-Prés have exquisite
★   taste and a superb respect for tradition and detail. Moreover, the rooms are at least twice the size of what you'll find at other hotels in the area for the same price. Much of the furniture was selected with a knowledgeable eye from the city's *brocantes* (second-hand dealers) and every room has its own, unique treasures. Doubles have separate sitting areas; four have kitchenettes. Breakfast is included in the rate. ⊠ *9 carrefour de l'Odéon, 75006,* ☎ *01–43–29–12–05,* FAX *01–46–33–45–30. 21 rooms and 1 suite, all with bath. Breakfast room, wine bar, air-conditioning, in-room safes, room service, baby-sitting, laundry service. AE, DC, MC, V. Métro: Odéon.*

$$–$$$ ⊞ **Le Clos Médicis.** This three-star hotel in St-Germain-des-Prés is richly decorated with Provence in mind. Rooms are small (except for the duplex) but laden with comforts, such as crisp terry-cloth robes and minibars. ⊠ *56 rue Monsieur-le-Prince, 75006,* ☎ *01–43–29–10–80,* FAX *01–43–54–26–90. 22 rooms and 1 duplex with bath, 15 rooms with shower. Bar, air-conditioning, in-room modem lines, minibars, no-smoking rooms, baby-sitting, laundry service, meeting rooms. AE, DC, MC, V. Métro: Luxembourg.*

$$–$$$ ⊞ **Fleurie.** This spiffy family-run hotel, on a quiet side street near place de l'Odéon, has pretty rooms in pastel colors and many modern luxury amenities, including marble-clad bathrooms with heated towel racks. Antiques, Oriental rugs, and rich upholsteries fill the 18th-century building. The staff is helpful. ✉ *32–34 rue Grégoire-de-Tours, 75006,* ☎ *01–53–73–70–70,* FAX *01–53–73–70–20. 29 rooms with bath. Bar, air-conditioning, in-room modem lines, in-room safes, baby-sitting, laundry service. AE, DC, MC, V. Métro: Odéon.*

$$–$$$ 🏨 **Hôtel de L'Abbaye.** This delightful hotel near St-Sulpice, in the heart of the Left Bank, was a convent in the 18th century. It has a stone-vaulted entrance. The first-floor rooms open onto a flower-filled garden; some of the ones on the top floor have oak beams and alcoves. The four duplexes with private terraces are more expensive. Breakfast is included. ✉ *10 rue Cassette, 75006,* ☎ *01–45–44–38–11,* FAX *01–45–48–07–86. 42 rooms and 4 suites, all with bath. Bar, breakfast room, air-conditioning, room service. AE, MC, V. Métro: St-Sulpice.*

$$–$$$ 🏨 **Relais St-Sulpice.** This fashionable little hotel attracts a savvy clientele of discerning taste. The decor is a stylish blend of various periods and regions—African artworks line the hallways; Provençal tiles adorn the bathrooms; Chinese engravings wink to Parisians' penchant for the Orient in the 1930s; heavy fabrics drape the windows; and thick, cotton-pique downy comforters envelop wrought-iron beds. There's a sauna downstairs, right off the atrium breakfast salon. Room 11 has a terrific view of St-Sulpice. ✉ *3 rue Garancière, 75006,* ☎ *01–46–33–99–00,* FAX *01–46–33–00–10. 26 rooms with bath. Air-conditioning, in-room modem lines, in-room safes, no-smoking rooms, sauna, meeting rooms, parking (fee). AE, DC, MC, V. Métro: Mabillon, St-Sulpice.*

$$ 🏨 **Atelier Montparnasse.** This Art Deco–inspired gem of a hotel was
★ designed with style and comfort in mind. Rooms are tastefully decorated and spacious and all the bathrooms feature mosaic reproductions of famous French paintings. The hotel is well situated in Montparnasse within walking distance of the Luxembourg Gardens and St-Germain-des-Prés. ✉ *49 rue Vavin, 75006,* ☎ *01–46–33–60–00,* FAX *01–40–51–04–21. 16 rooms and 1 triple, all with bath. Bar, room service, laundry service. AE, DC, MC, V. Métro: Vavin.*

$$ 🏨 **Manoir de St-Germain-des-Prés.** This stylish and extremely well-priced four-star hotel is right next to the Brasserie Lipp and across from the Café de Flore. Most rooms are done up in traditional 18th-century luxe, with wainscoting and rich upholsteries. Amenities promote genuine R&R: Jacuzzis, soundproof rooms, thirsty terry robes, and well-stocked minibars. ✉ *153 bd. St-Germain-des-Prés, 75006,* ☎ *01–42–22–21–65,* FAX *01–45–48–22–25. 32 rooms with bath. Bar, air-conditioning, in-room safes, minibars, no-smoking rooms, room service, hot tubs. AE, DC, MC, V. Métro: St-Germain-des-Prés.*

$–$$ 🏨 **Acacias St-Germain.** The rooms in this well-priced three-star hotel near Montparnasse are decorated in the *style Anglais* (English style), with sturdy pine furniture and summery upholstery. The staff is friendly and professional. Ask about weekend discounts. ✉ *151 bis rue de Rennes, 75006,* ☎ *01–45–48–97–38,* FAX *01–45–44–63–57. 33 rooms and 4 apartments with bath, 8 rooms with shower. In-room safes, no-smoking rooms, room service, baby-sitting, laundry service, meeting rooms, airport shuttle, parking (fee). AE, DC, MC, V. Métro: St-Placide.*

$–$$ 🏨 **Aramis-St-Germain.** This three-star hotel in the Best Western chain offers great value for the money. Decor is understated and classic French, featuring damask bedspreads and sturdy cherry-wood armoires. All the rooms are soundproof and equipped with cable TV and minibars; nine have whirlpool baths. Harvey's Piano Bar, on the ground floor, is popular with a smart business set. ✉ *124 rue de Rennes, 75006,* ☎ *01–45–48–03–75, 800/528–1234 in the U.S.,* FAX *01–45–44–99–29. 36 rooms with bath, 6 with shower. Bar, air-conditioning, minibars, laundry service, meeting room. AE, DC, MC, V. Métro: St-Placide.*

7ᵉ Arrondissement (Invalides/École Militaire)

See Left Bank Lodging map.

$$$–$$$$ ⊞ **Montalembert.** The Montalembert, a creation of hotel goddess,
   ★ Grace Leo-Andrieu, is one of Paris's most originally voguish boutique
hotels. Whether appointed with traditional or contemporary furnish-
ings, rooms are all about simple lines and chic luxury. A host of sig-
nature elements were designed especially for the hotel by the world's
hippest designers: quilts in bold navy-and-white stripes, Frette linens
and fabrics, Cascais marble bathrooms, and cast-bronze door handles.
Ask about special packages if you're staying for more than three nights.
⊠ *3 rue de Montalembert, 75007,* ☎ *01–45–49–68–68, 800/447–
7462 in the U.S.,* FAX *01–45–49–69–49. 41 rooms and 5 suites with
bath, 10 rooms with shower. Restaurant, bar, air-conditioning, in-
room safes, room service, in-room VCRs, baby-sitting, laundry service,
meeting rooms. AE, DC, MC, V. Métro: Rue du Bac.*

$$–$$$ ⊞ **Le Tourville.** Here is a rare find: an intimate four-star hotel at more
   ★ affordable prices. Each room has crisp, virgin-white damask upholstery
set against pastel or ocher walls, a smattering of antique bureaus and
lamps, original artwork, and fabulous old mirrors. Though most dou-
bles are priced at the low end of the $$ category, the four doubles with
lovely walk-out terraces nip into the $$$ bracket. Both junior suites
have Jacuzzis. The staff couldn't be more helpful. ⊠ *16 av. de Tourville,
75007,* ☎ *01–47–05–62–62, 800/528–3549 in the U.S.,* FAX *01–47–
05–43–90. 28 rooms and 2 junior suites, all with bath. Bar, air-con-
ditioning, laundry service. AE, DC, MC, V. Métro: École Militaire.*

$$ ⊞ **Hôtel du Cadran.** Colorful window boxes lend a welcoming touch
to this cheerful three-star hotel, which occupies a handsome corner build-
ing near the lively pedestrian market on rue Cler. The charming Madame
Chaine and her gracious staff go out of their way to ensure that every
guest enjoys his or her stay, from recommending a charming bistro to
booking theater tickets. Rooms are pretty and very comfortable. Ask
about special weekend rates. ⊠ *10 rue du Champ de Mars, 75007,* ☎
01–40–62–67–00, FAX *01–40–62–67–13. 42 rooms and 1 suite, all
with bath. Bar, air-conditioning, in-room safes, no-smoking rooms, meeting rooms, travel services. AE, DC, MC, V. Métro: École Militaire.*

$$ ⊞ **Hôtel de l'Université.** Rooms still have their original fireplaces and
are decorated with English and French antiques, in this 17th-century
town house between boulevard St-Germain and the Seine. Ask for one
with a terrace on the fifth floor. Those with showers are moderately
priced. ⊠ *22 rue de l'Université, 75007,* ☎ *01–42–61–09–39,* FAX *01–
42–60–40–84. 19 rooms with bath, 8 with shower. Air-conditioning,
in-room safes. AE, MC, V. Métro: Rue du Bac.*

$–$$ ⊞ **Solférino.** Across the street from the Musée d'Orsay, the two-star
Solférino is a charming little hotel with satellite TV and a number of
rooms in the $ category. The upbeat decor is frequently freshened, and
the breakfast lounge is skylighted. ⊠ *91 rue de Lille, 75007,* ☎ *01–
47–05–85–54,* FAX *01–45–55–51–16. 22 rooms with bath, 6 with
shower, 5 with shower and shared WC. AE, MC, V. Closed Dec. 25–
Jan. 1. Métro: Solférino.*

$ ⊞ **Champ de Mars.** Françoise and Stéphane Gourdal's comfortable two-
   ★ star hotel has rooms done in an attractive blue-and-yellow French
country-house style. All are equipped with satellite TV and CNN. The
two on the ground floor open onto a leafy courtyard. The neighborhood—near the Eiffel Tower and Invalides—is also difficult to beat.
⊠ *7 rue du Champ de Mars, 75007,* ☎ *01–45–51–52–30,* FAX *01–
45–51–64–36. 19 rooms with bath, 6 with shower. AE, MC, V.
Métro: École Militaire.*

8ᵉ Arrondissement (Champs-Elysées)

See Right Bank Lodging map.

$$$$ 🏨 **L'Astor.** Following a top-to-bottom makeover by the elite Westin-Demeure group, L'Astor has been reborn as a bastion of highly stylized, civilized chic. The Art Deco lobby is decked out in boldly patterned armchairs, huge mirrors, and clever ceiling frescoes. There's also a cozy bar; a small, neoclassic-inspired library; and a stunning trompe l'oeil dining room. Guest rooms are testimonials to the sober Regency style, with weighty marble fireplaces and mahogany furnishings. Several suites have walk-out balconies with superb vistas. The hotel's restaurant is supervised by the celebrated chef Joel Robuchon. ✉ *11 rue d'Astorg, 75008,* ☎ *01–53–05–05–05, 800/228–3000 in the U.S.,* 📠 *01–53–05–05–30. 132 rooms and 3 suites, all with bath. Restaurant, bar, air-conditioning, in-room modem lines, in-room safes, no-smoking rooms, room service, health club, laundry service. AE, DC, MC, V. Métro: Miromesnil, St-Augustin.*

$$$$ 🏨 **Le Bristol.** Luxury and discretion are its trump cards. The understated facade on rue du Faubourg St-Honoré might mislead the unknowing, but the Bristol ranks among Paris's top four hotels and has the prices to prove it. Some of the spaciously elegant rooms have authentic Louis XV and Louis XVI furniture and magnificent marble bathrooms. The public areas are filled with Old Master paintings, sculptures, sumptuous carpets, and tapestries. Service throughout is impeccable. ✉ *112 rue du Faubourg St-Honoré, 75008,* ☎ *01–53–43–43–00,* 📠 *01–53–43–43–01. 154 rooms and 41 suites, all with bath. Restaurant, bar, air-conditioning, in-room safes, room service, indoor pool, sauna, health club, laundry service, meeting rooms, free parking. AE, DC, MC, V. Métro: St-Philippe-du-Roule.*

$$$$ 🏨 **Crillon.** The Crillon, comprising two 18th-century town houses on place de la Concorde, is often called the crème de la crème of Paris's "palace" hotels. Marie-Antoinette took singing lessons here; one of the original *grands appartements,* now protected as national treasures, has been named after her. Rooms are lavishly (some might say overbearingly) decorated with Rococo and Directoire antiques, crystal and gilt wall sconces, and gold fittings. The sheer quantity of marble downstairs—especially in Les Ambassadeurs restaurant—is staggering. ✉ *10 pl. de la Concorde, 75008,* ☎ *01–44–71–15–00,* 📠 *01–44–71–15–02. 118 rooms and 45 suites, all with bath. 2 restaurants, 2 bars, tea shop, air-conditioning, in-room safes, no-smoking rooms, room service, exercise room, meeting rooms. AE, DC, MC, V. Métro: Concorde.*

$$$$ 🏨 **Lancaster.** The Lancaster—one of Paris's most venerable institutions—
★　has been meticulously transformed into one of the city's most modish, luxury hotels by its new owner, Grace Leo-Andrieu. The new decor seamlessly blends the traditional with the contemporary to evoke an overall feeling of timeless elegance. Every detail speaks of quality, from the hotel's specially commissioned line of scented bath products to the exquisite Porthault linens. Many of the suites pay homage to the hotel's colorful regulars from Garbo to Huston to Sir Alec Guinness. Marlene Dietrich's is decorated in lilac (her favorite color) and features a superb Louis XV desk. ✉ *7 rue de Berri, 75008,* ☎ *01–40–76–40–76, 800/447–7462 in the U.S.,* 📠 *01–40–76–40–00. 60 rooms and 8 suites, all with bath. Restaurant, bar, air-conditioning, in-room safes, room service, in-room VCRs, sauna, exercise room, baby-sitting, laundry service, meeting rooms. AE, DC, MC, V. Métro: George-V.*

$$$$ 🏨 **Plaza-Athénée.** The Plaza, with its distinctive turn-of-the-century facade, accented with wrought iron and red awnings, is tucked discreetly among the haute couture houses on avenue Montaigne, just a block from the Champs-Elysées. Rooms, overlooking either the courtyard or the tony, tree-lined avenue, are superb examples of the Louis XV, Louis XVI, or Regency styles. The brand new fitness club affords views of the Eiffel Tower. ⌧ *25 av. Montaigne, 75008,* ☎ *01–53–67–66–65, 800/223–6800 in the U.S.,* ℻ *01–53–67–66–66. 205 rooms and 65 suites, all with bath. 2 restaurants, bar, air-conditioning, in-room modem lines, in-room safes, no-smoking rooms, room service, beauty salon, health club, laundry service, meeting rooms. AE, DC, MC, V. Métro: Alma-Marceau.*

$$ 🏨 **Bradford-Elysées.** This turn-of-the-century three-star hotel, part of the Best Western chain, has been recently renovated to conserve its appealing, old-fashioned feel. An old wooden elevator carries you from the flower-filled lobby to the spacious, comfortable rooms, some equipped with Louis XVI–style furniture, brass beds, and fireplaces. ⌧ *10 rue St-Philippe-du-Roule, 75008,* ☎ *01–45–63–20–20, 800/528–1234 in the U.S.,* ℻ *01–45–63–20–07. 40 rooms with bath, 8 with shower. Air-conditioning, in-room safes, no-smoking rooms. AE, DC, MC, V. Métro: St-Philippe-du-Roule.*

$$ 🏨 **Résidence Monceau.** In one of the most privileged neighborhoods of Paris, within a stone's throw of the Parc Monceau, this friendly, fashionable hotel is a calm oasis of refined tranquility. Rooms are cozily draped in warm tones and the staff is efficient and professional. The breakfast garden, surrounded by ivy-covered trellises, makes a lovely place to start the day. ⌧ *85 rue du Rocher, 75008,* ☎ *01–45–22–75–11,* ℻ *01–45–22–30–88. 45 rooms with bath, 6 with shower. Bar, café, no-smoking rooms, travel services. AE, DC, MC, V. Métro: Villiers.*

9e Arrondissement (Opéra)

See Right Bank Lodging map.

$$$$ 🏨 **Grand Hôtel Inter-Continental.** Open since 1862, Paris's biggest luxury hotel has a facade that seems as long as the Louvre. The grand salon's Art Deco dome and the restaurant's painted ceilings are registered landmarks. The Art Deco rooms are spacious and light. The famed Café de la Paix is one of the city's great people-watching spots. ⌧ *2 rue Scribe, 75009,* ☎ *01–40–07–32–32, 800/327–0200 in the U.S.,* ℻ *01–42–66–12–51. 514 rooms and 39 suites, all with bath. 3 restaurants, 2 bars, air-conditioning, in-room safes, no-smoking rooms, room service, in-room VCRs, sauna, health club, laundry service, meeting rooms. AE, DC, MC, V. Métro: Opéra.*

11e Arrondissement (Bastille)

See Right Bank Lodging map.

$ 🏨 **Garden Hotel.** This family-run, two-star hotel is on a pretty garden square in a quiet residential neighborhood 10 minutes from Père Lachaise cemetery. Rooms are spotlessly clean; the ones in front have lovely views of the verdant square. All units have double-glazed windows to ensure quiet and are functionally decorated. The staff speaks little English. Bathtubs are half size. ⌧ *1 rue du Général-Blaise, 75011,* ☎ *01–47–00–57–93,* ℻ *01–47–00–45–29. 4 rooms with bath, 38 with shower. AE, MC, V. Métro: St-Ambroise.*

$ 🏨 **Résidence Alhambra.** The gleaming white facade, pretty back garden, and flower-filled window boxes of the two-star Alhambra brighten an otherwise lackluster neighborhood. The hotel is near the Marais and is accessible to five métro lines at place de la République. The smallish rooms are spartanly but tastefully furnished, and have satellite TV. In good weather, breakfast is served on the garden terrace. Prices are rock-bottom. ✉ *13 rue de Malte, 75011*, ☎ *01–47–00–35–52*, FAX *01–43–57–98–75. 10 rooms with bath, 48 with shower. AE, DC, MC, V. Métro: Oberkampf.*

12ᵉ Arrondissement (Bastille/Gare de Lyon)

See Right Bank Lodging map.

$$ ▦ **Le Pavillon Bastille.** Here's a smart address (across from the Opéra
★ Bastille) for savvy travelers who appreciate getting four-star perks for less. The transformation of this 19th-century hôtel particulier into a mod, colorful, high-design hotel garnered architectural awards and a fiercely loyal, hip clientele. The gracious staff pours on the romantic extras (4 PM checkout, fluffy Porthault towels, complimentary mini-bar) and every detail is pitch perfect, right down to the 17th-century fountain in the garden. ✉ *65 rue de Lyon, 75012*, ☎ *01–43–43–65–65, 800/233–2552 in the U.S.*, FAX *01–43–43–96–52. 24 rooms and 1 suite, all with bath. Bar, air-conditioning, in-room safes, minibars, room service. AE, DC, MC, V. Métro: Bastille.*

$–$$ ▦ **Modern Hôtel-Lyon.** Just a block from the Gare de Lyon, this cozy, family-run three-star hotel, open since 1903, has rooms decorated in pastel blues and lavenders. The owners are friendly and helpful. ✉ *3 rue Parrot, 75012*, ☎ *01–43–43–41–52*, FAX *01–43–43–81–16. 40 rooms and 1 suite with bath, 7 rooms with shower. In-room safes. AE, DC, MC, V. Métro: Gare de Lyon.*

$ ▦ **Jules-César.** This two-star hotel, opened in 1930, has a rather glitzy marble lobby. Rooms are more subdued; the ones facing the street are larger and brighter than those in the back. It's near Gare de Lyon and the Opéra Bastille. ✉ *52 av. Ledru-Rollin, 75012*, ☎ *01–43–43–15–88*, FAX *01–43–43–53–60. 4 rooms with bath, 44 with shower. DC, MC, V. Métro: Gare de Lyon, Ledru-Rollin.*

13ᵉ Arrondissement (Gobelins)

See Left Bank Lodging map.

$ ▦ **Résidence les Gobelins.** Warm, wicker-furnished rooms character-ize this small, simple two-star hotel, between place d'Italie and the Latin Quarter on a quiet side street. You can eat breakfast looking out on a small flower-filled garden. ✉ *9 rue des Gobelins, 75013*, ☎ *01–47–07–26–90*, FAX *01–43–31–44–05. 18 rooms with bath, 14 with shower. AE, DC, MC, V. Métro: Gobelins.*

14ᵉ Arrondissement (Montparnasse)

See Left Bank Lodging map.

$$ ▦ **Raspail-Montparnasse.** Rooms in this three-star hotel are named after the artists who made Montparnasse the art capital of the world in the '20s and '30s. All are decorated in pastel colors; five offer spectacular panoramic views of Montparnasse and the Eiffel Tower. Most rooms are at the low end of this price category. ✉ *203 bd. Raspail, 75014*, ☎ *01–43–20–62–86*, FAX *01–43–20–50–79. 28 rooms with bath, 10 with shower. Bar, air-conditioning, in-room safes, meeting rooms. AE, DC, MC, V. Métro: Vavin.*

$–$$ ▦ **Lenox-Montparnasse.** This hotel is in the heart of Montparnasse, just around the corner from the famous Dôme and Coupole brasseries, and close to the Luxembourg Gardens. Rooms vary considerably. The best have fireplaces, old mirrors, and exposed beams; others are dec-orated in a functional contemporary fashion. All have immaculate bathrooms. ✉ *15 rue Delambre, 75014*, ☎ *01–43–35–34–50*, FAX *01–*

43–20–46–64. 44 rooms and 6 suites with bath, 6 rooms with shower. Bar, laundry service. AE, DC, MC, V. Métro: Vavin.

$ ▨ **Istria.** This small, charming family-run hotel on a quiet side street was once a Montparnasse artists' hangout. It has a flower-filled courtyard and simple, clean, comfortable rooms with soft pastel-toned Japanese wallpaper. ⊠ *29 rue Campagne-Première, 75014,* ☎ *01–43–20–91–82,* FAX *01–43–22–48–45. 4 rooms with bath, 22 with shower. In-room safes, meeting rooms. AE, DC, MC, V. Métro: Raspail.*

$ ▨ **Midi.** Don't be put off by the facade and the reception area, which might make you think you're in a chain hotel; rooms here are comfortably furnished in French provincial style and have large floor-to-ceiling windows. Those facing the street are quite spacious. ⊠ *4 av. Réné-Coty, 75014,* ☎ *01–43–27–23–25,* FAX *01–43–21–24–58. 25 rooms with bath, 19 with shower. Refrigerators. MC, V. Métro and RER: Denfert-Rochereau.*

$ ▨ **Parc Montsouris.** This modest two-star hotel in a 1930s villa on a quiet residential street next to the lovely Parc Montsouris gets better every year. Rooms tend to be small, but clean, tastefully furnished, and equipped with satellite TV. Those with showers are very inexpensive. Suites sleep four. ⊠ *4 rue du Parc-Montsouris, 75014,* ☎ *01–45–89–09–72,* FAX *01–45–80–92–72. 28 rooms with bath, 7 suites with shower. AE, MC, V. Métro: Montparnasse-Bienvenue.*

15ᵉ Arrondissement (Champs de Mars)

See Left Bank Lodging map.

$ ▨ **Tour Eiffel Dupleix.** This comfortable, well-priced hotel has been recently revamped to feature modern bathrooms, cable TV with CNN, and double-glazed windows. Some rooms have great views of the Eiffel Tower, which is only a short walk away. The buffet breakfast is one of the city's least expensive. ⊠ *11 rue Juge, 75015,* ☎ *01–45–78–29–29,* FAX *01–45–78–60–00. 30 rooms with bath, 10 with shower. Laundry service, travel services. AE, DC, MC, V. Métro: Dupleix.*

16ᵉ Arrondissement (Trocadéro/Bois de Boulogne)

See Right Bank Lodging map.

$$$$ ▨ **Saint James Paris.** Called the "only château-hôtel in Paris," this gracious late-19th-century neoclassical mansion is surrounded by a lush
★ private park. The lavish Art Deco interior was created by jet-set designer André Putnam. Ten rooms on the third floor open onto a winter garden. The magnificent bar-library is lined with floor-to-ceiling oak bookcases and thousands of leather-covered tomes. The restaurant is reserved for guests; in warm weather, meals are served in the garden. The poshest option: booking one of the two duplex gatehouses. ⊠ *43 av. Bugeaud, 75116,* ☎ *01–44–05–81–81,* FAX *01–44–05–81–82. 24 rooms and 24 suites, all with bath. Restaurant, bar, air-conditioning, in-room safes, room service, sauna, health club, baby-sitting, laundry service, meeting rooms, free parking. AE, DC, MC, V. Métro: Porte Dauphine.*

$$$ ▨ **Alexander.** Everything about the Alexander smacks of Old Europe, from the 20-foot corniced ceilings and period wall sconces (which bathe everything in warm, rosy hues) to the old-fashioned cage elevator. The hotel has a smart address on one of Paris's finest shopping avenues. ⊠ *102 av. Victor Hugo, 75116,* ☎ *01–45–53–64–65; 800/888–4747 or 800/843–3311 in the U.S.;* FAX *01–45–53–12–51. 50 rooms with bath, 12 with shower. Air-conditioning, laundry service, parking (fee). AE, DC, MC, V. Métro: Victor Hugo.*

$–$$ 🏨 **Queen's Hotel.** One of only a handful of hotels in the tony residential
★ district near the Bois de Boulogne, Queen's is a small, comfortable two-
star hotel with a high standard of service. Each room focuses on a different 20th-century French artist. The rooms with baths have Jacuzzis.
☒ *4 rue Bastien-Lepage, 75016,* ☎ *01–42–88–89–85,* FAX *01–40–
50–67–52. 7 rooms with bath, 16 with shower. Air-conditioning, in-
room safes, no-smoking rooms. AE, DC, MC, V. Métro:
Michelange-Auteuil.*

$ 🏨 **Keppler.** Near the Champs-Elysées, on the edge of the 8ᵉ and 16ᵉ
arrondissements, this small two-star hotel in a 19th-century building
has some three-star amenities (like satellite TV) and extremely reasonable
prices. The spacious and airy rooms are simply decorated. ☒ *12 rue
Keppler, 75116,* ☎ *01–47–20–65–05,* FAX *01–47–23–02–29. 31
rooms with bath, 18 with shower. Bar, room service. AE, MC, V.
Métro: George-V.*

$ 🏨 **Kléber.** Between the Arc de Triomphe and Trocadéro, this lovely 19th-
century mansion benefits from the calm and greenery of nearby place
des Etats-Unis. The hotel has been recently redecorated with traditional
French fabrics and furnishings. Every room has satellite TV and those
on the second and fifth floors have balconies. ☒ *7 rue de Belloy,
75116,* ☎ *01–47–23–80–22,* FAX *01–49–52–07–20, 800/246–0041
in the U.S. 12 rooms and 1 suite with bath, 10 rooms with shower.
Bar, no-smoking rooms, laundry service. AE, DC, MC, V. Métro:
Kléber.*

17ᵉ Arrondissement (Monceau/Clichy)

See Right Bank Lodging map.

$$ 🏨 **Eber-Monceau.** This small hotel belongs to the Relais du Silence group,
which guarantees a quiet night's sleep. Just one block from the romantic
Parc Monceau, it attracts the smart media and fashion set. The engaging
host, Jean-Marc Eber, is delighted to welcome first-time visitors. Rooms
are tastefully furnished; ask for one overlooking the courtyard. ☒ *18
rue Léon Jost, 75017,* ☎ *01–46–22–60–70,* FAX *01–47–63–01–01.
8 rooms and 5 suites with bath, 5 rooms with shower. Bar, room ser-
vice, parking (fee). AE, DC, MC, V. Métro: Courcelles.*

$$ 🏨 **Etoile-Péreire.** The extremely congenial owner has created a unique,
★ intimate hotel, behind a quiet, leafy courtyard in a chic residential dis-
trict. It consists of two parts: a fin-de-siècle building on the street and
a 1920s annex overlooking an interior courtyard. Rooms and du-
plexes are decorated in deep shades of roses or blues with crisp, white
damask upholstery. The copious breakfast is legendary, featuring 40
assorted jams and jellies. The bar is always busy in the evening. ☒ *146
bd. Péreire, 75017,* ☎ *01–42–67–60–00,* FAX *01–42–67–02–90. 18
rooms and 5 duplex suites with bath, 3 rooms with shower. Bar, air-
conditioning in some rooms, no-smoking rooms, laundry service. AE,
DC, MC, V. Métro: Péreire.*

$$ 🏨 **Regent's Garden.** The large number of repeat visitors is a safe in-
dication that this hotel, near the Arc de Triomphe, is a special place.
Built in the mid-19th century by Napoléon III for his doctor, it is
adorned as you would imagine with marble fireplaces, mirrors, gilt fur-
niture, and cornicing. Be sure to request a room overlooking the gor-
geous garden, where breakfast is served in summer. ☒ *6 rue
Pierre-Demours, 75017,* ☎ *01–45–74–07–30,* FAX *01–40–55–01–
42. 39 rooms with bath. Lobby lounge, air-conditioning in some
rooms. AE, DC, MC, V. Métro: Ternes.*

$ 🏨 **Excelsior.** This endearing place is just a five-minute walk from
Montmartre and near more than a dozen bus and métro lines. The small,
spotless rooms are warmly furnished with rustic antiques and heavy

armoires. Request one overlooking the charming little garden. ⊠ *16 rue Caroline, 75017,* ☎ *01–45–22–50–95,* ℻ *01–45–22–59–88. 19 rooms with bath, 3 with shower. Laundry service. AE, V. Métro: Place de Clichy.*

$ 🏨 **L'Ouest.** Although this unpretentious two-star hotel overlooks the railroad near Pont-Cardinet station, you can be sure of a restful sleep, since all the rooms are soundproof. Some have more light and are more spacious than others, so be sure to make your preference known. The area may not have much to interest tourists, but Montmartre, Parc Monceau, and the *grands magasins* (department stores) are all within easy reach. ⊠ *165 rue de Rome, 75017,* ☎ *01–42–27–50–29,* ℻ *01–42–27–27–40. 16 rooms with bath, 32 with shower. Bar. AE, DC, MC, V. Métro: Rome, Villiers.*

$ 🏨 **Palma.** The friendly and efficient Couderc family runs this small and charming two-star hotel between the Arc de Triomphe and Porte Maillot. It's one of the best modest hotel deals in the city. Rooms are decorated with bright floral wallpaper; ask for a top-floor room with a view. ⊠ *46 rue Brunel, 75017,* ☎ *01–45–74–74–51,* ℻ *01–45–74–40–90. 13 rooms with bath, 24 with shower. 5 rooms with air-conditioning. AE, MC, V. Métro: Argentine.*

18ᵉ Arrondissement (Montmartre)

See Right Bank Lodging map.

$ 🏨 **Ermitage.** This elfin, family-run two-star hotel dates from Napoléon III and is filled with antiques. The building has only two stories, but the hilly Montmartre neighborhood ensures that some rooms have a nice view of Paris. ⊠ *24 rue Lamarck, 75018,* ☎ *01–42–64–79–22,* ℻ *01–42–64–10–33. 3 rooms with bath, 9 with shower. No credit cards. Métro: Lamarck-Caulaincourt.*

$ 🏨 **Regyn's Montmartre.** Despite the small rooms, this owner-run hotel on Montmartre's evocative place des Abbesses provides comfortable accommodations that are regularly refurbished. Each floor is dedicated to a Montmartre artist; poetic homages by local writers are featured in the hallways. Ask for a room on either of the top two floors for great views of either the Eiffel Tower or Sacré-Coeur. Courteous service and a relaxed atmosphere make this an attractive choice. ⊠ *18 pl. des Abbesses, 75018,* ☎ *01–42–54–45–21,* ℻ *01–42–23–76–69. 14 rooms with bath, 8 with shower. In-room safes. AE, MC, V. Métro: Abbesses.*

$ 🏨 **Utrillo.** This charming two-star hotel is on a quiet side street at the foot of Montmartre, near colorful rue Lepic. The prints and the marble-top breakfast tables in every room are charmingly old-fashioned. Whites and pastels lend a bright and spacious feel. Two rooms (numbers 61 and 63) have views of the Eiffel Tower. ⊠ *7 rue Aristide-Bruant, 75018,* ☎ *01–42–58–13–44,* ℻ *01–42–23–93–88. 5 rooms with bath, 25 with shower. Sauna. AE, DC, MC, V. Métro: Abbesses.*

19ᵉ Arrondissement (Buttes-Chaumont)

See Right Bank Lodging map.

$ 🏨 **Le Laumière.** Though it's some distance from the city center, the rock-bottom rates of this family-run, two-star hotel near the rambling Buttes-Chaumont park are hard to resist. Rooms are sleek but uninspiring, with modular furniture; some of the larger ones overlook the garden. The staff is exceptionally helpful. Ask about special rates. ⊠ *4 rue Petit, 75019,* ☎ *01–42–06–10–77,* ℻ *01–42–06–72–50. 18 rooms with bath, 36 with shower. MC, V. Métro: Laumière.*

Apartment Rentals

If you will be staying longer than a week, want to do your own cooking, or need a base large enough for a family, consider a furnished rental. Policies differ from company to company, but you can generally expect a minimum required stay of one week; a refundable deposit (expect $200–$500), payable on arrival; and weekly or biweekly maid service. The following is a list of good-value residence hotels, each with multiple properties in Paris. **Orion** (⊠ 30 pl. d'Italie, 75013, ☎ 01–40–78–54–54, 800/546–4777 or 212/688–9538 in the U.S.; FAX 01–40–78–54–55, 212/688–9467 in the U.S.). **Citadines Résidences Hôtelières** (⊠ 18 rue Favart, 75002, ☎ 01–44–50–23–23, FAX 01–44–50–32–50). **Adagio** (⊠ 20 esplanade Charles-de-Gaulle, 92000, Nanterre, ☎ 01–46–69–79–00, FAX 01–47–25–46–48). **Paris Appartements Services** (⊠ 69 rue d'Argout, 75002, ☎ 01–40–28–01–28, FAX 01–40–28–92–01).

U.S.-based agencies rent apartments in Paris. **French Experience** (⊠ 370 Lexington Ave., New York, NY 10017, ☎ 212/986–1115, FAX 212/986–3808). **Chez Vous** (⊠ 1001 Bridgeway, Suite 245, Sausalito, CA 94965, ☎ 415/331–2535, FAX 415/331–5296).

In Paris, the **Rothray** agency (⊠ 10 rue Nicolas Flamel, 74004, ☎ 01–48–87–13–37 or 01–40–28–91–84, FAX 01–42–78–17–72 or 01–40–26–34–33) has particularly pretty properties—for short- or long-term rental—in stylish districts like the Marais.

5 Nightlife and the Arts

Whether you love dancing the night away at a fashionable club, sipping Pernod at a crowded bar, or listening to music in a postmodern, state-of-the-art concert hall, Paris has it all. From gilded opera houses to low-key jazz clubs, trendy discos, and Art Deco cinemas, the City of Light shines at night.

THE ARTS

Updated by
Roberta
Beardsley

PARISIANS CONSIDER THEIR CITY a bastion of art and culture, and indeed it is. Enormous amounts of government money go into culture, but surprisingly, Paris is not quite on par with New York, London, or Milan for theater, opera, music, or ballet. Nonetheless, Parisian audiences are discerning, so standards are very high. Also, many international companies that you might not see elsewhere perform in Paris. The contemporary dance scene, too, is particularly exciting, as are the plethora of cinemas showing excellent French and American films.

The music season usually runs from September to June. Theaters also stay open at this time, but many productions are at summer festivals elsewhere in France. The weekly magazines *Pariscope* (which has an English section), *L'Officiel des Spectacles,* and *Figaroscope* (a supplement to *Le Figaro* newspaper) are published every Wednesday and give detailed entertainment listings. The booklet, **"Saison de Paris,"** available at the Office de Tourisme de la Ville de Paris or from the Maison de France (☞ Visitor Information *in* the Gold Guide, for both). The Paris Tourist Office's **24-hour hot line** in English (☎ 01–49–52–53–56) is another source of information about weekly events.

The best place to buy tickets is at the venue itself; try to purchase in advance, as many of the more popular performances sell out. Also try your hotel or a travel agency, such as **Paris-Vision** (⊠ 1 rue Auber, 9ᵉ, ☎ 01–40–06–01–00, métro Opéra). Tickets for some events can be bought at the **FNAC** stores—especially Alpha-FNAC (⊠ 1–5 rue Pierre Lescot, Forum des Halles, 3rd level down, 1ᵉ, ☎ 01–40–41–40–00, métro Châtelet-Les Halles). **Virgin Megastore** (⊠ 52 av. des Champs-Elysées, 8ᵉ, ☎ 01–44–78–44–08, métro Franklin-D.-Roosevelt) sells theater and concert tickets. Half-price tickets for many same-day theater performances are available at the **Kiosque Théâtre** (⊠ across from 15 pl. de la Madeleine, métro Madeleine), open Tuesday–Saturday 12:30–8 and Sunday 12:30–6; expect a line. There's another branch inside the Châtelet RER station, open Monday–Saturday.

Classical Music

Cité de la Musique (⊠ in the Parc de la Villette, 221 av. Jean-Jaurès, 19ᵉ, ☎ 01–44–84–44–84, métro Porte de Pantin) presents a varied program of classical and world music concerts in a postmodern setting.
IRCAM (⊠ 1 pl. Igor-Stravinsky, 4ᵉ, ☎ 01–44–78–48–43, métro Les Halles) gives concerts of contemporary classical music on the premises, at the Pompidou Center next door, or at the Cité de la Musique.
Salle Pleyel (⊠ 252 rue du Faubourg St-Honoré, 8ᵉ, ☎ 01–45–61–53–00, métro Ternes) was Paris's principal home of classical music before the new Opéra Bastille opened. The Paris Symphony Orchestra and other leading international orchestras still play here regularly.
Théâtre des Champs-Elysées (⊠ 15 av. Montaigne, 8ᵉ, ☎ 01–49–52–50–50, métro Alma-Marceau) is worthy of a visit based solely on architectural merit and ambience; this elegantly restored, plush Art Deco temple hosts concerts and ballet as well as plays.

Paris also has a never-ending stream of free or inexpensive lunchtime and evening church concerts, ranging from organ recitals to choral music and orchestral works. Some are scheduled as part of the **Festival d'Art Sacré** (☎ 01–44–70–64–10, for information) between mid-November and Christmas. Check the weekly listings for information; telephone numbers for most church concerts vary with the organizer. **Ste-Chapelle** (⊠ 4 bd. du Palais, 1er, métro Cité) holds outstanding candlelit concerts, though not in winter; make reservations well in advance. At **Notre-Dame** (⊠ Ile de la Cité, 4e, métro Cité) you can combine sightseeing with good listening. Other churches with classical concerts include: **St-Eustache** (⊠ rue du Jour, 1er, métro Les Halles). **St-Germain-des-Prés** (⊠ 3 pl. St-Germain-des-Prés, 6e, métro St-Germain-des-Prés). **St-Louis-en-l'Ile** (⊠ 19 rue St-Louis-en-l'Ile, 4e, métro Pont-Marie). **St-Roch** (⊠ 296 rue St-Honoré, 1er, métro Tuileries). **St-Germain l'Auxerrois** (⊠ pl. du Louvre, 1er, métro Louvre-Rivoli).

Museums are another place to find classical concerts: The **Musée d'Orsay,** (⊠ 1 rue de Bellechasse, 7e, ☏ 01–45–49–48–14, RER Musée d'Orsay) regularly holds small-scale concerts (song cycles, piano recitals, or chamber music) at lunchtime or in the early evening. For lovers of early music, the **Musée du Moyen Age** frequently stages atmospheric events (⊠ 6 pl. Paul Painlevé, 5e, ☏ 01–43–25–62–00, métro Cluny–La Sorbonne).

Dance

As a rule, more avant-garde or up-and-coming choreographers can be found in the smaller dance spaces around the Bastille and the Marais and in theaters in the nearby suburbs. Classical ballet can be found in places as varied as the opera house and the sports stadium. Check the weekly guides for listings.

Opéra Garnier (⊠ pl. de l'Opéra, 9e, ☏ 01–40–01–17–89, métro Opéra) is the sumptuous home of the well-reputed Paris Ballet, as well as host to many major foreign dance troupes.
Palais des Congrès (⊠ pl. de la Porte Maillot, 17e, ☏ 01–40–68–00–05, métro Porte Maillot) is a large, modern hall that presents a classical repertoire to a family audience.
Palais des Sports (⊠ pl. de la Porte de Versailles, 15e, ☏ 01–44–68–69–70, métro Porte de Versailles), a circular building dating from the 1970s, often stages ballet performances and large-scale spectacles.
Théâtre de la Bastille (⊠ 76 rue de la Roquette, ☏ 01–43–57–42–14, 11e, métro Bastille) merits mention as an example of the innovative activity in the Bastille area; it has an enviable record as a launch pad for tomorrow's modern dance stars.
Théâtre de la Ville (⊠ 2 pl. du Châtelet, 4e, métro Châtelet and ⊠ 31 rue des Abbesses, 18e, métro Abbesses, ☏ 01–42–74–22–77 for both) has a varied international dance program.

Film

Parisians are far more addicted to film as an art form than Londoners or New Yorkers. There are hundreds of cinemas in the city showing contemporary and classic French and American movies, as well as an array of independent, international, and documentary films. A number of theaters, especially in principal tourist areas such as the Champs-Elysées, the boulevard des Italiens near the Opéra, St-Germain-des-Prés, and Les Halles, run English-language films. Check the weekly guides for a movie of your choice with the initials "v.o." or "v.o.s.t.f.," which means *version original/sous titrés français,* or not dubbed. Cinema admission runs from 37 to 51 francs; some cinemas have reduced rates on certain days or for early shows; others offer reductions with purchase of a multiple entry card. Most theaters will post two show times: the *séance,* the commercials, previews, and, sometimes, short films before the film; and the feature presentation, which usually starts 10–25 minutes later.

There are a number of cinemas for big-screen fanatics. **Gaumont Grand Ecran** (⊠ 30 pl. d'Italie, 13ᵉ, ☎ 01–45–80–77–00, métro Place d'Italie). **Grand Rex** (⊠ 1 bd. Poissonière, 2ᵉ, ☎ 08–36–68–70–23, métro Bonne Nouvelle). **Kinopanorama** (⊠ 60 av. de la Motte-Piquet, 15ᵉ, ☎ 01–43–06–50–50, métro La Motte Picquet Grenelle). **Max Linder Panorama** (⊠ 24 bd. Poissonière, 9ᵉ, ☎ 01–48–24–88–88, métro Rue Montmartre). **UGC Ciné Cité Les Halles** (⊠ Forum des Halles, Level 3, access by the Porte du Jour near the St-Eustache church, 1ᵉʳ, ☎ 08–36–68–68–58, métro Les Halles). **La Pagode** (⊠ 57 bis rue de Babylone, 7ᵉ, ☎ 01–45–55–48–48, métro François-Xavier), a cinema in a Chinese-style pagoda, is a national monument and well worth a visit (plus it has a pleasant café).

The Latin Quarter is the realm of small theaters showing classic and independent films, although there are also other cinemas all over the city with similar programming. Showings are often organized around retrospectives (check "Festivals" in weekly guides). Following is a list of some of the cinemas in the area. **Action Christine Odéon** (⊠ 4 rue Christine, 6ᵉ, ☎ 01–43–29–11–30, métro Odéon). **Action Ecoles** (⊠ 23 rue des Ecoles, 5ᵉ, ☎ 01–43–25–72–07, métro Maubert-Mutualité). **L'Entrepôt** (⊠ 7–9 rue Francis de Pressensé, 14ᵉ, ☎ 08–36–68–05–87, métro Pernety). and the **MacMahon** (⊠ 5 av. MacMahon, 14ᵉ, ☎ 01–43–29–79–89, métro Etoile).

Classics and obscure films that attract real movie buffs are shown at the **Centre Pompidou** (⊠ Salle Garance, pl. Georges-Pompidou, 4ᵉ, ☎ 01–42–78–37–29, métro Rambuteau). At the **Cinéma des Cinéastes,** (⊠ 7 av. de Clichy, 17ᵉ, ☎ 01–53–42–40–00, métro Place de Clichy) you can see special previews of feature films, as well as documentaries, short subjects, and rarely shown movies, in an old cabaret transformed into a movie theater and wine bar by three contemporary French directors. The **Vidéothèque de Paris** (⊠ Forum des Halles, Porte St-Eustache entrance, 1ᵉʳ, ☎ 01–40–26–34–30, métro Les Halles) organizes thematic viewings of its archives of films and videos on the city of Paris. The **Cinémathèque Française** (⊠ Musée du Cinéma, corner of rue Albert de Mun and av. du Président Wilson, in the Palais de Chaillot, ☎ 01–45–53–74–39, métro Trocadéro) has a reference library, photography collection, and an outstanding assortment of films.

Géode (⊠ at the Cité des Sciences et de l'Industrie, Parc de la Villette, 30 av. Corentin-Cariou, 19ᵉ, ☎ 01–40–05–70–00, métro Porte de la Villette) shows wide-angle Omnimax films—usually documentaries—on a 1,000-square-meter spherical surface. In summer, the stars in the sky rival those of the screen as old favorites are projected outdoors on a large screen at the **Parc de la Villette** (métro Porte de Pantin or La Villette). Films are listed in the weekly guides.

Opera

Getting tickets to the Opéra de la Bastille or the Opéra Garnier can be difficult on short notice, so it is a good idea to plan ahead. Get the program of performances in the Paris Tourist Office's "Saison de Paris" booklet (☞ *above*), then write to the Opéra de la Bastille (⊠ 120 rue de Lyon, 75012) well in advance, giving several choices of nights and performances. If the response is affirmative, just pick up your tickets before the performance. A word of caution: Buying from a scalper is not recommended, as there have been reports of people selling counterfeit tickets.

Opéra de la Bastille (⌧ pl. de la Bastille, 11ᵉ, ☎ 01–47–73–13–00, métro Bastille) has taken over the role as Paris's main opera house from the Opéra Garnier. It has had its share of start-up and management problems, and many feel it is not living up to its promise of grand opera at affordable prices (which range from 60 to 590 francs).

Opéra Comique (⌧ 5 rue Favart, 2ᵉ, ☎ 01–42–96–12–20, métro Richelieu-Drouot) is a lofty old hall that presents excellent comic operas and lightweight musical entertainments.

Opéra Garnier (⌧ pl. de l'Opéra, 9ᵉ, ☎ 01–40–01–17–89, métro Opéra) still hosts occasional performances of the Paris Opéra.

Théâtre Musical de Paris (⌧ pl. du Châtelet, 1ᵉʳ, ☎ 01–40–28–28–28, métro Châtelet), better known as the Théâtre du Châtelet, offers opera and ballet for a wider audience than the Opéra Garnier, at more reasonable prices.

Theater

A number of theaters line the Grand Boulevards between Opéra and République, but there is no Paris equivalent to Broadway or the West End. Shows are mostly in French.

Bouffes du Nord (⌧ 37 bis bd. de la Chapelle, 10ᵉ, ☎ 01–46–07–34–50, métro La Chapelle) has wonderful experimental productions.

Café de la Gare (⌧ 41 rue du Temple, 4ᵉ, ☎ 01–42–78–52–51, métro Rambuteau) is a fun spot to experience a particularly Parisian form of theater, the *café-théâtre*—a mixture of satirical sketches and variety show riddled with slapstick humor, performed in a café setting. You need a good grasp of French.

La Cartoucherie (⌧ in the Bois de Vincennes, ☎ 01–43–74–24–08, métro Château de Vincennes, then take the shuttle bus), a complex of three theaters in a former munitions factory, turns cast and spectators into an intimate theatrical world. Go early for a simple meal; the cast often helps serve.

Chez Michou (⌧ 80 rue des Martyrs, 18ᵉ, ☎ 01–46–06–16–04, métro Abbesses) is another spot for café-théâtre, but this Montmartre venue is pricier than Café de la Gare (☞ *above*).

Comédie Française (⌧ pl. André-Malraux, 1ᵉʳ, ☎ 01–44–58–15–15, métro Palais-Royal) is a distinguished venue that stages classical drama. You can reserve seats in person about two weeks in advance, or turn up an hour beforehand and wait in line for cancellations.

MC93 Bobigny (⌧ 1 bd. Lenine, Bobigny, ☎ 01–41–60–72–72, métro Bobigny–Pablo Picasso), in a working class neighborhood north of Paris, often stages top-flight English and American productions.

Nouveau Théâtre Mouffetard (⌧ 73 rue Mouffetard, 5ᵉ, ☎ 01–43–31–11–99, métro Monge) is home to inexpensive and popular modern drama productions.

Théâtre de la Huchette (⌧ 23 rue de la Huchette, 5ᵉ, ☎ 01–43–26–38–99, métro St-Michel) is a highlight for Ionesco admirers; this tiny Left Bank theater is where the playwright's short modern plays make a deliberate mess of the French language.

Théâtre Mogador (⌧ 25 rue de Mogador, 9ᵉ, ☎ 01–53–32–32–00, métro Trinité), one of Paris's most sumptuous theaters, has musicals and other productions with popular appeal.

Théâtre de l'Odéon (⌧ pl. de l'Odéon, 6ᵉ, ☎ 01–44–41–36–36, métro Odéon) hosts first-rate companies from all over Europe; subtitles (in French) are part of the program.

Théâtre de la Renaissance (⌧ 20 bd. St-Martin, 10ᵉ, ☎ 01–42–08–18–50, métro Strasbourg-St-Denis) was once home to Belle Epoque star Sarah Bernhardt (she was manager from 1893 to 1899). Come here to see French comedies.

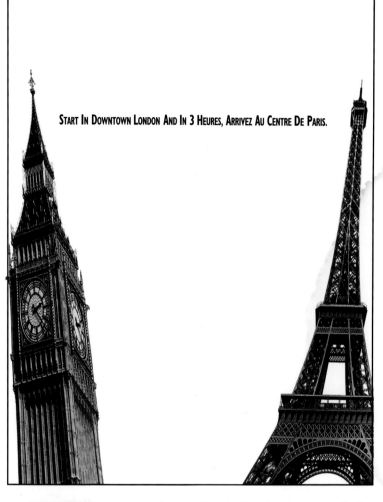

START IN DOWNTOWN LONDON AND IN 3 HEURES, ARRIVEZ AU CENTRE DE PARIS.

Rail Europe

Imagine traveling directly between London and Paris with no connections to run for, no busses to board, no taxis to hail. In fact, the only thing you have to change is the tongue you speak upon arrival.

That's exactly what you'll experience aboard the high-speed Eurostar passenger train.

Board the Eurostar at the center of one city, travel through the new Channel Tunnel, and arrive directly in the center of the other. Simple as that. And at speeds of up to 200 miles per hour, the entire trip lasts just three short hours. We can also get you between London and Brussels in three and a quarter.

For more information, contact your travel agent or Rail Europe at 1-800-EUROSTAR.

If a quick, comfortable trip between London and Paris is on your itinerary, you'll find we speak your language perfectly.

EUROSTAR. DIRECT.   **CALL 1-800-EUROSTAR**

Eurostar is a service provided together by the railways of Belgium, Britain and France

Circus

There's no need to know French to enjoy the circus. Tickets range from 40 to 180 francs. The venues change frequently, so it is best to check one of the weekly guides. **Cirque National Alexie Gruss** (✉ no fixed address, ☎ 01–40–36–08–00, for information) remains an avowedly old-fashioned production with showy and often aristocratic horsemen. From tigers to yaks, dogs, and clowns, **Cirque Diana Moreno Bormann** (✉ Jardin d'Acclimatation, Bois de Boulogne, ☎ 01–45–01–51–22, métro Sablons) is good for all ages; performances are Wednesday and Saturday afternoons. **Cirque de Paris** (✉ 115 av. Charles de Gaulle, Villeneuve-la-Garenne, ☎ 01–47–99–40–40, métro Porte de Clignancourt, then Bux 137) offers "A Day at the Circus": a peek behind the scenes in the morning, lunch with the artists, and a performance in the afternoon. **Cirque d'Hiver** (✉ 110 rue Amelot, 11ᵉ, ☎ 01–47–00–12–25, métro Filles du Calvaire), constructed in 1852 as a circus hall, is now only occasionally home to the circus; more often fashion shows and parties are held here.

Puppet Shows

On most Wednesday, Saturday, and Sunday afternoons, the Guignol, the French equivalent of Punch and Judy, can be seen going through their ritualistic battles in a number of Paris's parks, including **Champs de Mars** (métro Ecole Militaire) and **Parc Montsouris** (métro Porte d'Orléans). The **Jardin du Luxembourg** (métro Vavin) and the **Jardin d'Acclimatation** (métro Sablons) both have year-round, weather-proof spaces. The **Marionnettes des Champs-Elysées** (✉ Rond Point des Champs-Elysées, at the corner of avs. Matignon and Gabriel, 8ᵉ, ☎ 01–42–57–43–34, métro Champs-Elysées–Clemenceau) also gives performances.

NIGHTLIFE

So you've immersed yourself in culture all day and you want a night out on the town. The hottest spots are around Pigalle—despite its reputation as a seedy red-light district—and the Bastille and Marais areas. The Left Bank has a bit of everything. The Champs-Elysées is making a comeback, though the clientele remains predominantly foreign. On weeknights, people are usually home after closing hours at 2 AM, but weekends mean late-night partying. Take note, though: The last métro runs between 12:30 and 1 AM (but you can always take a cab).

Bars de Nuit

More and more, Parisians seem to be bypassing clubs and heading for bars when out on the town. The success of the bar scene is understandable—the best of the category have character, witty waiters, local color, and inventive cocktails at prices that permit consumption without counting. The variety of bar is also impressive—bars serving light food, moody late-night bars, bars with DJs, and bars with live music. Bar hours vary, so be sure to call ahead.

Bastille/Marais

Café de la Plage (✉ 59 rue de Charonne, 11ᵉ, ☎ 01–47–00–35–39, métro Ledru-Rollin) has jazz in the cellar and Guinness at the bar.
Le Casbah (✉ 18 rue de la Forge-Royale, 11ᵉ, ☎ 01–43–71–71–89, métro Faidherbe-Chaligny) has more than a touch of Casablanca in its denlike atmosphere; upstairs there is a bar and restaurant; downstairs, a dance club.

China Club (⊠ 50 rue de Charenton, 12ᵉ, ☎ 01–43–43–82–02, métro Ledru-Rollin) has three floors of bars and a restaurant with lacquered furnishings and a colonial Orient theme.

Opium Café (⊠ 5 rue Elzevir, 4ᵉ, ☎ 01–40–29–93–40, métro St-Paul) will carry you through dinner and dancing in a baroque but relaxed atmosphere.

Le Reservoir (⊠ 16 rue de la Forge Royale, 11ᵉ, ☎ 01–43–56–39–60, métro Faidherbe-Chaligny), in a yawning space where sewing machines once hummed, has an immense bar and occasional musical guests.

Sanz Sans (⊠ 49 rue du Faubourg St-Antoine, 11ᵉ, ☎ 01–44–75–78–78, métro Bastille) has added a new twist to bar life—the "actors" on the upstairs lounge's gilt-framed video screen are really the habitués of the downstairs bar.

Pigalle/Montmartre

Châo-Bâ (⊠ 22 bd. de Clichy, 18ᵉ, ☎ 01–46–06–72–90, métro Pigalle) is a spacious, two-tiered café-bar with Asian decor and mock bamboo furniture.

Le Dépanneur (⊠ 27 rue Fontaine, 9ᵉ, ☎ 01–40–16–40–20, métro Blanche) caters to a gin- and tequila-drinking yuppie crowd and stays open all night.

Moloko (⊠ 26 rue Fontaine, 9ᵉ, ☎ 01–48–74–50–26, métro Blanche), a smoky late-night bar with several rooms, a mezzanine, a jukebox, and a small dance floor, is a popular spot.

Champs-Elysées/Opéra

Barfly (⊠ 49–51 av. George V, 8ᵉ, ☎ 01–53–67–84–60, métro George V) has its followers among the business and fashion crowd who come to this extremely narrow place for a sushi fix, as well as to see and be seen.

Buddha Bar (⊠ 8 rue Boissy d'Anglas, 8ᵉ, ☎ 01–53–05–90–00, métro Concorde), with its imposing Buddha contemplating the fashionable crowd, has a spacious mezzanine bar that overlooks the dining room where cuisines, east and west, meet somewhere in California.

Le Forum (⊠ 4 bd. Malesherbes, 8ᵉ, ☎ 01–42–65–37–86, métro Madeleine), a discreet, archetypal French cocktail bar, has one of the best selections of cocktails and whiskeys in Paris.

Harry's New York Bar (⊠ 5 rue Daunou, 2ᵉ, ☎ 01–42–61–71–14, métro Opéra), a cozy, wood-paneled hangout popular with expatriates, is haunted by the ghosts of Ernest Hemingway and F. Scott Fitzgerald.

Montparnasse

Le Closerie des Lilas (⊠ 171 bd. de Montparnasse, 6ᵉ, ☎ 01–43–54–21–68, RER Port Royal) has served more than one generation of poets and intellectuals, as the brass plaques around the bar attest. The piano plays until one in the morning.

Le Rosebud (⊠ 11 bis rue Delambre, 14ᵉ, ☎ 01–43–20–44–13, métro Vavin) is a jazzy cult spot for the *jeunesse dorée* (young and fashionable) of Montparnasse; it's also renowned for its late-night chili con carne.

Utopia (⊠ 79 rue de l'Ouest, 14ᵉ, ☎ 01–43–22–79–66, métro Pernety) has live rhythm and blues and country almost every night.

Elsewhere

Café de la Musique (⊠ 213 av. Jean Juarès, at Parc de la Villette, 19ᵉ, métro Porte de Pantin) offers a large choice of cocktails and limited brasserie offerings in a comfortable setting inspired by the 40s. Varied musical menus include live jazz on Wednesday.

La Ginguette Pirate (⊠ quai de la Gare, 13ᵉ, ☎ 01–44–24–89–89, métro quai de la Gare) began as a model of a Chinese junk sitting on a piano and became a real Chinese junk with a piano moored here. Listen to live rock or salsa nightly; on Saturday there is a modest cover.

Hotel Bars

Highly popular among the nostalgic, as well as people looking for a quiet place to talk, are the many hotel bars in the city, including: **Bristol** (⊠ 112 rue du Faubourg St-Honoré, 8ᵉ, ☎ 01–53–43–43–42, métro Miromesnil), **Lutétia** (⊠ 45 bd. Raspail, 6ᵉ, ☎ 01–49–54–46–46, métro Sèvres-Babylone), **Normandy** (⊠ 7 rue de l'Echelle, 1ᵉʳ, ☎ 01–42–60–61–08, métro Palais-Royal), and the **Ritz** (⊠ 15 pl. Vendôme, 1ᵉʳ, ☎ 01–43–16–30–30, métro Opéra).

Boîtes de Nuit

Paris's *boîtes de nuit* (nightclubs) are both expensive and exclusive—it's best to know someone to get through the door. But the less affluent '90s have been a humbling experience for more than a few clubs. Some have survived by offering clubgoers more, including meals, theme nights, and special events. Given the fragility of a club's life, it's best to check before going out. Many clubs are closed Monday and some on Tuesday; by Wednesday most are functioning at full swing.

Bastille/Marais

Les Bains (⊠ 7 rue du Bourg-l'Abbé, 3ᵉ, ☎ 01–48–87–01–80, métro Etienne-Marcel), a forever-trendy hot spot with controversial new decor, combines bar, restaurant, and club, and is hard to get into; it helps to be famous, look like a model, or have a reservation at the restaurant. It's open every day of the week.

Le Balajo (⊠ 9 rue de Lappe, 11ᵉ, ☎ 01–47–00–07–87, métro Bastille), in an old Java ballroom, offers a bit of everything: salsa, techno, retro, even *bal musette*, the accordion music so evocative of Montmartre street balls.

La Java (⊠ 105 rue du Faubourg du Temple, 10ᵉ, ☎ 01–42–02–20–52, métro Belleville), where Edith Piaf and Maurice Chevalier made their names, offers live Latin music and Cuban jam sessions on Thursday and Friday night.

Opus Café (⊠ 167 quai de Valmy, 10ᵉ, ☎ 01–40–34–70–00, métro Jean Juarès) shelters a youngish crowd seeking escape from techno-rap in a stunning loftlike space.

Pigalle/Montmartre

Bus Palladium (⊠ 6 rue Fontaine, 9ᵉ, ☎ 01–42–81–31–81, métro Blanche) invites women free on Tuesdays and adds striptease to the program on Wednesdays; on other nights it caters to a more general clientele. Fear no techno; the house music is rock in all its variations.

Le Palace (⊠ 8 rue du Faubourg-Montmartre, 9ᵉ, ☎ 01–42–46–10–87, métro rue Montmartre) is a legendary two-story haunt; at press time (1997) it had closed, and a reopening date had not yet been set.

Le Temple (⊠ 9 pl. Pigalle, 9ᵉ, ☎ 01–48–74–27–11, métro Pigalle), a new addition to the night scene, has two bars and two dance floors, a mixed gay and hetero clientele, and techno music.

Latin Quarter/Montparnasse

Chez Félix (⊠ 23 rue Mouffetard, 5ᵉ, ☎ 01–47–07–68–78, métro Monge) pulls in aficionados of live Brazilian music on Saturday nights.

Their formula is a prix-fixe dinner with the show and dancing afterwards.

Dancing la Coupole (✉ 100 bd. du Montparnasse, 14ᵉ, ☎ 01–43–20–14–20, métro Vavin) has retro and disco on weekends; and on Tuesday, salsa, preceded by an optional refresher course—an idea which seems to have breathed new life into this monument.

Zed Club (✉ 2 rue des Anglais, 6ᵉ, ☎ 01–43–54–93–78, métro Maubert-Mutualité) is a prime rock-and-roll and bebop venue for all ages.

Champs-Elysées/Monceau

Keur Samba (✉ 79 rue La Boétie, 8ᵉ, ☎ 01–43–59–03–10, métro St-Philippe-du-Roule) has African decor and rhythms, a tiny dance floor, and an exclusive clientele who stays until dawn.

Niel's (✉ 27 av. Ternes, 17ᵉ, ☎ 01–47–66–45–00, métro Ternes) numbers top models and showbiz glitterati among its regulars. Music ranges from rap to techno to mainstream disco.

Eiffel Tower

Le Colonial (✉ moored at Port Debilly opposite the Eiffel Tower, 16ᵉ, ☎ 01–53–23–98–98, métro Pont de l'Alma) offers a port in the storm for those looking for an alternative to the Pigalle scene. The sizable disco has replaced the first-class cabins.

Gay and Lesbian Bars and Clubs

Gay and lesbian bars and clubs are mostly concentrated in the Marais and include some of the hippest addresses in the city. However, trendy clubs fall in and out of favor at lightning speed, and one-night discos and tea dances are always popping up, so check the local papers to see what's hot.

For Men and Women

Amnésia Café (✉ 42 rue Vieille-du-Temple, 4ᵉ, ☎ 01–42–72–16–94, métro Rambuteau) has an underlit bar and art deco ceiling paintings that attract a young, yuppie gay and lesbian crowd.

Banana Café (✉ 13 rue de la Ferronnerie, 1ᵉʳ, ☎ 01–42–33–35–31, métro Les Halles) has a trendy, energetic, and scantily clad mixed crowd; dancing on the tables is the norm.

Les Planches (✉ 36 rue Doudeauville, 18ᵉ, ☎ 01–42–54–12–56, métro Château Rouge) offers two roomy lounges and a summer terrace for evening get-togethers.

Queen (✉ 102 av. des Champs-Elysées, 8ᵉ, ☎ 01–53–89–08–90, métro George V) is currently one of the most talked about nightclubs in Paris: Gays, lesbians, and heterosexuals are all lining up to get in. Monday is disco night, with house music on other days.

Mostly Men

Club 18 (✉ 18 rue de Beaujolais, 1ᵉʳ, ☎ 01–42–97–52–13, métro Pyramides), the oldest gay disco in Paris, took on a modern look in 1993 and is as popular and casual as ever, particularly on theme nights.

Le Milk (✉ 3 Cité Bergère, 9ᵉ, ☎ 01–42–46–50–98, métro rue Montmartre) is a basement spot bathed in blue and green underwater decor. Clients can access the Palace (☞ *above*) through a backdoor.

Quetzal Bar (✉ 10 rue de la Verrerie, 4ᵉ, ☎ 01–48–87–99–07, métro Hôtel-de-Ville) gleams with lots of chrome, blue lighting, and pick-me-up smiles. It's packed and smoky on weekends.

Mostly Women

Au Vieux Casque (✉ 19 rue Bonaparte, 6ᵉ, ☎ 01–43–54–99–46, métro St-Germain-des-Prés) serves bistro food at reasonable prices. The decor is cozy and the ambience is friendly and frequently boisterous.

Champmesle (⊠ 4 rue Chabanais, 2ᵉ, ☎ 01–42–96–85–20, métro Bourse) is the hub of lesbian nightlife, with a dusky back room reserved for women only.

L'Enfer (⊠ 34 rue du Départ, 14ᵉ, ☎ 01–42–79–94–94, métro Montparnasse) reserves prime time, Friday and Saturday nights, for a women-only disco crowd. Men get their chance to take in the flashing laser show on Thursday and Sunday. Wednesday the doors are open to everyone.

Pubs

Pubs wooing English-speaking clients with a selection of beers are becoming increasingly popular with Parisians. They are also good places to find reasonably priced food at off-hours.

Académie de la Bière (⊠ 88 bis bd. de Port Royal, 5ᵉ, ☎ 01–43–54–66–65, RER Port-Royal) serves 145 brews and good french fries and *moules marinière* (mussels cooked in white wine).

Bar Belge (⊠ 75 av. de St-Ouen, 17ᵉ, ☎ 01–46–27–41–01, métro Guy Môquet) is an authentically noisy Flemish drinking hole.

The Bowler (⊠ 13 rue d'Artois, 8ᵉ, ☎ 01–45–61–16–60, métro St-Philippe-du-Roule) is the latest bang in the Paris pub explosion: Beer and food are served in the evening in this big space.

The Cricketers (⊠ 41 rue des Mathurins, 8ᵉ, ☎ 01–40–07–01–45, métro St-Augustin), owned by Graham Gooch, the legendary captain of the English cricket team, replies to the virtual Irish monopoly on Paris pubs with amber ales from Adnams of Sussex. Cricket memorabilia adorn the walls.

Finnegan's Wake (⊠ 9 rue des Boulangers, 5ᵉ, ☎ 01–46–34–23–65, métro Jussieu) attracts a mixed Franco-British clientele with its Guinness on tap, Irish music, and dancing in the vaulted cellar on Thursday night.

Kitty O'Shea's (⊠ 10 rue des Capucines, 2ᵉ, ☎ 01–40–15–08–08, métro Opéra) has authentic pub trappings and Guinness on tap.

The Mayflower (⊠ 49 rue Descartes, 5ᵉ, ☎ 01–43–54–56–47, métro Cardinal Lemoine) is a wood-paneled, leather-benched favorite among Scotchophile Left Bankers, astounded by the sippability of its 101 whiskeys. There's also a large list of international beers.

Wine Bars

Paris wine bars are the perfect place to enjoy a glass (or bottle) of wine with a plate of cheese or charcuterie. Bar owners are often true wine enthusiasts ready to dispense expert advice. Most Paris wine bars also serve light meals, which in French terms means three courses in the 120- to 180-franc range. Hours can vary widely, so it's best to check ahead if your heart is set on a particular place; most, however, close around 10 PM.

Aux Bons Crus (⊠ 7 rue des Petits-Champs, 1ᵉʳ, ☎ 01–42–60–06–45, métro Bourse) is a cramped, narrow venue with an authentic Parisian feel (it dates from 1905).

Le Baron Rouge (⊠ 1 rue Théophile-Roussel, 12ᵉ, ☎ 01–43–43–14–32, métro Ledru-Rollin) is a dark, noisy haunt, where wine spills from the barrel. It's every bit as rambunctious as the nearby place d'Aligre (famous for its market).

Jacques Mélac (⊠ 42 rue Léon-Frot, 11ᵉ, ☎ 01–43–70–59–27, métro Charonne) is named after the jolly host who harvests grapes from the vine outside and bottles several of his own wines (☞ Chapter 3).

Le Moulin à Vins (⊠ 6 rue Burq, 18ᵉ, ☎ 01–42–52–81–27, métro Abbesses) serves up wines from the southwest and the Rhone valley and sturdy bistro cuisine. Stop by and elbow your way in among the locals at the bar.

La Robe et le Palais (⊠ 13 rue des Lavandières-Ste-Opportune, 1ᵉʳ, ☎ 01–45–08–07–41, métro Châtelet) offers over 120 wines from all over France, served *au compteur* (according to the quantity consumed), as well as good, creative light dishes.

Le Rubis (⊠ 10 rue du Marché St-Honoré, 1ᵉʳ, ☎ 01–42–61–03–34, métro Tuileries) is a resolutely old-time wine bar, which is the most crowded during the day. During rush hour it's best to be smoke resistant.

La Tartine (⊠ 24 rue de Rivoli, 4ᵉ, ☎ 01–42–72–76–85, métro St-Paul) provides cheap wine and *tartines* (large open-face sandwiches) in a tatty, almost seedy, turn-of-the-century bar that has earned antihero status among the rebel cognoscenti.

Willi's Wine Bar (⊠ 13 rue des Petits-Champs, 1ᵉʳ, ☎ 01–42–61–05–09, métro Bourse), a small, London-style venue popular with English speakers, takes its wine, and sometimes itself, just a little too seriously; good Rhône wines and an inventive menu are served.

Jazz Clubs

The French take jazz seriously, and Paris is one of the world's great jazz cities, with plenty of variety, including some fine, distinctive local talent. Most jazz clubs are in the Latin Quarter or around Les Halles. For nightly schedules, consult the specialty magazine *Jazz Hot* or *Jazz Magazine*. Remember that nothing gets going until 10 or 11 PM and that entry prices vary widely from about 40 francs to more than 100 francs.

Latin Quarter/St-Germain

Le Bilboquet (⊠ 13 rue St-Benoît, 6ᵉ, ☎ 01–45–48–81–84, métro St-Germain-des-Prés) is where mostly French musicians play mainstream jazz in a faded Belle Epoque decor.

Caveau de la Huchette (⊠ 5 rue de la Huchette, 5ᵉ, ☎ 01–43–26–65–05, métro St-Michel) is a smoke-filled shrine to the Dixieland beat.

Le Montana (⊠ 28 rue St-Benoît, 6ᵉ, ☎ 01–45–48–93–08, métro St-Germain-des-Prés), in a restored Art Deco building, concentrates on traditional jazz with occasional forays into country and blues.

Le Petit Journal (⊠ 71 bd. St-Michel, 5ᵉ, ☎ 01–43–26–28–59, RER Luxembourg) has long attracted leading exponents of New Orleans jazz; it serves good food, too.

La Villa (⊠ 29 rue Jacob, 6ᵉ, ☎ 01–43–26–60–00, métro St-Germain-des-Prés) attracts serious pianists and jazz musicians to its stylish setting.

Les Halles/Gare du Nord

Au Duc des Lombards (⊠ 42 rue des Lombards, 1ᵉʳ, ☎ 01–42–33–22–88, métro Les Halles) offers modern contemporary jazz in an ill-lit, romantic bebop venue with decor inspired by the Paris métro.

Le Baiser Salé (⊠ 58 rue des Lombards, 1ᵉʳ, ☎ 01–42–33–37–71, métro Les Halles) attracts a younger crowd with salsa, rhythm and blues, fusion, and funk.

New Morning (⊠ 7 rue des Petites-Ecuries, 10ᵉ, ☎ 01–45–23–51–41, métro Château-d'Eau) is a premier spot for serious fans of avant-garde jazz, folk, and world music; decor is spartan, the mood reverential.

Le Petit Opportun (⊠ 15 rue des Lavandières-Ste-Opportune, 1ᵉʳ, ☎ 01–42–36–01–36, métro Les Halles), in a converted bistro, sometimes features top-flight American soloists with French backup.

Le Sunset (⊠ 60 rue des Lombards, 1ᵉʳ, ☎ 01–40–26–46–50, métro Châtelet) delivers modern jazz with mostly French or local musicians; on Sunday night there's a featured vocalist.

Champs-Elysées

Lionel Hampton Jazz Club (⊠ Méridien Hotel, 81 bd. Gouvion-St-Cyr, 17ᵉ, ☎ 01–40–68–30–42, métro Porte Maillot), named for the zingy xylophonist loved by Parisians, hosts a roster of international jazz musicians in a spacious, comfortable atmosphere.

Rock, Pop, and World Music Venues

Unlike French jazz, French rock is not generally considered to be on a par with its American and British cousins. Even so, Paris is a great place to catch some of your favorite groups because concert halls tend to be smaller and tickets can be less expensive. It's also a good spot to see all kinds of world music. Most places charge from 90 to 120 francs for entrance and get going around 11 PM.

Le Bataclan (⊠ 50 bd. Voltaire, 11ᵉ, ☎ 01–47–00–30–12, métro Oberkampf) is a legendary venue for live rock, rap, and reggae in an intimate setting with a disco that gets going after-hours.

Casino de Paris (⊠ 16 rue de Clichy, 9ᵉ, ☎ 01–49–95–99–99, métro Trinité), once a favorite with Serge Gainsbourg, has a horseshoe balcony and a cramped, cozy, music-hall feel.

La Cigale (⊠ 124 bd. Rochechouart, 18ᵉ, ☎ 01–42–23–15–15, métro Pigalle) often plays host to up-and-coming French rock bands.

Divan du Monde (⊠ 75 rue des Martyrs, 18ᵉ, ☎ 01–44–92–77–66, métro Pigalle) is on every music fan's list. The crowd varies according to the music of the evening: reggae, soul, funk, or salsa.

Elysée Montmartre (⊠ 72 bd. Rochechouart, 18ᵉ, ☎ 01–44–92–45–45, métro Anvers) dates from Gustave Eiffel, its builder, who, it's hoped, liked a good party. With a following as diverse as the music, and a new techno sound system, it provides a new definition of the old *bal populaire*.

Hot Brass (⊠ Parc de la Villette, 211 av. Jean Jaurès, 19ᵉ, ☎ 01–42–00–14–14, métro Porte de Pantin) often features American musicians on its varied program, including modern jazz, fusion, funk, salsa, world music, and hip-hop. Dancing begins after the concert.

Olympia (⊠ 28 bd. des Capucines, 9ᵉ, ☎ 01–47–25–49–45, métro Madeleine), a legendary venue once favored by Jacques Brel and Edith Piaf, still hosts leading French singers.

Palais Omnisports de Paris-Bercy (⊠ rue de Bercy, 12ᵉ, ☎ 01–44–68–44–68, métro Bercy) is a large venue where you'll find leading English and American groups.

Zenith (⊠ Parc de la Villette, 19ᵉ, ☎ 01–42–08–60–00, métro Porte-de-Pantin) is a large concert hall that primarily stages rock shows; check posters and listings for details.

Cabarets

Paris's cabarets are household names, shunned by worldly Parisians and loved by tourists, who flock to the shows. You can dine at many of them: prices range from 200 francs (simple admission plus one drink) to more than 750 francs (dinner plus show). For 400 to 500 francs, you get a seat plus half a bottle of champagne.

L'Ane Rouge (⊠ 3 rue Laugier, 17ᵉ, ☎ 01–43–80–79–97, métro Ternes) is a typical French cabaret playing to a mixed Parisian and foreign crowd, where the emphasis is on laughs and entertainment, with a host of singers, magicians, comedians, and ventriloquists.

Au Lapin Agile (⊠ 22 rue des Saules, 18ᵉ, ☎ 01–46–06–85–87, métro Lamarck-Caulaincourt), in Montmartre, considers itself the doyen of cabarets. Picasso once paid for a meal with one of his paintings. Prices are lower than elsewhere, as this is more of a large bar than a full-blown cabaret.

Caveau des Oubliettes (⊠ 52 rue Galande, 5ᵉ, ☎ 01–44–07–06–51, métro St-Michel), where you can listen to Edith Piaf songs in a medieval cellar that was once the dungeon of a prison, serves up minstrels, troubadours, and wenches as the wait staff.

Crazy Horse (⊠ 12 av. George V, 8ᵉ, ☎ 01–47–23–32–32, métro Alma-Marceau) is one of the best-known clubs for pretty girls and raunchy dance routines with lots of humor and few clothes.

Eléphant Bleu (⊠ 49 rue de Ponthieu, 8ᵉ, ☎ 01–42–25–17–61, métro Franklin-D.-Roosevelt) is a cabaret-cum-restaurant with an exotic (often Asian) touch to most of its shows.

Folies Bergère (⊠ 32 rue Richer, 9ᵉ, ☎ 01–44–79–98–98, métro Cadet), a legend since the days of Manet, is now a new-and-improved cabaret that returns to its music-hall origins, helped by ornate costumes and masterful lighting.

Lido (⊠ 116 bis av. des Champs-Elysées, 8e, ☎ 01–40–76–56–10, métro George V) stars the famous Bluebell Girls; the owners claim no show this side of Las Vegas can rival it for special effects.

Madame Arthur (⊠ 75 bis rue des Martyrs, 18ᵉ, ☎ 01–42–54–40–21, métro Pigalle) stages a wacky, burlesque transvestite-and-drag show that's not for the faint-hearted.

Moulin Rouge (⊠ 82 bd. de Clichy, 18ᵉ, ☎ 01–46–06–00–19, métro Blanche), that old favorite at the foot of Montmartre, mingles the Doriss girls, the cancan, and crocodiles in an extravagant spectacle.

Nouvelle Eve (⊠ 25 rue Fontaine, 9ᵉ, ☎ 01–48–74–69–25, métro Pigalle) has a postwar music-hall flavor, with songs, dance, and magicians.

Paradis Latin (⊠ 28 rue du Cardinal Lemoine, 5ᵉ, ☎ 01–43–25–28–28, métro Cardinal Lemoine) is perhaps the liveliest, busiest, and trendiest cabaret on the Left Bank.

Rôtisserie de l'Abbaye (⊠ 22 rue Jacob, 6ᵉ, ☎ 01–46–33–50–05, métro St-Germain-des-Prés) is a venue for French, English, and American songs accompanied by the guitar in a medieval setting.

Casino

Casino d'Enghien (⊠ 3 av. de Ceinture, ☎ 01–34–12–90–00), the nearest public casino, is by the lake at Enghien-les-Bains, 16 km (10 mi) north of Paris. For admittance, take an ID, put on a jacket and tie, and leave your sports shoes at home.

After-Hours Dining

Chances are that some of your nocturnal forays will have you looking for sustenance at an unlikely hour. If so, you might find it handy to know that there are restaurants open round the clock. *See* Chapter 3 for more suggestions.

L'Alsace (⊠ 39 av. des Champs-Elysées, 8ᵉ, ☎ 01–53–93–97–00, métro Franklin-D.-Roosevelt), a smart, if characterless, brasserie-restaurant, serves seafood and sauerkraut to famished night owls.

Au Chien Qui Fume (⊠ 33 rue du Pont-Neuf, 1ᵉʳ, ☎ 01–42–36–07–42, métro Les Halles), open until 2 AM, has a chocolate mousse worth waiting up for.

Au Pied de Cochon (⊠ 6 rue Coquillière, 1ᵉʳ, ☎ 01–40–13–77–00, métro Les Halles), near St-Eustache church, once catered to the all-night workers at the adjacent Paris food market. Its Second Empire decor has been restored, and traditional dishes like pig's trotters and chitterling sausage still grace the menu.

Le Congrès (⊠ 80 av. de la Grande-Armée, 17ᵉ, ☎ 01–45–74–17–24, métro Porte-Maillot), a lesser-known haunt beyond the Arc de Triomphe, is worth checking out if you're in search of a late-night T-bone steak.

Grand Café des Capucines (⊠ 4 bd. des Capucines, 9ᵉ, ☎ 01–43–12–19–00, métro Opéra), whose exuberant turn-of-the-century dining room matches the mood of the neighboring Opéra, serves excellent oysters, fish, and meat dishes at hefty prices.

K.O.H. Tapis Rouge (⊠ 67 rue du Faubourg-St-Martin, 10e, ☎ 01–42–45–87–36, métro Château d'Eau) started out as a carpet store in 1784. Regulars include theater people and cabaret dancers. With space for 300 diners, it is a good address for large groups.

6 Shopping

When shopping in Paris you will find that every neighborhood reflects a unique attitude and style. From the designer extravagance of avenue Montaigne and rue Faubourg St-Honoré to the hip attitude of Les Halles, the blink-and-you'll-miss-it trends of the Bastille, the avant-garde designers of the Marais, and the classic sophistication of St-Germain, Paris offers something for every taste.

Updated by
Suzanne
Rowan
Kelleher

WINDOW-SHOPPING is one of Paris's greatest spectator sports. Tastefully displayed wares—luscious cream-filled éclairs, lacy lingerie, exquisite clothing, and gleaming copper pots—entice the eye and awaken the imagination. Happily, shopping opportunities in Paris are endless and geared to every taste. You can price emerald earrings at Cartier, spend an afternoon browsing through bookstalls along the Seine, buy silk-lined gloves at Dior, tour the high-gloss department stores, or haggle over prices in the sprawling flea markets on the outskirts of town.

For many, perfume and designer clothing are perhaps the most coveted Parisian souvenirs. However, even on haute couture's home turf, bargains are surprisingly elusive. It's best to know prices before coming, to avoid the slings and arrows of international exchange rates. A Pierre Cardin tie or a Lalique bottle of L'Air du Temps may be cheaper at the mall back home, although it won't be as much fun to buy.

Bargain hunters should watch for the word *soldes* (sales). The two main sale seasons are January and July. Until recently, the typical French markdown was meager, but the recession has forced the average discount to 30%–50% off during sale seasons. Also look for goods marked *dégriffé*—designer labels, often from last year's collection, for sale at a deep discount.

While sightseeing, visit the gift shops in Paris's museums: The best offer a superb selection of books, posters, accessories, and jewelry, along with excellent reproductions from the museum's collection.

Credit Cards

Credit cards are more widely used in France than in the United States. Even the corner newsstand or flea market are likely to honor plastic for purchases over 100 francs. Visa is the most common and preferred card, followed closely by MasterCard/EuroCard. American Express, Diners Club, and Access are accepted in the larger international stores.

Duty-Free Shopping

A value-added tax of 20.6%, known in France as the TVA or *détaxe,* is imposed on most consumer goods. Non–European Union residents, aged 15 and over, who stay in France and/or the EU for fewer than six months can reclaim part of this tax. To qualify, your purchases in a single shop must total at least 1,200 francs. The amount of the refund varies from shop to shop but usually hovers between 13% and 16%. You may opt to be reimbursed by check, but a refund credited directly to your credit card is the easiest and fastest way to receive your money. The major department stores have simplified the process with special détaxe desks where the *bordereaux* (export sales invoices) are prepared. Most high-profile shops with international clients have détaxe forms, but stores are not required to do this paperwork. If the discount is extremely important to you, ask if it is available before making your purchase. There is no refund for food, wine, and tobacco. Invoices and bordereaux forms must be presented to French customs upon leaving the country. The items purchased should be available for inspection.

Mailing Purchases Home

Smaller shops are reluctant to mail purchases overseas. Mailing goods oneself is quite easy—all French post offices sell self-sealing mailing boxes—but postage is costly. Remember that if you are claiming a Value Added Tax deduction (☞ *above*), you must have the goods with you when you leave the country.

Shopping Areas

Avenue Montaigne

This exclusive, elegant boulevard is a showcase of international haute-couture houses. Italian moguls Prada and Dolce & Gabbana have joined Chanel, Dior, Nina Ricci, Jil Sander, Guy Laroche, Jean-Louis Scherrer, Emanuel Ungaro, Céline, Valentino, MaxMara, Genny, Krizia, Escada, Thierry Mugler, and Hanae Mori. Here you'll also find accessories by S. T. Dupont, Loewe, Salvatore Ferragamo, and Louis Vuitton. Yves Saint-Laurent and Givenchy are nearby, on avenues Marceau and George-V, respectively, and you'll find Versace on rue François I.

Bastille

Scores of trendy boutiques are clustered between art galleries, bars, and furniture stores in this gentrified neighborhood. Jean-Paul Gaultier has a boutique on rue Faubourg St-Antoine and hot, young newcomer Christophe Lemaire is installed on the rue St-Sabin.

Champs-Elysées

Cafés and movie theaters keep the once chic Champs-Elysées active 24 hours a day, but the invasion of exchange banks, car showrooms, and fast-food chains has lowered the tone. Four glitzy 20th-century arcade malls (Galerie du Lido, Le Rond-Point, Le Claridge, and Elysées 26) capture most of the retail action.

Left Bank

After decades of clustering on the Right Bank's venerable shopping avenues, the high-fashion houses are now storming the Rive Gauche. Ever since Louis Vuitton, Giorgio Armani, Thierry Mugler, Christian Dior Men, and Romeo Gigli set up Left Bank shops in 1996, anyone who's anyone has rushed to followed suit. (Sonia Rykiel and Yves Saint-Laurent arrived fashionably early in the 1970s). This immensely walkable district between rue de Grenelle and rue de Rennes is also known for its top-quality shoe shops (Maud Frizon, Charles Jourdan, Stéphane Kélian, and Harel).

Les Halles

Most of the narrow pedestrian streets on the former site of Paris's wholesale food market are lined with fast-food joints, sex shops, jeans outlets, and garish souvenir stands, but rue du Jour (featuring MaxMara, Agnès B., and Junior Gaultier boutiques) is an attractive exception. The fabulously quirky Comme des Garçons has shops for both sexes on rue Etienne-Marcel. In the middle of the action is the Forum des Halles, a multilevel underground shopping mall, which used to be a nightmarish mash of noisy teens until it attracted higher-quality merchants and a clutch of promising designers.

Louvre–Palais-Royal

The elegant and eclectic shops clustered in the 18th-century arcades of the Palais-Royal sell antiques, toy soldiers, Shiseido cosmetics, dramatic art jewelry from Siki, and even vintage designer dresses. The glossy marble Carrousel du Louvre mall, beneath the Louvre, is lit by an immense inverted glass pyramid. Shops, including Virgin Megastore, the Body Shop, and Esprit, along with a lively international food court, are open on Sunday—still a rare convenience in Paris.

Le Marais

Between the pre-Revolution mansions and tiny kosher food stores that characterize this area are scores of trendy gift shops and clothing stores. Avant-garde designers Azzedine Alaïa, Lolita Lempicka, Issey Miyake, and Romeo Gigli have boutiques within a few blocks of the stately place des Vosges and the Picasso and Carnavalet museums. A growing number of Marais shops are open on Sunday afternoons.

Montparnasse

The bohemian mecca for artists and writers in the '20s and '30s, Montparnasse is better known for bars and restaurants than shops. The commercial center near the train station has a Galeries Lafayette outlet, but it's too charmless to attract many tourists. Rue d'Alésia on the southern fringe of Montparnasse is known for discount clothing shops.

Opéra to Madeleine

Three major department stores—Au Printemps, Galeries Lafayette, and the British Marks & Spencer—define boulevard Haussmann, behind Paris's ornate 19th-century Opéra Garnier. Place de la Madeleine is home to two luxurious food stores, Fauchon and Hédiard. Steps away, on boulevard de la Madeleine, is a classy 75-shop mall, Les Trois Quartiers. Lalique and Baccarat Crystal also have opulent showrooms near the Eglise de la Madeleine.

Passy–Victor Hugo

The bourgeois and conservative 16ᵉ arrondissement attracts predictably classic and upscale retailers, most of whom are centered on rue de Passy and place Victor Hugo. A handful of secondhand shops in this wealthy area offer exceptionally good deals. Réciproque, on rue de la Pompe, is one of the biggest and best discount haunts in Paris.

Place Vendôme and Rue de la Paix

The magnificent 17th-century place Vendôme, home of the Ritz Hotel, and rue de la Paix, leading north from Vendôme, have attracted the world's most elegant jewelers: Cartier, Boucheron, Buccellati, Van Cleef and Arpels, Répossi, Mellerio, Mauboussin, and Mikimoto.

Place des Victoires

This graceful, circular plaza near the Palais-Royal is the playground of cutting-edge fashion icons such as Kenzo, Victoire, and Thierry Mugler. Avant-garde boutiques like Chantal Thomass, Jean-Charles de Castelbajac, Absinthe, and En Attendant les Barbares have fanned into the side streets; Jean-Paul Gaultier's flagship shop is in the nearby Galerie Vivienne arcade. One of the hottest new emporiums to pop up in the neighborhood, Le Shop, at 3 rue d'Argout, rents retail space to hip, up-and-coming designers.

Rue du Faubourg St-Honoré

The presence of the Elysée Palace and the official residences of the American and British ambassadors means this chic shopping and residential street is well patrolled by the police. The Paris branch of Sotheby's and renowned antiques galleries such as Didier Aaron add artistic flavor. Boutiques include Hermès, Lanvin, Karl Lagerfeld, Reveillon Furs, Louis Feraud, and Christian Lacroix.

Department Stores

Paris's top department stores offer both convenience and style. Most are open Monday through Saturday from about 9:30 AM to 7 PM, and some are open until 10 PM one weekday evening. All six major stores listed below have multilingual guides, international welcome desks, détaxe offices, and restaurants. Most are on the Right Bank, near the Opéra and the Hôtel de Ville; the notable exception is Au Bon Marché on the Left Bank.

Au Bon Marché (⊠ 22 rue de Sèvres, 7ᵉ, ☎ 01–44–39–80–00, métro Sèvres-Babylone), founded in 1852, is an excellent hunting ground for linens, table settings, and high-quality furniture on the Left Bank. The

Right Bank Shopping

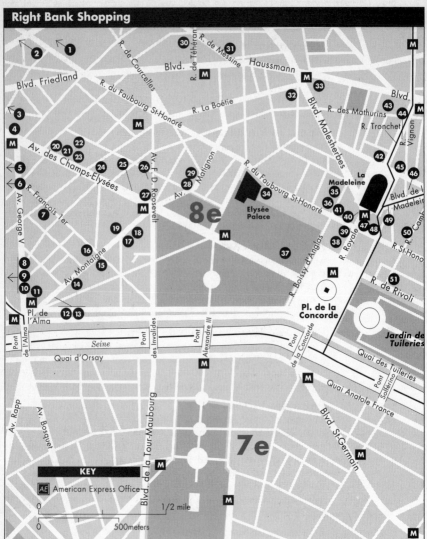

Accessoires à Soie, **3**
A la Mère de Famille, **68**
Agnès B., **90**
Anna Lowe, **29**
Annick Goutal, **53**
Argenterie des Francs-Bourgeois, **101**
Artcurial, **28**
Arts-Céramiques, **74**
Au Nain Bleu, **48**
Au Printemps, **61**
Baccarat Crystal, **72**
Bazar de l'Hôtel de Ville, **107**
Brentano's, **78**

Brummel, **62**
Carrousel du Louvre Mall, **112**
Cartier, **56, 59**
Cassegrain, **33**
Catherine Baril, **9**
Le Cave Augé, **41**
Chanel, **14, 50**
Chantal Thomass, **81**
Charvet, **57**
Christian Dior, **15**
Christofle, **39, 60**
Christophe Lemaire, **102**
La Droguerie, **89**

Du Pareil Au Méme, **63**
L'Eclaireur, **96**
Elysées 26, **25**
Façonnable, **37**
Fauchon, **45**
FNAC, **2, 91**
Forum des Halles, **91**
Gagliani, **52**
Galerie du Claridge, **21**
Galerie Jean Fournier, **93**
Galerie Laage-Salomon, **104**
Galerie Lelong, **30**

Galerie du Lido, **4**
Galerie Louis Carré, **31**
Galerie du Rond-Point, **27**
Galerie Véro-Dodat, **110**
Galerie Vivienne, **77**
Galerie Yvonne Lambert, **103**
Galeries Lafayette, **66**
Geneviève Lethu, **98**
Givenchy, **11**
Guerlain, **23**
Les Halles Montmartre, **75**
Hédiard, **42**

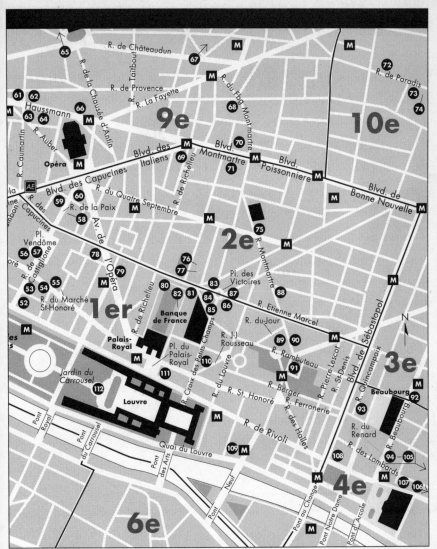

168

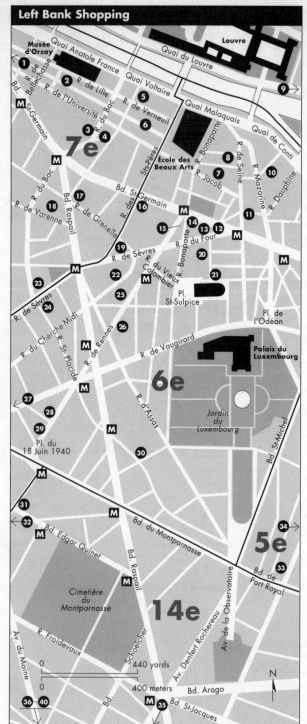

Left Bank Shopping

new ground-floor Balthazar men's shop feels like a smart boutique. La Grande Epicerie, one of the largest groceries in Paris and a gourmet's mecca, stocks the best of French wines, chocolates, foie gras, and cheeses. The basement is a treasure trove for books, records, classy stationery, and artsy gifts.

Au Printemps (⊠ 64 bd. Haussmann, 9ᵉ, ☎ 01–42–82–50–00, métro Havre-Caumartin, Opéra, or Auber) has three newly revamped floors of women's fashion featuring hot designers like Helmut Lang, Dolce & Gabbana, and the Spanish line, Zara. Free fashion shows are held on Tuesday (all year) and Friday (March–October) at 10 AM under the cupola on the 7th floor of La Mode, the building dedicated to women's and children's fashion. The three-store complex also includes La Maison, for housewares and furniture, and Brummel, a six-floor emporium devoted to menswear. Flo Prestige, the celebrated Parisian brasserie chain, runs the in-house restaurant.

Bazar de l'Hôtel de Ville (⊠ 52–64 rue de Rivoli, 4ᵉ, ☎ 01–42–74–90–00, métro Hôtel de Ville), better known as BHV, houses an enormous basement hardware store that sells everything from doorknobs to cement mixers. The fashion offerings are minimal, but BHV is noteworthy for quality household goods, home decor materials, and office supplies.

Galeries Lafayette (⊠ 40 bd. Haussmann, 9ᵉ, ☎ 01–42–82–34–56, métro Chaussée d'Antin, Opéra, or Havre-Caumartin; ⊠ Centre Commercial Montparnasse, 15ᵉ, ☎ 01–45–38–52–87, métro Montparnasse-Bienvenue) carries nearly 80,000 fashion labels under its roof, including rising stars like Mariot Chanet, Ann Demeulemeester, and Marcel Marongiou. Free fashion shows are held every Wednesday at 11 AM (for reservations, call ☎ 01–48–74–02–30). Along with the world's largest perfumery, the main store boasts the new "Espace Lafayette Maison," a huge Yves Taralon–designed emporium dedicated to the art of living *à la française*.

Marks & Spencer (⊠ 35 bd. Haussmann, 9ᵉ, ☎ 01–47–42–42–91, métro Havre-Caumartin, Auber, or Opéra; ⊠ 88 rue de Rivoli, 4ᵉ, ☎ 01–44–61–08–00, métro Hôtel de Ville) is a British chain chiefly noted for its moderately priced basics (underwear, socks, sleep- and sportswear). Its excellent English grocery store and take-out food service are enormously popular with Parisians.

La Samaritaine (⊠ 19 rue de la Monnaie, 1ᵉʳ, ☎ 01–40–41–20–20, métro Pont-Neuf or Châtelet), a sprawling five-store complex, carries everything from designer fashions to cuckoo clocks but is especially known for kitchen supplies, housewares, and furniture. Its most famous asset is the rooftop café in Building 2 that offers a marvelous view of Notre-Dame.

Budget

Monoprix or Prisunic are French dime stores—with scores of branches throughout the city—that stock inexpensive everyday items like toothpaste, groceries, toys, typing paper, and bath mats—a little of everything. Both chains carry inexpensive children's clothes of surprisingly good quality. Most Parisians dash into their neighborhood stores at least once a week.

Tati (⊠ central location at 140 rue de Rennes, 6ᵉ, ☎ 01–45–48–68–31, métro St-Placide), with outlets throughout the city, is known for its bargain-basement prices and hectic, jumbled sales floors. Shop carefully, as goods—from clothes to kitchen utensils—vary in quality. The store recently introduced a hip "La Rue Est à Nous" line of trendy teen fashions.

Specialty Shops

Art and Antiques

Art galleries and antiques shops are scattered throughout the city, though some that offer items from a specific period are clustered in certain neighborhoods. Many contemporary art galleries can be found around the Pompidou Center, the Picasso Museum, and the Bastille Opera. Often these galleries are in the courtyard of a building, the only sign of their presence a small plaque; take it as an invitation to push through the double doors. Galleries around St-Germain aren't as avant-garde, though some could certainly fit on either side of the river. The carré Rive Gauche (métro St-Germain-des-Prés, Rue du Bac), an area that shelters dozens of art and antique galleries on its narrow lanes, is a good place to start. Works by old masters and established modern artists dominate the galleries around rue du Faubourg St-Honoré and avenue Matignon. To plot your course, get the free map published by the Association des Galeries; it's available at many of the galleries listed below.

Artcurial (⊠ 9 av. Matignon, 8ᵉ, ☎ 01–42–99–16–16, métro Champs-Elysées–Clemenceau), which has the feel of a museum shop, sells artist designed decorative objects. Exhibits by artists such as Bram van Velde and Zao Wou-Ki are held regularly in the Grande Galerie.

Galerie Arnoux (⊠ 27 rue Guénégaud, 6ᵉ, ☎ 01–46–33–04–66, métro Odéon), one of many galleries on this street, specializes in abstract painting of the '50s, as well as young painters and sculptors who work in this tradition.

Galerie Berès (⊠ 17 quai Voltaire, 7ᵉ, ☎ 01–42–60–72–68, métro Rue du Bac) specializes in graphic arts of the Far East, in particular Japanese prints, as well as 19th-century French painting.

Galerie Claude Bernard (⊠ 5 rue des Beaux-Arts, 6ᵉ, ☎ 01–43–26–97–07, métro Mabillon) is very established, particularly in the domain of traditional figurative work. It also publishes a large number of catalogs available here or by mail.

Galerie Dina Vierny (⊠ 36 rue Jacob, 6ᵉ, ☎ 01–42–61–32–83, métro Mabillon) reflects the interests of the owner whose collection includes Maillol, Rodin, Matisse, and Poliakoff. More of her collection art can be seen at the Musée Maillol (☞ Chapter 2).

Galerie Jean Fournier (⊠ 44 rue Quincampoix, 4ᵉ, ☎ 01–42–77–32–31, métro Rambuteau) began in the late '40s and grew up with the abstract movement; it's on a street with a number of other galleries.

Galerie Laage-Salomon (⊠ 54 rue du Temple, 4ᵉ, ☎ 01–42–78–11–71, métro Hôtel de Ville) shows a well-known, very international group of artists, such as Per Kirkeby, Georg Baselitz, and A. R. Penck.

Galerie Lelong (⊠ 13–14 rue de Téhéran, 8ᵉ, ☎ 01–45–63–13–19, métro Miromesnil) also has galleries in New York and Zurich, each offering a slightly different mix of contemporary artists.

Galerie Louis Carré (⊠ 10 av. de Messine, 8ᵉ, ☎ 01–45–62–57–07, métro Miromesnil) has a long history of promoting French artists, including Bazaine, but it is not lost in the past. Recent expositions have been witty and innovative.

Galerie Maeght (⊠ 42 rue du Bac, 7ᵉ, ☎ 01–42–22–22–83, métro Rue du Bac) is the Paris shop of the Foundation Maeght in St-Paul-de-Vence. You can find paintings, as well as books, prints, and reasonably priced posters.

Galerie Samy Kinge (⊠ 54 rue de Verneuil, 6ᵉ, ☎ 01–42–61–19–07, métro Rue du Bac) specializes in the realists and new realists, as well as young artists representing various traditions.

Galerie Templon (✉ in the courtyard of 30 rue Beaubourg, 3ᵉ, ☎ 01–42–72–14–10, métro Rambuteau) was the first to bring American artists to Paris in the '60s; now it represents many artists, including the French sculptor, César.

Galerie Yvon Lambert (✉ 108 rue Vielle du Temple, 3ᵉ, ☎ 01–71–42–09–33, métro Filles de Calvaire) exhibits challenging minimalist and conceptualist artists in an extraordinary space.

Louvre des Antiquaires (✉ 2 pl. du Palais-Royal, 1ᵉʳ, métro Palais-Royal) is an elegant multifloor complex where 250 of Paris's leading dealers showcase their rarest objects, including Louis XV furniture, tapestries, and antique jewelry. The center is open Tuesday to Sunday; it's closed Sunday in July and August.

Viaduc des Arts (✉ 9-147 av. Daumensil, 12ᵉ, métro Ledru-Rollin) houses dozens of art galleries and traditional artisans' boutiques under the arches of a 19th-century stone train viaduct. There are gilders, sculptors, porcelain specialists, metal craftsmen, painters, and even launderers.

Bags, Scarves, and Accessories

Hermès (✉ 24 rue du Faubourg St-Honoré, 8ᵉ, ☎ 01–40–17–47–17, métro Concorde) was established as a saddlery in 1837 and went on to create the famous, eternally chic Kelly bag, for Grace Kelly. The magnificent silk scarves—truly fashion icons—are legendary for their rich colors and intricate designs, which change yearly. During biannual sales, in January and July, the astronomical prices are slashed by up to 50%.

Longchamp (✉ 390 rue St-Honoré, 1ᵉʳ, ☎ 01–42–60–00–00, métro Concorde) sells bags and leather goods of excellent quality and impeccable taste. Its name has tremendous cachet with the famously brand-conscious Parisians.

Losco (✉ 20 rue de Sévigné, 4ᵉ, ☎ 01–48–04–39–93, métro St-Paul) allows customers to design their own high-quality belt by mixing and matching buckles and straps. There is a wide selection of styles and colors. Prices are reasonable.

Louis Vuitton (✉ 54 av. Montaigne, 8ᵉ, ☎ 01–45–62–90–43, métro Franklin-D.-Roosevelt; ✉ 78 av. Marceau, 8ᵉ, ☎ 01–47–20–47–00, métro George-V; ✉ 6 pl. St-Germain-des-Prés, 6ᵉ, ☎ 01–45–49–62–32, métro St-Germain-des-Prés) catapulted back to the fashion pinnacle by persuading designers like Helmut Lang, Vivienne Westwood, and Azzedine Alaïa to create a daring new series of bags with the famous monogrammed canvas. The results are anything but over-exposed. The postmodern Left Bank boutique was designed by Anouska de Hempel.

Souleiado (✉ 78 rue de Seine, 6ᵉ, ☎ 01–43–54–62–25, métro Odéon; ✉ 83 av. Paul Doumer, 16ᵉ, ☎ 01–42–24–99–34, métro La Muette) is *the* name for scarves, quilted bags, and linens in traditional, richly colored Provençal patterns.

DISCOUNT

Accessoires à Soie (✉ 21 rue des Acacias, 17ᵉ, ☎ 01–42–27–78–77, métro Argentine) is where savvy Parisians buy superb silk scarves in all shapes and sizes. The wide selection includes many big-name designers, and everything costs about half of what you'd pay elsewhere.

Bookstores (English-Language)

The scenic open-air bookstalls along the Seine, selling secondhand books (mostly in French), prints, and souvenirs, are a major tourist attraction. Numerous French-language bookshops are found in the scholarly Latin Quarter and the publishing district, St-Germain-des-Prés. For English-language books, try the following:

Brentano's (⊠ 37 av. de l'Opéra, 2ᵉ, ☎ 01–42–61–52–50, métro Opéra) is stocked with everything from classics to children's titles.

Galignani (⊠ 224 rue de Rivoli, 1ᵉʳ, ☎ 01–42–60–76–07, métro Tuileries), founded in 1802, was the first English bookstore on the continent. It is a trove of exquisite art and history books.

Shakespeare & Company (⊠ 37 rue de la Bûcherie, 5ᵉ, no phone, métro St-Michel), the sentimental Left Bank favorite, specializes in expatriate literature. The staff tends to be rather pretentious, but the shelves of secondhand books hold real bargains. Poets often give readings upstairs.

Tea & Tattered Pages (⊠ 24 rue Mayet, 6ᵉ, ☎ 01–40–65–94–35, métro Duroc) sells cheap, secondhand paperbacks, plus new books (publishers' overstock) at low prices. Tea and brownies are served, and browsing is encouraged.

Village Voice (⊠ 6 rue Princesse, 6ᵉ, ☎ 01–46–33–36–47, métro Mabillon), known for its selection of contemporary authors, hosts regular literary readings.

W. H. Smith (⊠ 248 rue de Rivoli, 1ᵉʳ, ☎ 01–44–78–88–89, métro Concorde) carries an excellent range of travel and language books, cookbooks, and fiction for adults and children.

Clothing (Women's)

CLASSIC CHIC

No matter, say the French, that fewer and fewer of their top couture houses are still headed by compatriots. It's the chic elegance, the classic ambience, the je ne sais quoi, that remains undeniably Gallic.

Chanel (⊠ 42 av. Montaigne, 8ᵉ, ☎ 01–47–23–74–12, métro Franklin-D.-Roosevelt; ⊠ 31 rue Cambon, 1ᵉʳ, ☎ 01–42–86–28–00, métro Tuileries), the most successful of all the houses, is helmed by Karl Lagerfeld, a master at updating Coco's signature look with fresh colors and free-spirited silhouettes.

Christian Dior (⊠ 30 av. Montaigne, 8ᵉ, ☎ 01–40–73–56–07, métro Franklin-D.-Roosevelt) installed the flamboyant British designer, John Galliano, as head designer after his triumphant run at Givenchy. His wonderfully dramatic creations are sparkling homages to Dior's elegance.

Givenchy (⊠ 3 av. George V, 8ᵉ, ☎ 01–44–31–50–00, métro Alma-Marceau) made headlines when it chose another bad boy Briton, Alexander McQueen, to take over where Galliano left off. Across the street at No. 8, Givenchy Boutique presents slightly more affordable versions of the designer's elegant ready-to-wear.

Nina Ricci (⊠ 39 av. Montaigne, 8ᵉ, ☎ 01–49–52–56–00, métro Franklin-D.-Roosevelt) designs, with the trademark bow, are supremely ladylike; the lingerie is luxuriantly romantic. Ricci Club, for men, is next door.

TRENDSETTERS

L'Eclaireur (⊠ 3 rue des Rosiers, 4ᵉ, ☎ 01–48–87–10–22, métro St-Paul) works with an international crop of rising young avante-garde designers and has an uncanny gift for spotting tomorrow's fashion stars.

Jean-Paul Gaultier (⊠ 6 rue Vivienne, 2ᵉ, ☎ 01–42–86–05–05, métro Bourse or Palais-Royal), who made his name as Madonna's irreverent clothier, continues to create outrageously attention-getting garments for men and women. The less-expensive "Junior" boutiques are at 30 rue Faubourg St-Antoine, in the Bastille district, and at 7 rue du Jour, near Les Halles.

Lolita Lempicka (⊠ 13 bis rue Pavée, 4ᵉ, ☎ 01–42–74–50–48, métro St-Paul) serves up sharp suits and whimsical silk dresses. Studio Lolita, which sells last season's items at a discount, is across the street.

Thierry Mugler (✉ 45 rue du Bac, 6ᵉ, ☎ 01–45–44–44–44, métro Rue du Bac; ✉ 10 pl. des Victoires, 2ᵉ, ☎ 01–42–60–06–37, métro Bourse or Palais-Royal; ✉ 49 av. Montaigne, 8ᵉ, ☎ 01–47–23–37–62, métro Franklin-D.-Roosevelt) moved his empire to the Left Bank and brought his trademark curve-hugging shapes with him. His new Mugler Trade Mark line is a younger, funkier, and gentler-priced look.

Victoire (✉ 12 pl. des Victoires, 2ᵉ, ☎ 01–42–61–09–02, métro Bourse or Palais-Royal; menswear at ✉ 10–12 rue du Col. Driant, 1ᵉʳ, ☎ 01–42–97–44–87, métro Palais-Royal) is a discreet boutique with a knack for identifying new trends. What you buy here will be so far ahead of its time that you'll wear it for years. The Victoire menswear shop is a few steps away.

CHIC AND CASUAL

Agnès B. (✉ 3, 6, and 10 rue du Jour, 1ᵉʳ, ☎ 01–45–08–56–56, métro Les Halles) makes knitwear separates in neutral colors that are wardrobe basics for young Parisians. Her various lines are sold as follows: children at No. 2, women at No. 3, men at No. 6, and the teenage line at No. 10.

Christophe Lemaire (✉ 4 rue Chérubini, 2ᵉ, ☎ 01–47–03–39–00, métro Quatre Septembre) trained with Lacroix, St-Laurent, and Michel Klein and is now the name to watch among the new generation of French designers. His comfort-chic message is highlighted by his use of pajama fabrics.

Inès de la Fressange (✉ 14 av. Montaigne, 8ᵉ, ☎ 01–47–23–08–94, métro Franklin-D.-Roosevelt; ✉ 81 rue des St-Pères, 6ᵉ, ☎ 01–45–44–99–66, métro St-Germain-des-Prés), the former Chanel supermodel, recently expanded her empire of impeccably-tailored fashions to include colorfully chic home decor.

Jil Sander (✉ 52 av. Montaigne, 8ᵉ, ☎ 01–44–95–06–70, métro Franklin-D.-Roosevelt) is a German designer known for well-cut suits and separates with savvy, ultrasimple lines.

Sonia Rykiel (✉ 175 bd. St-Germain, 6ᵉ, ☎ 01–49–54–60–60, métro St-Germain-des-Prés; ✉ 70 rue du Faubourg St-Honoré, 8ᵉ, ☎ 01–42–65–20–81, métro Concorde; ✉ 64 rue d'Alésia, 14ᵉ, ☎ 01–43–95–06–13, métro Alésia) designs stylish, knitted separates and dresses for active women. The shop on rue d'Alésia sells last season's collection at a significant discount.

Tara Jarmon (✉ 18 rue du Four, 6ᵉ, ☎ 01–46–33–26–60, métro St-Sulpice) is a Canadian designer who has garnered plaudits from Paris's trendwatchers. Her understated knee-length coats are especially popular.

Clothing (Men's)

Brummel (✉ Au Printemps department store, 64 bd. Haussmann, 9ᵉ, ☎ 01–42–82–50–00, métro Havre-Caumartin or Opéra) is Paris's menswear fashion leader: six floors of suits, sportswear, underwear, coats, ties, and accessories in all price ranges.

Charvet (✉ 28 pl. Vendôme, 1ᵉʳ, ☎ 01–42–60–30–70, métro Opéra) is the Parisian equivalent of a Savile Row tailor: a conservative, aristocratic institution famed for made-to-measure shirts and exquisite ties and accessories.

Façonnable (✉ 9 rue du Fauboug St-Honoré, 8ᵉ, ☎ 01–47–42–72–60, métro Concorde) sells fashionable town and weekend clothes for young urbanites.

Kenzo (✉ 3 pl. des Victoires, 2ᵉ, ☎ 01–40–39–72–03, métro Bourse; ✉ 17 bd. Raspail, 7ᵉ, ☎ 01–42–22–09–38, métro Rue du Bac) brings exuberant color and fantasy to his menswear collections. Move on if you're looking for a classic three-piece suit.

Lanvin (⊠ 15 rue du Faubourg St-Honoré, 8ᵉ, ☎ 01–44–71–33–33, métro Madeleine) offers elegant tailoring, sophisticated sportswear, and a chic little in-house café. The branch for women is at No. 22.

Clothing (Children)

Almost all the top designers offer minicouture, but you can expect to pay upwards of 1,200 francs for each wee outfit. Here's where mere mortal Parisian parents shop to keep their kids looking chic.

Du Pareil Au Même (⊠ 15 and 23 rue des Mathurins, 8ᵉ, ☎ 01–42–66–93–80, métro Havre-Caumartin; ⊠ 7 rue St-Placide, 6ᵉ, ☎ 01–40–49–00–33, métro St-Placide; ⊠ 135 av. Emile Zola, 15ᵉ, ☎ 01–40–59–48–82, métro Emile Zola) is a moderately priced chain selling well-made, adorable basics in soft, brightly colored jersey and cotton. Sizes and styles range from newborn to young teen.

Natalys (⊠ 32 rue St-Antoine, 4ᵉ, ☎ 01–48–87–77–42, métro St-Paul; ⊠ 92 av. des Champs-Elysées, 8ᵉ, ☎ 01–43–59–17–65, métro George-V), a major French chain, sells clothing, toys, furniture, and accessories for newborns and grade-school children.

Pom d'Api (⊠ 28 rue du Four, 6ᵉ, ☎ 01–45–48–39–31, métro St-Sulpice) stocks quality French and Italian footwear for babies and preteens, as well as miniversions of Doc Martens and Timberlands.

Clothing (Resale)

Catherine Baril (⊠ 14 and 25 rue de la Tour, 16ᵉ, ☎ 01–45–20–95–21, métro Passy) has one-of-a-kind, barely worn haute couture and designer ready-to-wear. No. 25 is devoted to menswear.

Réciproque (⊠ 89, 92, 95, 97, 101, and 123 rue de la Pompe, 16ᵉ, ☎ 01–47–04–30–28, métro Rue de la Pompe) is Paris's largest and most exclusive swap shop. There's not much in the way of service or space, but savings on all the Ricci, Dior, Chanel, Mugler—are significant. The newest shop, at No. 92, specializes in leather goods. The store is closed Sundays and Mondays and the end of July through August.

Clothing (Discount)

Rue d'Alésia, in the 14ᵉ arrondissement (métro Alésia), is the main place to find shops selling last season's items at a discount; Anna Lowe, on avenue Matignon in the 8ᵉ, and Mendès, on rue Montmartre in the 2ᵉ, are the notable exceptions. Be forewarned: Most of these shops are much more downscale than their elegant sister shops and dressing rooms are not always provided.

Anna Lowe (⊠ 35 av. Matignon, 8ᵉ, ☎ 01–43–59–96–61, métro Miromesnil) is a treasure trove for women who adore classic designer names (Valentino, Armani, Givenchy, Lacroix, Montana) but appreciate the substantial savings on new ready-to-wear designer labels and one-of-a-kind haute couture gowns. Unlike most discounters, this elegant shop will do alterations.

Cacharel Stock (⊠ 114 rue d'Alésia, 14ᵉ, ☎ 01–45–42–53–04) offers impressive savings (up to 50% off) on men's, women's, and children's clothing (plus even bigger markdown sales racks on the second floor).

Chipie Stock (⊠ 82 rue d'Alésia, 14ᵉ, ☎ 01–45–42–07–52) has jeans and sweaters for the whole family.

Dorothée bis Stock (⊠ 74 rue d'Alésia, 14ᵉ, ☎ 01–45–42–17–11) significantly marks down selected gowns and sportswear.

Majestic by Chevignon (⊠ 12 rue d'Alésia, 14ᵉ, ☎ 01–45–43–40–25) discounts Chevignon casual wear for all ages at up to 40% off.

Mendès (⊠ 65 rue Montmartre, 2ᵉ, ☎ 01–42–36–83–32, métro Sentier) sells last season's Yves Saint-Laurent Rive Gauche and Variations lines at half price. Christian Lacroix designs are also sold here at discount prices.

SR Store (⊠ 64 rue d'Alésia, 14ᵉ, ☎ 01–43–95–06–13) slices 50% off last year's prices on Sonia Rykiel fashions for men, women, and children and still manages to chop another 20%–30% off during the sales in January and July. The sporty, lower-priced "Inscription" line designed by Sonia's daughter, Nathalie, is also sold here.

Cosmetics

When it comes to *le maquillage* (makeup), Parisian women swear by those two beloved dime stores, **Monoprix** and **Prisunic** (☞ *above*). Both are goldmines for inexpensive, good-quality cosmetics (but the Prisunic branch at ⊠ 109 rue de la Boétie, 8ᵉ, métro St-Philippe-du-Roule, is the best-stocked). Brand names to look for are Bourjois, whose products are made in the Chanel factories, and Arcancil.

Make Up For Ever (⊠ 5 rue de la Boétie, 8ᵉ, ☎ 01–42–65–48–57, métro St-Augustin) is a must-stop for makeup artists, models (Kate Moss is a regular), and actresses (Madonna has dropped in, too). The ultrahip selection spans 40 shades of foundation, 100 eye shadows, 24 glittering powders, and scores of fake eyelashes.

Drugstores

Pharmacie Anglo-Américaine (⊠ 6 rue Castiglione, 1ᵉʳ, ☎ 01–42–60–72–96, métro Palais-Royal) stocks foreign medicines and is open daily 9–7:30.

Pharmacie Dérhy (⊠ 84 av. des Champs-Elysées, 8ᵉ, ☎ 01–45–62–02–41, métro Georges-V) is open 24 hours a day, 365 days a year.

Pharmacie Européenne de la Place Clichy (⊠ 6 pl. Clichy, 9ᵉ, ☎ 01–48–74–65–18, métro Place de Clichy) is open 24 hours, seven days a week.

Fabrics

Madura (⊠ 66 rue de Rennes, 6ᵉ, ☎ 01–45–44–71–30, métro St-Sulpice) is full of gorgeous materials and creative ideas for decorating the smart Parisian home.

Marché St-Pierre (⊠ 2 rue Charles Nodier, 18ᵉ, ☎ 01–46–06–92–25, métro Anvers), a raucous, five-floor warehouse in Montmartre, supplied designers like Kenzo in his salad days. Its inventory runs the gamut from fine brocades to fake furs, and there are often good specials on cheap end-of-bolt upholstery and fabrics. The market is open Monday through Saturday afternoon.

Food and Wine

A la Mère de Famille (⊠ 35 rue du Faubourg-Montmartre, 9ᵉ, ☎ 01–47–70–83–69, métro Cadet) is an enchanting shop well versed in French regional specialties and old-fashioned bonbons, sugar candy, and more.

Le Cave Augé (⊠ 116 bd. Haussmann, 8ᵉ, ☎ 01–45–22–16–97, métro St-Augustin), one of the best wine shops in Paris since 1850, is just the ticket whether you're looking for a rare vintage for a vinophile friend or a seductive Bordeaux for a tête-à-tête. English-speaking Marc Sibard is a knowledgeable and affable adviser.

Fauchon (⊠ 26 pl. de la Madeleine, 8ᵉ, ☎ 01–47–42–60–11, métro Madeleine), established in 1886, sells renowned pâté, honey, jelly, and private-label champagne. Hard-to-find foreign foods (U.S. pancake mix, British lemon curd) are also stocked. Try the particularly delectable pastries and chocolates in the café.

Galeries Lafayette Gourmet (⊠ 40 bd. Haussmann, 9ᵉ, ☎ 01–42–82–34–56, métro Chausée-d'Antin or Opéra), with its gold shopping carts and bistro-style snack bar serving caviar and smoked salmon, is as chic as Fauchon and Hédiard, but less intimidating.

La Grande Epicerie (⊠ 38 rue de Sèvres, 7ᵉ, ☏ 01–44–39–80–00, métro Sèvres-Babylone), on the ground floor of Au Bon Marché, stocks an extensive array of fine French foodstuffs.

Hédiard (⊠ 21 pl. de la Madeleine, 8ᵉ, ☏ 01–42–66–44–36, métro Madeleine), established in 1854, was famous in the 19th century for its high-quality imported spices. These—along with rare teas and beautifully packaged house brands of jam, mustard, and cookies—are still sold in this handsome shop.

Jadis et Gourmande (⊠ 49 bis av. Franklin-D.-Roosevelt, 8ᵉ, ☏ 01–42–25–06–04, métro Franklin-D.-Roosevelt; ⊠ 27 rue Boissy d'Anglas, 8ᵉ, ☏ 01–42–65–23–23, métro Madeleine; ⊠ 88 bd. de Port-Royal, 5ᵉ, ☏ 01–43–26–17–75, métro Port-Royal) sells an impressive range of novelty chocolates and will even personalize gift bars.

La Maison du Chocolat (⊠ 52 rue François 1ᵉʳ, 8ᵉ, ☏ 01–47–23–38–25, métro Franklin-D.-Roosevelt; ⊠ 8 bd. de la Madeleine, 9ᵉ, ☏ 01–47–42–86–52, métro Madeleine; ⊠ 225 rue du Faubourg St-Honoré, 8ᵉ, ☏ 01–42–27–39–44, métro Ternes) is heaven for cocoa purists. Take home chocolates, ice cream, and other treats, or meet a friend in the tearoom at the one on rue du Faubourg St-Honoré for sinfully rich hot chocolate and chocolate-mousse frappés.

P. L. Poujauran (⊠ 20 rue Jean-Nicot, 7ᵉ, ☏ 01–47–05–80–88, métro La Tour–Maubourg) is loved for its delicious black-olive and whole grain breads. Its mini taster loaves are the answer if you can't bring yourself to choose just one.

Poilâne (⊠ 8 rue du Cherche-Midi, 6ᵉ, ☏ 01–45–48–42–59, métro St-Sulpice) produces the most famous bread in the world. The chewy sourdough loaves are sold in hundreds of Paris restaurants and shops and are airmailed to the United States and Tokyo every day.

Housewares

Argenterie des Francs-Bourgeois (⊠ 17 rue des Francs-Bourgeois, 4ᵉ, ☏ 01–42–72–04–00, métro St-Paul), a dusty secondhand shop, sells old-fashioned silver settings from estates and grand hotels by the kilo. The inexpensive bracelets made of Victorian silver spoons and forks make marvelous gifts.

Baccarat Crystal (⊠ 30 bis rue de Paradis, 10ᵉ, ☏ 01–47–70–64–30, métro Château-d'Eau or Gare de l'Est) may not have many bargains, but this elegant, red-carpeted showroom with an in-house museum is worth a visit.

Christofle (⊠ 24 rue de la Paix, 2ᵉ, ☏ 01–42–65–62–43, métro Opéra; ⊠ 9 rue Royale, 8ᵉ, ☏ 01–49–33–43–00, métro Concorde or Madeleine), founded in 1830, is *the* name to know in French silver.

Geneviève Lethu (⊠ 28 rue St-Antoine, 4ᵉ, ☏ 01–42–74–21–25, métro St-Paul) sells tea services, potpourri mixtures, and table linens for your real or imagined country house. There is also a small store in the basement of Galeries Lafayette.

Lalique (⊠ 11 rue Royale, 8ᵉ, ☏ 01–42–66–52–40, métro Madeleine) crystal vases and statuettes are prized for their sinuous, romantic forms and delicate design.

Point à la Ligne (⊠ 25 rue de Varenne, 7ᵉ, ☏ 01–42–84–14–45, métro Rue du Bac; ⊠ 67 av. Victor Hugo, 16ᵉ, ☏ 01–45–00–87–01, métro Victor Hugo) specializes in modestly priced, beautiful candles and candleholders. There is also a small store in the basement of Galeries Lafayette.

Porthault (⊠ 18 av. Montaigne, 8ᵉ, ☏ 01–47–20–75–25, métro Franklin-D.-Roosevelt) makes hand-embroidered table linens, luxurious Old World–style sheets, and sumptuous layettes.

La Tuile à Loup (⊠ 35 rue Daubenton, 5ᵉ, ☎ 01–47–07–28–90, métro Censier-Daubenton) is a darling Left Bank shop jam-packed with traditional pottery, faience, basketry, and gift items from every region of France.

La Vaissellerie (⊠ 80 bd. Haussmann, 8ᵉ, ☎ 01–45–22–32–47, métro Havre-Caumartin; ⊠ 85 rue de Rennes, 6ᵉ, ☎ 01–42–22–61–49, métro Rennes; ⊠ 92 rue St-Antoine, 4ᵉ, ☎ 01–42–72–76–66, métro St-Paul; ⊠ 332 rue St-Honoré, 1ᵉʳ, ☎ 01–42–60–64–50, métro Tuileries) is chockablock with the sort of ingenious kitchen accoutrements that the French do so well, priced below what you would pay for such creativity back home.

DISCOUNT

Shoppers with style numbers, pocket calculators, and comparison prices from home often profit from serious savings on fine porcelain in the showrooms on Rue de Paradis (métro Gare de l'Est) in the 10ᵉ arrondissement.

Arts-Céramiques (⊠ 15 rue de Paradis, 10ᵉ, ☎ 01–48–24–83–70) has special promotional sales in its back room.

La Tisanière (⊠ 21 rue de Paradis, 10ᵉ, ☎ 01–47–70–22–80) sells china seconds.

Jewelry

Most of the big names are near the place Vendôme. Designer costume and semiprecious jewelry are sold in most avenue Montaigne and rue du Faubourg St-Honoré boutiques.

Cartier (⊠ 7 and 23 pl. Vendôme, 1ᵉʳ, ☎ 01–42–61–55–55, métro Opéra) has two less-formal "Les Must" boutiques, which carry lighters, pens, watches, key-chains, and other gift items.

La Droguerie (⊠ 9 rue du Jour, 1ᵉʳ, ☎ 01–45–08–93–27, métro Les Halles) is a do-it-yourselfer's paradise, with all the latest in beads, bangles, and baubles—plus ribbons, strings, and clasps—to make your own jewelry statement.

Siki (⊠ 33–35 rue de Valois, 1ᵉʳ, ☎ 01–42–60–61–10, métro Palais-Royal) sells extraordinary semiprecious costume jewelry that mixes exotic African themes with haute couture classic tradition.

Lingerie

Chantal Thomass (⊠ 1 rue Vivienne, 1ᵉʳ, ☎ 01–40–15–02–36, métro Bourse or Palais-Royal) sets the right mood for her trademark black-lace hosiery, satin corsets, and feather-trimmed negligees in this plush, pink-velvet boutique that resembles a Victorian bordello.

Natari (⊠ 7 pl. Vendôme, 1ᵉʳ, ☎ 01–42–96–22–94, métro Opéra or Concorde) seduces all, with selections for every pocketbook. Movie-star lingerie and peignoir sets come in pure silk or washable synthetic.

Music

FNAC (⊠ Forum des Halles, 1ᵉʳ, ☎ 01–40–41–40–00, métro Les Halles; ⊠ 26 av. Ternes, 17ᵉ, ☎ 01–44–09–18–00, métro Ternes; ⊠ 136 rue de Rennes, 6ᵉ, ☎ 01–49–54–30–00, métro St-Placide) is a high-profile French chain selling music and books, and photo, TV, and audio equipment at good prices, by French standards.

Virgin Megastore (⊠ 52–60 av. des Champs-Elysées, 8ᵉ, ☎ 01–49–53–50–00, métro Franklin-D.-Roosevelt; ⊠ Carrousel du Louvre mall, 99 rue de Rivoli, 1ᵉʳ, ☎ 01–49–53–52–90, métro Palais-Royal) has acres of CDs and tapes, plus a book division and a trendy café upstairs.

Perfumes

Annick Goutal (⊠ 14 rue de Castiglione, 1ᵉʳ, ☏ 01–42–60–52–82, métro Concorde) sells this exclusive signature perfume line.

Guerlain (⊠ 68 av. des Champs-Elysées, 8ᵉ, ☏ 01–47–89–71–84, métro Franklin-D.-Roosevelt; ⊠ 47 rue Bonaparte, 6ᵉ, ☏ 01–43–26–71–19, métro Mabillon) boutiques are the only authorized Paris outlets for legendary perfumes like Shalimar, Jicky, Vol de Nuit, Mitsouko, Chamade, and the latest, Champs-Elysées.

DISCOUNT

The airport duty-free shops are still your best bet for minor purchases. But if you're going to spend more than about 1,200 francs, it's worthwhile to seek out the top discounters. Don't forget to claim your détaxe!

Les Halles Montmartre (⊠ 85 rue Montmartre, 2ᵉ, ☏ 01–42–33–11–13, métro Bourse) routinely discounts its wide range of perfumes and cosmetics by 30%–40%.

Michel Swiss (⊠ 16 rue de la Paix, 2nd Floor, 2ᵉ, ☏ 01–42–61–61–11, métro Opéra; ⊠ 24 av. de l'Opéra, 1ᵉʳ, ☏ 01–47–03–49–11, métro Pyramides) offers savings of up to 25% on perfumes, designer jewelry, and fashion accessories. There's no storefront window; enter the courtyard to take the elevator upstairs.

Shoes

Laurent Mercadel (⊠ 31 rue Tronchet, 8ᵉ, ☏ 01–42–66–00–48, métro Opéra; ⊠ 3 pl. des Victoires, 1ᵉʳ, ☏ 01–45–08–84–44, métro Bourse) has classic styles for both men and women, updated to stay at the fashion forefront.

Stéphane Kélian (⊠ 23 bd. de la Madeleine, 1ᵉʳ, ☏ 01–42–96–01–84, métro Madeleine; ⊠ 6 pl. des Victoires, 2ᵉ, ☏ 01–42–61–60–74, métro Bourse) creates chic, high-style, comfortable shoes for men and women.

DISCOUNT

Mi-Prix (⊠ 27 bd. Victor, 15ᵉ, ☏ 01–48–28–42–48, métro Porte-de-Versailles) is an unruly jumble of end-of-series designer shoes and accessories from the likes of Maud Frizon, Philippe Model, Walter Steiger, and Chantal Thomass, priced at up to 60% below retail.

Stationery

Cassegrain (⊠ 422 rue St-Honoré, 8ᵉ, ☏ 01–42–60–20–08, métro Concorde; ⊠ 81 rue des St-Pères, 6ᵉ, ☏ 01–42–22–04–76, métro Sèvres-Babylone) is the last word on the beautifully engraved cards and elegant stationery so ubiquitous in French families of stature. The desk accessories and inexpensive glass-nib writing pens make great gifts.

Marie Papier (⊠ 26 rue Vavin, 6ᵉ, ☏ 01–43–26–46–44, métro Vavin) sells an extraordinary variety of colored, marbled, and Japanese writing paper and notebooks, plus every kind of stylish writing accessory you could dream of.

Toys

Au Nain Bleu (⊠ 406–410 rue St-Honoré, 8ᵉ, ☏ 01–42–60–39–01, métro Concorde) is a high-price wonderland of elaborate dollhouses, miniature sports cars, and enchanting hand-carved rocking horses.

Shopping Arcades

Paris's 19th-century commercial arcades, called *passages,* are the forerunners of the modern shopping mall. Glass roofs, decorative pillars, and inlaid mosaic floors make these spaces charming. Shops range from the avant-garde (Gaultier and Yukii Tori designs in the luxurious Galerie Vivienne) to the genteel (embroidery supplies and satin ribbons at Le Bonheur des Dames in the Passage Jouffroy). The major arcades are in the 1er and 2e arrondissements on the Right Bank. The patient browser will find all sorts of dusty curiosity shops tucked into the alleys, with such items as rare stamps, secondhand books, and even antique canes.

Galerie Véro-Dodat (✉ 19 rue Jean-Jacques Rousseau, 1er, métro Les Halles) has painted ceilings and slender copper pillars.

Galerie Vivienne (✉ 4 rue des Petits-Champs, 2e, métro Bourse), between the Stock Exchange (Bourse) and the Palais-Royal, is home to a range of interesting shops, an excellent tearoom, and Cave Legrand, a quality wine shop.

Passage Jouffroy (✉ 12 bd. Montmartre, 9e, métro Montmartre) is full of shops selling toys, postcards, antique canes, perfumes, original cosmetics, and dried flowers: Try Pain d'Epices (✉ No. 29) and Au Bonheur des Dames (✉ No. 39).

Passage Verdeau (✉ 12 bd. Montmartre, 9e, métro Montmartre) is across the street from Passage Jouffroy and has shops selling antique cameras, toy soldiers, and rare gemstones.

Passage des Panoramas (✉ 11 bd. Montmartre, 2e, métro Montmartre), opened in 1800, is the oldest of them all.

Passage des Pavillons (✉ 6 rue de Beaujolais, 1er, métro Palais-Royal) is near the Palais-Royal gardens.

Passage des Princes (✉ 97 rue de Richelieu, 2e, métro Richelieu-Drouot) contains an espresso bar.

Markets

Food Markets

Paris's open-air food markets are among the city's most colorful attractions. Fruits and vegetables are piled high in vibrant pyramids. The variety of cheeses is always astounding. The lively—and somewhat chaotic—atmosphere that reigns in most markets makes them a sight worth seeing, even if you don't want or need to buy anything. Every *quartier* (neighborhood) has at least one, although many are open only a few days each week. Sunday morning, till 1 PM, is usually a good time to go; Monday they are likely to be closed.

Many of the better-known markets are in areas you'd visit for sightseeing: **rue de Buci** (6e, métro Odéon; open daily) near St-Germain-des-Prés; **rue Mouffetard** (5e, métro Monge; best on weekends) near the Jardin des Plantes; and **rue Lepic** in Montmartre (18e, métro Blanche or Abbesses; best on weekends). The **Marché d'Aligre** (12e, métro Ledru-Rollin), open Monday mornings and weekends, is a bit farther out, beyond the Bastille on rue d'Aligre; Parisians from all over the city know it and love it, but you won't see many tourists in this less affluent area of town. Foods are mostly ethnic, particularly North African. The prices come tumbling down as the morning draws to a close.

Flea Markets

Le Marché aux Puces St-Ouen (métro Porte de Clignancourt), on Paris's northern boundary, still attracts the crowds when it opens on weekends and Monday, but its once unbeatable prices are now a feature of the past. This century-old labyrinth of alleyways packed with antiques dealers' booths and junk stalls spreads for over a square mile. The clothing is downscale, but there are excellent finds in the bins of old prints and vintage advertisements. Early birds often pick up the most worthwhile loot. But be warned—if there's one place in Paris where you need to know how to barter, this is it! For lunch, stop for mussels and fries in one of the rough-and-ready cafés.

There are other, less-impressive flea markets on the southern and eastern slopes of the city—at **Porte de Montreuil** and **Porte de Vanves**—but they have a depressing amount of real junk and are best avoided, except by obsessive bargain hunters.

Flower and Bird Markets

Paris's main flower market is in the heart of the city on the Ile de la Cité (métro Cité), between Notre-Dame and the Palais de Justice. It's open every day except Sunday, when a bird market takes its place. Birds and a host of other animals are also sold in the shops and stalls on quai de la Mégisserie on the Right Bank of the Seine (métro Pont-Neuf). Other colorful flower markets are held beside the Madeleine church (métro Madeleine) and on place des Ternes (métro Ternes), down the road from the Arc de Triomphe. Both are open daily except Monday.

Stamp Market

Philatelists head for Paris's unique stamp market on avenue Marigny and avenue Gabriel (métro Champs-Elysées–Clemenceau) overlooking the gardens at the bottom of the Champs-Elysées. On sale are vintage postcards and stamps from all over the world. It is open Thursdays, weekends, and public holidays.

7 Side Trips from Paris

The soft light of the region around Paris inspired painters and kings alike. Corot, Cézanne, and van Gogh took up residence here, as did Louis XIV, who built one of France's most spectacular châteaux at Versailles. Here, too, Gothic architecture reached a pinnacle in the soaring spires of Chartres and Senlis.

EVEN THOUGH PARIS HAS SO MUCH TO SEE, you might
consider taking a short trip outside the city. The region around the capital, known as Ile-de-France, of-
fers as much stimulation as the capital, but with less frenzy. Though
Ile-de-France is not actually an island (*île*), it is figuratively isolated from
the rest of France by three rivers—the Seine, the Oise, and the Marne—
that weave majestic, meandering circles around its periphery. Remarkably, this area contains more than 10 million people—almost
one-fifth of France's entire population. This type of statistic conjures
up visions of a gray, never-ending suburban sprawl, but nothing could
be further from the truth.

Updated by
Simon Hewitt

Grand cathedrals and stately châteaux dot the lush, rolling landscape.
The kings and clerics who ruled France liked to escape from the capital now and then: Châteaux went up at Versailles, Fontainebleau, Chantilly, and Thoiry; abbeys and cathedrals soared skyward in Chartres,
Reims, Senlis, and Laon. The region never lost favor with the powerful, partly because its many forests—large chunks of which still stand—
harbored sufficient game to ensure a kill for even bloated, cosseted
monarchs. First Fontainebleau, in humane Renaissance proportions,
then Versailles, on a minion-crushing, Baroque scale, reflected the
royal desire to transform hunting lodges into palatial residences.

Painters from the Barbizon School loved this verdant region for its soft
light. Established in the mid-19th century in the village of Barbizon,
the school created a naturalistic painting style that inspired the Impressionists. The Impressionists, in turn, influenced van Gogh, who came
to Auvers-sur-Oise to paint in the late 19th century.

In 1992 Disney brought its own kind of kingdom to this region: Disneyland Paris. Since then, the park has emerged as France's leading tourist
attraction, with 11 million visitors a year. Getting from the capital to
Disneyland Paris and the other attractions in this region is easy: Most
are within an hour of central Paris and almost all are easily accessible
by train.

AUVERS-SUR-OISE

Cézanne, Pissarro, Corot, Daubigny, and Berthe Morisot all painted
in Auvers in the second half of the 19th century. But it is Vincent van
Gogh whose memory haunts every nook and cranny of this pretty riverside village. Van Gogh moved here from Arles in 1890 to be with his
brother, Theo. Little has changed since the summer of 1890, during
the last 10 weeks of van Gogh's life, when he painted no fewer than
70 pictures then shot himself behind the village château. He is buried
next to his brother in a simple, ivy-covered grave in the village cemetery. The whole village is peppered with plaques marking the spots that
inspired van Gogh's art; the plaques bear reproductions of his paintings, enabling you to compare his final works with the scenes as they
are today. After years of indifference and neglect, van Gogh's last
abode has been turned into a shrine. The château is now home to a
stunning high-tech exhibit on the Impressionist era. You can also visit
the medieval village church, subject of one of van Gogh's most famous
paintings, *L'Eglise d'Auvers,* and admire Osip Zadkine's powerful
modern statue of van Gogh in the village park.

The Auberge Ravoux, the inn where van Gogh stayed, was opened to
the public as the **Maison de van Gogh** in 1993, after painstaking
restoration. A dingy staircase leads up to the tiny, spartan, wood-

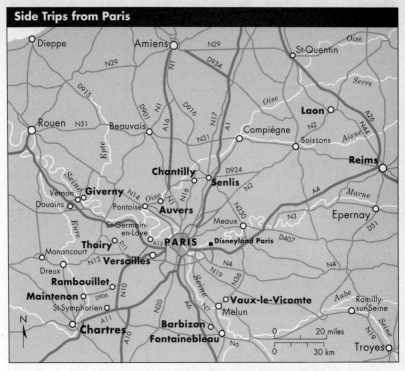

floored attic where van Gogh stored some of modern art's most famous pictures under the bed in which he breathed his last. A short film retraces van Gogh's time at Auvers, and there is a well-stocked souvenir shop. Stop for a drink or for lunch at the ground-floor restaurant, complete with glasswork, lace curtains, and wall decor carefully modeled on the original designs (☞ *Dining, below*). ⊠ *pl. de la Mairie*, ☎ *01– 34–48–07–79.* ⊡ *30 frs.* ☉ *Tues.–Sun. 10–6.*

Serious art lovers should visit the modest **Musée Daubigny** to admire the drawings, lithographs, and occasional oils by local 19th-century artists. It's opposite the Maison de van Gogh, above the tourist office. ⊠ *Manoir des Colombières, rue de la Sansonne*, ☎ *01–30–36–80– 20.* ⊡ *20 frs.* ☉ *Wed.–Sun. 2:30–6:30 (summer), 2–5:30 (winter).*

The landscapist Charles-François Daubigny, a precursor of the Impressionists, lived in Auvers from 1861 until his death in 1878. You can visit the **Atelier Daubigny,** his studio, and admire the remarkable array of mural and roof paintings by Daubigny and fellow artists Camille Corot and Honoré Daumier. ⊠ *61 rue Daubigny*, ☎ *01–34– 48–03–03.* ⊡ *20 frs.* ☉ *Easter–Oct., Tues.–Sun. 2–6:30.*

The elegant 17th-century village château, set above split-level gardens, is now home of the **Voyage au Temps des Impressionistes.** At this museum devoted to the Impressionists, you will receive a set of infrared headphones (English available), with commentary that progresses as you Journey Through the Impressionist Era past various tableaux of Belle Epoque life. Although there are no Impressionist originals—500 reproductions pop up on screen—some say this is one of France's most imaginative, enjoyable, and innovative museums. Some of the special effects—talking mirrors, computerized cabaret dance girls, a train ride past Impressionist landscapes—rival Disney at its best. ⊠

rue de Léry, ☎ *01–34–48–48–48.* ✆ *55 frs, 130 frs family.* ☉
May–Oct., daily 10–8; Nov.–Apr., Tues.–Sun. 10–5:30.

The small **Musée de l'Absinthe** near the château contains publicity posters
and other Belle Epoque artifacts evoking the history of absinthe—a forerunner of today's anise-based aperitifs, like Ricard and Pernod. Before
it was banned in 1915 because of its effects on the nervous system, absinthe was France's national drink. A famous painting by Edgar Degas
shows two absinthe drinkers; van Gogh probably downed a few glasses
at the Auberge Ravoux. ✉ *44 rue Callé,* ☎ *01–30–36–83–26.* ✆
25 frs. ☉ *Oct.–May, weekends 11–6; June–Sept., Wed.–Sun. 11–6.*

Dining

$$ ✕ **Auberge Ravoux.** The place where van Gogh used to eat is the ob-
vious choice for lunch. The 140-franc three-course menu changes reg-
ularly and usually includes a fish or meat dish. There's also a good-value
wine list. But it is the setting and the history that make eating here spe-
cial. ✉ *pl. de la Mairie,* ☎ *01–34–48–05–47. Reservations essen-
tial. AE, DC, MC, V.*

Auvers-sur-Oise A to Z

Arriving and Departing

BY CAR
Auvers is 38 km (24 mi) northwest of Paris. Take highway A1, then
A15 toward Pontoise; then head east along N184 to Méry-sur-Oise and
pick up the N328, which crosses the river to Auvers.

BY TRAIN
There are two trains every hour to Auvers from Gare du Nord; a
change is necessary, and journey time can vary from 60 to 90 minutes.
There is a quicker (53 minutes) but more infrequent service from Gare
St-Lazare, involving a change at Pontoise.

Visitor Information

Auvers-sur-Oise Office de Tourisme (✉ rue de la Sansonne, opposite
the Maison de van Gogh, 95430 Auvers-sur-Oise, ☎ 01–30–36–
10–06).

CHANTILLY AND SENLIS

Chantilly, with its forest and château, and nearby Senlis, with its cathe-
dral and old town, lie just 30 minutes north of Paris and provide a per-
fect setting for a day away from the capital. Although separated by just
a few miles of forest, the two towns are very different. Senlis has nar-
row, winding medieval streets and one of the Gothic style's most ele-
gant spires. Chantilly is spacious and aristocratic; its stately moated
château is fronted by France's premier racecourse and palatial Baroque
stables.

Chantilly

Romantic Chantilly has a host of attractions: a faux Renaissance
château, eye-popping art collection, splendid Baroque stables, classy
racecourse, and vast (nearly 16,000-acre) forest. Yet it attracts far
fewer sightseeing hordes than Versailles or Fontainebleau.

Although the lavish exterior may be overdone—the style is 19th-cen-
tury Renaissance pastiche—the **Château de Chantilly** is photogenic be-
hind its moat. Housed here is the **Musée Condé,** an outstanding
collection of medieval manuscripts and European paintings, including
masterpieces by Raphael, Watteau, and Ingres. ☎ *03–44–57–03–62.*

▨ *35 frs.* ⊘ *Mar.–Oct., Wed.–Mon. 10–6; Nov.–Feb., 10:30–12:45 and 2–5. Orchestra performance every afternoon during the summer and Christmas holidays.* ▨ *80 frs.*

The majestic 18th-century **Grandes Ecuries** are the grandest stables in France and still in use as the **Musée Vivant du Cheval** (Living Museum of the Horse), with 30 horses and ponies performing dressage exercises for admiring visitors. The stables, next to the racecourse, opposite the château, were designed by Jean Aubert to accommodate 240 horses and 500 hounds for stag and boar hunts in the forests nearby. ✉ *7 rue du Connétable,* ☎ *03–44–57–40–40.* ▨ *50 frs.* ⊘ *Wed.–Mon. 10:30–5:30.*

Dining

$$ ✕ **Relais Condé.** The classiest restaurant in Chantilly—across from the racecourse—has a reasonable prix-fixe menu (155 francs) that makes it a suitable lunch spot. Chef Jacques Legrand's lively menu includes lobster terrine and duck breast with honey and spices. ✉ *42 av. du Maréchal-Joffre,* ☎ *03–44–57–05–75. Reservations essential. AE, V. Closed Tues.*

Senlis

This ancient town has a maze of crooked streets to explore beneath the svelte soaring spire of its Gothic cathedral.

The **Cathédrale Notre-Dame** dates from the second half of the 12th century. The superb spire—arguably the most elegant in France—was added around 1240 and has recently been cleaned and restored to its original splendor. This is one of France's oldest (and narrowest) cathedrals. ✉ *pl. du Parvis.*

The **Musée de la Vénerie** (Hunting Museum) stands on the grounds of the ruined royal castle across from the cathedral. One of France's few full-fledged hunting museums, it displays related artifacts, prints, and paintings, including excellent works by 18th-century animal portraitist Jean-Baptiste Oudry. ✉ *Château Royal,* ☎ *03–44–53–00–80.* ▨ *14 frs; grounds only, 6 frs.* ⊘ *Mid-Jan.–mid-Dec., Wed. 2–6, Thurs.–Mon. 10–noon and 2–6.*

Dining

$$ ✕ **Les Gourmandins.** This cozy two-floor restaurant in old Senlis serves interesting dishes, such as fricassee of burbot with mushrooms, and has a fine wine list. The 125-franc prix-fixe menu is ideal for a weekday lunch. ✉ *3 pl. de la Halle,* ☎ *03–44–60–94–01. V. Closed Tues. and last 3 wks in Aug. No dinner Mon.*

Chantilly and Senlis A to Z

Arriving and Departing

BY CAR

Take the highway A1 to Senlis from Paris (Porte de la Chapelle), 50 km (31 mi) away; Chantilly is 10 km (6 mi) west along pretty D924.

BY TRAIN

Chantilly is about 30 minutes from Gare du Nord; there is at least one train every hour. A shuttle bus links Chantilly to Senlis (25 minutes).

Visitor Information

Chantilly Office du Tourisme (✉ 23 av. Maréchal-Joffre, 60500 Chantilly, ☎ 03–44–57–08–58); **Senlis Office du Tourisme** (✉ 1 pl. du Parvis Notre-Dame, 60300 Senlis, ☎ 03–44–53–06–40).

CHARTRES, MAINTENON, AND RAMBOUILLET

The noble, soaring spires of Chartres compose one of the most famous sights in Europe. Try to catch a glimpse of them surging out of the vast, golden grain fields of the Beauce as you approach from the northeast. Maintenon, with its château and ruined aqueduct, and Rambouillet, a stately town whose château has a lake and extensive park land, are within easy reach of Chartres by road or rail.

Chartres

Although Chartres is chiefly visited for its magnificent Gothic cathedral with world-famous stained-glass windows, the whole town—one of the prettiest in France, with old houses and picturesque streets—is worth leisurely exploration. Ancient streets tumble down from the cathedral to the river Eure; the view of the rooftops beneath the cathedral from rue du Pont-St-Hilaire is particularly charming.

Chartres Cathedral is the sixth church to occupy the same spot. It dates mainly from the 12th and 13th centuries; the previous, 11th-century building burned down in 1194. A well-chronicled outburst of religious fervor followed the discovery that the Virgin's relic had miraculously survived unsinged. Reconstruction went ahead at a breathtaking pace. Just 25 years were needed for Chartres cathedral to rise again, and it has remained substantially unchanged ever since.

Worship on the site of the cathedral goes back to before the Gallo-Roman period; the crypt contains a well that was the focus of Druid ceremonies. The original cult of the fertility goddess merged into that of the Virgin Mary with the arrival of Christianity. In the late 9th century, King Charles the Bold presented Chartres with what was believed to be the tunic of the Virgin. This precious relic attracted hordes of pilgrims, and Chartres swiftly became—and has remained—a prime destination for the faithful. Pilgrims trek to Chartres from Paris on foot to this day.

The lower half of the facade is all that survives from the 11th-century Romanesque church. (The Romanesque style is evident in the use of round, rather than pointed, arches.) The main door—the **Portail Royal**—is richly sculpted with scenes from the life of Christ. The flanking towers are also Romanesque, though the upper part of the taller of the two **spires** (380 feet as against 350 feet) dates from the start of the 16th century, and its fanciful flamboyance contrasts with the stumpy solemnity of its Romanesque counterpart. The **rose window** above the main portal dates from the 13th century. The three windows below it contain some of the finest examples of 12th-century stained glass in France.

The interior is somber, and your eyes will need time to adjust to the dark. Their reward will be a view of the gemlike richness of the stained glass, dominated by the famous deep "Chartres blue." The oldest window, and perhaps the most stunning, is **Notre Dame de la Belle Verrière** (literally, Our Lady of the Lovely Window), in the south choir. It is well worth taking a pair of binoculars to pick out the details. If you wish to know more about stained-glass techniques and the motifs used, visit the small exhibit in the gallery opposite the north porch. The vast black-and-white medieval pattern on the floor of the nave is the only one of its kind to have survived from the Middle Ages. The faithful were expected to travel along its entire length (some 300 yards) on their knees.

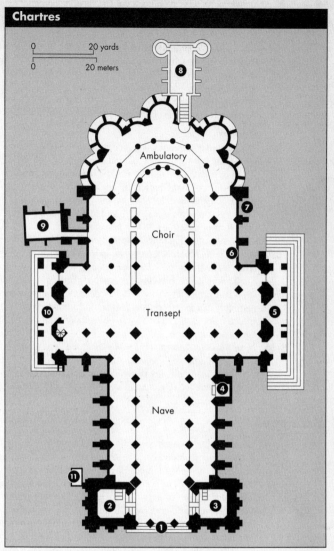

Chartres

Guided tours of the crypt start from the **Maison de la Crypte** opposite the south porch. The Romanesque and Gothic chapels running around the crypt have recently been stripped of the 19th-century paintings that used to disfigure them. You will also be shown a 4th-century Gallo-Roman wall and some 12th-century wall paintings. ⊠ *16 cloître Notre-Dame*, ☎ *02–37–21–56–33.* ▦ *10 frs.* ☽ *Guided tours of crypt: Easter–Oct., daily at 11, 2:15, 3:30, 4:30, 5:15; Nov.–Easter, daily at 11, 4. English guide 30 frs.*

The **Musée des Beaux-Arts** is a handsome 18th-century building just behind the cathedral—it used to serve as the bishop's palace. Its varied collection includes Renaissance enamels, a portrait of Erasmus by Holbein, tapestries, armor, and some fine, mainly French paintings of the 17th, 18th, and 19th centuries. There is also a room devoted to the forceful 20th-century works of Maurice de Vlaminck, who lived in the region. ⊠ *29 cloître Notre-Dame*, ☎ *02–37–36–41–39.* ▦

10 frs (20 frs for special exhibitions). ☉ *Apr.–Oct., Wed.–Mon. 10–6; Nov.–Mar., Wed.–Mon. 10–noon and 2–5.*

The Gothic **Église St-Pierre** near the River Eure has magnificent medieval windows from a period (circa 1300) not represented at the cathedral. The oldest stained glass here, portraying Old Testament worthies, is to the right of the choir and dates from the late 13th century. There is more fine stained glass (17th century) to admire at the **Eglise St-Aignan** on rue des Grenets, around the corner. ⊠ *rue St-Pierre.*

Dining

$$$ ✕ **Château d'Esclimont.** This magnificent restored Renaissance château, owned by the Relais & Châteaux chain, is frequented by high-profile Parisian businesspeople. Enjoy the luxuriant grounds, with lawns and lake, after you eat the rich cuisine. Lamb with asparagus, hare fricassee (in season), and lobster top the menu. It's 6 km (4 mi) west of the Ablis exit on expressway A11 and about 24 km (15 mi) from Chartres (and Rambouillet). ⊠ *St-Symphorien-le-Château*, ☎ *02–37–31–15–15. Reservations essential. Jacket and tie. MC, V.*

$$$ ✕ **La Vieille Maison.** Close to Chartres cathedral, in the same narrow street as Le Buisson Ardent (☞ *below*), this intimate spot has a flower-filled patio. The menu changes regularly but invariably includes regional specialties, such as truffles and asparagus with chicken. Prices, though justified, can be steep; the 160-franc lunch menu is a good bet. ⊠ *5 rue au Lait*, ☎ *02–37–34–10–67. Jacket and tie. AE, MC, V. Closed Sun. evening, Mon.*

$–$$ ✕ **Le Buisson Ardent.** This wood-beamed restaurant offers a prix-fixe menu, imaginative food, and attentive service in a quaint old street near Chartres cathedral. Try the chicken ravioli with leeks or the rolled beef with spinach. ⊠ *10 rue au Lait*, ☎ *02–37–34–04–66. AE, DC, MC, V. No dinner Sun.*

Maintenon

The River Eure snakes northeast from Chartres to Maintenon. The town's Renaissance **Château** once belonged to Louis XIV's mistress and morganatic spouse, Madame de Maintenon. Her private apartments are open to visitors. The square, 12th-century **keep** is the sole vestige of a fortress that once occupied this site. The formal gardens stretch behind the château to the ivy-covered arches of the ruined **aqueduct**—one of the Sun King's most outrageous projects. His aim: to provide the ornamental ponds in the gardens of Versailles (48 km/30 mi away) with water from the Eure. In 1684, some 30,000 men were signed up to construct a three-tier, 5-km (3-mi) aqueduct as part of this project. Many died of fever before the enterprise was called off in 1689. ⊠ *pl. Aristide-Briand*, ☎ *02–37–23–00–09.* 🎟 *30 frs.* ☉ *Apr.–Oct., Wed.–Mon. 2–6; Nov.–Mar., weekends 2–5.*

Rambouillet

Surrounded by a huge forest, Rambouillet was once the residence of kings and dukes. Today the **Château de Rambouillet** belongs to the French president, although he is seldom in residence. Most of the buildings date from the early 18th century, but the brawny **Tour François I**, named for the king who breathed his last here in 1547, was part of the 14th-century fortified castle that first stood on this site. The château backs a lake; you can stroll around it and explore the extensive grounds, which contain a sheepfold and dairy. 🎟 *27 frs.* ☉ *Wed.–Mon. 10–11:30 and 2–5:30.*

Chartres, Maintenon, and Rambouillet A to Z

Arriving and Departing

BY CAR

The A10/A11 expressways link Paris to Chartres, 88 km (55 mi) away. Maintenon is 19 km (12 mi) and Rambouillet is 43 km (27 mi) northeast of Chartres via D906. If you are coming from Paris, take A13 toward Versailles, then A12/N10 to Rambouillet (total distance 53 km/33 mi); D906 leads to Maintenon (total distance 77 km/48 mi).

BY TRAIN

There are hourly trains from Paris (Gare Montparnasse) to Chartres (travel time is 50–70 minutes, depending on service). Many of the trains between Paris and Chartres stop at Maintenon (50 minutes) and Rambouillet (35 minutes) and there is an hourly service between Rambouillet and Paris (Gare Montparnasse).

Guided Tours

Paris Vision (⊠ 214 rue de Rivoli, Paris, ☎ 01–42–60–31–25) and **Cityrama** (⊠ 4 pl. des Pyramides, Paris, ☎ 01–44–55–61–00) feature half-day trips to Chartres (250 frs) and combined excursions to Chartres and Versailles (435 frs) on Tuesday and Saturday. Additional trips are scheduled in summer; call for information.

Visitor Information

Chartres (⊠ pl. de la Cathédrale, 28000 Chartres, ☎ 02–37–21–50–00); **Maintenon** (⊠ 2 pl. Aristide-Briand, 28130 Maintenon, ☎ 02–37–23–05–04); **Rambouillet** (⊠ 8 pl. de la Libération, 78120 Rambouillet, ☎ 01–34–83–21–21).

DISNEYLAND PARIS

In April 1992 American pop culture secured a mammoth outpost just 32 km (20 mi) east of Paris. Disneyland Paris, on 1,500 acres in Marne-la-Vallée, has thousands of hotel rooms, a convention center, sports facilities, an entertainment and shopping complex, and, of course, the theme park itself. Although great fanfare greeted the opening of the park, the resort has had its share of troubles: image problems, reports of technical glitches, feuds with neighbors objecting to noisy fireworks, and—initially—low attendance levels. Economic woes were partially to blame: The devaluation of currency in Great Britain, Italy, and Spain in late 1992 made a trip to the park a costly venture for many Europeans. In 1994 Disney responded with an about-face: a new name (it had been called Euro Disney), a tumble in admission prices, and the sale of alcohol in theme-park restaurants. These changes, plus the 10 additional attractions opened since 1992, have reversed the slide.

The theme park is made up of five "lands": Main Street U.S.A., Frontierland, Adventureland, Fantasyland, and Discoveryland. The central theme of each land is relentlessly echoed in every detail, from attractions to restaurant menus to souvenirs.

Main Street U.S.A. is the scene of the Disney Parades held every afternoon and—during holiday periods—every evening, too.

Top attractions at **Frontierland** are the chilling Phantom Manor, haunted by holographic spooks, and the thrilling runaway mine train of Big Thunder Mountain, a roller coaster that plunges wildly through floods and avalanches in a setting meant to evoke Monument Valley.

Whiffs of Arabia, Africa, and the West Indies give **Adventureland** its exotic cachet; the spicy meals and snacks served here rank among the best food in the theme park. Don't miss the Pirates of the Caribbean, an exciting mise-en-scène populated by eerily human, computer-driven figures, or Indiana Jones and the Temple of Doom, a breathtaking ride that relives some of our luckless hero's most exciting moments.

Fantasyland charms the youngest park goers with familiar cartoon characters from such Disney classics as Snow White, Pinocchio, Dumbo, and Peter Pan. The focal point of Fantasyland, and indeed Disneyland Paris, is Sleeping Beauty's Castle, a 140-foot, bubble-gum pink structure topped with 16 blue- and gold-tipped turrets. Officially known as Le Château de la Belle au Bois Dormant, the château has a design allegedly inspired by illustrations from a medieval Book of Hours. The castle's dungeon conceals a scaly, green, 2-ton dragon who rumbles and grumbles in his sleep and occasionally rouses to roar—an impressive feat of engineering that terrifies every tot in the crowd!

Discoveryland is a futuristic setting for high-tech Disney entertainment. Robots on roller skates welcome you as you bound for Star Tours, a pitching, plunging, sense-confounding ride through intergalactic space. Space Mountain, Disney's latest attraction, pretends to catapult riders through the Milky Way.

For entertainment outside the theme park, check out **Festival Disney,** a vast pleasure mall designed by architect Frank Gehry. Featured are American-style restaurants (crab shack, diner, deli, steak house), a disco, and a dinner theater where Buffalo Bill stages his **Wild West Show** twice nightly. An 18-hole golf course is open to the public (for information, call 01–60–45–68–04). ☎ *Disneyland Paris (prices vary according to season): 120–195 frs.* ⊙ *Mid-June–mid-Sept., daily 9–10; mid-Sept.–mid-June, daily 10–6; Dec. and spring school holidays, daily 10–9.*

Dining

$–$$ ✕ **Disneyland Restaurants.** Disneyland Paris is peppered with places to eat, ranging from snack bars and fast-food joints to five full-service restaurants—all with a distinguishing theme. In addition, all Disney hotels and Festival Disney have restaurants that are open to the public. But since these are outside the theme park, it is not recommended that you waste time traveling to them for lunch. Wine and beer are served in the theme park's five sit-down restaurants, as well as in the hotels and restaurants outside the park. Eateries serve nonstop as long as the park is open. *AE, DC, MC, V at sit-down restaurants; no credit cards at others.*

Disneyland Paris A to Z

Arriving and Departing

BY BUS

Shuttle buses link Disneyland Paris to Roissy (56 km/35 mi) and Orly (50 km/31 mi) airports. The fare is 68 francs one-way.

BY CAR

The Strasbourg-bound A4 expressway leads from Paris to Disneyland Paris, at Marne-la-Vallée, a journey of 32 km (20 mi) that in normal traffic will take about 30 minutes. The 4-km (2½-mi) route from the expressway to the entrance of the theme park is clearly marked. Day visitors must head for the *Parking Visiteurs,* which costs 40 francs per car and is 600 yards from the theme-park entrance.

Disneyland Paris's suburban train station (Marne-la-Vallée-Chessy) is just 100 yards from the entrance to both the theme park and Festival Disney. Trains run every 10 to 20 minutes from RER-A stations in central Paris: Charles de Gaulle–Etoile, Auber, Châtelet–Les Halles, Gare de Lyon, and Nation. The trip takes about 40 minutes and costs 72 francs round-trip (including the métro to the RER). A TGV station next to the RER station has trains running direct from Lille, Lyon, and Marseille.

Visitor Information

Contact **Walt Disney World Central Reservations** (✉ Box 10, 100 Lake Buena Vista, FL 32830-0100, ☎ 407/934–7639) or **Disneyland Paris S.C.A.** (✉ Central Reservations Office, BP 104, 77777 Marne-la-Vallée, Cedex 4, France, ☎ 01–60–30–60–30, FAX 01–49–30–71–00).

FONTAINEBLEAU, BARBIZON, AND VAUX-LE-VICOMTE

Fontainebleau, with its historic château, is a favorite place for excursions, especially since a lush forest (containing the painters' village of Barbizon) and the superb Baroque château of Vaux-le-Vicomte are close by.

Fontainebleau

Like Chambord in the Loire Valley or Compiègne to the north of Paris, Fontainebleau earned royal esteem as a hunting base. As at Versailles, a hunting lodge once stood on the site of the current château, along with a chapel built in 1169 and consecrated by exiled (later murdered and canonized) English priest Thomas à Becket.

The **Château de Fontainebleau** you see today dates from the 16th century, although additions were made by various royal incumbents through the next 300 years. The palace was begun under the flamboyant Renaissance king, François I, the French contemporary of England's Henry VIII. The king hired Italian artists Il Rosso (a pupil of Michelangelo) and Primaticcio to embellish his château. In fact, they did much more: By introducing the pagan allegories and elegant lines of Mannerism to France, they revolutionized French decorative art. Their extraordinary frescoes and stuccowork can be admired in the **Galerie François-I** and the glorious **Salle de Bal,** which was completed under Henri II, François's successor.

Although Sun King Louis XIV's architectural fancy was concentrated on Versailles, he commissioned Mansart to design new pavilions and had André Lenôtre replant the gardens at Fontainebleau, where he and his court returned faithfully in the fall for the hunting season. However, it was Napoléon who made a Versailles out of Fontainebleau, by spending lavishly to restore it to its former glory. He held Pope Pius VII prisoner here in 1812, signed the second Church-State concordat here in 1813, and, in the cobbled Cour des Adieux, bade farewell to his Old Guard in 1814 as he began his brief exile on the Mediterranean island of Elba. Another courtyard—the **Cour de la Fontaine**—was commissioned by Napoléon in 1812 and adjoins the Etang (or pond) des Carpes. Ancient carp are alleged to swim here, although Allied soldiers drained the pond in 1915 and ate all the fish, and, in the event they missed some, Hitler's hordes did likewise in 1940.

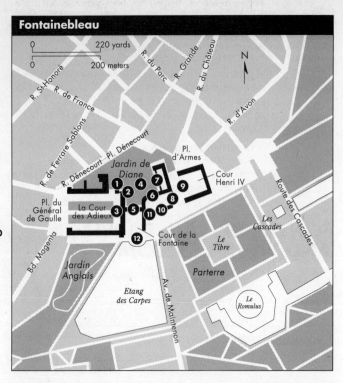

The famous Horseshoe Staircase that dominates the **Cour du Cheval Blanc,** or Courtyard of the White Horse (which later came to be called the Cour des Adieux, or Courtyard of Farewell), was built by Androuet du Cerceau for Louis XIII (1610–43). The **Porte Dauphine** is the most beautiful of the various gateways that connect the complex of buildings; its name commemorates the fact that the Dauphin—the heir to the throne, later Louis XIII—was christened under its archway in 1606.

Napoléon's apartments occupied the first floor. You can see a lock of his hair, his Légion d'Honneur medal, his imperial uniform, the hat he wore on his return from Elba in 1815, and one bed in which he definitely did spend a night (almost every town in France boasts a bed in which the emperor supposedly snoozed). There is also a throne room—Napoléon spurned the one at Versailles, a palace he disliked, establishing his imperial seat in the former **King's Bedchamber**—and the **Queen's Boudoir,** known as the Room of the Six Maries (occupants included ill-fated Marie-Antoinette and Napoléon's second wife, Marie-Louise). Highlights of other salons include 17th-century tapestries, marble reliefs by Jacquet de Grenoble, and paintings and frescoes by the versatile Primaticcio.

The jewel of the interior, though, is the ceremonial ballroom, or **Salle de Bal,** nearly 100 feet long and dazzlingly decorated with 16th-century frescoes and gilding. It is luxuriantly wood-paneled, and a gleaming parquetry floor reflects the patterns in the ceiling. Like the château as a whole, the room exudes a sense of elegance and style—but on a more intimate, human scale than at Versailles: This is Renaissance, not Baroque. ⊠ *pl. du Gal-de-Gaulle,* ☎ *01–64–22–27–40.* ▦ *32 frs; gardens free.* ◷ *Wed.–Mon. 9:30–5; gardens 9–dusk.*

Dining

$$$ ✕ **Le Beauharnais.** Opposite the château, in the Aigle Noir hotel, this restaurant serves classic French fare in a grand setting; try the duck with marjoram. Prix-fixe menus are set at 195 and 300 francs. There's a tranquil garden for alfresco dining in summer. ✉ *27 pl. Napoléon-Bonaparte,* ☎ *01–64–22–32–65. Jacket and tie. AE, DC, MC, V. Closed last 2 wks of Dec.*

Barbizon

On the western edge of the 62,000-acre Forest of Fontainebleau lies the village of Barbizon, home to a number of mid-19th-century landscape artists, whose innovative outdoor style paved the way for the Impressionists. Corot, Millet, Théodore Rousseau, Daubigny, and Diaz, among others, all painted here, repairing to the Auberge du Père Ganne after working hours to brush up on their social life. Father Ganne's inn still stands and is now the **Musée de l'École de Barbizon** (Barbizon School Museum). The museum contains a few original works as well as information about the village as it was in the 19th century. ✉ *92 Grande-Rue,* ☎ *01–60–66–22–27.* 🎫 *25 frs., joint ticket with the Maison-Atelier Théodore Rousseau,* ☞ *below.* ✿ *Wed.–Mon. 10–12:30 and 2–5.*

Farther along the main street, you can soak up the arty mood at Millet's studio, the **Maison J. F. Millet** (✉ 27 Grande-Rue, ☎ 01–60–66–21–55, ✿ Wed.–Mon. 9:30–12:30 and 2–5:30). The **Maison-Atelier Théodore Rousseau** (✉ 55 Grande-Rue, ☎ 01–60–66–22–38, ✿ Wed. and Fri.–Mon. 10–12:30 and 2–5) is another painter's house-cum-studio; temporary exhibits are now staged here.

Dining

$–$$ ✕ **Le Relais de Barbizon.** Solid home-cooked meals are served outdoors. Among the offerings are duckling with cherries, and lamb with parsley. Expect crowds in midsummer. The five-course, 140-franc weekday menu is an excellent value. ✉ *2 av. Charles-de-Gaulle,* ☎ *01–60–66–40–28. MC, V. Closed Wed. No dinner Tues.*

Vaux-le-Vicomte

The majestic **Château de Vaux-le-Vicomte,** started in 1656 by court finance wizard Nicolas Fouquet, is one of the most impressive buildings in the Ile-de-France. The construction process was monstrous: Villages were razed, then 18,000 workmen were called in to execute the plans of architect Louis Le Vau, decorator Charles Le Brun, and landscape gardener André Lenôtre. The house-warming party was so lavish that star guest Louis XIV, tetchy at the best of times, threw a jealous fit. He hurled Fouquet in the slammer and promptly began building Versailles to prove just who was boss.

Decoration of the château's landmark feature, the **cupola,** was halted at Fouquet's arrest, and the ceiling of the oval **Grand Salon** beneath remains depressingly blank. Le Brun's major achievement is the ceiling of the **Chambre du Roi,** depicting *Time Bearing Truth Heavenwards.* The word "squirrel" in French is *écureuil,* but in local dialect they were known as *fouquets*; they appear here (along the frieze) and throughout the château, a sly visual tribute to the château's hapless founder. Le Brun's other masterwork is the ceiling in the **Salon des Muses,** a brilliant allegorical composition painted in glowing, sensuous colors surpassing anything he achieved at Versailles.

A clever **exhibition,** complete with life-size wax figures, explains the rise and fall of Nicolas Fouquet. Although accused by Louis XIV and subsequent historians of megalomania and shady financial dealings, he was apparently condemned on little evidence by a court eager to please the jealous, irascible monarch. The exhibition continues in the basement, whose cool, dim rooms used to store food and wine and house the château's staff. The **kitchens,** a more cheerful sight with their gleaming copperware and old menus, are also down here.

Lenôtre's stupendous, studiously restored **gardens** contain statues, waterfalls, and fountains. There is also a **Musée des Equipages**—stocked with carriages, saddles, and a smithy—near the entrance. ⊠ *Domaine de Vaux-le-Vicomte, 77950 Maincy,* ☎ *01–64–14–41–90.* ⊠ *54 frs; grounds only, 30 frs.* ☉ *Château Apr.–Oct., daily 10–6. Candlelight visits May–Oct., Sat. 8:30–11 pm (68 frs).*

Fontainebleau, Barbizon, and Vaux-le-Vicomte A to Z

Arriving and Departing

BY CAR
From Paris, take A6, then N7 to Fontainebleau from Porte d'Orléans or Porte d'Italie (total distance 72 km/45 mi). Barbizon is 8 km (5 mi) northwest of Fontainebleau. From Fontainebleau take N7; the Barbizon exit is clearly marked. Vaux-le-Vicomte is 21 km (13 mi) north of Fontainebleau. Take N6 to Melun, then N36 northeast (direction Meaux), turning right after 1½ km (1 mi) or so along D215.

BY TRAIN
Fontainebleau is about 50 minutes from Paris (Gare de Lyon); take a bus to complete the 3-km (2-mi) trip from the station (Fontainebleau-Avon) to the château. Vaux-le-Vicomte is a 7-km (4-mi) taxi ride from the nearest station at Melun, served by regular trains from Paris and Fontainebleau. The taxi ride costs about 80–100 francs. Barbizon is, unfortunately, not accessible by train.

Guided Tours
Paris Vision and **Cityrama** offer half-day trips to Fontainebleau and Barbizon (☞ Guided Tours *in* Chartres, Maintenon, and Rambouillet, *above*). The cost is 300 francs and the tours depart Wednesday, Friday, and Sunday at 1:30.

Visitor Information
Fontainebleau (⊠ 31 pl. Napoléon-Bonaparte, 77300 Fontainebleau, ☎ 01–64–22–25–68); **Barbizon** (⊠ 55 Grande Rue, 77630 Barbizon, ☎ 01–60–66–41–87); **Vaux-le-Vicomte** (⊠ Domaine de Vaux-le-Vicomte, 77950 Maincy, ☎ 01–64–14–41–90).

GIVERNY

The charming village of Giverny has become a place of pilgrimage for art lovers. It was here that Claude Monet lived for 43 years, until his death in 1926 at the age of 86. After decades of neglect, his pretty pink house with green shutters, the **Maison de Claude Monet,** his studios, and his garden with its famous lily pond have been lovingly restored—thanks to gifts from around the world and in particular from the United States. Late spring is perhaps the best time to visit, when the apple trees are in blossom and the garden is a riot of color. Try to avoid summer weekends and afternoons in July and August, when the limited capacity of Monet's home and gardens is pushed to the limit by busloads of tourists.

Monet was brought up in Normandy and, like many of the other Impressionists, was attracted by the soft light of the Seine Valley. After several years at Argenteuil, just north of Paris, he moved downriver to Giverny in 1883 along with his two sons, his mistress Alice Hoschedé (whom he later married), and her six children. By 1890, a prospering Monet was able to buy the house outright. Three years later, he purchased another plot of land across the lane to continue his gardening experiments, diverting the River Epte to make a pond.

Monet's house has a warm family feeling that may come as a welcome break after visiting stately French châteaux. The rooms have been restored to Monet's original designs: the kitchen with its blue tiles, the buttercup-yellow dining room, and Monet's bedroom on the second floor. There are reproductions of his own works, and some of the Japanese prints Monet avidly collected, displayed around the house. His studios are also open for viewing.

The **garden,** with flowers spilling out across the paths, is as cheerful and natural as the house—quite unlike formal French gardens. The enchanting water garden, with its water lilies, bridges, and rhododendrons, is across the lane that runs to the side of the house and can be reached through a tunnel. The lilies and Japanese bridges became special features of his garden and now help to conjure up an image of a grizzle-bearded Monet dabbing cheerfully at his canvases—capturing changes in light and weather in a way that was to have a major influence on 20th-century art. From Giverny, Monet enthusiasts may want to continue up the Seine Valley to the site of another of his celebrated painting series: Rouen Cathedral. ⊠ *84 rue Claude-Monet,* ☎ *02–32–51–94–65.* ▣ *38 frs; gardens only, 27 frs.* ☉ *Apr.–Oct., Tues.–Sun. 10–6 (gardens 10–noon and 2–6).*

The spacious, airy **Musée Américain,** endowed by Chicago art patrons Daniel and Judith Terra, displays works by American Impressionists who were influenced by—and often studied with—Claude Monet. ⊠ *99 rue Claude-Monet,* ☎ *02–32–51–94–65.* ▣ *30 frs.* ☉ *Apr.–Oct., Tues.–Sun. 10–6.*

Dining

$$$ ✕ **Château de Brécourt.** Part of the stylish Relais & Châteaux chain, this 17th-century brick château on extensive grounds is a popular spot for people who drive to Giverny. Some of the creative items on the menu are smoked salmon-and-crab cakes, turbot with caviar, and pears in a flaky pastry roasted in honey for dessert. It's 11 km (7 mi) west of Giverny (via D181 at Douains, near Pacy-sur-Eure). ⊠ *Douains,* ☎ *02–32–52–40–50. AE, DC, MC, V.*

$$ ✕ **Les Jardins de Giverny.** This commendable restaurant, close to Monet's house, has an old-fashioned dining room overlooking a rose garden. The inventive dishes include foie gras laced with applejack, and seafood terrine with a mild pepper sauce. ⊠ *1 rue Milieu,* ☎ *02–32–21–60–80. AE, V. Closed Mon. and Feb. No dinner Sun.*

Giverny A to Z

Arriving and Departing

BY CAR
Take expressway A13 from Paris to the Vernon exit (D181). Cross the Seine in Vernon and follow D5 to Giverny (total distance 84 km/52 mi).

BY TRAIN
Take the train from Paris (Gare St-Lazare) to Vernon (50 minutes). Giverny is 5½ km (3½ mi) away by bus or taxi.

Guided Tours

Guided excursions are organized by **American Express** (✉ 11 rue Scribe, Paris, ☎ 01–47–77–77–37) and the **RATP Tourist Office** (✉ pl. de la Madeleine, Paris, ☎ 01–40–06–71–45), on either a half-day or full-day basis, combined with trips to Rouen.

REIMS AND LAON

Champagne and cathedrals make a trip to the renowned city of Reims, and the lesser-known hilltop town of Laon, an ideal two-day break in the northeast of Paris. Both have historic links with royalty: Laon was once capital of France—12 centuries ago—and Reims was the setting for the coronations of the French kings (Charles X's was the last, in 1825).

Reims

Reims is best known as the center of the champagne industry. Several major producers have their headquarters here, and you can visit their chalky, labyrinthine cellars that tunnel beneath the city. Reims cathedral is one of the most historic in France, although restoring it to medieval glory, after its partial destruction during World War I, has taken most of the century. Despite much indifferent postwar rebuilding, Reims is rich with attractions dating from Roman times to the modern era.

The glory of Reims's **Cathédrale Notre-Dame** is its facade. Its proportions are curiously deceptive; the building is actually considerably larger than it appears. Above the north (left) door is the **Smiling Angel,** a delightful statue whose kindly expression threatens to turn into an acid-rain scowl: Pollution has succeeded war as the ravager of the building. The postcard shops nearby have views of the cathedral after World War I, and on seeing the destruction, you'll understand why restoration here is an ongoing process. The high, solemn nave is at its best in the summer, when the lower walls are adorned with 16th-century tapestries relating the Life of the Virgin. The east-end windows were designed by Marc Chagall.

With the exception of the 15th-century towers, most of the original building was constructed in the hundred years after 1211. A stroll around the outside gives the impression of harmony and discipline, almost belying all the decorative richness. The east end presents an idyllic vista across well-tended lawns. There are spectacular light shows both inside (40 frs) and outside (free) the cathedral in July and August. ✉ *cours Anatole-France.* ☉ *Daily 8–7. Guided tours in English available.*

The **Palais du Tau,** the former archbishop's palace next to the cathedral, contains tapestries, coronation robes, and several outstanding statues removed from the cathedral's facade before they fell off. There are excellent views of the cathedral from the upper stories. ✉ *2 pl. du Cardinal-Luçon,* ☎ *03–26–47–74–39.* 💷 *26 frs.* ☉ *Daily 10–noon and 2–6; winter, weekdays 10–noon and 2–5.*

The **Musée des Beaux-Arts,** Reims's fine-arts museum, has an outstanding painting collection crowned by 27 Corots and David's celebrated portrait of Revolutionary leader Marat dead in his bath. Nine Boudins and Jongkinds are among the finer Impressionist works here. ✉ *8 rue Chanzy,* ☎ *03–26–47–28–44.* 💷 *12 frs.* ☉ *Wed.–Mon. 10–noon and 2–6.*

The 11th-century **Basilique St-Rémi,** devoted to the 5th-century saint who gave his name to the city, is nearly as long as the cathedral; its interior seems to stretch away into the dim distance. The Gothic choir has retained much of its original 12th-century stained glass. ✉ *53 rue Simon.* ◷ *Daily 8–noon and 2–6.*

Several producers run tours of their **champagne cellars,** combining video presentations with guided walks through their cavernous, chalk-hewn underground warehouses. Few, however, show much generosity when it comes to pouring out samples of bubbly; **Mumm** is an exception. ✉ *34 rue du Champ-de-Mars,* ☎ *03–26–49–59–69.* ◷ *Daily 9:30–noon and 2–5; closed weekends in winter.*

If you don't mind paying for samples, the most spectacular cellars are those of **Taittinger.** ✉ *9 pl. St-Nicaise,* ☎ *03–26–85–84–33.* 🎫 *15 frs.* ◷ *Guided 1-hr tours weekdays 9:30–noon and 2–4:30; weekends 9–11 and 2–5; closed weekends in winter.*

The **Chapelle Foujita** opened in 1966 across from the Mumm Cellars. It was decorated by Paris-based Japanese artist Tsuguharu Fujita (1886–1968), a member of the Montparnasse set in the '20s who converted to Catholicism and was baptized in Reims. ✉ *33 rue du Champ-de-Mars,* ☎ *03–26–40–06–96.*

It was in the well-preserved, map-covered **Salle de Guerre** (War Room) near the railroad station, where Eisenhower established Allied headquarters, that the German surrender was signed in May 1945 at the end of World War II. ✉ *12 rue Franklin-Roosevelt.* 🎫 *12 frs.* ◷ *Apr.–Sept., Wed.–Mon. 10–noon and 2–6; Oct.–Mar., Wed.–Mon. 10–noon.*

The **Porte Mars,** an impressive Roman arch adorned with faded bas-reliefs depicting Jupiter, Romulus, and Remus, looms up just across from the railroad station.

Dining and Lodging

$$$$ ✕ **Boyer.** Gérard Boyer is one of the most highly rated chefs in France. Duck, foie gras in pastry, and truffles figure among his delicious specialties. The setting, not far from the Basilique St-Rémi, is magnificent, too: a 19th-century château, built for the champagne firm Pommery, surrounded by an extensive, well-tended park. ✉ *Château des Crayères, 64 bd. Henry-Vasnier,* ☎ *03–26–82–80–80. Reservations essential. Jacket and tie. AE, DC, MC, V. Closed Mon. and Dec. 25–mid-Jan. No lunch Tues.*

$$–$$$ ✕🏨 **Gambetta.** This small hotel near the cathedral has clean, comfortable rooms and a fine restaurant, Le Vonelly, where owners Brigitte and Pascal Géraudel serve a 190-franc menu featuring scallop salad with spinach and roast duck with cabbage. ✉ *9–13 rue Gambetta,* ☎ *03–26–47–41–64,* 📠 *03–26–47–22–43. AE, MC, V. Closed Mon. and mid-Aug. No dinner Sun.*

Laon

Laon occupies a spectacular hilltop site 40 km (25 mi) northwest of Reims and is known as the Crowned Mountain on account of the many-towered silhouette of its venerable cathedral. This enchanting old town is at last emerging from decades of lethargy to become one of northern France's leading tourist attractions.

Laon's **Cathédrale Notre-Dame** was constructed from 1160 to 1235 and is a superb example of early Gothic architecture. The light interior gives the impression of immense length (120 yards in total). The flat east end—an English-inspired feature—is unusual in France. The second-floor galleries that run around the building are typical early Gothic; you can visit them (and the towers) with a guide from the tourist office on the cathedral square. The airy elegance of the five remaining towers is audacious by any standard and highly unusual: French medieval architects preferred to concentrate on soaring interiors and usually allowed for just two towers at the west end. You don't have to be an architectural scholar to appreciate the sense of movement about Laon's west-end facade compared with the more placid, two-dimensional feel of Notre-Dame in Paris. Look for the stone bulls protruding from the towers, a tribute to the stalwart beasts who carted the blocks of stone from quarries far below.

The medieval **ramparts,** the old fortification walls, lie virtually undisturbed by passing traffic and provide a ready-made route for a tour of old Laon as well as panoramic views of the plains below.

A notable and well-preserved survivor from medieval times is the **Chapelle des Templiers,** a small, octagonal 12th-century chapel on the grounds of the town museum. ⊠ *32 rue Georges-Ermant.* ⊠ *12 frs.* ⊙ *Apr.–Sept., Wed.–Mon. 10–noon and 2–6; Oct.–Mar., Wed.–Mon. 10–noon and 2–5.*

Dining

$$ ✕ **La Petite Auberge.** You can expect some imaginative nouvelle dishes from chef Willy-Marc Zorn in this 18th-century-style restaurant close to the station in Laon's *ville basse* (lower town). Pigeon, fillet of plaice with champagne vinegar, and frozen nougat are among the choices. ⊠ *45 bd. Pierre-Brossolette,* ☎ *03–23–23–02–38. AE, V. Closed Sun. and Aug. No lunch Sat.*

Reims and Laon A to Z

Arriving and Departing

BY CAR

Expressway A4 heads east to Reims, 144 km (90 mi) from Paris, on its way to Strasbourg. The Belgium-bound N2 links Paris to Laon, 140 km (87 mi) away. The N44 highway links Laon to Reims, a 40-km (25-mi) trip. If you're not in a hurry, leave the N44 at Corbény and explore the Chemin des Dames.

BY TRAIN

Trains run daily between Laon and Reims from the SNCF stations and take 35–55 minutes. The Paris–Laon route (from Gare du Nord, not Gare de l'Est) takes up to two hours. The Paris (Gare de l'Est) to Reims trip takes 90 minutes.

Visitor Information

Reims (⊠ 2 rue Guillaume-de-Machault, 51100 Reims, ☎ 03–26–47–25–69); **Laon** (⊠ pl. du Parvis, 02000 Laon, ☎ 03–23–20–28–62).

THOIRY

Thoiry, 40 km (25 mi) west of Paris, is an ideal day-trip destination, especially for families with children. It offers a splendid combination of history and culture—chiefly in the form of a superbly furnished 16th-century château with its own archives and gastronomy museum—and outdoor adventure, in the form of a safari park with more than 800 wild animals, including lions and elephants.

The **Château de Thoiry** was built by Philibert de l'Orme in 1564. Its handsome Renaissance facade is set off by **gardens** landscaped by Lenôtre in the disciplined French fashion; for contrast, there is also a less formal Jardin Anglais (English Garden). Owners Vicomte de La

Panouse and his American wife, Annabelle, have restored the château and grounds to their former glory and opened both to the public. Highlights of the interior include the grand staircase; the 18th-century Gobelins tapestries in the dining room, which were inspired by the adventures of Don Quixote, and the Green and White Salon, with an old harpsichord, portraits, and tapestries.

The distinguished history of the Panouse family—one member, Comte César, fought in the American Revolution—is retraced in the **Archive Museum,** where papal bulls and Napoléonic letters are displayed side by side with missives from Thomas Jefferson and Benjamin Franklin. Since 1984 the château pantries have housed a **Museum of Gastronomy,** whose *pièces montées* (banquet showpieces) re-create the designs of the premier 19th-century chef, Antoine Carême (his clients included George IV of England and the emperors of Austria and Russia). One is more than 15 feet high and took eight months to confect. Engravings, old copper pots, and early recipe books are also on display.

You can stroll at leisure around the picturesque grounds, stop off at the Pré Angélique to watch a cricket match (summer weekends) or admire giraffes, wolves, and—from the safety of a raised footbridge—the world's first *ligrons,* a cross between a lion and a tiger. There is an exploratory play area for children, featuring giant burrows and cobwebs. For obvious reasons, pedestrians are not allowed into the **Bear Park** or the **African Reserve.** Keep your car windows closed if you want to remain on peaceful terms with marauding lions, rhinos, elephants, and megahorned Watusi cattle. ☏ *01–34–87–52–25.* ✉ *Château 30 frs. Château, park, and game reserve 78–99 frs.* ☉ *Summer, weekdays 10–6, weekends 10–6:30; winter, daily 10–5.*

Dining

$ ✕ **Commerce.** This bar on Thoiry's main street has an attractive upstairs dining room where locals in the know come for hearty weekday lunches. There's a choice of entrées from an extensive buffet—pâté, salami, and carrot salad are staple favorites—followed by a sturdy main course, such as steak and chips or beef Wellington. ✉ *rue de la Porte-St-Martin,* ☏ *01–34–87–40–18. No credit cards. Closed Sat. No dinner.*

$ ✕ **Etoile.** This restaurant, in a dowdy hotel on the main street just 300 yards from the château, has special tourist and children's menus, as well as a wide selection of à la carte items. Robust, traditional French dishes are served: steak, chicken, fish, and pâté. ✉ *38 rue de la Porte-St-Martin,* ☏ *01–34–87–40–21. AE, DC, MC, V. Closed Mon.*

Thoiry A to Z

Arriving and Departing

BY CAR

Take highway A13 from Paris; then follow signs for Dreux along A12/N12. Just past Pontchartrain, D11 heads off right toward Thoiry (total distance from Paris: 44 km/27 mi).

BY TRAIN

Trains run every hour or so from Paris (Gare Montparnasse) to Montfort-L'Amaury (35 minutes), 8 km (5 mi) from Thoiry (a 10-minute taxi ride, ☏ 01–34–86–01–51). A special shuttle bus operates to and from the château on Sundays in summer (call the château for details).

VERSAILLES

Paris in the 17th century was a rowdy, rabble-ridden city. Louis XIV hated it and set about in search of a new power base. He settled on Versailles, 24 km (15 mi) west of Paris, where his father had a small château–hunting lodge.

Today the **Château de Versailles** seems monstrously big, but it wasn't large enough for the army of 20,000 noblemen, servants, and hangers-on who moved in with Louis. A new city—a new capital, in fact—had to be constructed from scratch to accommodate them. Tough-thinking town planners promptly dreamt up vast mansions and avenues broader than the Champs-Elysées—all in bicep-flexing Baroque.

It was hardly surprising that Louis XIV's successors rapidly felt out of sync with their architectural inheritance. The Sun King's successors, Louis XV and Louis XVI, preferred to cower in small retreats in the gardens, well out of the mighty château's shadow. The two most famous of these structures are the Petit Trianon, a model of classical harmony and proportion built by Louis XV; and the Hameau, where Marie-Antoinette could play at being a shepherdess amid the ersatz rusticity of her Potemkin hamlet.

The contrast between the majestic and the domesticated is an important part of Versailles's appeal, but pomp and bombast dominate the mood here, and you won't need reminding that you're in the world's grandest palace—or one of France's most popular tourist attractions. The park outside is the ideal place to get your breath back. Lenôtre's gardens represent formal landscaping at its most rigid and sophisticated.

The château was built under court architects Le Vau and Mansart between 1662 and 1690; the entrance is through the gilt-and-iron gates from the huge place d'Armes. In the center of the building, across the sprawling cobbled forecourt, are the rooms that belonged to the king and queen. The two wings were occupied by the royal children and princes; attendants were up in the attics.

The highlight of the tour, for many, is the **Galerie des Glaces** (Hall of Mirrors), fully restored to its original dazzle. It was here that Bismarck proclaimed the unified German Empire in 1871, and the controversial Treaty of Versailles, asserting Germany's responsibility for World War I, was signed in 1919. The **Royal Bedchambers** are formal; the **Petits Appartements,** where royal family and friends lived, are on a more human scale. The intimate **Opéra Royal,** the first oval hall in France, was designed for Louis XV. Touch the "marble" loges—they're actually painted wood. The chapel, built by Mansart, is a study in white-and-gold solemnity. ☎ *01-30-84-74-00.* ✉ *Château 45 frs.* ☉ *Tues.–Sun. 9–6:30; winter, Tues.–Sun. 9–5:30. Opéra Royal 9:45–3:30 (tours every 15 mins).*

The 250-acre **château park** includes woods, lawns, flower beds, statues, lakes, and fountains. The fountains play on Sundays from May through September, making a fabulous spectacle. ✉ *Free (25 frs for fountains).* ☉ *Grounds daily 7–dusk.*

At one end of the Petit Canal, about 1½ km (1 mi) from the château, stands the **Grand Trianon,** built by Jules Hardouin-Mansart in the late 1680s. This pink-marble pleasure palace is sometimes used to entertain visiting heads of state; at other times it is open to the public. ✉ *25 frs.* ☉ *Oct.–Apr., Tues.–Fri. 10–5:30; May–Sept., Tues.–Sun. 10–6:30.*

Apollo
Basin, **10**

Château, **1**

Enceladus
Basin, **9**

Grand
Trianon, **11**

Les Grands
Apparte-
ments, **2**

Hameau, **13**

Latona
Basin, **6**

Neptune Basin;
Dragon
Basin, **7**

Obelisk
Basin, **8**

Orangerie, **4**

Petit
Trianon, **12**

Water Mirror
Basin, **5**

Water
Terrace, **3**

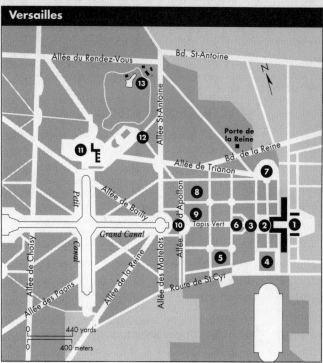

Versailles

The **Petit Trianon,** close to the Grand Trianon, is a sumptuously furnished neoclassical mansion erected in the 1760s by architect Jacques
Gabriel. Louis XV had a superb botanical garden planted here; some
of the trees from that era survive today. Louis XVI presented the Petit
Trianon to Marie-Antoinette, who spent lavish sums creating an ide-
alized world nearby, the charming *hameau,* a hamlet of thatched-roof
cottages, complete with watermill, lake, and pigeon loft. ⊠ *15 frs.* ☉
Oct.–Apr., Tues.–Fri. 10–5:30; May–Sept., Tues.–Sun. 10–6:30.

Versailles, the town, is often overlooked. You might be exhausted
from exploring the palace and park, but the town's broad, leafy boulevards are also agreeable places to stroll. The **Cathédrale St-Louis** is an
austere edifice with a powerful two-tiered facade; it was built from 1743
to 1754 and contains fine paintings and an organ loft. The sturdy
Baroque church of **Notre-Dame** was built from 1684 to 1686 by Jules
Hardouin-Mansart as the parish church for Louis XIV's brand-new
town; the Sun King even deigned to lay the foundation stone. The wide-
ranging **Musée Lambinet,** housed near Notre-Dame church in an imposing 18th-century mansion, has a maze of cozy rooms furnished with
paintings, weapons, fans, and porcelain. ⊠ *54 bd. de la Reine,* ☎ *01–
39–50–30–32.* ⊠ *25 frs.* ☉ *Tues.–Sun. 2–6.*

Dining

$$$$ ✕ **Les Trois Marches.** One of the best-known restaurants in the Paris
area is now in the Trianon Palace Hotel, near Versailles. Chef Gérard
Vié serves creative dishes such as duckling roasted with vinegar and
honey. The prix-fixe (260 francs) weekday lunch is the most affordable option. If you're in a hurry, try the Brasserie La Fontaine in the
garden (expect to pay 150–200 francs for a three-course meal). ⊠ *1
bd. de la Reine,* ☎ *01–39–50–13–21. Reservations essential. Jacket
and tie. AE, DC, MC, V. Closed Sun., Mon., and Aug.*

$$ ✕ **Quai No. 1.** Barometers, sails, and model boats fill this small, charming seafood restaurant. In summer you can enjoy your meal on the terrace. Home-smoked salmon is a specialty; any dish on the two prix-fixe menus is a good value. ⊠ *1 av. de St-Cloud,* ☎ *01–39–50–42–26. MC, V. Closed Mon. No dinner Sun.*

Versailles A to Z

Arriving and Departing

BY CAR

Versailles is 16 km (10 mi) west of Paris. Take highway A13 from Porte d'Auteuil, on the west side of Paris; then follow the signs to Versailles.

BY TRAIN

There are three train routes from Paris to Versailles (20–30 minutes). The RER-C to Versailles Rive-Gauche takes you closest to the château (600 yards away via av. de Sceaux). The other trains run from Gare St-Lazare to Versailles Rive-Droite (closer to the Trianons, but 1 km/¾mi from the château via rue du Maréchal-Foch and av. de St-Cloud) and from Gare Montparnasse to Versailles-Chantiers (1 km/¾ mi to the château via rue des Etats-Généraux and av. de Paris).

Guided Tours

Paris Vision and **Cityrama** (☞ Guided Tours *in* Chartres, Maintenon, and Rambouillet, *above*) offer half- and full-day guided bus tours of Versailles, Fontainebleau, Barbizon, and Chartres. Trips cost from 200 francs (half day) to 440 francs (full day).

8 Portraits of Paris

Paris at a Glance: A Chronology

Imagine Paris

Books and Videos

PARIS AT A GLANCE: A CHRONOLOGY

ca. 200 BC   The Parisii—Celtic fishermen—live on the Ile de la Cité.

52   Romans establish a colony, Lutetia, on the Ile de la Cité, which soon spreads to both Seine banks. Under the Romans, Paris becomes a major administrative and commercial center, its situation on a low, defensible crossing point on the Seine making it a natural communications nexus.

ca. AD 250   St-Denis, first bishop of Paris and France's patron saint, is martyred in Christian persecutions.

451   The hordes of Attila the Hun are said to be halted before reaching Paris by the prayers of Ste-Geneviève (died 512); in fact they are halted by an army of Romans and mercenaries. Few traces of the Roman era in Paris remain. Most of those that do are from the late empire, including the catacombs of Montparnasse and the baths that form part of the Cluny Museum.

The Merovingian Dynasty (486–751)

507   Clovis, king of the Franks and founder of the Merovingian dynasty, makes Paris his capital. Many churches are built, including the abbey that will become St-Germain-des-Prés. Commerce is active; Jewish and Asian colonies are founded along the Seine.

The Carolingian Dynasty (751–987)

Under the Carolingians, Paris ceases to be the capital of France and sinks into political insignificance, but it remains a major administrative, commercial, and ecclesiastical center—and, as a result of the last, one of the foremost centers of culture and learning west of Constantinople.

845–87   Parisians restore the fortifications of the city, which are repeatedly sacked by the Vikings (up to 877).

The Capetian Dynasty (987–1328)

987   Hugh Capet, Count of Paris, becomes king. Paris, once more the capital, grows in importance. The Ile de la Cité is the seat of government, commerce makes its place on the Right Bank, and a university develops on the Left Bank.

1140–63   The Gothic style of architecture appears at St-Denis: Notre-Dame, begun in 1163, sees the style come to maturity. In the late 12th century streets are paved.

1200   Philippe-Auguste charters a university, builds walls around Paris, and constructs a fortress, the first Louvre.

1243–46   The Ste-Chapelle is built to house the reputed crown of thorns brought by Louis IX (St. Louis) from Constantinople.

1253   The Sorbonne is founded, to become a major theological center.

The Valois Dynasty (1328–1589)

1348–49   The Black Death and the beginning of the Hundred Years' War bring misery and strife to Paris.

1364–80   Charles V works to restore prosperity to Paris. The Bastille is built to defend new city walls. The Louvre is converted into a royal palace.

1420–37 After the battle of Agincourt, Henry V of England enters Paris. Joan of Arc leads an attempt to recapture the city (1429). Charles VII of France drives out the English (1437).

1469 The first printing house in France is established at the Sorbonne.

1515–47 François I imports Italian artists, including Leonardo da Vinci, to work on his new palace at Fontainebleau, bringing the Renaissance to France. François resumes work on the Louvre and builds the Hôtel de Ville in the new style. The Tour St-Jacques (bell tower) is completed (all that now remains of the church of St-Jacques-de-la-Boucherie).

1562–98 In the Wars of Religion, Paris remains a Catholic stronghold. On August 24, 1572, Protestant leaders are killed in the St. Bartholomew's Day Massacre.

The Bourbon Dynasty (1589–1789)

1598–1610 Henri IV begins his reign after converting to Catholicism: "Paris is worth a mass." He embellishes Paris, laying out the Renaissance place des Vosges, first in a new Parisian style of town planning that will last till the 19th century. In 1610, Henri is assassinated. His widow, Marie de Medicis, begins the Luxembourg Palace and Gardens.

1624 Cardinal Richelieu is appointed minister to Louis XIII and concludes the ongoing religious persecution by strictly imposing Catholicism on the country. In 1629 he begins construction of the Palais-Royal.

1635 The Académie Française is founded.

1643–1715 Reign of Louis XIV, the Sun King. Paris rebels against him in the Fronde uprisings (1648–52). During most of his reign, he creates a new palace at Versailles, away from the Paris mobs. It is the largest royal complex in Europe, the symbolic center of a centralized French state. His minister of finance, Colbert, establishes the Gobelins factory-school for tapestries and furniture (1667). André Lenôtre transforms the Jardin de Tuileries (Tuileries Gardens) and lays out the Champs-Elysées (1660s). Louis founds the Hôtel des Invalides (1670). Ile St-Louis is created out of the merger of two islands in the Seine.

1715–89 During the reigns of Louis XV and Louis XVI, Paris becomes the European center of culture and style. Aristocrats build town houses in new fashionable quarters (Faubourg St-Honoré). The Rococo style gains popularity.

1783 New outer walls of Paris are begun, incorporating customs gatehouses to control the flow of commerce into the city. The walls, which include new parks, triple the area of Paris.

The Revolution and the First Empire (1789–1848)

1789–99 The French Revolution begins as the Bastille is stormed on July 14, 1789. The First Republic is established. Louis XVI and his queen, Marie-Antoinette, are guillotined in place de la Concorde. Almost 2,600 others perish in the same way during the Terror (1793–94). The transformation of Ste-Geneviève's church into the Panthéon is completed.

1799–1814 Napoléon begins to convert Paris into a neoclassical city—the Empire style. The Arc de Triomphe and the first iron bridges across the Seine are built. In 1805 he orders the completion of the Louvre Museum.

1815 The Congress of Vienna ensures the restoration of the Bourbon dynasty following the fall of Napoléon.

1828–42 Urban and political discontent causes riots and demonstrations in the streets. Yet another uprising replaces Charles X with Louis-Philippe's liberal monarchy in 1830. Napoléon's remains are returned to Paris in 1840.

1848 Europe's "Year of Revolutions" brings more turmoil to the Paris streets.

The Second Empire and the Second Republic (1852–71)

In 1852 further additions to the Louvre are made. Under Napoléon III, the Alsatian town planner, Baron Haussmann, guts large areas of medieval Paris to lay out broad boulevards linking important squares. Railroad stations and the vast covered markets at Les Halles are built.

1862 Victor Hugo's *Les Misérables* is published in Paris while the liberal author remains in exile by order of Napoléon III.

1870–71 Franco-Prussian War; Paris is besieged by Prussian troops; starvation is rampant—each week during the winter, 5,000 people die. The Paris Commune, an attempt by the citizens to take power in 1871, results in bloody suppression and much property damage (the Tuileries Palace is razed). Hugo returns to Paris.

The Third Republic (1875–1944)

1875 The Paris Opéra, Paris's first permanent theater, is inaugurated after 15 years of construction.

1889 The Eiffel Tower is built for the Paris World Exhibition.

1900 The International Exhibition in Paris popularizes the curving forms of Art Nouveau with the entrance for the newly opened Paris métro.

1910 Sacré-Coeur (Montmartre) is completed.

1914–18 World War I. The Germans come within 9 mi of Paris (so close that Paris taxis are used to carry troops to the front).

1919 The Treaty of Versailles is signed, formally ending World War I.

1925 International Decorative Art exhibition consecrates the restrained, sophisticated design style now known as Art Deco.

1918–39 Between the wars, Paris attracts artists and writers, including Americans Ernest Hemingway and Gertrude Stein. Paris nourishes Existentialism, a philosophical movement, and major modern art movements—Constructivism, Dadaism, Surrealism.

1939–45 World War II. Paris falls to the Germans in 1940. The French government moves to Vichy and collaborates with the Nazis. The Resistance movement uses Paris as a base. The Free French Army, under Charles de Gaulle, joins with the Allies to liberate Paris after D day, August 1944.

The Fourth and Fifth Republics (1944–present)

1944–46 De Gaulle moves the provisional government to Paris.

1958–69 De Gaulle is president of the Fifth Republic.

1960s–70s Paris undergoes physical changes: Dirty buildings are cleaned, beltways are built around the city, and expressways are driven through the heart of it, even beside the Seine, in an attempt to solve traffic problems. Major new building projects (especially La Défense) are banished to the outskirts.

1962 De Gaulle grants Algeria independence; growing tensions with immigrant workers in Paris and other cities.

1968 Parisian students declare the Sorbonne a commune in riots that lead to de Gaulle's resignation.

1969 Les Halles market is moved and its buildings demolished.

1970s Paris, with other Western capitals, becomes the focus of extreme leftist and Arab terrorist bomb outrages.

1977 Beaubourg (Centre Pompidou) opens to controversy, marking a high point in modern political intervention in the arts and public architecture.

1981 François Mitterrand (1916–96) is elected president. Embarks on a major building program throughout the city.

1986 Musée d'Orsay opens in the former Gare d'Orsay train station, housing hitherto scattered collections of 19th-century art and design.

1988 President Mitterrand is elected to a second term.

1989 Paris celebrates the bicentennial of the French Revolution. The Grande Arche (La Défense) and the Opéra Bastille are completed. The Louvre's glass pyramid is completed in the first phase of major renovations designed by architect I. M. Pei.

1990 Cognacq-Jay museum reopens in the Marais.

1991 Edith Cresson becomes France's first female prime minister.

1992 Disneyland Paris opens in Marne-la-Vallée near Paris.

1993 After nine years of painstaking renovations by Pei, the Richelieu wing of the Louvre is opened to the public, doubling the museum's exhibition space and allowing 25% more works to be displayed. The completion of the Channel Tunnel between England and France is announced.

1994 The Grande Galerie de l'Evolution reopens after 30 years at the Jardin des Plantes. The Champs-Elysées's face-lift is completed, with more trees, wider sidewalks, designer street furniture, and art-nouveau newsstands. Extra sculpture section, with mainly Italian and German late-medieval and Renaissance works, opens in Denon wing of the Louvre. Paris–London rail link via Channel Tunnel becomes operational.

1995 The Cité de la Musique, a giant music academy with a new auditorium, is completed at La Villette. Mayor Jacques Chirac replaces François Mitterrand as the president of France. Paris becomes the focus of extremist terrorist bomb attacks.

1996 Late President Mitterrand's last large project, the Bibliothèque Nationale François Mitterrand, or new national library, opens. Nearby, a new bridge across the Seine from Gare de Lyon to Gare d'Austerlitz is finished. The Tuileries Gardens' flower-lift is completed. The disastrous fire in the Channel Tunnel undermines confidence in the already debt-plagued system, but repairs are made and the Eurostar train resumes service.

1997 President Jacques Chirac calls early elections, a socialist coalition wins the majority, and Lionel Jospin becomes prime minister. The futuristic Stade de France in St-Denis is completed, just in time for the 1998 Soccer World Cup.

IMAGINE PARIS

IN THE PLACE DU Tertre, behind the Sacré-Coeur, which dominates the northern skyline of Paris, dozens of painters display their canvases of the Seine, the Notre Dame, the Boulevards. Cheap, kitsch and in real oil paint. Not entirely insincere, however. The intentions of poor art are simply kinder than those of great art. One or two tourists occasionally buy a canvas, but the more interesting trade is in portraits.

Strolling between the café tables of the little *place,* other painters politely accost the foreign and provincial visitors. A drawing while you wait in charcoal or Conté. The price may be as high as a hundred dollars. A surprising number of tourists agree, stand on the street corner for a quarter of an hour to be drawn, pay up, and go away happy. Why?

The answer has to lead us to another question. Why do people visit art galleries all over the world? Art appreciation? I don't believe it. People really go to the great museums to look at those who once lived, to look at the dead. By the same token, the tourists who pose, standing still for a long quarter of an hour on a sidewalk in the Place du Tertre, believe that their likeness, if "caught," is already being preserved for the future, their old age, their grandchildren. A hundred dollars to be there when the angels come marching in is not so expensive.

What of course is derisory in this commerce is the carefully encouraged hint that the portraits being made in the Place du Tertre have somehow been "authenticated" by Renoir, Van Gogh, Utrillo, Picasso and all the other great painters who, half a century or more ago, worked and drank and went hungry in the same quarter, within shouting distance of the little *place.* This, however, is an art-critical point, and has little to do with the ontological wager that a likeness, once caught, carries the mystery of a Being.

The mystery of Paris. How can I draw a likeness of the city? Not the official one, stamped on the coins of history. Something more intimate. The date of my birth shows that I was conceived in a hotel somewhere between the Madeleine and the Opéra.

The Madeleine was much admired when it was built in the nineteenth century because it resembled a bank more than a church. It was a monument to worldliness, keeping a proper distance from the original Madeleine's washing of a preacher's dusty feet. Today, inside, it is like a half-empty warehouse for every sort of broken public promise.

I prefer to think that the hotel in 1926 was nearer to the Opéra. Perhaps where, today, two storeys down in a basement, there's a tea-dance every afternoon. The strobing coloured lights gyrate in a circle; the mirror wall along the side of the dance floor reflects the turning dancers. The music is retro—waltzes, tangos, foxtrots. It's an old-fashioned Aladdin's cave of glitter, where time, dates, age, are put aside (not forgotten) between 4 and 7 PM.

Men of a certain age in well-cut suits come to relax and dance with women they've never met before. The women, younger, genteel and a little disappointed with life, come in the hope of meeting a kind widower. They are not tarts. They dream of becoming wives or understanding mistresses. There's a bar, but scarcely anyone drinks. The first pleasure is dancing, and everyone dances exceptionally well.

Both the women and the men pride themselves on being experts in life without illusion. In this expertise there is a typical Parisian fastidiousness. A chic. What is touching is that, entwined with the music, between 4 and 7 PM, an unreasonable hope still intermittently flickers and persists there.

In 1926 when I was conceived, I was a hope without any expertise, embalmed in sweet illusions, for my parents were not Parisians. To them the city was a simple honeymoon. To me it's the capital of the country in which I've lived for twenty-five years. Yet what distinguishes Paris from any other city has perhaps not changed so much. How to draw its likeness?

Take the first metro from a suburb early on a summer morning. The first swallows flying. The dustbins under the trees not yet emptied. An incongruous small cornfield between apartment blocks. The suburbs of Paris demand a portrait to themselves. Among them you find the only remaining details from the world as painted by the Impressionists. They are anachronistic, makeshift, and look as if they've been constructed out of contraband. They were marginal long before the word became fashionable. A man sleepily clipping the hedge of his tiny front garden, still in his pajamas. Beehives. A take-away hamburger counter, not yet open, but with the smell of yesterday's oil. Rich Parisians don't live in the suburbs: they live in the center. They take the train.

There's little traffic there yet. The cars parked along the streets are like silent toy ones. On a corner the smell of fresh croissants wafts from a patisserie. Time to get dressed. In a greengrocer's shop two men are arranging fruit and vegetables as if they were millinery. An uncle in a café is looking through a magnifying glass at the stock prices in the morning paper. He doesn't have to ask for a cup of coffee which is brought to him. The last street is being washed. Where's the towel, Maman?

This strange question floats into the mind because the heart of Paris is like nothing so much as the unending interior of a house. Buildings become furniture, courtyards become carpets and arrases, the streets are like galleries, the boulevards conservatories. It is a house, one or two centuries old, rich, bourgeois, distinguished. The only way of going out, or shutting the door behind you, is to leave the centre.

The vast number of little shops, artisans, boutiques, constitute the staff of the house, its servants, there day and night for its hourly upkeep. Their skills are curiously interrelated: hairdressing and carving, needlework and carpentry, tailoring and masonry, lace-making and wrought-iron work, dressmaking and painting. Paris is a mansion. Its dreams are the most urban and the most furnished in the world.

Sufficient to look at Balzac's study. (Now a museum in the Rue Raynouard, 16ème.) The room is not extravagant. Far from it. But it is furnished, enclosed, papered, polished, very claustrophobic. Yet this is highly appropriate to the city's imagination: Balzac's novels are about property, the human heart, destiny, and the natural

meeting place for all these forces in Paris is the *salon*. The battlefields are beds, carpets, counters. Everything made in Paris is for indoor use. Even the marvelous silvery light of the typical Paris sky is like a framed skylight.

Who lives in this mansion which is Paris? Every city has a sex and an age which have nothing to do with demography. Rome is feminine. So is Odessa. London is a teenager, an urchin, and, in this, hasn't changed since the time of Dickens.

PARIS, I BELIEVE, is a man in his twenties in love with an older woman. Somewhat spoilt by his mother, not so much with kisses as with purchases: well-cooked food, fine shoes, after-shave lotion, leather-bound books, chic envelopes. He discusses everything, he is handsome—perhaps, for once, the word "debonaire" is the right one, and he has a special courage: life is enacted on a stage and he wishes to be exemplary, whatever the risk. His father was his first example of an Expert. Now he has become one himself. There's a complicity between the two men, but also a slight anxiety, for they risk having the same mistress. She also is Paris, and if every city has its own unique smile, in Paris it is hers.

I try to think of a well-known painting containing such a smile but cannot find one. Walking in the city, you see it often. The Boulevard de Charonne is working-class, hot in summer, without shade. A large woman in a floral dress with hefty arms is drinking a beer on the sidewalk at a café table. Under the table is a black mongrel dog with pointed ears to whom she feeds the peanuts she has bought from a machine. A neighbour passes, stops at the table. The woman goes to the counter to buy her friend a lemonade. "She's pretty, your Maman!" says the neighbour to the dog. When the woman comes back with the lemonade, her friend, laughing, says to her: "I'd be happy to be guided by you—so long as the lead wasn't too short!" And the woman in the floral dress, who must be in her seventies, smiles that inimitable smile of indulgent but lucid experience.

Often cemeteries are unexpectedly revealing about the life of the living. And this is true of the Père Lachaise. One needs a map, for it is large. Sections are built like towns—with streets, crossroads, pavements: each house is a tomb or mausoleum. The dead rest there in furnished property, still protected from the vast exterior. Each tomb has a license and a number: Concession Perpétuelle Numéro...It is the most urban and the most secular cemetery.

Where, for example, would you find a father's grave with an inscription ordered by the family declaring: "President of the Society of High Class Masculine Hairdressing. World Champion. 1950–80"?

ASHRINE OF PROPERTY this cemetery, certainly. But also one of popular heroes: the last 147 Communards summarily shot against a wall here in 1871; Sarah Bernhardt; Edith Piaf; Chopin. Every day people come to visit them and to listen to their silence.

There is another, more mysterious shrine, which is our reason for coming: the grave of Victor Noir. In 1870, Prince Pierre Bonaparte, cousin of Emperor Napoleon III, wrote an article in a reactionary Corsican journal attacking the good faith of the radical Paris paper called *La Revanche*. The editor sent Victor Noir and another journalist to ask the prince for an apology. Instead, Pierre Bonaparte seized his pistol and shot Victor Noir dead. The popular outrage provoked by this murder of political pique transformed a relatively unknown young man into a national hero, and the sculptor Jules Dalou made an effigy for his tombstone. Life-size, cast in bronze, it shows Victor Noir—twenty-two years old—dead on the ground, an instant after the pistol shot has been fired. Division ninety-two, Père Lachaise.

Dalou was a realist, making in sculpture works whose vision has something in common with Courbet's paintings: the same kind of fullness in the bodies and limbs depicted, the same close attention to realistic details of costume, a similar corporeal weight. The two artists were friends and both had to go into exile after the fall of the Commune, which they had actively supported.

Victor Noir lies there with the abandon of the two girls in Courbet's *Demoiselles au Bord de la Seine*. The only difference being that the man has died at that very instant—his blood still hot—whereas the girls are overcome by drowsiness and the langour of their day-dreams.

An elegant tall hat lies on the ground beside him. His handsome face is still proud of his own courage, believing it will be rewarded by the love of women. (Each generation of young men knows that, from time to time, the mansion is transformed into an improvised theatre, on whose stage history is played out—often to the death.) His coat is open, the top button of his tight trousers is undone. His soft-skinned, well-manicured hands lie unclenched, expecting to touch or to be touched only by what is fine.

The effigy is moving and strange in its integrity, for it gives the impression that the death it shows has somewhere been selected with the same fastidiousness as the shirt or boots.

Beneath the sky of the cemetery the bronze has turned a dull green. In three places, however, the metal is shiny and gold-coloured where it has been polished by innumerable caresses and kisses. For certain sections of the populace, Victor Noir has become a talisman, a fetish, promising fertility, potency, success, continuity. People come all the while to seek his aid, to touch his example.

The three places where the bronze metal shines are his mouth, the pointed toes of his superbly elegant boots, and, most brilliantly of all, the protuberance which his sex makes against his tight trousers.

Perhaps a likeness of the city of Paris begins there in the south-east corner of the Père Lachaise cemetery . . .

— John Berger

John Berger is a novelist, short story writer, nonfiction essayist, and author of several volumes of art criticism. His six volumes of essays include *Keeping a Rendezvous*, from which this essay is excerpted, *The Sense of Sight*, and *Ways of Seeing*. Born in London, Berger now calls a small village in the French Alps home.

BOOKS AND VIDEOS

Books

For a look at the American expatriates in Paris between the wars, read *Sylvia Beach and the Lost Generation* by Noel R. Fitch or *A Moveable Feast* by Ernest Hemingway. Flaubert's *Sentimental Education* includes excellent descriptions of Paris and its environs, as do many Zola novels. Other recommended titles include Charles Dickens's *A Tale of Two Cities*, Henry James's *The Ambassadors*, Colette's *The Complete Claudine*, Hemingway's *The Sun Also Rises*, and Gertrude Stein's *Paris, France*. George Orwell's *Down and Out in Paris and London* gives a stirring account of life on a shoestring in these two European capitals between the world wars. More essays about Paris by some of the 20th century's greatest writers are excerpted in *A Place in the World Called Paris*.

Jules Verne's *Paris in the Twentieth Century* provides a view from the past of Paris in the future. A history of Paris from the Revolution to the Belle Epoque can be found in Johannes Willms's *Paris: Capital of Europe*. Two memoirs by Americans who have lived in Paris include Art Buchwald's *I'll Always Have Paris* and Edmund White's *Our Paris*. *Paris Notebooks* by Mavis Gallant is a collection of her observations about Paris life. *Between Meals* by A. J. Leibling looks at the fine art of eating in Paris. Two unconventional guides to Paris, real and imagined, are Karen Elizabeth Gordon's witty and surreal *Paris Out of Hand* and Lawrence Osborne's unusual *Paris Dreambook*.

For those who like it hot, try Henry Miller's *Tropic of Cancer* or *The Diary of Anaïs Nin*, by Miller's lover. For a racy read about three generations of women in Paris, take along *Mistral's Daughter* by Judith Krantz. Diane Johnson's *Le Divorce* is a comedy of manners set in Paris. Helen MacInnes's *The Venetian Affair* and Alan Furst's *The World at Night* are two spy thrillers that wind through Paris.

Videos

For a glimpse of Paris before you go, you may wish to rent one of the following films: *A Bout de Souffle* ("Breathless," 1960; in French), by Jean-Luc Godard, about a car thief who kills a policeman and then flees with his American girlfriend; *An American in Paris* (1951; in English), a Hollywood musical with Gershwin tunes that gives you the feel of Paris years ago; *Charade* (1953; in English), a comic thriller starring Cary Grant and Audrey Hepburn; *Diva* (1981; in French), a surreal story about a singer in Paris who becomes involved in murder and drug smuggling; *Everyone Says I Love You* (1996; in English), a Woody Allen musical with Paris, New York, and Venice as its backdrop; and *La Femme Nikita* (1990; in French), a noir thriller with Anne Parillaud as a sexy killer.

More films include *Forget Paris* (1995; in English), by Billy Crystal, who plays an NBA referee who falls in love with Debra Winger on a trip to Paris; *French Kiss* (1995; in English), a Lawrence Kasdan comedy with Kevin Kline as a French jewel thief who meets Meg Ryan on a plane to Paris; *Funny Face* (1957; in English), a Roger Edens musical with Audrey Hepburn and Fred Astaire in Paris; *Last Tango in Paris* (1972; in English), a Bertolucci film starring Marlon Brando about a middle-aged man and young French girl who fall in love; *Ready to Wear* (1994; in English), a Robert Altman film with Tim Robbins, Julia Roberts, Sophia Loren, and many stars of the fashion industry; *'Round Midnight* (1986; in English and French), a Bertrand Tavernier film about a troubled jazz musician in Paris played by Dexter Gordon; and *Zazie Dans le Métro* (1960; in French), a Louis Malle film about the adventures of a 10-year-old girl on vacation in Paris—and the chaos she creates.

FRENCH VOCABULARY

One of the trickiest French sounds to pronounce is the nasal final *n* sound (whether or not the *n* is actually the last letter of the word). You should try to pronounce it as a sort of nasal grunt—as in "huh." The vowel that precedes the *n* will govern the vowel sound of the word, and in this list we precede the final *n* with an *h* to remind you to be nasal.

Another problem sound is the ubiquitous but untransliterable *eu,* as in *bleu* (blue) or *deux* (two), and the very similar sound in *je* (I), *ce* (this), and *de* (of). The closest equivalent might be the vowel sound in "put," but rounded.

Words and Phrases

	English	French	Pronunciation

Basics

	English	French	Pronunciation
Yes/no	Oui/non	wee/nohn
Please	S'il vous plaît	seel voo **play**
Thank you	Merci	mair-**see**
You're welcome	De rien	deh ree-**ehn**
That's all right	Il n'y a pas de quoi	eel nee ah pah de **kwah**
Excuse me, sorry	Pardon	pahr-**dohn**
Sorry!	Désolé(e)	day-zoh-**lay**
Good morning/ afternoon	Bonjour	bohn-**zhoor**
Good evening	Bonsoir	bohn-**swahr**
Goodbye	Au revoir	o ruh-**vwahr**
Mr. (Sir)	Monsieur	muh-**syuh**
Mrs. (Ma'am)	Madame	ma-**dam**
Miss	Mademoiselle	mad-mwa-**zel**
Pleased to meet you	Enchanté(e)	ohn-shahn-**tay**
How are you?	Comment ça va?	kuh-mahn-sa-**va**
Very well, thanks	Très bien, merci	tray bee-ehn, mair-**see**
And you?	Et vous?	ay **voo**?

Numbers

one	un	uhn
two	deux	deuh
three	trois	twah
four	quatre	**kaht**-ruh
five	cinq	sank
six	six	seess
seven	sept	set
eight	huit	wheat
nine	neuf	nuff
ten	dix	deess
eleven	onze	ohnz
twelve	douze	dooz

thirteen	treize	trehz
fourteen	quatorze	kah-**torz**
fifteen	quinze	kanz
sixteen	seize	sez
seventeen	dix-sept	deez-**set**
eighteen	dix-huit	deez-**wheat**
nineteen	dix-neuf	deez-**nuff**
twenty	vingt	vehn
twenty-one	vingt-et-un	vehnt-ay-**uhn**
thirty	trente	trahnt
forty	quarante	ka-**rahnt**
fifty	cinquante	sang-**kahnt**
sixty	soixante	swa-**sahnt**
seventy	soixante-dix	swa-sahnt-**deess**
eighty	quatre-vingts	kaht-ruh-**vehn**
ninety	quatre-vingt-dix	kaht-ruh-vehn-**deess**
one-hundred	cent	sahn
one-thousand	mille	meel

Colors

black	noir	nwahr
blue	bleu	bleuh
brown	brun/marron	bruhn/mar-**rohn**
green	vert	vair
orange	orange	o-**rahnj**
pink	rose	rose
red	rouge	rooje
violet	violette	vee-o-**let**
white	blanc	blahnk
yellow	jaune	zhone

Days of the Week

Sunday	dimanche	**dee**-mahnsh
Monday	lundi	**luhn**-dee
Tuesday	mardi	**mahr**-dee
Wednesday	mercredi	**mair**-kruh-dee
Thursday	jeudi	**zhuh**-dee
Friday	vendredi	**vawn**-druh-dee
Saturday	samedi	**sahm**-dee

Months

January	janvier	**zhahn**-vee-ay
February	février	**feh**-vree-ay
March	mars	marce
April	avril	a-**vreel**
May	mai	meh
June	juin	zhwehn
July	juillet	**zhwee**-ay
August	août	oot
September	septembre	sep-**tahm**-bruh
October	octobre	awk-**to**-bruh
November	novembre	no-**vahm**-bruh
December	décembre	day-**sahm**-bruh

Useful Phrases

Do you speak . . . English?	Parlez-vous . . . anglais?	par-lay **voo** **ahn**-glay
I don't speak . . . French	Je ne parle pas . . . français	zhuh nuh parl **pah** frahn-**say**
I don't understand	Je ne comprends pas	zhuh nuh kohm-prahn **pah**
I understand	Je comprends	zhuh kohm-**prahn**
I don't know	Je ne sais pas	zhuh nuh say **pah**
I'm American/ British	Je suis américain/ anglais	zhuh sweez a-may-ree-**kehn**/ahn-**glay**
What's your name?	Comment vous appelez-vous?	ko-mahn voo za-pell-ay-**voo**
My name is . . .	Je m'appelle . . .	zhuh ma-**pell** . . .
What time is it?	Quelle heure est-il?	kel air eh-**teel**
How?	Comment?	ko-**mahn**
When?	Quand?	kahn
Yesterday	Hier	yair
Today	Aujourd'hui	o-zhoor-**dwee**
Tomorrow	Demain	duh-**mehn**
This morning/ afternoon	Ce matin/cet après-midi	suh ma-**tehn**/set ah-pray-mee-**dee**
Tonight	Ce soir	suh **swahr**
What?	Quoi?	kwah
What is it?	Qu'est-ce que c'est?	kess-kuh-**say**
Why?	Pourquoi?	**poor**-kwa
Who?	Qui?	kee
Where is . . .	Où se trouve . . .	oo suh **troov**
the train station?	la gare?	la gar
the subway?	la station de?	la sta-**syon** duh
station?	métro?	may-**tro**
the bus stop?	l'arrêt de bus?	la-**ray** duh **booss**
the airport?	l'aérogare?	lay-ro-**gar**
the post office?	la poste?	la post
the bank?	la banque?	la bahnk
the hotel?	l'hôtel?	lo-**tel**
the store?	le magasin?	luh ma-ga-**zehn**
the cashier?	la caisse?	la **kess**
the museum?	le musée?	luh mew-**zay**
the hospital?	l'hôpital?	lo-pee-**tahl**
the elevator?	l'ascenseur?	la-sahn-**seuhr**
the telephone?	le téléphone?	luh tay-lay-**phone**
Where are the rest rooms?	Où sont les toilettes?	oo sohn lay twah-**let**
Here/there	Ici/là	ee-**see**/la
Left/right	A gauche/à droite	a goash/a drwaht
Straight ahead	Tout droit	too drwah

Is it near/far?	C'est près/loin?	say pray/lwehn
I'd like . . .	Je voudrais . . .	zhuh voo-**dray**
a room	une chambre	ewn **shahm**-bruh
the key	la clé	la clay
a newspaper	un journal	uhn zhoor-**nahl**
a stamp	un timbre	uhn **tam**-bruh
I'd like to buy . . .	Je voudrais acheter . . .	zhuh voo-**dray** **ahsh**-tay
a cigar	un cigare	uhn see-**gar**
cigarettes	des cigarettes	day see-ga-**ret**
matches	des allumettes	days a-loo-**met**
dictionary	un dictionnaire	uhn deek-see-oh-**nare**
soap	du savon	dew sah-**vohn**
city map	un plan de ville	uhn plahn de **veel**
road map	une carte routière	ewn cart roo-tee-**air**
magazine	une revue	ewn reh-**vu**
envelopes	des enveloppes	dayz ahn-veh-**lope**
writing paper	du papier à lettres	dew pa-pee-**ay** a **let**-ruh
airmail writing paper	du papier avion	dew pa-pee-**ay** a-vee-**ohn**
postcard	une carte postale	ewn cart pos-**tal**
How much is it?	C'est combien?	say comb-bee-**ehn**
It's expensive/cheap	C'est cher/pas cher	say share/pa share
A little/a lot	Un peu/beaucoup	uhn peuh/bo-**koo**
More/less	Plus/moins	plu/mwehn
Enough/too (much)	Assez/trop	a-say/tro
I am ill/sick	Je suis malade	zhuh swee ma-**lahd**
Call a . . . doctor	Appelez un . . . médecin	a-play uhn mayd-**sehn**
Help!	Au secours!	o suh-**koor**
Stop!	Arrêtez!	a-reh-**tay**
Fire!	Au feu!	o fuh
Caution!/Look out!	Attention!	a-tahn-see-**ohn**

Dining Out

A bottle of . . .	une bouteille de . . .	ewn boo-**tay** duh
A cup of . . .	une tasse de . . .	ewn **tass** duh
A glass of . . .	un verre de . . .	uhn **vair** duh
Ashtray	un cendrier	uhn sahn-dree-**ay**
Bill/check	l'addition	la-dee-see-**ohn**
Bread	du pain	dew pan
Breakfast	le petit-déjeuner	luh puh-**tee** day-zhuh-**nay**
Butter	du beurre	dew burr
Cheers!	A votre santé!	ah vo-truh sahn-**tay**
Cocktail/aperitif	un apéritif	uhn ah-pay-ree-**teef**

Dinner	le dîner	luh dee-**nay**
Special of the day	le plat du jour	luh plah dew **zhoor**
Enjoy!	Bon appétit!	bohn a-pay-**tee**
Fixed-price menu	le menu	luh may-**new**
Fork	une fourchette	ewn four-**shet**
I am diabetic	Je suis diabétique	zhuh swee dee-ah-bay-**teek**
I am on a diet	Je suis au régime	zhuh sweez oray-**jeem**
I am vegetarian	Je suis végé-tarien(ne)	zhuh swee vay-zhay-ta-ree-**en**
I cannot eat . . .	Je ne peux pas manger de . . .	zhuh nuh **puh** pah mahn-**jay** deh
I'd like to order	Je voudrais commander	zhuh voo-**dray** ko-mahn-**day**
I'm hungry/thirsty	J'ai faim/soif	zhay fahm/swahf
Is service/the tip included?	Le service est-il compris?	luh sair-**veess** ay-teel com-**pree**
It's good/bad	C'est bon/mauvais	say bohn/mo-**vay**
It's hot/cold	C'est chaud/froid	say sho/frwah
Knife	un couteau	uhn koo-**toe**
Lunch	le déjeuner	luh day-zhuh-**nay**
Menu	la carte	la cart
Napkin	une serviette	ewn sair-vee-**et**
Pepper	du poivre	dew **pwah**-vruh
Plate	une assiette	ewn a-see-**et**
Please give me . . .	Merci de me donner . . .	Mair-**see** deh meh doe-**nay**
Salt	du sel	dew sell
Spoon	une cuillère	ewn kwee-**air**
Sugar	du sucre	dew **sook**-ruh
Waiter!/Waitress!	Monsieur!/Mademoiselle!	muh-**syuh**/mad-mwa-**zel**
Wine list	la carte des vins	la **cart** day van

MENU GUIDE

French	English

General Dining

Dîner	Dinner
Déjeuner	Lunch
Entrée	Appetizer/Starter
Garniture au choix	Choice of vegetable side
Menu à prix fixe	Fixed-price menu
Petit déjeuner	Breakfast
Plat du jour	Special of the day
Selon arrivage	When available
Supplément/En sus	Extra charge
Sur commande	Made to order

Breakfast

Céréale	Cereal
Confiture	Jam
Miel	Honey
Oeuf à la coque	Boiled egg
Oeufs au bacon	Bacon and eggs
Oeufs au jambon	Ham and eggs
Oeufs sur le plat	Fried eggs
Oeufs brouillés	Scrambled eggs
Omelette (nature)	Omelet (plain)
Petits pains	Rolls
Tartine	Bread with butter or jam

Appetizers/Starters

Anchois	Anchovies
Andouille(tte)	Chitterling sausage
Assiette de charcuterie	Assorted pork products
Crudités	Mixed raw vegetable salad
Escargots	Snails
Hors-d'oeuvres variés	Assorted appetizers
Jambon	Ham
Jambon de campagne	Smoked ham
Jambonneau	Cured pig's knuckle
Mortadelle	Bologna sausage
Pâté	Liver puree blended with meat
Quenelles	Light dumplings (fish, fowl, or meat)
Saucisson	Dried sausage
Terrine	Pâté sliced and served from an earthenware pot

Salads

Salade de thon	Tuna salad
Salade mixte	Mixed salad
Salade niçoise	Green salad with tuna, potatoes, and anchovies
Salade verte	Green salad

Soups

Bisque	Shellfish soup
Bouillabaisse	Fish and seafood stew
Crême de . . .	Cream of . . .
Julienne	Vegetable soup
Potage/Soupe	Soup
Potage parmentier	Thick potato soup
Pot-au-feu	Stew of meat and vegetables
Ragoût	Stew, usually beef
Soupe du jour	Soup of the day
Soupe à l'oignon gratinée	French onion soup
Soupe au pistou	Provençal vegetable soup
Velouté de . . .	Cream of . . .
Vichyssoise	Cold leek and potato cream soup

Fish and Seafood

Anguille	Eel
Bar	Bass
Bourride	Fish stew from Marseilles
Brandade de morue	Creamed salt cod
Brochet	Pike
Cabillaud	Fresh cod
Calmar	Squid
Carpe	Carp
Coquilles St-Jacques	Scallops
Crabe	Crab
Crevettes	Shrimp
Daurade	Sea bream
Écrevisses	Prawns/crayfish
Éperlans	Smelt
Harengs	Herring
Homard	Lobster
Huîtres	Oysters
Langouste	Spiny lobster
Langoustine	Dublin bay prawn (scampi)/lobster
Lotte	Monkfish
Lotte de mer	Angler
Loup	Catfish
Maquereau	Mackerel
Matelote	Fish stew in wine
Merlan	Whiting
Morue	Cod
Moules	Mussels
Palourdes	Clams
Perche	Perch
Poulpe	Octopus
Raie	Skate
Rascasse	Scorpion-fish
Rouget	Red mullet
Saumon	Salmon
Sole	Sole
Thon	Tuna
Truite	Trout

Meat

Agneau	Lamb
Ballotine	A cut of meat that has been boned, stuffed, and rolled
Blanquette de veau	Veal stew with a white-sauce base
Boeuf	Beef
Boeuf à la Bourguignonne	Beef stew
Boudin blanc	Sausage made with white meat
Boudin noir	Sausage made with pig's blood
Boulettes de viande	Meatballs
Brochette	Kabob
Cassoulet	Casserole of white beans and meat
Cervelle	Brains
Châteaubriand	Double fillet steak
Côtelettes	Chops
Choucroute garnie	Sausages and cured pork served with sauerkraut
Contre-filet	Loin strip steak
Côte de boeuf	T-bone steak
Côte	Rib
Cuisses de grenouilles	Frogs' legs
Entrecôte	Rib or rib-eye steak
Épaule	Shoulder
Escalope	Cutlet
Filet	Fillet steak
Foie	Liver
Gigot	Leg
Langue	Tongue
Médaillon	Tenderloin steak
Pavé	Thick slice of boned beef
Pieds de cochon	Pig's feet
Porc	Pork
Ragoût	Stew
Ris de veau	Veal sweetbreads
Rognons	Kidneys
Saucisses	Sausages
Selle	Saddle
Steak/steack	Steak
Steak tartare	Raw minced meat
Tournedos	Tenderloin of T-bone steak
Veau	Veal
Viande	Meat

Methods of Preparation

À point	Medium
À l'étouffée	Stewed
Au four	Baked
Bien cuit	Well-done
Bleu	Very rare
Bouilli	Boiled
Braisé	Braised
Frit	Fried
Grillé	Grilled

Rôti	Roast
Saignant	Rare
Sauté/poêlée	Sautéed

Game and Poultry

Blanc de volaille	Chicken breast
Caille	Quail
Canard/caneton	Duck/duckling
Cerf/chevreuil	Venison (red/roe)
Coq au vin	Chicken stewed in red wine
Dinde/dindonneau	Turkey/young turkey
Faisan	Pheasant
Grive	Thrush
Lapin	Rabbit
Lièvre	Wild hare
Oie	Goose
Perdrix/perdreau	Partridge/young partridge
Pigeon/pigeonneau	Pigeon/squab
Pintade/pintadeau	Guinea fowl/young guinea fowl
Poularde	Fattened pullet
Poule au pot	Chicken stewed with vegetables
Poulet	Chicken
Poussin	Spring chicken
Sanglier/marcassin	Wild boar/young wild boar
Volaille	Fowl

Vegetables

Artichaut	Artichoke
Asperge	Asparagus
Aubergine	Eggplant
Carottes	Carrots
Champignons	Mushrooms
Chou-fleur	Cauliflower
Chou (rouge)	Cabbage (red)
Choux de Bruxelles	Brussels sprouts
Courgette	Zucchini
Cresson	Watercress
Endive	Endive
Épinard	Spinach
Haricots blancs/verts	White kidney/French beans
Laitue	Lettuce
Lentilles	Lentils
Maïs	Corn
Oignons	Onions
Petits pois	Peas
Poireaux	Leeks
Poivrons	Peppers
Pomme de terre	Potato
Radis	Radishes
Tomates	Tomatoes

Potatoes, Rice, and Noodles

Pâtes	Pasta
Pommes (de terre)	Potatoes

allumettes	*matchstick fries*
dauphine	*mashed and deep-fried*
duchesse	*mashed with butter and egg yolks*
en robe des champs	*in their skin*
frites	*french fries*
mousseline	*mashed*
nature/vapeur	*boiled/steamed*
Riz	Rice

Sauces and Preparations

Béarnaise	Vinegar, egg yolks, white wine, shallots, tarragon
Béchamel	White sauce
Bordelaise	Mushrooms, red wine, shallots, beef marrow
Bourguignon	Red wine, herbs
Chasseur	Wine, mushrooms, onions, shallots
Diable	Hot pepper
Forestière	Mushrooms
Hollandaise	Egg yolks, butter, vinegar
Indienne	Curry
Madère	With Madeira wine
Marinière	White wine, mussel broth, egg yolks
Meunière	Brown butter, parsley, lemon juice
Périgueux	With goose or duck liver puree and truffles
Poivrade	Pepper sauce
Provençale	Onions, tomatoes, garlic
Tartare	Mayonnaise flavored with mustard and herbs
Vinaigrette	Vinegar dressing

Fruits and Nuts

Abricot	Apricot
Amandes	Almonds
Ananas	Pineapple
Banane	Banana
Brugnon	Nectarine
Cacahouètes	Peanuts
Cassis	Black currants
Cerises	Cherries
Citron	Lemon
Citron vert	Lime
Dattes	Dates
Figues	Figs
Fraises	Strawberries
Framboises	Raspberries
Fruits secs	Dried fruit
Groseilles	Red currants
Mandarine	Tangerine
Marrons	Chestnuts
Melon	Melon
Mûres	Blackberries

Myrtilles	Blueberries
Noisettes	Hazelnuts
Noix de coco	Coconut
Noix	Walnuts
Orange	Orange
Pamplemousse	Grapefruit
Pastèque	Watermelon
Pêche	Peach
Poire	Pear
Pomme	Apple
Pruneaux	Prunes
Prunes	Plums
Raisins secs	Raisins
Raisins blancs/noirs	Grapes green/purple

Desserts

Coupe (glacée)	Sundae
Crêpe	Thin pancake
au chocolat	*with chocolate*
à la confiture	*with jam*
au sucre	*with sugar*
suzette	*simmered in orange juice and flambéed with orange liqueur*
Crème brûlée	Custard with caramelized topping
Crème caramel	Caramel-coated custard
Crème Chantilly	Whipped cream
Flan	Caramel-coated custard
Gâteau au chocolat	Chocolate cake
Glace	Ice cream
Mousse au chocolat	Chocolate mousse
Pastilla	Flaky pastry
Profiterole	Small cream puff filled with ice cream
Sabayon	Egg-and-wine-based custard
Tarte aux pommes	Apple pie
Tarte tatin	Upside-down, caramelized apple tart
Tourte	Layer cake
Vacherin glacé	Ice-cream cake

Alcoholic Drinks

À l'eau	With water
Avec des glaçons	On the rocks
Kir	Chilled white wine mixed with black-currant syrup
Bière	Beer
blonde/brune	Light/dark
Calvados	Apple brandy from Normandy
Eau-de-vie	Brandy
Kirsch	Cherry brandy
Liqueur	Cordial
Poire William	Pear brandy
Porto	Port
Sec	Straight
Vin	Wine

sec	dry
brut	very dry
léger	light
doux	sweet
rouge	red
rosé	rosé
mousseux	sparkling
blanc	white

Nonalcoholic Drinks

Café	Coffee
noir	black
crème	with steamed milk/cream
au lait	with steamed milk
décaféiné	caffeine-free
express	espresso
Chocolat chaud	Hot chocolate
Eau minérale	Mineral water
gazeuse	carbonated
non gazeuse	still
Jus de . . .	. . . juice (☞ Fruits and Nuts, above)
Lait	Milk
Limonade	Lemonade
Schweppes	Tonic water
Thé	Tea
au lait/au citron	with milk/lemon
glacé	Iced tea
Tisane	Herb tea

INDEX

Airport Network

Your
Window
To The
World
While You're
On The
Road

Keep in touch when you're traveling. Before you take off, tune in to CNN Airport Network. Now available in major airports across America, CNN Airport Network provides nonstop news, sports, business, weather and lifestyle programming. Both domestic and international. All piloted by the top-flight global resources of CNN. All up-to-the-minute reporting. And just for travelers, CNN Airport Network features intriguing segments such as "Travel Facts." With an information source like Fodor's this series of fascinating travel trivia will definitely make time fly while you're waiting to board. SO KEEP YOUR WINDOW TO THE WORLD WIDE OPEN. ESPECIALLY WHEN YOU'RE ON THE ROAD. TUNE IN TO CNN AIRPORT NETWORK TODAY.